AF322613

Capture the Natural World in Watercolor

35+ Simple Tutorials for Painting Epic Animals, Botanicals, and More

Anastasiia Morozova

Creator of Natura Illustrata

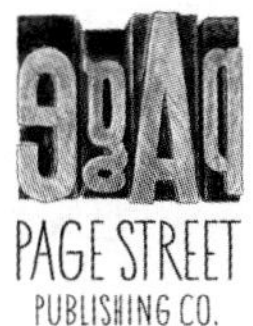

PAGE STREET
PUBLISHING CO.

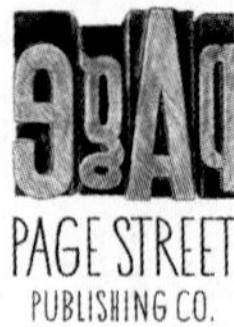

PAGE STREET
PUBLISHING CO.

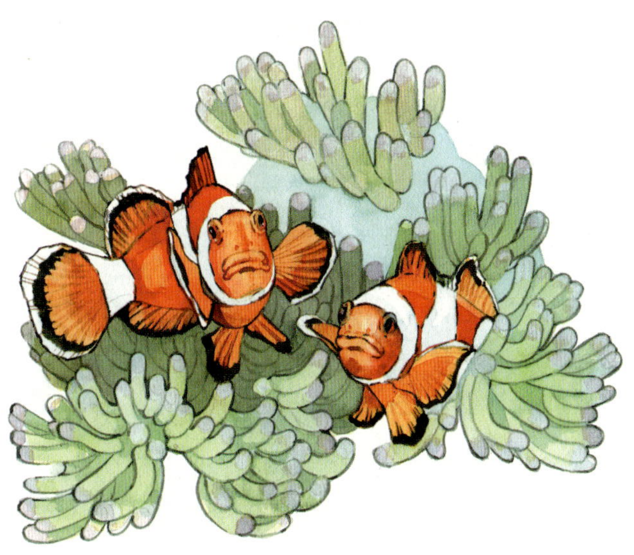

Dedication

To my husband, who believed in me from day one and empowered me to pursue my creative path and mission to teach others. To my family, who sparked my passion and curiosity for nature, travel, and the beauty of the world—especially my parents, grandmothers, and godmother. And to those who doubt themselves—the regret of never trying will outweigh the struggles or fear of failure, so start now and have fun!

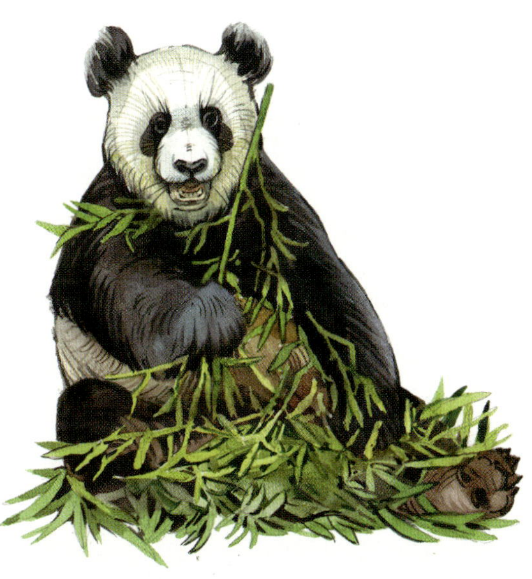

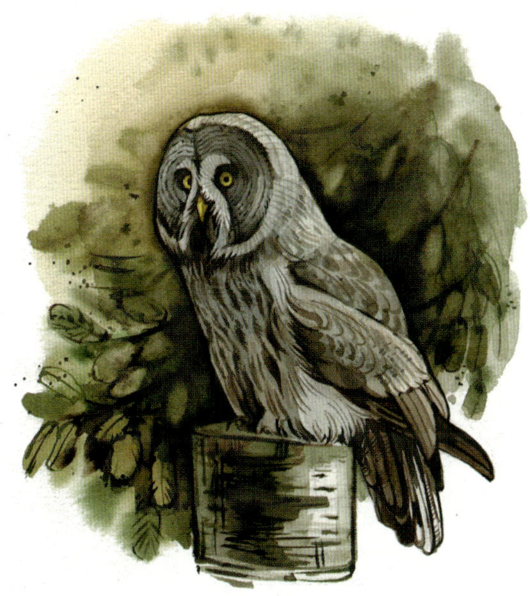

Table *of* Contents

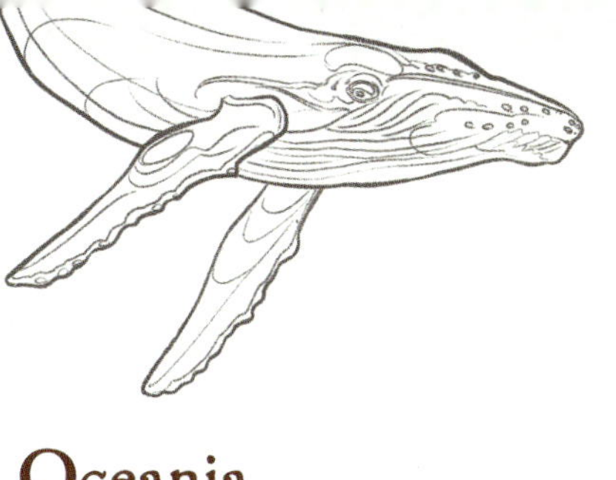

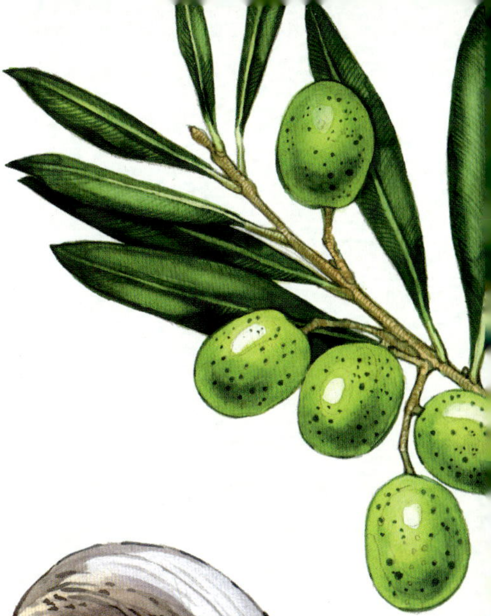

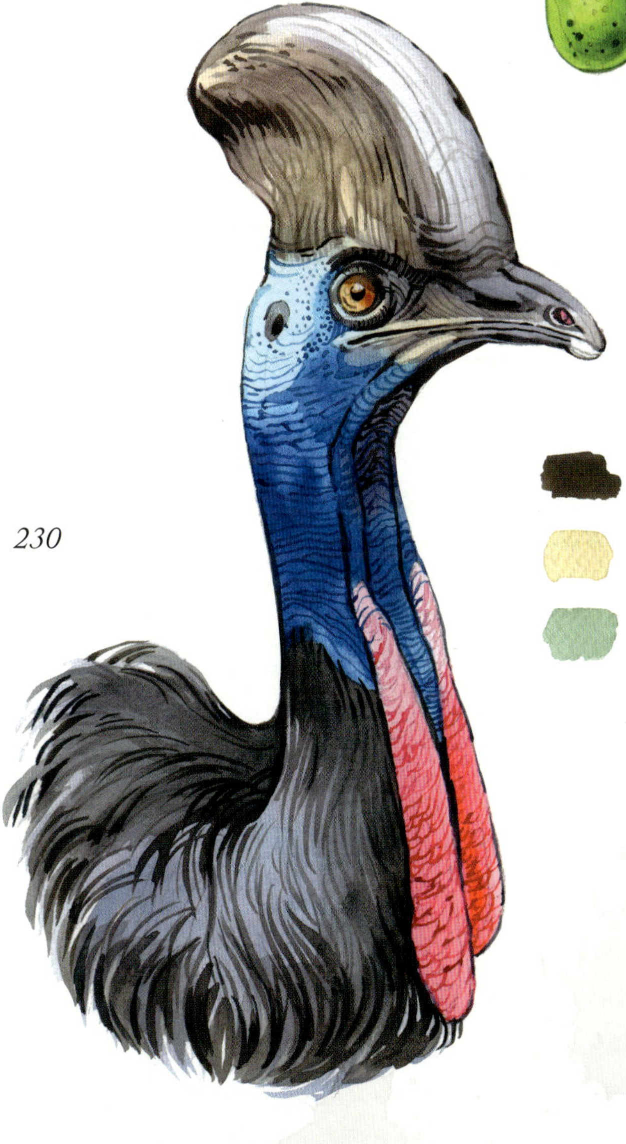

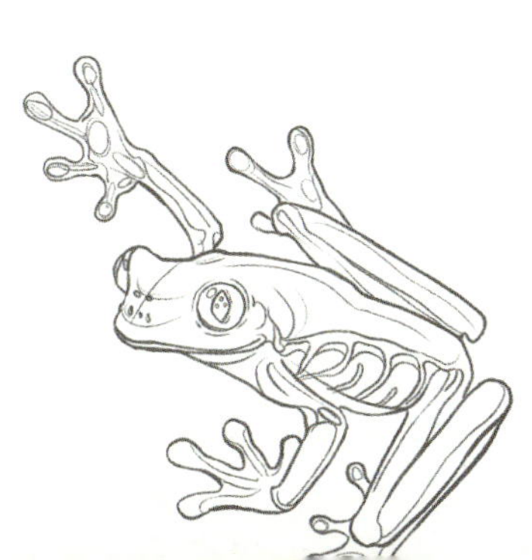

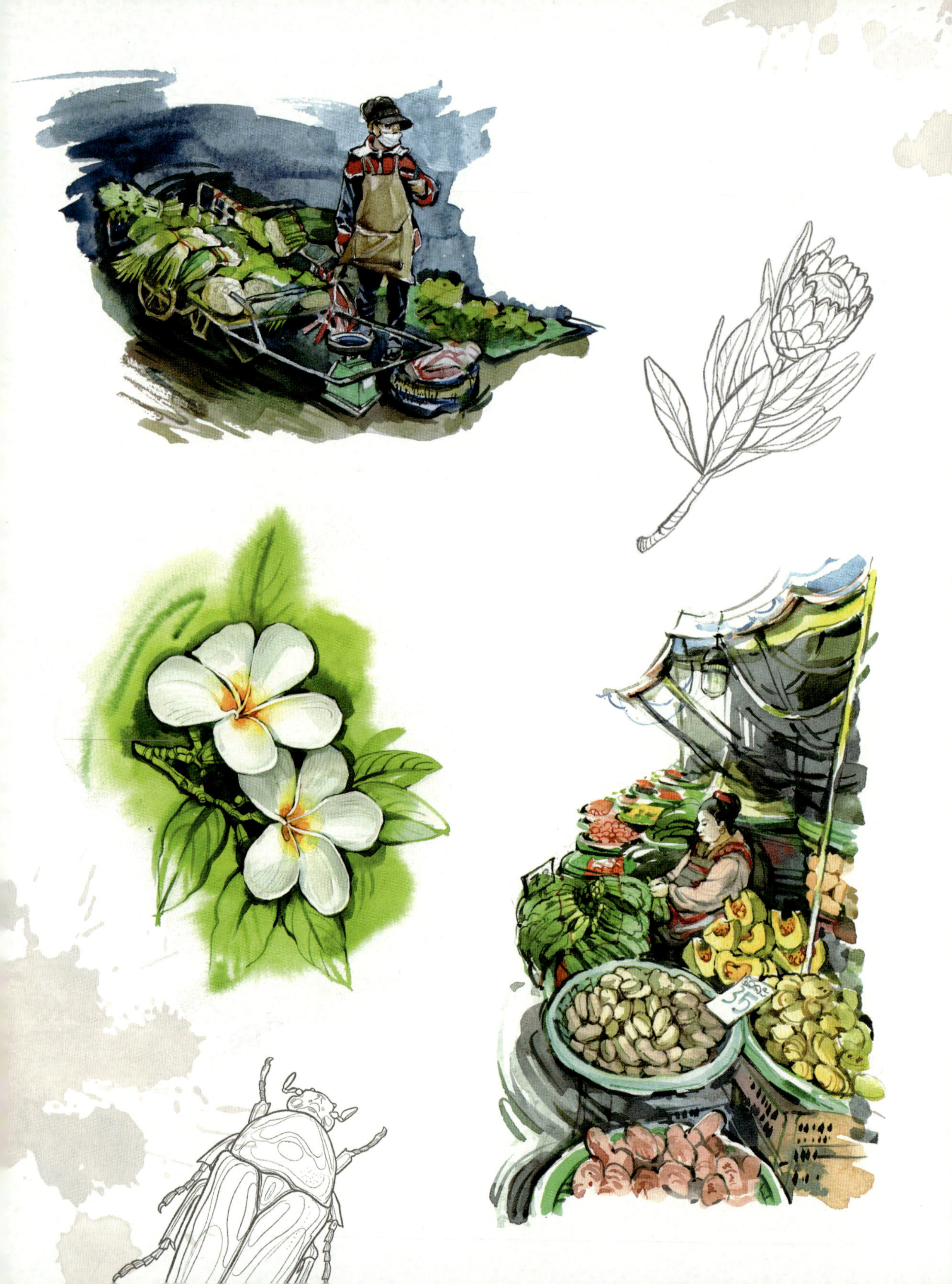

Introduction

Dear Reader,

Welcome aboard! I'm so glad you (or the person who gave this to you) chose this book from among many others, and I believe there's a special reason for that. First and foremost, you are a creative individual who loves bringing beauty into the world. That's fantastic because in this book, I'll be guiding you to build your skills in one of the most unique artistic techniques: watercolor painting. Whether you're a complete beginner or an experienced painter, you're in the right place, and I'm excited to share the secrets of this versatile medium with you.

Second, perhaps you also love traveling, or you're simply curious about the world. If so, I'm confident you'll find a lot to enjoy in this book. You'll discover that watercolor isn't just for studio work—it's also an amazing travel companion! Watercolor is perfect for capturing the essence of your travels, and you'll learn how to use this medium to its fullest potential.

Lastly, I suspect you have a special sensitivity and love for nature. This book will take you on a journey across the seven continents, exploring the incredible natural world of our planet. From scorching deserts to the depths of the oceans, from dense rainforests to icy mountain peaks, we'll dive into the diversity of nature and apply what we learn while illustrating these beautiful subjects.

If you're new to watercolor and feel a bit overwhelmed, don't worry—I'll guide you through every step! While the book focuses on watercolor techniques, I've included a few initial tips on drawing as well. If you're a complete beginner and struggle with sketching, there's no need to stress. On page 19, you'll find a QR code that gives you access to templates you can trace. Now, let's jump in and paint our way across the natural world!

Anastasia Morozova

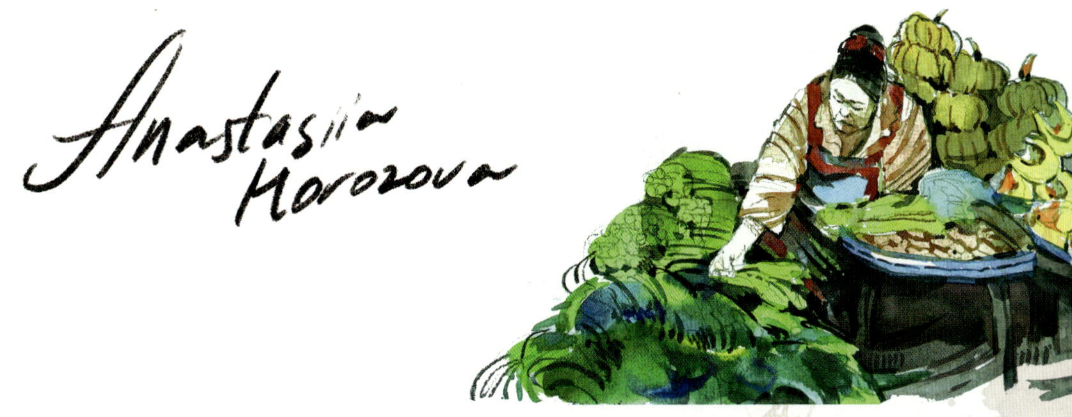

Create Anywhere
Supplies for Travel and Studio

Packing for your next trip or just wondering what art supplies to choose for watercolor painting at home? Well, you're in the right place! In this section, I'll walk you through all the essential art supplies for watercolor painting that are suitable for studio work and travel.

Watercolor Paper

Probably the most important aspect of watercolor painting is paper. The quality of your paper directly influences the ease of your painting process and the final result, so I highly recommend investing in good-quality paper. I recommend using 100 percent cotton paper for these tutorials, as we will use layering techniques in most of the paintings and certain steps and effects may not turn out the way they should on cellulose paper. My favorite brands are Arches® (a higher-end French brand) and Baohong® (a more affordable Chinese brand), which are both great for our watercolor needs.

There are two main types of watercolor paper: hot-press and cold-press. Hot-press paper has a smooth, almost textureless surface, while cold-press paper has a bit of texture. For better results, I recommend one of these two options:

1. Hot-press paper with a satin finish (no texture) or

2. Cold-press paper with a fine texture

The second option is better for beginners, but if you have experience with watercolor, you can choose either based on your preference.

Watercolor paper comes in different thicknesses, usually indicated in pounds or grams per square meter (gsm or g/m²). The higher the weight or gram count, the thicker the paper. For our purposes, 140 lb (300 gsm), which is considered medium thickness, works well. This is what I used for the tutorials in this book.

Watercolor paper is available in various forms, including pads, sketchbooks, or loose sheets. Pads glued on four sides are the most expensive option, as they help prevent buckling. Sketchbooks are perfect for travel or outdoor sketching. The price of a sketchbook depends on the brand, material (cotton fibers are more expensive than cellulose), and size. For a more cost-effective option, consider buying large sheets of watercolor paper and cutting them to the size you need. It's also a great way to test a brand and decide if you like the paper since personal preferences vary. If you're on a budget or just starting, Baohong pads are similar in quality to Arches at a lower price.

What I've used for the tutorials in this book:

- **Arches paper in sheets:** 140 lb (300 gsm), 100% cotton, hot-press with satin (smooth) finish. I cut the sheets to the desired size, and for all the tutorials in this book, I used 10 x 7–inch (25 x 18–cm) sheets.

- **Baohong pads:** 140 lb (300 gsm), 100% cotton, satin finish, sized 10 x 7 inches (25 x 18 cm). This is an artist's watercolor paper. You can identify this paper pad by its muted red cover.

Watercolor Paints

The quality of watercolor paint is crucial for the success of your painting. First and foremost, avoid using amateur or children's watercolors. These will not provide the desired effect and will likely be a waste of your time and paper. Instead, make sure you invest in student-grade or, even better, professional-grade paints.

Watercolors typically come in two forms: pans or tubes. The pigment in pans is hard and dry, so you need to activate it with water first. The color in tubes is more liquid, but keep in mind that you still need to dilute it with water.

These forms are similar in quality, so you can use either or combine both if you prefer. If you want to use a travel color palette (page 11), you'll likely need to fill it with your own colors (these palettes are often sold with empty pans, which means you'll need watercolors from tubes to fill the pans). As for brand, any professional-grade watercolor will work well. I regularly use: Daniel Smith, Winsor & Newton®, White Nights by Nevskaya Palitra, Holbein®, and Sennelier.

If you don't have a standard professional water-color set yet, I recommend investing in a 24-color set from your chosen brand or purchasing individual tubes or pans from the list I provide. However, buying a pre-composed set might be more cost-effective. In this book, I used a standard 24-color set of tubes from Nevskaya Palitra called White Nights, along with indigo from Winsor & Newton. If you're using a different brand, don't worry—just refer to the swatches and find the closest match in your set. To the right is the complete list of the colors I used across all the tutorials in this book, divided into most frequently used and occasionally used:

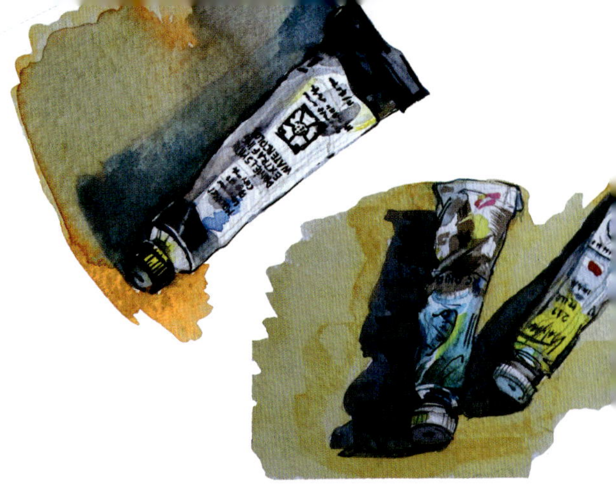

Note: The colors listed below are followed by a corresponding code number from the Nevskaya Palitra–White Nights range. This makes it easier to find the exact color or choose a similar shade from what you already have on hand.

Most Frequently Used

Cadmium Yellow Medium #201

Cadmium Lemon #203

Yellow Ochre #218

Cadmium Red Light #302

Carmine #319

Sepia #413

Raw Sienna #405

Ultramarine #511

(or Cobalt Blue #508)

Indigo #516 (not included in the White Nights by Nevskaya Palitra set, but you can purchase it separately)

Green #725

Ruby #323

Green Light #717

Quinacridone Lilac #609

Cerulean Blue #503

Emerald Green #713

Turquoise Blue #507

Brushes

The most frequently used brushes for watercolor are round. I prefer synthetic brushes, as long as they have a sharp tip. The brushes I used in all the tutorials in this book are limited-edition custom brushes I created in collaboration with Craftamo. Feel free to purchase separate brushes or use the ones you already have as long as they meet the following criteria:

- Round

- Synthetic or mixed bristles (natural + synthetic hair)

- Sharp point

Here are some brands I've tried and recommend: DaVinci Paint Co., Escoda®, Etchr, and White Nights by Nevskaya Palitra (although they can be hard to find online).

The most frequently used brush sizes in this book are 10, 8, 6, 4, and 2. I also like using a mop brush (number 14 in my Craftamo set) with a pointy tip for painting large areas using the wet-on-wet technique (page 17).

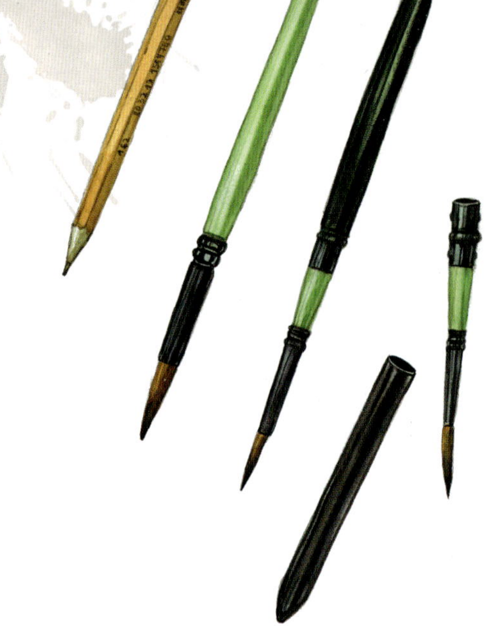

Different brands use different systems for numbering brushes, so I suggest having at least one large brush (in the range of 10 to 6), one medium brush (6 to 4), and one small brush with a pointy tip (size 3 or smaller). While I'll often suggest brush sizes to use, don't be afraid to use a different size if it feels intuitive for you; just keep in mind that the smallest brush is best for the tiniest details, such as whiskers or veins on petals. With just three brushes, you can complete all the tutorials in this book.

Note: If you're traveling with your brushes, make sure to use a brush holder to prevent the tips from bending or getting damaged. Another option is to use travel brushes, which have handles that also serve as protective lids. My Craftamo set includes two travel brushes (sizes 6 and 10).

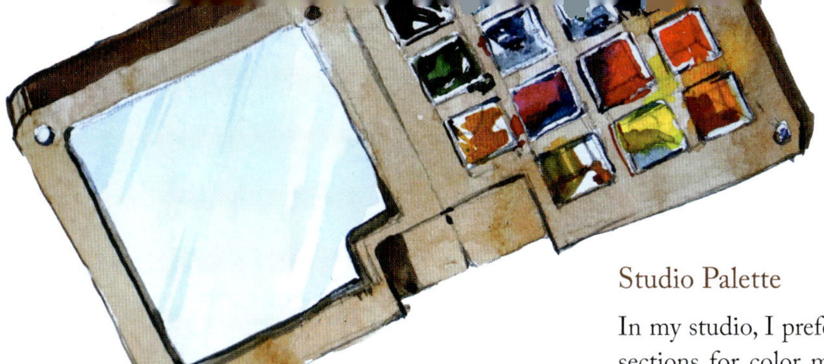

Palette

I suggest having one palette for travel and one for studio work.

Travel Palette

I use a small foldable travel palette for my trips. This is a personal preference, and most of my students love this suggestion because of the flexibility and versatility of these palettes. It fits in any bag, and you can easily clip it to your sketchbook during outdoor sketching, which eliminates the need to hold it in your hands. One side of the palette holds the watercolor pans (it usually comes with empty pans, so you'll need to fill them with your own watercolors from tubes), and the other side has a ceramic surface that serves as a mixing area for the colors.

My current palette holds 15 colors, which is more than enough for my travel needs. The mixing area is quite small, and you might need some time to get used to it and find the best method that works for you. What I typically do is wipe the palette clean if I run out of space for new colors so I can create a clean area again. You can find travel palettes online; searching for "small foldable travel paint palette" often brings up good options. Search for "portable watercolor palette" and you'll find the one I use or something similar. The illustration above shows the exact palette I used daily during my five-month trip to Southeast Asia and three months in South America, and I loved it!

Studio Palette

In my studio, I prefer a larger palette with several sections for color mixing. I also use this kind of palette when I'm working on bigger pieces and will need a lot of color mixing to complete the painting. If you don't have a ceramic palette, you can use a regular ceramic plate or the inside lid of a metal watercolor set box. Avoid using plastic palettes because the color doesn't behave as desired on them—it tends to pool together, making it difficult to see the true color. Additionally, plastic palettes stain easily and need to be replaced often, so I suggest sticking with ceramic palettes instead.

Pencils

To paint something with watercolor, you need to draw it first. The main quality to consider when choosing the right pencil is hardness, which is indicated by the symbol H (hard), B (soft), or HB (medium). The number before the letter indicates the level of hardness or softness. For example, just "H" with no number is the softest among the hardest pencils. If there is a number before it (e.g., 2H, 4H, 6H, etc.), the larger the number, the harder the pencil. Soft pencils follow the same principle: The larger the number, the softer the pencil, with the softest being 9B. The softer the pencil, the more easily it leaves a mark on paper and the darker the mark will be. Soft pencils are easier to smudge, which can be used for artistic purposes but not necessarily in our case.

For regular drawing and following the tutorials in this book, you will need to use pencils in this range: HB, B, or 2B. There are a variety of brands available on the market, and some of my favorites are Koh-I-Noor® and Faber-Castell®.

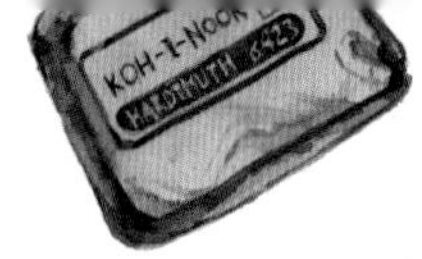

Erasers

There are several types of erasers available on the market. Instead of using a regular eraser, I recommend purchasing a kneadable (or kneaded) eraser. It's softer than a normal eraser and gentler on your paper. It's square when you first purchase it, but once you hold it in your hands, you'll notice that you can easily squeeze and mold it. I suggest creating a ball or cylinder.

This eraser has two functions: erasing mistakes like a regular eraser and lifting off excess pencil marks if your drawing is too bold or dark. To do this, roll the kneaded eraser in your hands to create a log. Then, roll it gently against the surface of your drawing multiple times. You will see that the eraser will lift off the excess pencil, softening and lightening your lines. This is often a good thing to do right before moving on to painting. Here are the brands I recommend: Koh-I-Noor and Faber-Castell.

Water Container

If you're painting in your studio, I recommend using a large glass jar, which is heavy, making it more difficult to accidentally spill your water. It's also better to have a larger container to avoid replacing the water too frequently.

During outdoor sketching, I use a small spray bottle in two ways: I spray water onto my palette, and then wipe it with a paper towel to clean the palette between the colors (since travel palettes are usually small), or I use it to clean my brush. To do that, I hold the brush against the palette, spray water on it, and rub the brush against the palette to remove the color. I then dry everything with a paper towel and repeat the process until the brush is clean. Always replace your water once it becomes dirty to avoid impacting your colors.

Masking Fluid

Masking fluid is optional, and we will only use it for a few tutorials (Fly Agaric Mushroom [page 55] and Giant Panda [page 160]). Masking fluid is used to protect certain areas of your paper, allowing you to paint on top of them without leaving any marks. For example, imagine the fly agaric mushroom cap with white spots. Without masking fluid, you would have to carefully avoid each of these spots, making the process long and tedious. However, if you cover these spots with masking fluid before painting, you can apply the red paint to the entire cap, white spots included. After everything dries, simply peel off the masking fluid and you will reveal the perfectly white surface underneath. Masking fluid can make the painting process easier, and I want to show you the possibilities of this technique. However, this tool is not required, so don't worry if you don't have it.

Other Supplies

Paper towels: We will use these constantly to remove excess water or color from the brush, clean the palette, and correct mistakes. I always have paper towels with me when I'm painting—in my studio or during travels.

Pencil sharpener or utility knife: Use these to sharpen your pencils.

That's it for the art supplies! I bet your hands are already itching to paint! But before we dive into our global painting adventure, let me introduce you to some important watercolor painting techniques that we'll be using throughout this book.

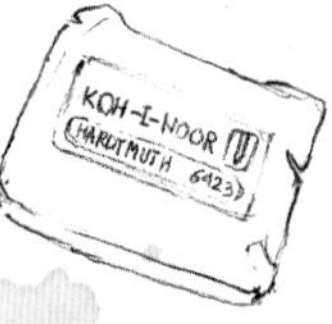

Main Watercolor Principles and Techniques

Before diving deeper into the creative process, it's essential to understand a few key concepts about watercolor. This understanding will help you fully appreciate the medium's unique qualities and use them to your advantage.

Watercolor Principles

As the name suggests, watercolor relies on two fundamental elements: water and pigment. Water plays a pivotal role, activating the pigment and determining the flow, transparency, and luminosity of the color. The amount of water you use directly influences how the pigment behaves on the paper, affecting the intensity and movement of your colors. More water creates lighter, more translucent washes, allowing the white of the paper to shine through and adding a luminous quality to the work. On the other hand, less water results in more saturated, darker hues, with the pigment more concentrated on the surface.

Even when using more liquid watercolors from tubes, adding water remains essential for using them correctly. Watercolor's reliance on water and its unique interplay with pigment is what sets it apart and creates vibrant results. Let's explore these principles together.

The Translucency of Watercolor

The main quality of watercolor that sets it apart from other painting mediums is translucency, or the ability of the paint to let light pass through the pigment layer. Many other painting mediums, such as acrylic, gouache, or oil, tend to be more opaque. The transparency of watercolor allows underlying layers of color—as well as the white of the paper—to shine through, giving the painting a sense of depth, luminosity, and vibrancy. This unique characteristic encourages layering and color blending, allowing artists to create paintings with a glowing quality that is difficult to achieve with other mediums. The interplay between pigment, water, and paper is essential to this effect, making watercolor a medium that thrives on its fluidity and transparency.

This gradient was created by layering the same color.

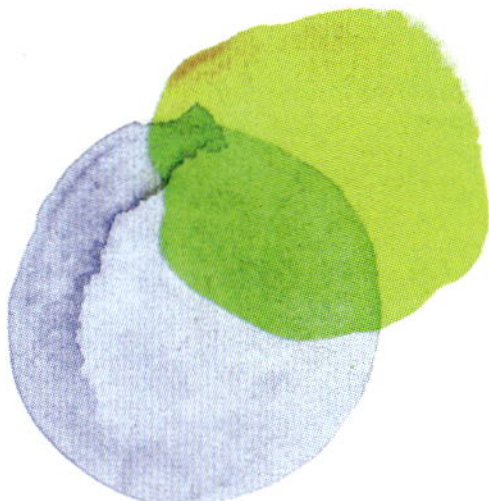

The translucency of the layers lets underlying colors interact, as seen with blue over yellow—creating green.

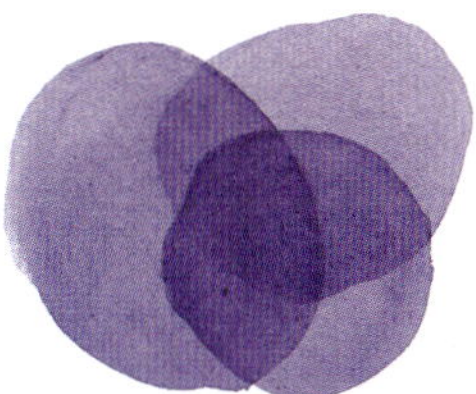

By layering the same color, the area with the most layers becomes the darkest.

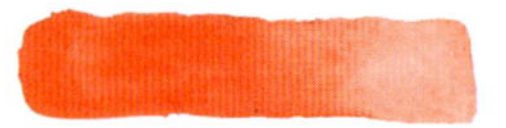

Cadmium red has a warm orange undertone.

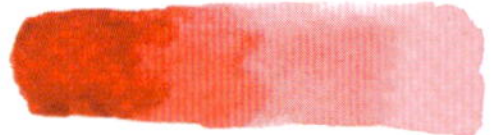

Carmine has a cool pink undertone.

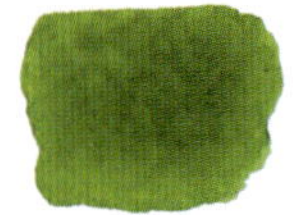

A warm green created by mixing green and cadmium yellow

A cool green created by mixing green and ultramarine

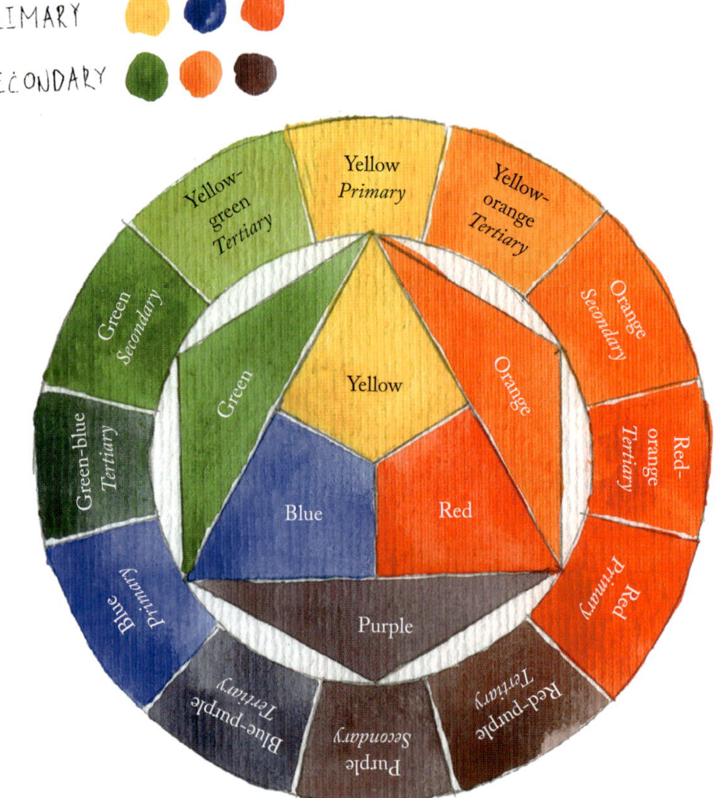

Color Mixing

Mixing colors is an essential part of watercolor painting, enabling you to achieve more nuanced and complex shades. I recommend following this simple rule: Limit your mixes to no more than four colors, with two to three being the ideal range. This ensures your mixtures remain clean and vibrant. Adding too many colors can lead to muddy, dull results.

Color mixing is a vast topic, but a few key concepts can make a big difference. One fundamental idea is the distinction between warm and cold colors. It's often intuitive—blue is cool, orange is warm—but even within a single color, such as red, there are warm and cool variations. For instance, cadmium red leans toward orange and is considered warm, while carmine has a pinkish undertone, making it cooler. This applies to other colors as well; for example, a green mixed with yellow will appear warmer than one mixed with blue. Understanding color mixing will help you as we discuss warm and cool colors in the tutorials.

Another important principle we'll rely on is working with the primary colors: yellow, blue, and red. These are called "primary" because you cannot create them by mixing other colors. However, by combining two primary colors, you can produce a secondary color. For example, mixing yellow and red gives you orange, while blue and red make purple. Throughout the book, we'll often mix and layer primary and secondary colors to create a variety of tones and explore their interactions. These foundational principles of color mixing will enrich your watercolor journey and help you create harmonious, dynamic artwork.

White in Watercolor

In watercolor, white is not typically used as a pigment but is instead the result of the white paper showing through the transparent layers of paint. This is a defining feature of the medium, as it relies on the natural white surface to create highlights. Unlike other painting mediums, where white paint can be mixed in to lighten colors, watercolor requires a delicate balance of controlling the flow of water and pigment to ensure the white of the paper remains a vital part of the artwork.

Some watercolor brands do offer a white pigment in their sets, but to me, it doesn't make much sense to use it. White is not traditionally used in classical watercolor painting because it will not make your colors lighter but rather more opaque and even muddy, losing the luminosity, freshness, and clarity that are characteristic of the medium.

The absence of white paint means that artists must carefully plan their compositions, using the unpainted paper to preserve areas of brightness and light. Another way to protect the white of the paper is by using masking fluid (page 12). The Fly Agaric Mushroom (page 55) and Giant Panda (page 160) are great examples of when this approach can be helpful.

Black in Watercolor

The use of pure black in watercolor is something I personally avoid, and it's a rule I picked up from my art school days. My teachers were quite traditional about this, and although I've evolved in many ways over the years, I still find that avoiding pure black helps enhance my work. It's a guideline I also encourage my students to follow.

In watercolor, there's rarely a need for pure black, as you can achieve rich dark tones by deepening other colors. Using dark blues, greens, purples, or browns to create shadows and depth results in more complex and refined shades, giving the work a sense of warmth and subtlety. These dark hues preserve the transparency and luminous quality that defines watercolor, while pure black can often look flat or stark, disrupting the vibrancy and delicacy of the piece.

By relying on other dark colors, you not only maintain the integrity of watercolor's airy lightness, but you also create richer, more nuanced shadows and textures that feel more alive and harmonious.

Essential Watercolor Techniques

Before diving into the tutorials, let's take a moment to explore some of the main watercolor techniques. These foundational methods are the building blocks of watercolor painting, and mastering them will greatly enhance your confidence and control over the medium.

I highly recommend practicing these techniques beforehand, especially if you're new to watercolor or if some of them feel unfamiliar. This practice will help you approach the tutorials with ease, ensuring a smoother and more enjoyable painting experience.

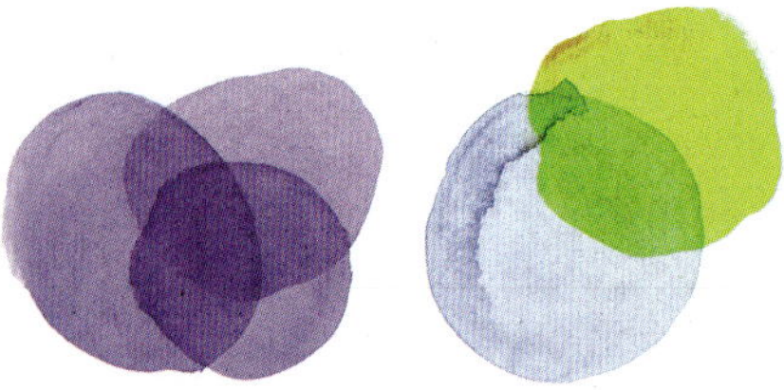

Layering can be done using the same color
or different colors.

Washes and Layering

Washes and layering are fundamental tools in
watercolor that allow you to build depth, create
smooth gradients, and add richness to your artwork. A wash refers to a thin, even layer of diluted
paint applied to the paper, often used for backgrounds, skies, or setting a base tone. Washes can
be flat, where the color is consistent throughout,
or graded, where it transitions smoothly from
dark to light or between colors.

Layering (also known as glazing), on the other
hand, involves applying multiple washes on top
of each other once the previous layer is dry. This
technique is essential for creating dimension,
adjusting tones, and adding complexity to your
painting. Because of watercolor's transparency,
each layer interacts with the ones beneath it,
allowing you to build subtle color variations and
depth while maintaining luminosity.

A gradient is a soft transition—
here it transitions from light to
dark purple.

Notice the hard edges of this flower
created using the wet-on-dry technique.

Wet-on-Dry

The wet-on-dry technique involves applying wet
paint onto dry paper or a dry layer of paint. This
method offers greater control and precision, as the
wet paint doesn't spread across the surface as it
does in the wet-on-wet technique (page 17) and
creates crisp, well-defined edges. It is ideal for
achieving sharp lines, textures, and well-defined
shapes—making it preferable for line work, final
details, and adding contrast to a painting. Wet-
on-dry is a highly versatile technique and remains
one of the most commonly used approaches in
watercolor painting.

To use this technique, start by ensuring your paper
or previous layer is completely dry. Then, load your
brush with wet paint and apply it directly onto
the dry surface, allowing the strokes to retain their
shape and intensity. For sharp edges and greater
control, make sure the paint is sufficiently liquid
but not too watery, as excess water can cause the
paint to puddle. On the other hand, too little
water will result in a dry, broken stroke that lacks
fluidity. Finding the right balance is key to achieving smooth, crisp results.

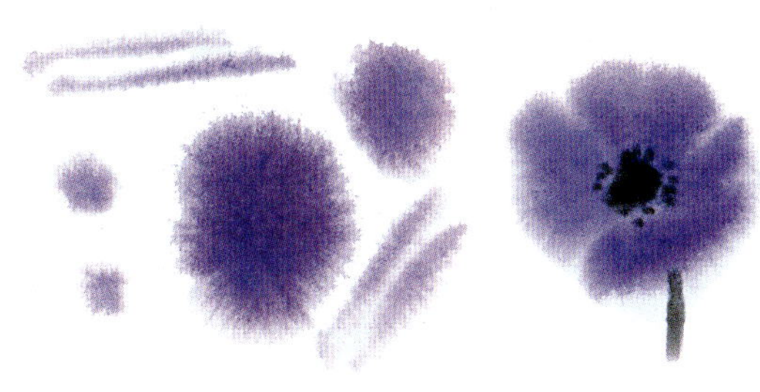

Notice the soft edges of this flower
created using the wet-on-wet technique.

Wet-on-Wet

The wet-on-wet technique involves applying wet paint onto wet paper or a wet layer of paint. This method allows the colors to flow and blend together organically, creating soft transitions and gradients. It's ideal for achieving smooth washes, atmospheric effects, and blending colors seamlessly—making it perfect for backgrounds, skies, and other areas where you want to create fluid, soft edges. Wet-on-wet is one of the most expressive techniques in watercolor painting, offering a spontaneous and flowing approach. We will often use this technique in the first stages of the process, as it is the best method for giving a subject volume from the very first steps.

To use this technique, begin by wetting your paper with clean water using a large brush, ensuring even coverage without pooling water. Then, load your brush with watercolor and apply it onto the wet surface. The paint will spread and move, creating soft edges and blends.

If you add a very thick layer of color to the wet surface, you will notice prominent blooming effects; the color will mainly remain in place and won't spread too much due to the high concentration of pigment. It's important to keep this trick in mind, as it's how we will create texture on the surface of the petals on the Mule Ear Orchid (page 37).

The key to mastering the wet-on-wet technique is understanding that the amount of water on both the paper and in your color mix will strongly influence the final result. I suggest practicing with this technique to get a feel for how it works.

One important factor to consider is that the effect of this technique changes as the paper dries. To experiment with this, create a medium-dark color mix, and use the same mix throughout the entire experiment. Then, cover three separate areas on your paper with water. Apply the mix to the first area immediately. Wait one to two minutes before applying the same mix to the second area, and then wait three to five minutes before applying the mix to the third area. You'll notice that the level of dryness of your paper strongly influences the effect, even though you used the same color mix.

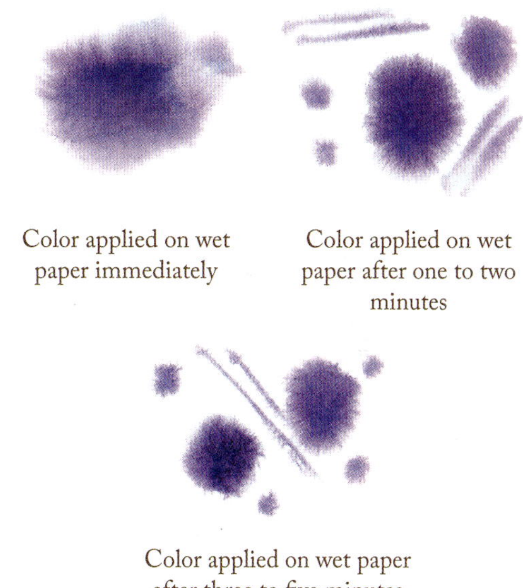

Color applied on wet
paper immediately

Color applied on wet
paper after one to two
minutes

Color applied on wet paper
after three to five minutes

Keep in mind that temperature and humidity will also have a significant impact on the behavior of watercolor, especially when using the wet-on-wet technique. In warm, dry spaces, the paper and color tend to dry much quicker, while in cool, humid environments, the paint remains wet for a much longer time.

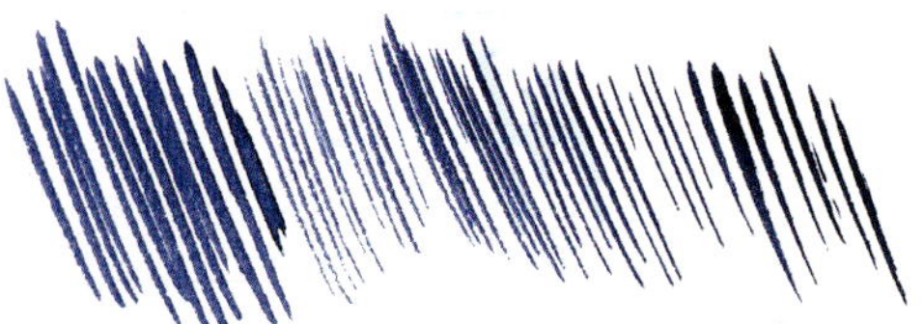

Thin dry brushed strokes

Lifting

Dry Brushing

Dry brushing involves using a relatively dry brush with a small amount of paint to create texture and final details. The key to this technique is the minimal amount of water in the color—just enough to create a mark. This allows the bristles to catch on the textured surface of the paper, leaving behind a distinct, often scratchy or grainy effect. The result is a subtle, almost broken stroke that can add depth and contrast to your painting. It's especially effective for creating rough textures, such as fur, hair, or the intricate veins on leaves and petals. We will often use this technique at the very last stages of painting, in combination with a very thin brush or by using the very tip of a brush.

To master dry brushing, you need to experiment with different amounts of paint and pressure, adjusting the technique to your desired outcome. Keep in mind that the smoother your paper, the subtler the texture, while a rougher paper surface produces a more pronounced, expressive effect.

Lifting

Lifting involves removing or lightening areas of paint. This technique is ideal for creating highlights, correcting mistakes, or softening hard edges. To lift off paint, you can use a clean, slightly damp brush or a paper towel to gently blot or scrub the paint from the surface. It's important to work quickly, as watercolor absorbs into the paper over time and becomes more difficult to lift once it dries. For a more precise effect, you can use a clean, stiff-bristled brush to scrub at the surface, removing some of the pigment without disturbing the paper too much.

The lifting effect will be more visible with darker colors than lighter ones due to the greater contrast between the area where the color was lifted and the original wash (see the illustrations above).

Hard edges (before applying the smoothing technique)   Soft edges (after applying the smoothing technique)

Smoothing Edges

This technique is used to soften or blend harsh, hard edges into a more seamless transition. This technique is particularly useful for creating a natural or fluid look, especially in areas where we see color transitions in different natural subjects.

To smooth out edges, you need to work quickly while the paint is still wet. Using a clean, damp brush, gently run it along the edge of the painted area, blending the color into the surrounding wet or dry surface. For dry areas, you can lightly mist the surface with water before softening the edges, allowing the pigment to reactivate and flow on the paper. You'll notice that I refer to this technique in almost every tutorial, so it is essential to practice it before starting the projects.

Sketching

Sketches allow you to plan out your composition and refine your subject's outline and major details before painting. In each tutorial, I provide sketching instructions, showing you how to build up your guide lines before honing your final drawing. You want to leave some space around your sketch—this gives your subject some space to breathe and you the opportunity to create a background, as with the Snowy Albatross (page 215), or add in additional elements, like in the Koala tutorial on page 194.

Note that in this book, I have darkened my pencil sketches in the first few steps of each tutorial for easy visibility. When you sketch, keep your pencil lines light so that they don't shine through your watercolor washes.

Tracing

Tracing with a lightbox, through a window, or using tracing paper allows you to quickly transfer a drawing onto your preferred watercolor paper, saving you the effort of starting from scratch.

If you're a beginner or simply want to jump straight into painting without the need to draw the subjects, use the QR code on this page. Scan it with your mobile device to access the page on my website where you can download the ready-to-transfer drawings alongside the instructions on how to use them. If you're having trouble using the QR code, just enter this link in your browser to access the same page: anastasiiamorozova.com/transfer-drawings-book.

These are the main principles and techniques we will be using throughout the entire book. If you'd like, you can practice them a bit before diving into the projects to feel more confident during the painting process. However, remember that the best way to learn is by doing, so even if you don't feel completely ready, don't worry—you'll have plenty of opportunities to practice throughout the tutorials.

With every natural subject you paint, you'll notice your skills and confidence growing. I hope you're as excited as I am, and I look forward to seeing you in the next chapters, where we'll start bringing your watercolor paintings to life!

Main Watercolor Principles and Techniques   19

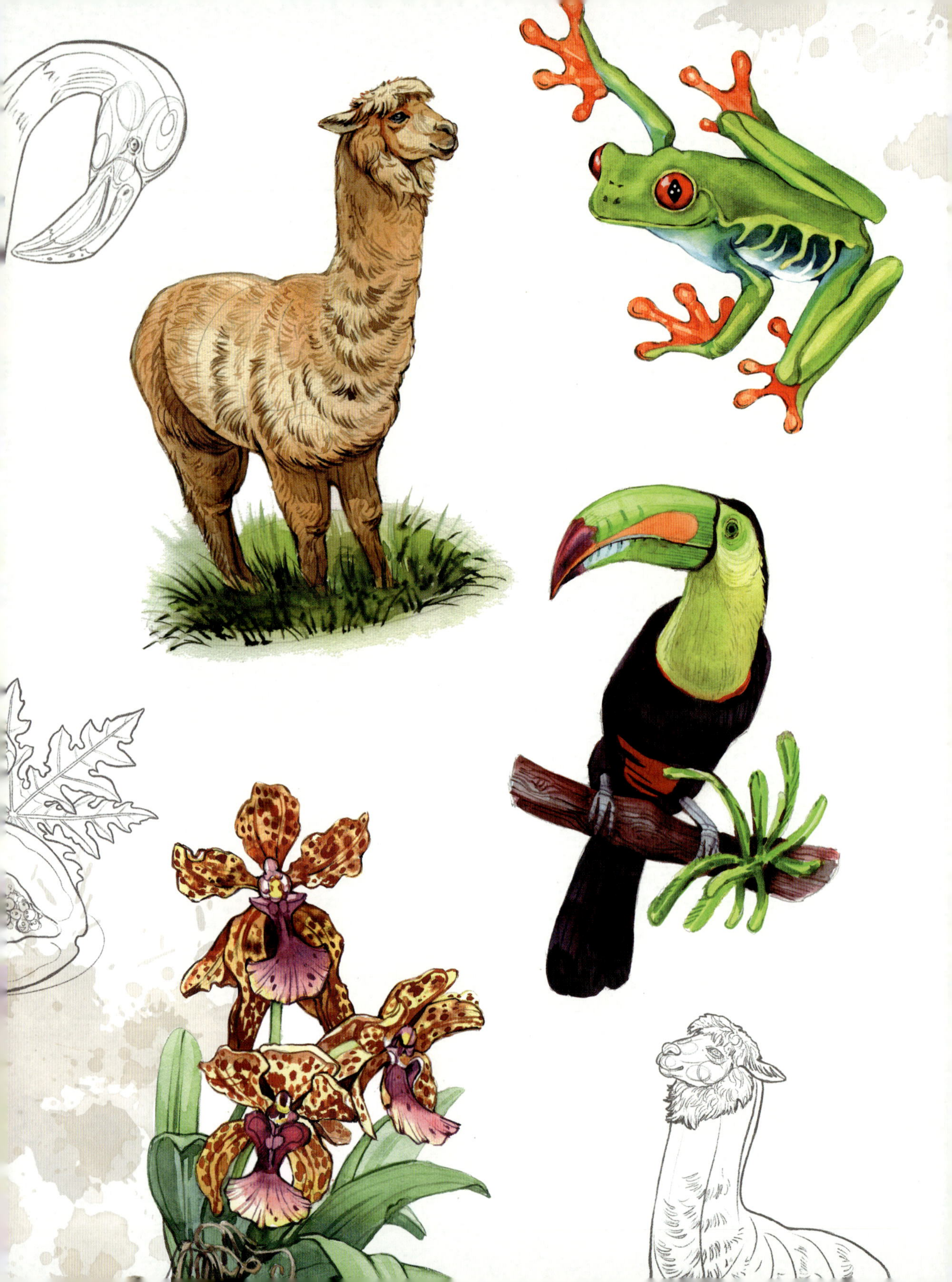

South America
From Rainforests to Mountaintops

Welcome to our illustrated journey through the vibrant and exhilarating continent of South America! This land is bursting with diversity, from the towering peaks of the Andes to the lush green expanses of the Amazon Rainforest. South America's landscapes are as varied as its wildlife, offering everything from salt deserts to tropical forests. This continent is also the birthplace of many foods we consider staples today, like tomatoes, potatoes, and corn. But it's the fruit that really steals the show here. One such fruit is the Papaya (page 23), the first tutorial of this chapter.

After painting this vibrant fruit, we'll explore the wonders of the Brazilian Amazon! This primary rainforest is a complex, interwoven ecosystem, and each plant and animal plays a vital role in its balance. For instance, the trees don't just tower above the forest floor; they also create the perfect environment for delicate and striking orchids like the Mule Ear Orchid (page 37). While orchids may be a familiar sight in homes around the world, few people realize they are native to the deep, humid Amazon Rainforest, where they rely on other plants for survival. As we venture deeper into the jungle, we'll encounter some of the rainforest's most fascinating creatures, including the Red-Eyed Tree Frog (page 27) and the charismatic Toucan (page 33), both of which we'll be bringing to life in our tutorials.

Continuing our adventure, we'll journey to the highlands of Bolivia and the awe-inspiring Salar de Uyuni, the world's largest salt flat. Although it may seem barren at first, this startling landscape is home to resilient and beautiful creatures like the Flamingo (page 43), which gets its distinctive pink color from the tiny red krill it eats in the salty lakes.

No South American adventure would be complete without the iconic Alpaca (page 47), native to the highlands of Peru. These adorable creatures, part of the camelid family, have evolved to thrive in extreme conditions, even drinking salty water from high-altitude lakes! Domesticated by ancient civilizations, alpacas play an integral role in the local culture. Their wool is prized for being softer and warmer than sheep's wool. The alpaca is so beloved that it's considered a symbol of good fortune, and many local people dress them in elaborate clothing, much like their own traditional attire.

With so many wonders to explore and paint, this chapter promises to be an unforgettable journey! Prepare your brushes and get ready for a splash of color and culture as we dive into the beauty of South America.

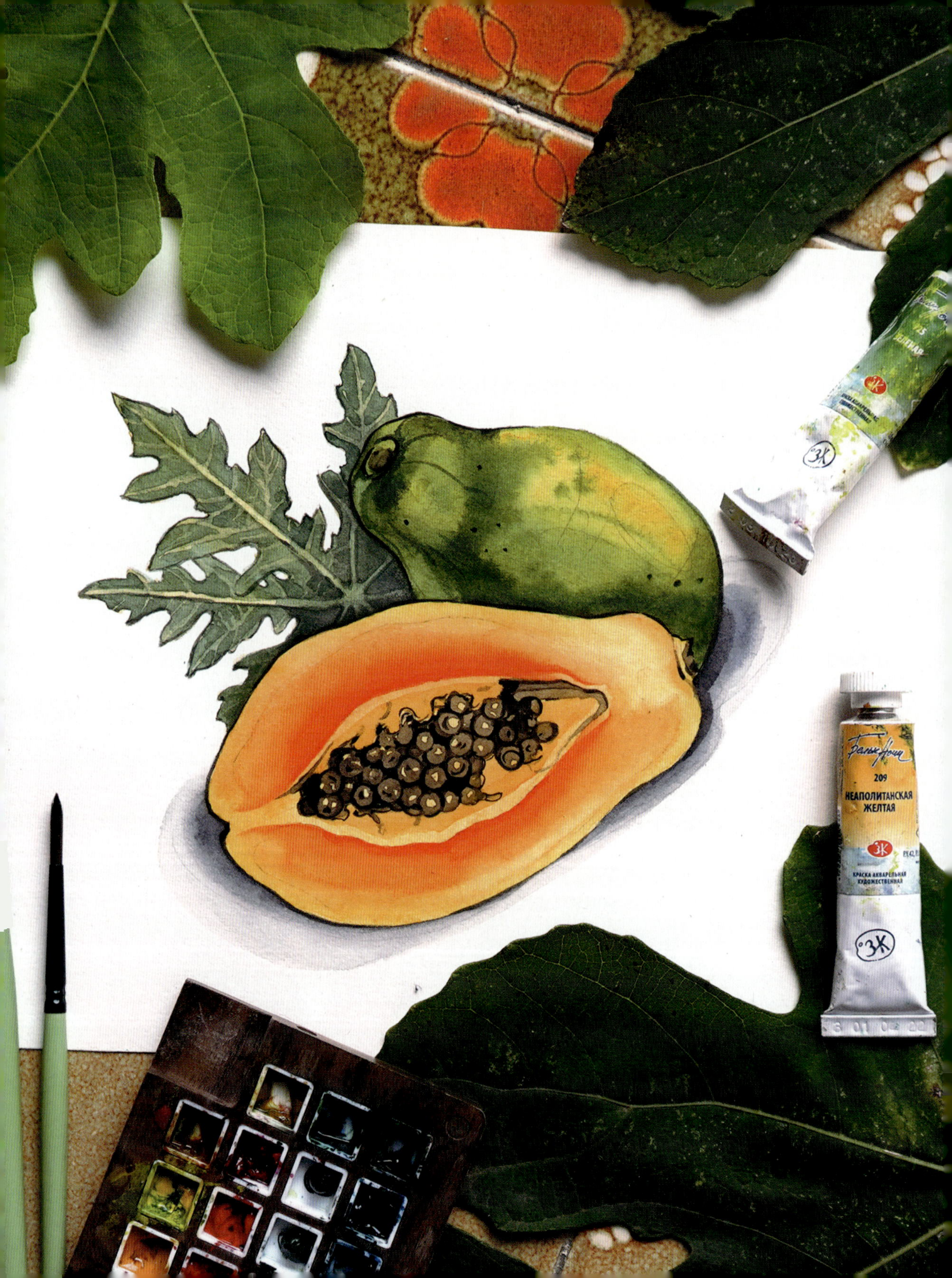
209
НЕАПОЛИТАНСКАЯ
ЖЕЛТАЯ
КРАСКА АКВАРЕЛЬНАЯ
ХУДОЖЕСТВЕННАЯ

Papaya

Fruits and vegetables are perfect subjects for artists, especially for beginners, as they offer a wealth of texture and colors. The papaya, with its vibrant orange flesh and smooth skin, is a perfect subject to practice. Native to southern Mexico and Central America, this tropical fruit is often referred to as the "fruit of the angels" due to its sweet, delicate flavor. What's fascinating is that the papaya tree isn't actually a tree but a large herb that can grow up to 10 feet (3 m) tall in just a year under ideal conditions. In this tutorial, you'll learn how to capture the subtle gradients of color in the fruit's flesh, the contrast with its black seeds, and the smooth texture of the skin. You'll also practice creating an interesting composition by adding leaves and a drop shadow, bringing depth and life to your painting.

Colors Needed

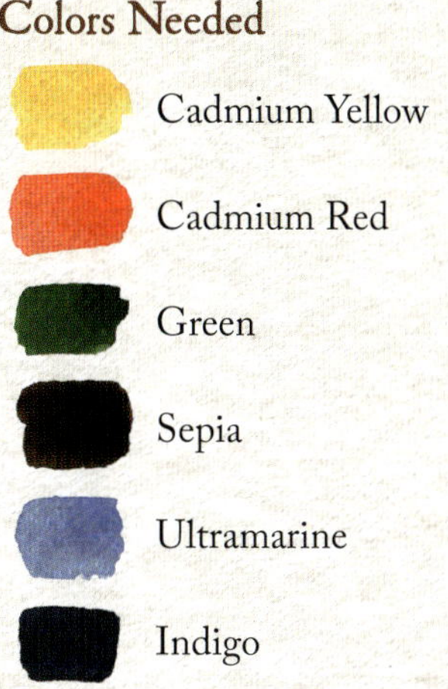

Suggested Paper Orientation: Horizontal

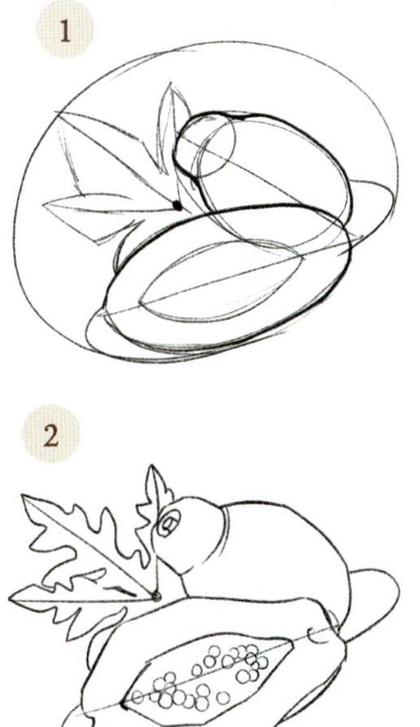

Step 1: Draw one large oval with two intersecting ovals that will represent two fruits at the base of the large oval. Add a smaller pointed oval in the center of the front papaya. Outline the leaf with three lines starting from the left intersection of the fruits, extending in three different directions (to the left, straight, and to the right). Add more detail to the leaf by outlining it with three triangles at the tips, with the largest one in the center. Refine the shape of the fruits by adding a center line to each, and give them a cast shadow using two ovals. Enhance the realism of the back fruit by adding a small oval at its tip.

Step 2: Erase the big oval, as we no longer need it. Separate the leaf into smaller sections and give it pointy tips. Refine the tip of the back papaya, adding a circle where the remains of the stem connect with the fruit. Refine the shape of the front (cut-open) papaya, and add the seeds to the center with small circles.

Step 3: Give the lines on the leaf some thickness and create lateral veins. Draw smaller spikes in between the bigger ones to refine the leaf's edges. Add texture to the back papaya using lines that go across its surface. Add a line to visually separate the oval tip from the wider body, and outline the highlight areas on the body and the top of the papaya with ovals. Finish the front papaya by adding an internal border and refining the stem and seeds. Your drawing is complete.

Step 4: Create two mixes:

- Mix A: cadmium yellow + a touch of cadmium red + water (more pigment than water) = yellow

- Mix B: cadmium yellow + more cadmium red + water (more pigment than water) = orange

Apply Mix A to the entire surface of the bottom (cut) papaya. While this layer dries, prepare Mix C:

- Mix C: green + a touch of cadmium yellow + water = light green

Once the first layer is dry, cover the surface of the top (whole) papaya with the same Mix A, and while the paint is still wet, apply Mix C to most areas, leaving some brighter spots on the top right side, a bit on the tip, and another spot on the top left. Then, get back to the lower papaya and apply a bold stroke of Mix B outside of the seed area. Make sure that the middle is thicker than the sides. While this is still wet, wash your brush and smooth out the edges using clean water until you have a seamless color blend from orange (closer to the inside part) to yellow (closer to the external part).

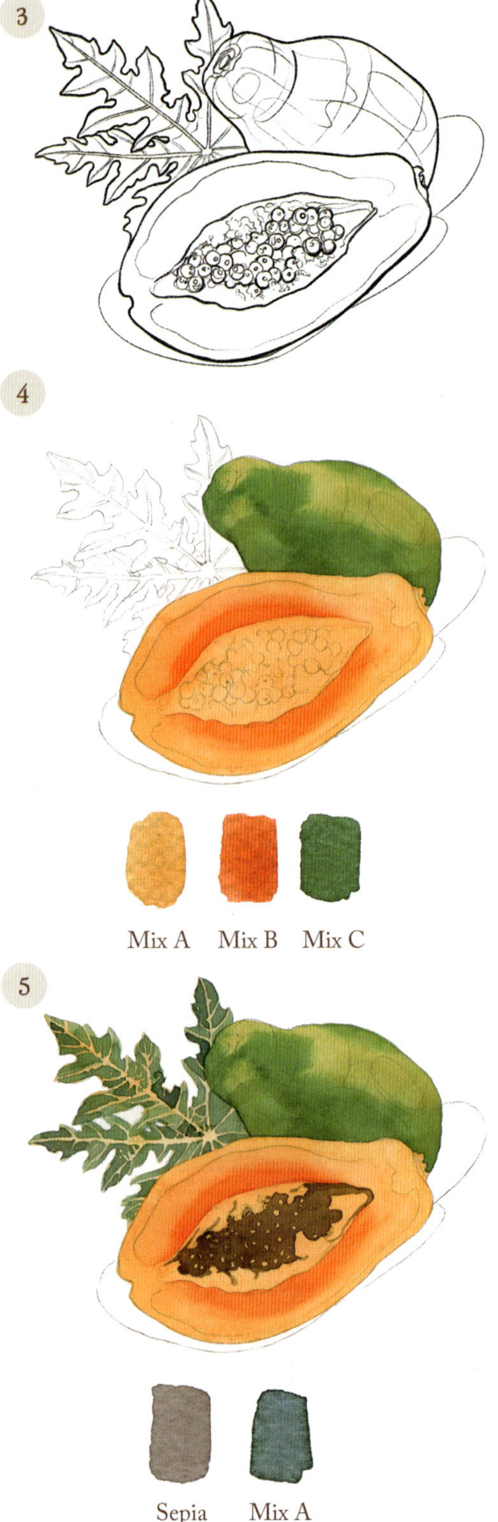

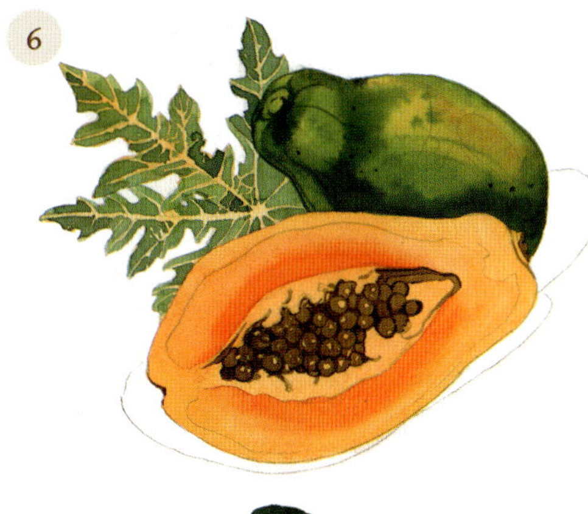

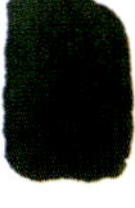

Mix A

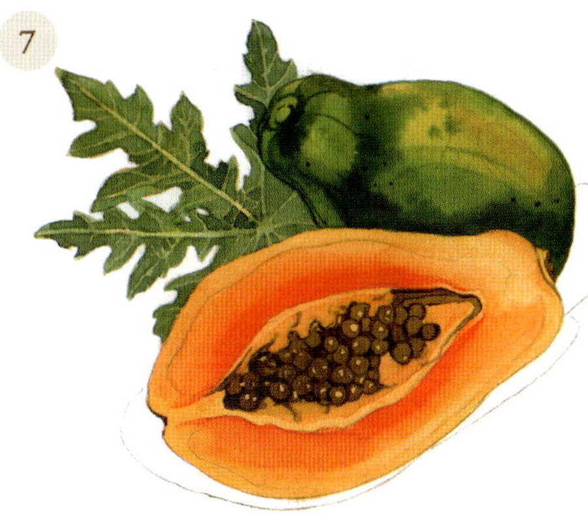

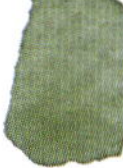

Mix A

Step 5: Cover the entire leaf with Mix 4A from the previous step. While this dries, mix sepia with water and apply this to the seeds in the bottom papaya. Then, mix another color for the leaf:

- Mix A: green + ultramarine + water = green

With a small brush, apply Mix A to the entire leaf, avoiding the veins. Leave the veins a bit bolder for now, as we will address them in the next steps.

Step 6: Let's focus on giving more volume to the top papaya. Cover it with Mix 4A, then darken it using Mix 4C. Add some dots and lines to imitate the skin's texture. Once this layer dries, add some final texture by using an even darker color mix:

- Mix A: Mix 4C (green + a touch of cadmium yellow + water) + more green + a touch of indigo + almost no water = dark green

Use Mix A and the very tip of your small brush to add thin lines that underline the shape of the papaya, especially on its upper part where the smaller initial portion transitions into the larger spherical body. Add some random dots in a few areas for more interest. Then, take the sepia mixed with water used in the previous step to outline the individual seeds and the tips of the cut papaya.

Step 7: Create a new mix:

- Mix A: green + indigo + water = light blue-green

Apply Mix A to the whole surface of the leaf, leaving the two main veins untouched. Then, add even more saturation to the cut papaya with Mix 4B and repeat the same process as in Step 4, intensifying the orange gradation even more.

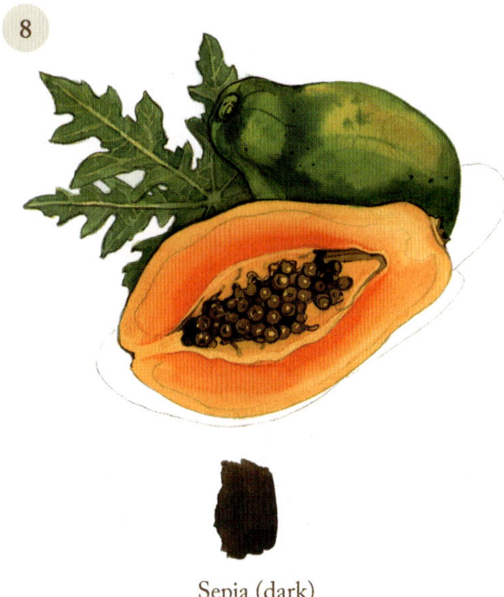

Sepia (dark)

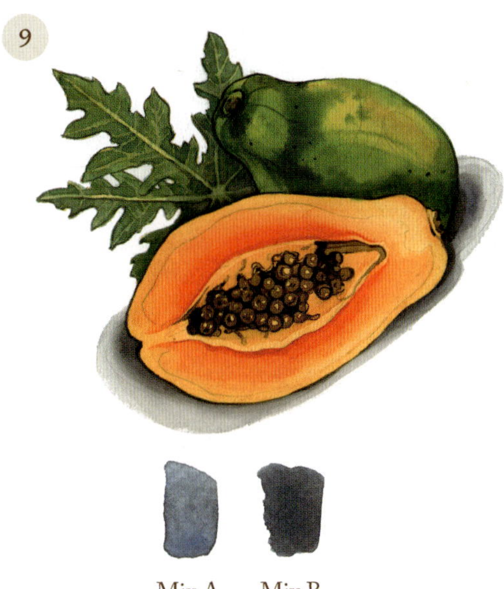

Mix A   Mix B

Step 8: Add shadow to the lower part of the leaf where it meets the fruits using Mix 7A. Then, add more pigment to the mix to create a darker color. Use this darker mix and the tip of your small brush to outline the leaf and veins with very thin lines. Make sure the outline is not uniform, with breaks in some places to create a more natural and organic look. Next, add final touches to the seeds of the papaya using a dark sepia (sepia with a touch of water). Use the same color to outline the top of the bottom papaya. Let dry completely.

Step 9: Paint the shadows around the fruits. Mix two gray colors:

- Mix A: ultramarine + sepia + water = gray
- Mix B: ultramarine + sepia + water (more pigment than water) = dark gray

Apply the lighter Mix A around the fruits, then smooth the edges for a seamless transition. Next, introduce the darker Mix B closer to the fruits. As a final touch, make the orange near the opening even more vibrant. Add more cadmium red to Mix 4B to intensify the color, and a thin line of this color to the two lower borders of the opening. No need to smooth out the edges this time. Your painting is ready!

Red-Eyed Tree Frog

The red-eyed tree frog is a vibrant and eye-catching amphibian, famous for its striking red eyes and bright green body. Found in the rainforests of Central America, it's known for its ability to blend into the leaves while hiding from predators during the day. In this tutorial, you will learn how to represent colorful and vibrant subjects realistically, creating distinct areas of color and patterns on the frog without making the final painting feel scattered or unharmonious. Let's dive in!

Colors Needed

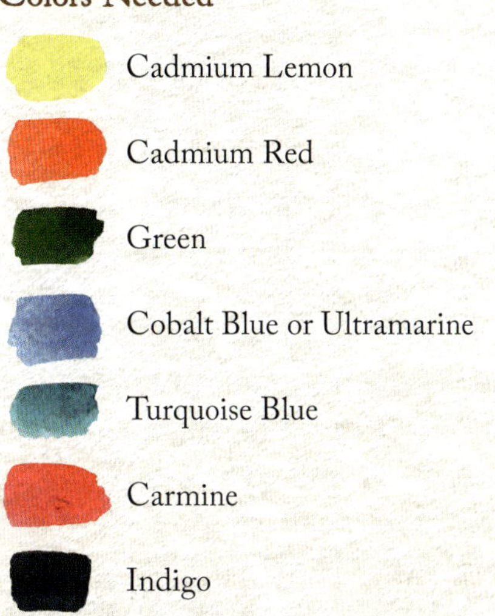

Cadmium Lemon

Cadmium Red

Green

Cobalt Blue or Ultramarine

Turquoise Blue

Carmine

Indigo

Suggested Paper Orientation: Vertical

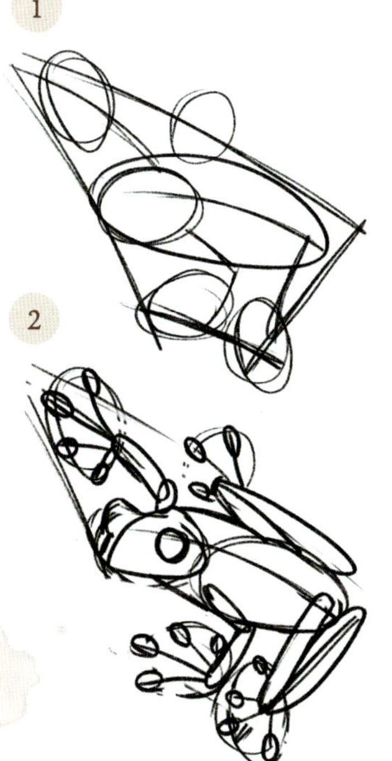

Step 1: Draw a diagonal oval with the left side slightly higher than the right; this will be the frog's body. Inside this oval, give the body a guide line and outline the head with a circle on the left side of the body oval.

Create some long guide lines to position the legs and add ovals for feet. You should end up with an irregular trapezoid. Then, position the "hands" with ovals, which will help you connect the hands to the body and define the position of the arms.

Step 2: Define the line on the head and the eyeline, and then position the eyes. Begin defining the legs with long ovals. Outline the individual fingers with small ovals, and then connect them to the arms with lines. We will use these lines as a base to outline the fingers in the next step. Then, make the tip of the head more pointed and outline the back eye with a bump.

Step 3: Refine the general outline of the frog before adding the final details to the body and legs. Give the fingers a more realistic appearance by adding two parallel lines to the outline, which will add thickness to the fingers. Outline the pattern on the belly, ensuring that the top of the pattern nearly matches the line of the body. Next, draw four perpendicular lines extending from this pattern to the lower side of the belly. Add lines along the length of the legs and arms, following their natural shape; these lines will help us define the light and shadow areas more easily while painting. Once you're happy with your drawing, you can move to the painting process!

Step 4: Use your medium brush and start with two colors. Obtain a light yellow mix by combining cadmium lemon with water. Then, create a mix:

- Mix A: cadmium lemon + cadmium red + water = medium orange

Apply the light yellow mix to the stripes on the belly, around the eye, on the nose, and to the highlights on the legs. Apply Mix A to the fingers and let this dry.

Step 5: While the previous layer dries, mix some colors for this step:

- Mix A: cadmium lemon + green + water = light green
- Mix B: cadmium lemon + cobalt blue or ultramarine + water = green

Apply Mix A to the top part of the body. Once you approach the yellow pattern and the lower part of the eye, switch to Mix B and continue covering the top portion of the body and head with this color.

(Step 5 continued)

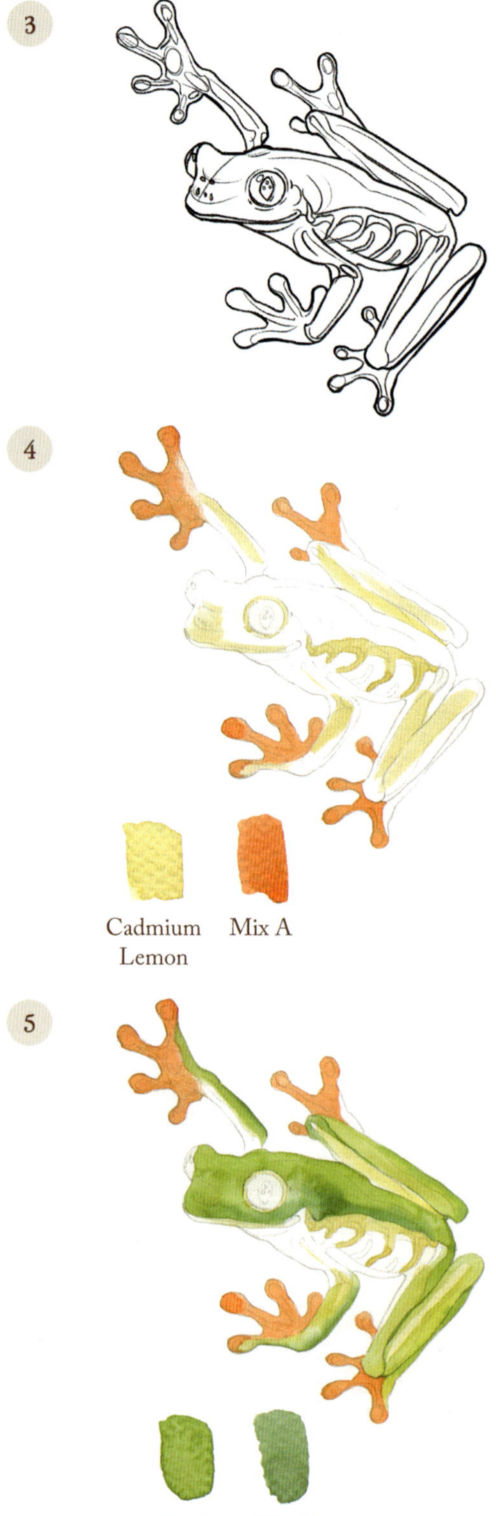

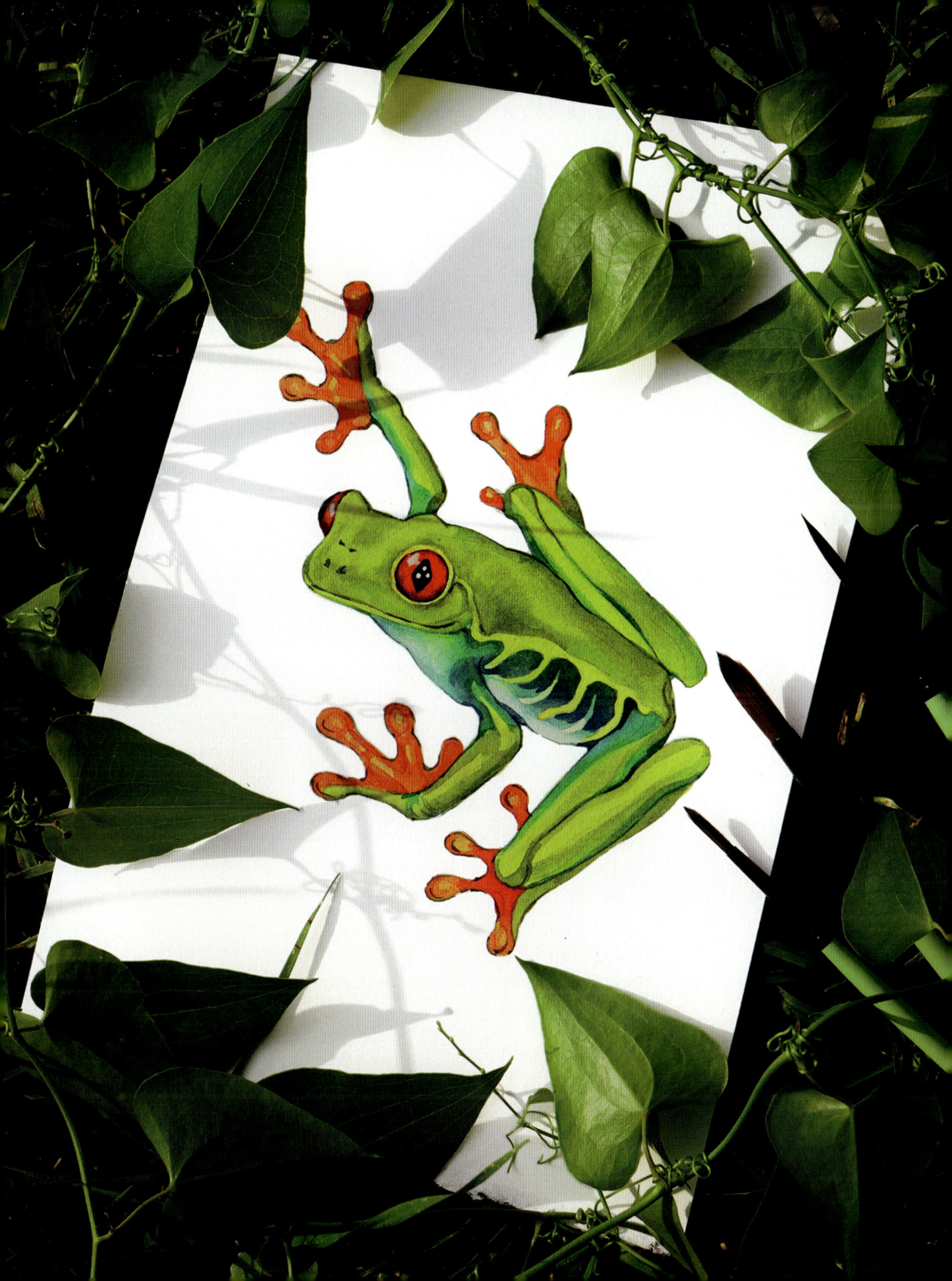

Using a similar principle, cover the right half of the top left leg with Mix A, then add Mix B to the upper right side of the leg. Let this color blend into the lighter green to create a gradient from light to dark green. Do the same thing on the lower left legs, but cover only the lower part of them and leave the top parts untouched for now. Then, proceed with the back legs. As before, start with Mix A, but this time, make sure to add Mix B not only to the right part of the leg but also to the folds between the two parts of the legs.

Step 6: While the previous layer dries, create a new bright blue mix by combining turquoise blue with water. Apply this color to the left side of the top left leg and smooth the edges for a seamless transition. Also, apply the turquoise blue to the left part of the lower right leg, to the right side of the hip, and to the left side of the hip. Finally, apply the color to the lower part of the belly, making sure to avoid the yellow pattern and the two white stripes on it. Once you almost reach the end of the belly, switch to water to create a blend from darker to lighter blue. Do the same as you get closer to the mouth; switch to water at that point and continue to paint the area under the head with water. Let this layer dry before proceeding.

Step 7: In this step, we will add color to the eyes and more details to the fingers. Prepare a bright saturated red with cadmium red and water, as well as a new color mix:

- Mix A: carmine + indigo + water = burgundy

We will also need more of Mix A from Step 4 for this step. Start by covering the eyes of the frog with cadmium red, except for the pupil and the highlight. While the red is still wet, add Mix A to the sides of the eye, especially on the lower side.

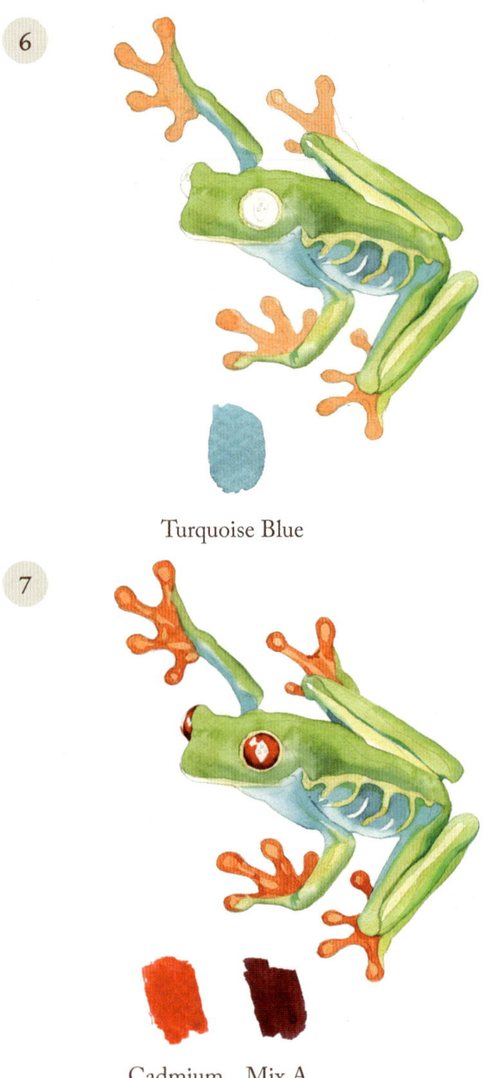

Turquoise Blue

Cadmium   Mix A
Red

Let this dark color slightly blend into the saturated red color of the eye. This will help create a light and shadow effect on the eye. Then, take Mix 4A and apply it to the fingers, leaving the round highlights on the tips and a long highlight on some of the fingers untouched.

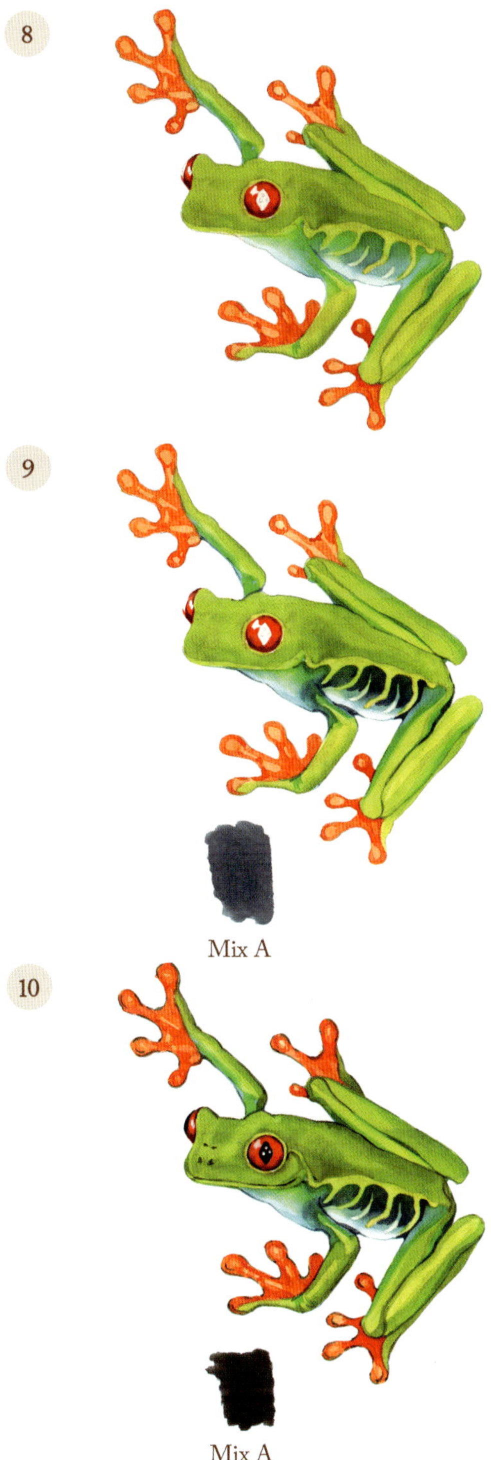

Mix A

Mix A

Step 8: Apply Mix 5A to all the legs, the head, and the top part of the body, also covering the yellow pattern. Once you have covered it, switch to water to keep the belly white. Let this layer dry completely before proceeding.

Step 9: Create a new dark blue color:

- Mix A: indigo + turquoise blue + water = dark blue

Apply Mix A to the top part of the belly under the yellow pattern, then smooth out the edges. The lower part of the belly should remain white. Next, apply a thin line of this color under the mouth and smooth out the edges for a seamless transition. Use the tip of your brush to add this color to the lower left arm that's close to the belly. Use the tip of your brush to add very thin lines of this color in the folds of the legs.

Step 10: Smooth the white highlight on the red part of the eyes with a tiny amount of water so it looks more unified with the rest of the eyes. Next, mix a dark color for the pupils. You can use any dark color you want, but I'm using the following mixture:

- Mix A: carmine + indigo + green + almost no water = dark purple (almost black)

Apply Mix A to the pupils, making sure to leave a couple of tiny white highlights on the pupil of the right eye untouched. Then, use Mix 5B to add details to the frog in the areas around the eyes, the forehead, and in some areas of the legs. Use Mix 9A to underline the opening of the mouth with a thin line. Add the nostrils and the fine details to the outlines of the fingers with the same color. Ensure that the outlines are very thin and irregular—regular lines can make the painting look flat. Use Mix 9A to make the outline of the eye more visible, which will help the eye pop even more. After this, your painting is ready!

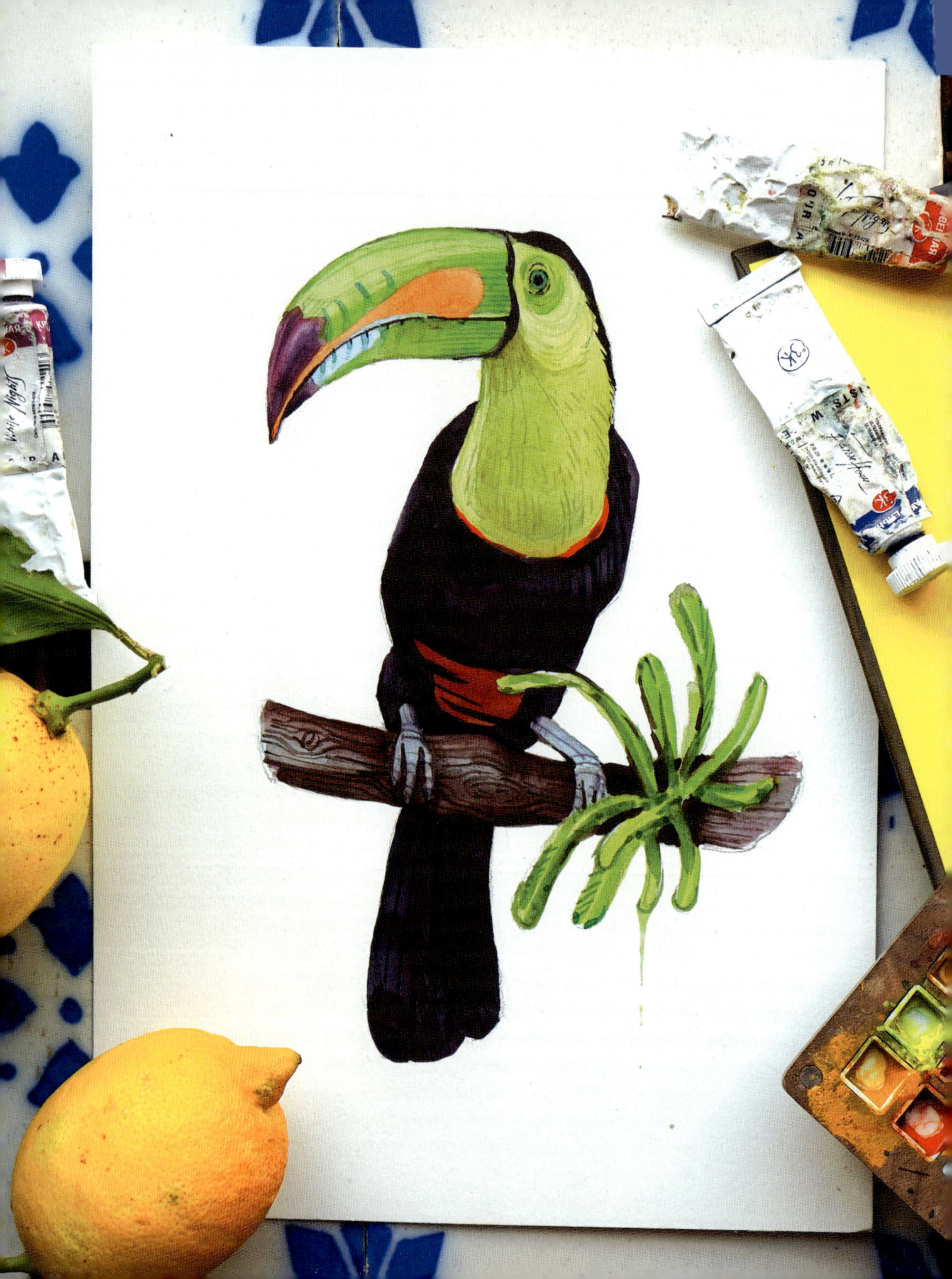

Toucan

This colorful, exotic bird is a visual delight! Native to Central and South America, the toucan is renowned for its strikingly large, vibrant beak, which can be up to one-third of its body length. Despite its size, the beak is surprisingly lightweight due to its unique honeycomb structure. In this tutorial, you'll learn how to paint this charismatic bird realistically, ensuring its proportions are accurate. One of the key lessons here is that you don't need pure black to paint dark areas. For the toucan's black feathers and beak, we'll use various colors, resulting in a richer, more vibrant, and harmonious look.

Colors Needed

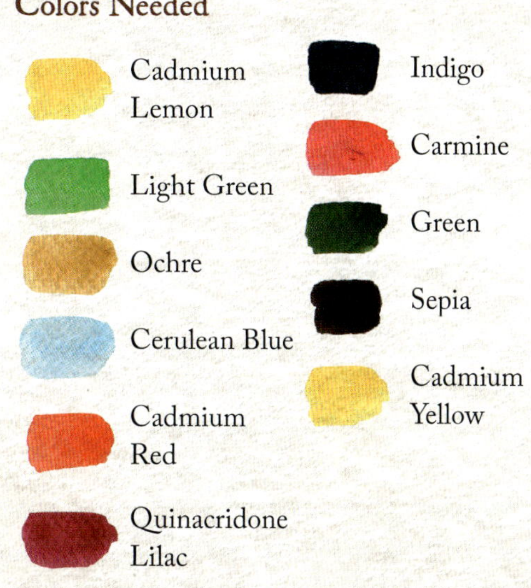

Suggested Paper Orientation: Vertical

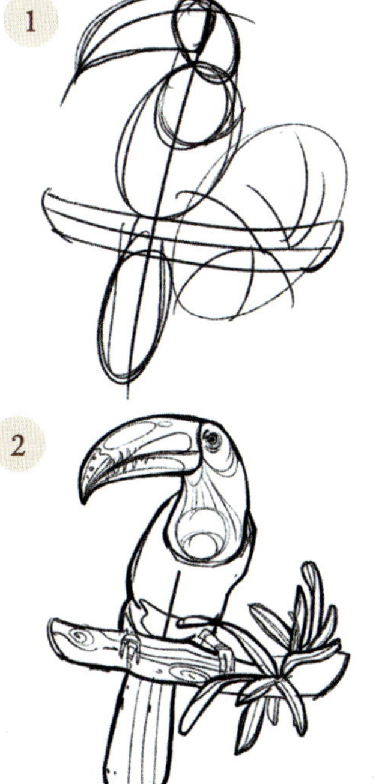

Step 1: Draw a vertical line that will represent the center of the bird. Then, make a horizontal line two-thirds of the way from the top of the vertical line. This line will show the center of the branch the toucan is sitting on. Draw ovals for the bird's body and tail, and add a horizontal curved line to represent the beak. Add an oval for the neck and one for the head. Outline the sides of the beak and give the branch some thickness by adding two parallel lines, one above and one below the center line. Finally, draw an oval on the right side of the toucan to represent the plant, and add some lines going in different directions to represent the direction of the leaves of the plant.

Step 2: Connect the ovals to shape the neck, making it more recognizable and realistic. Place the eye, outline the base of the beak, and add the beak "mouth." Refine the shape of the tail and add some leaves to the plant, angling them in different directions. Sketch the position of the legs where they attach to the branch. Once you're happy with the general shapes, define the body shape more clearly.

(Step 2 continued)

Add details to the eye, including the pupil and some circles around it. Enhance the beak with an oval for the orange spot, vertical lines representing the pattern, and an outline for the black tip. Add more details to the legs and the plant, refining the branch with a curvier outline and adding texture.

Step 3: Create a bright yellow color by combining cadmium lemon and water. Then, create a new mix:

- Mix A: cadmium lemon + light green + water = light green

Apply the yellow color to the entire surface of the head and neck, including the eye. While still wet, apply Mix A to the eye and the lower left side of the neck to outline the shadow cast by the beak. Whether or not the first layer has dried, apply Mix A to the beak, covering all areas except for the oval representing the orange spot, the area on the lower side of the beak that will be blue, and the tip of the beak. Apply Mix A to the plant as well. Wait for this layer to dry.

Step 4: Create these mixes:

- Mix A: cadmium lemon + green + ochre + water = medium green-brown
- Mix B: same as Mix A (above) but with more pigment and less water = darker green-brown

With a medium brush, wet the entire neck area with water, then add Mix A right under the beak and on the lower side of the neck, blending these areas while leaving the left and right sides lighter. If the darker color starts to spread too much, lift it with a clean, dry brush. Add a bit of Mix B under the beak and on the lower part of the neck.

Mix cerulean blue with water and apply it to the white area on the lower side of the beak. Then, create a new mix:

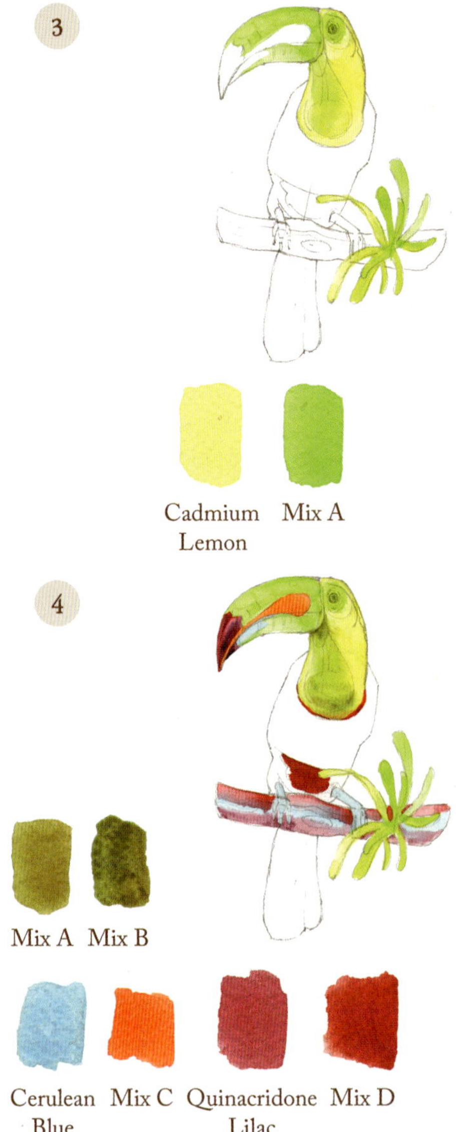

- Mix C: cadmium lemon + cadmium red + water = orange

Apply Mix C to the top area of the beak that was left white, extending this color in a line toward the tip of the beak. Using the tip of your brush, apply the same color where the neck transitions into the body. To color the tip of the beak, mix quinacridone lilac with water and apply it to the tip and the small lower portion of the beak's tip.

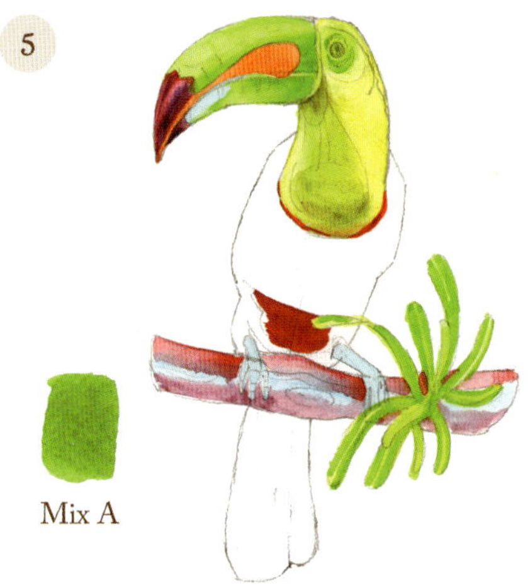

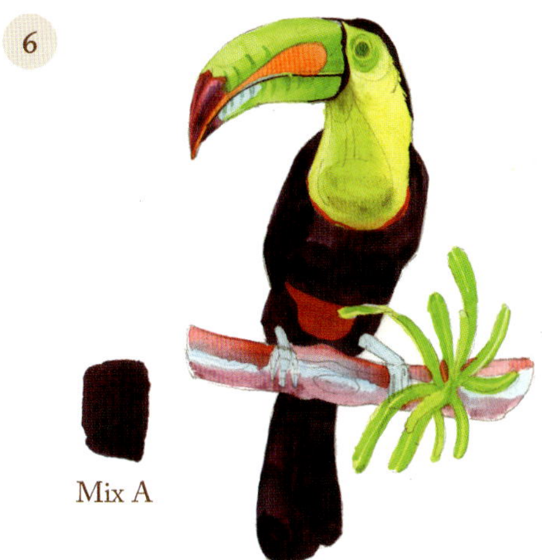

For a darker shade, add some indigo to Mix 3A, and while the tip is still wet, apply this darker color to the left-side center and small lower portion of the beak's tip to create volume.

Now, use the same cerulean blue and water mix from before and apply it to the legs. Let them dry. Wet the branch with water, avoiding the plant and legs. While still wet, apply the cerulean blue mix to the center, then use the quinacridone lilac and water mix on the upper and lower sides of the branch. Finally, create:

- Mix D: quinacridone lilac + carmine + water = red

Apply it to the bird's belly.

Step 5: Create a new mix:

- Mix A: cadmium lemon + green + water = darker green

Using your medium brush, apply Mix A to the lower side of the beak, avoiding the blue part and the tip. Add the same color near the eye and to the top side of the beak, leaving a thin line to separate the top and lower sides of the beak. Paint around the orange spot, avoiding the area near the top border of the beak. With a clean, damp brush, smooth the edges between the new darker

green color and the lighter one applied previously to create a seamless transition. Use Mix A to darken the edges of most of the leaves, leaving a thin line in the center of each one to represent the vein. Leaving a few of the front leaves completely bright helps add dimension to the plant.

Step 6: Create a new mix for the body:

- Mix A: quinacridone lilac + indigo + green + water = dark purple (this should be the darkest color we've mixed so far)

Apply this color to the entire remaining body, avoiding the red spot on the belly. Using the very tip of your small brush, add this color to the head of the bird, creating a thin line on the right side. You can also use the tip of your brush to outline some feathers in this area. With the same small brush, outline the part of the beak where it connects to the face. Then, add an even thinner line above the light blue line to separate the tip portion of the beak from the lower portion.

Cover the eye with the cerulean blue mixed with water from Step 4. Use the same color to create texture on the beak by adding curved perpendicular lines on both sides of the opening. Go over the blue area while doing this, but avoid the orange.

Step 7: In this step, we will add the final details. Let's start by finishing the branch. Create a new mix:

- Mix A: quinacridone lilac + sepia + water = medium warm brown-red

With a medium brush, cover the whole surface of the branch with this color, making sure not to completely cover the highlight area. While the first layer of the branch is drying, create a new color:

- Mix B: green + cadmium yellow + a touch of indigo (or any other blue) + water = medium green

Apply this to the center of the plant and create texture with thin lines using the same color. Use the same color to accentuate the texture at the base of the toucan's beak, applying very thin, long horizontal lines.

Now, let's add some final texture to the yellow part of the bird's body. Use Mix 4A, the tip of your small brush, and very thin, short strokes to create texture around the eye and on the neck, following the natural movement and anatomy of the bird. At this stage, the branch has probably dried, so add the final texture to it using the same red-brown Mix A as before, but in a more saturated version—you can darken the color by adding more of the same pigments or a touch of sepia or indigo. Use thin, wavy lines with the tip of your brush to imitate wood texture. Use the same color to add the final details to the feet, applying short horizontal strokes to make the outline of the feet more visible in some places. Darken this color even further by adding more carmine and sepia, and use it to darken the area of the branch near the plant.

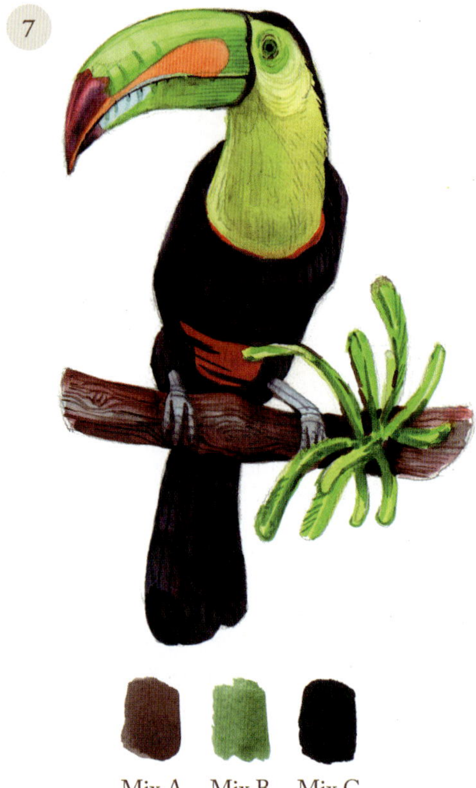

Next, mix the darkest color we've created so far, which should be the same as Mix 6A we used for the dark part of the body but with even more dark pigment:

- Mix C: quinacridone lilac + more indigo + green + water = darker purple

Use this color to add the final details to the face, such as the pupil and the eyelids, using the very tip of your small brush. Use the same color to add the last touches to the body, such as short horizontal lines on the red spot on the belly and long vertical lines on the tail to better outline the feathers. Add some strokes to the body to emphasize the feather texture as well. Your painting is now complete!

Mule Ear Orchid

The mule ear orchid is a fascinating flower named for its petals that resemble the long ears of a mule. Native to tropical regions of the Americas, this orchid thrives in humid environments like rainforests and mountain ranges. Despite its delicate appearance, it's a resilient flower known for its charming, spotted petals that make it a unique subject for painting. In this tutorial, you will learn how to draw and paint the orchid's complex petals, focusing on creating the distinct spotted texture. You'll practice the wet-on-wet technique (page 17), experimenting with pigment concentration to control the size and color of the spots.

Colors Needed

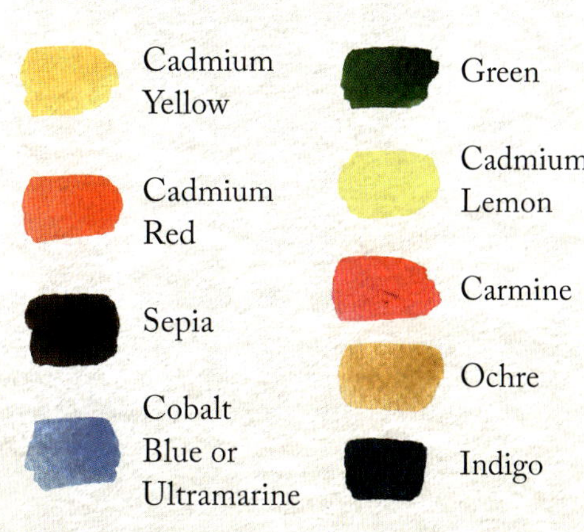

Suggested Paper Orientation: Vertical

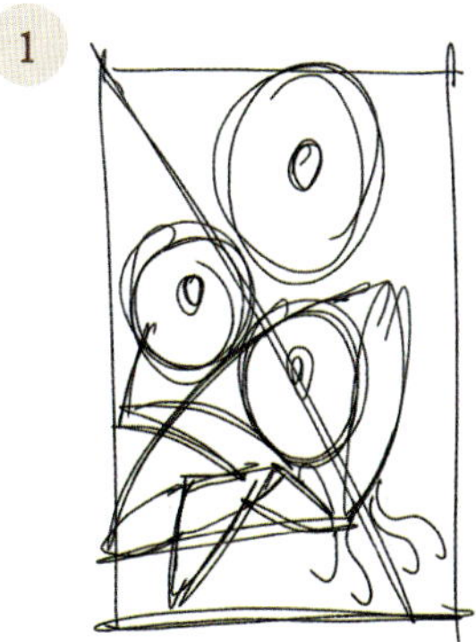

Step 1: Draw a rectangle that's one and a half times taller than it is wide. Draw a diagonal line from the top left corner to the bottom right corner. This line will guide you in placing the circles that represent the blooms. Draw a large circle in the upper-right portion of the rectangle; it should touch the top edge of the rectangle and come close to the diagonal guide line. Place one smaller bloom to the left of the largest circle's tip and then another lower down. The lowest bloom should be positioned around the center of the rectangle, with the diagonal line cutting through it. Add small circles to the center of each bloom to mark where the pistils will go. Draw long, pointy ovals for the leaves. Begin by sketching a curvy line that connects the leaf farthest to the left to the leaf farthest to the right. Then, position the individual leaves, ensuring they face different directions. Keep in mind that the front-left leaf is folded, so make sure to capture this feature at this stage. Outline the roots using wavy lines at the bottom right corner of the rectangle.

Step 2: Outline the individual petals, beginning with the top. Keep in mind that each bloom has three upper petals and three lower petals, with the lower center petal having a distinct shape. Outline the petals using pointy ovals, and for the lower center petal, use a thin cylinder at the base with a semicircular end. Add more details to the leaves by drawing lines on them. Add more roots and make them thicker, with parallel lines next to the initial ones.

Refine the shape of the petals, transforming them from simple ovals into more organic and intricate forms.

Step 3: Refine the outlines of the leaves and flowers, paying special attention to the individual petals. Make the outlines slightly bolder than the internal lines. Add spot textures to the petals by using small circles and ovals, placing them randomly across the surface to create a natural and detailed look. Add more intricate details to the petals, particularly the stand-alone lower petal. Create folds on it and enhance its shape by adding long vertical lines extending from its semicircular tip. Increase the spot texture on the petals, and finish adding details on the leaves and roots.

Step 4: Let's create the color mixes for the blooms. Create a bright yellow by mixing cadmium yellow with water. Then, create this mix:

- Mix A: cadmium yellow + cadmium red + sepia + water = medium khaki

Cover the petals of the top flower with the bright yellow, avoiding the lower center petal. While the paint is still wet, use Mix A to add a spot pattern to the petals with the tip of your brush. Don't worry if some areas of the petals have dried—just continue adding texture. On wet paper, you'll achieve blooming effects, while on dry paper, you'll create hard edges. We're aiming for a variety of textures to achieve an organic look, so the combination works in your favor. Repeat for the remaining two flowers.

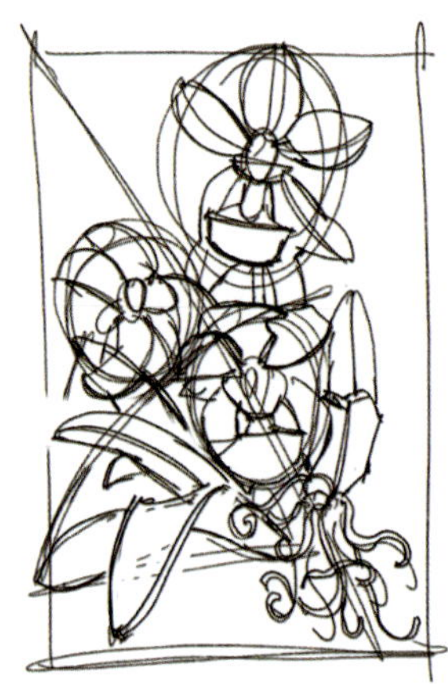

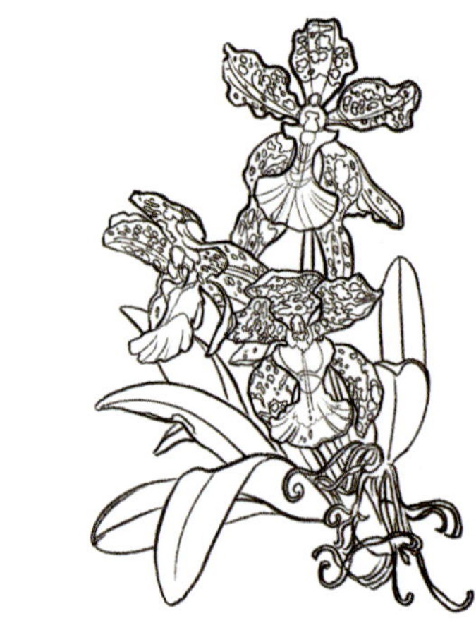

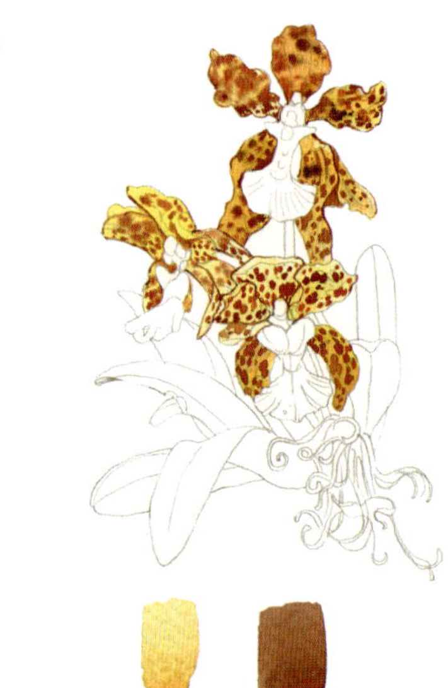

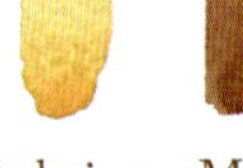

Cadmium   Mix A
Yellow

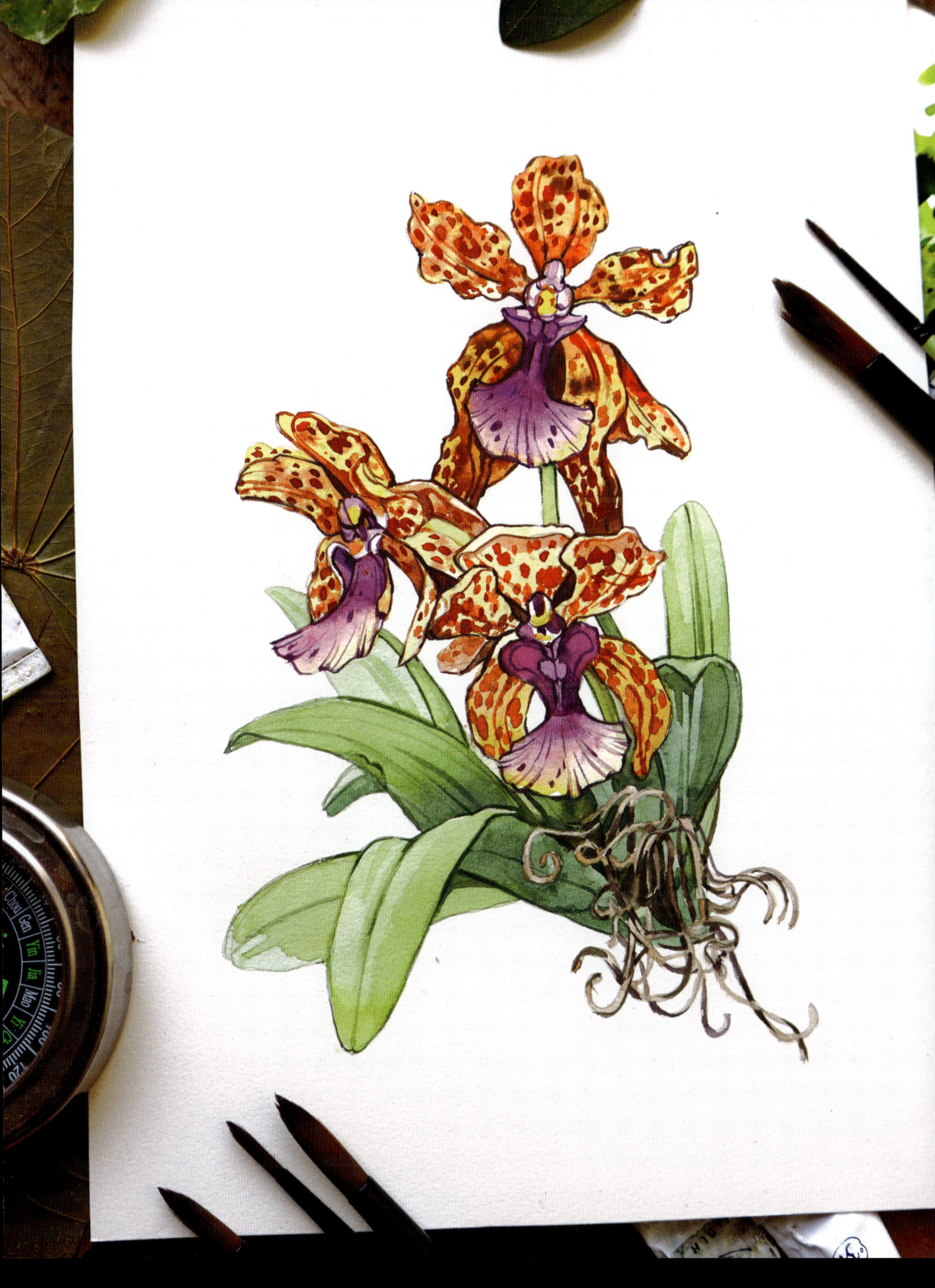

Step 5: Mix three shades of green for the leaves:

- Mix A: cobalt blue or ultramarine + green + a touch of cadmium lemon + water = light, watery green
- Mix B: Mix A (above) + more cadmium lemon + more water = light yellow-green
- Mix C: cobalt blue or ultramarine + green + water = medium, cool green

With your medium brush, apply Mix A to the tips of the leaves. Halfway down the leaf, transition to Mix C. Use this method for the two upper-left leaves. For the lower-left leaf, which is behind the others, apply only Mix A. On the top of the folded leaf, use Mix B for the area closer to the viewer and Mix C for the back portion, as it is darker and in shadow. On the right side, use Mix B for the back leaf and Mix A for the front leaf. Next, use Mix A and the tip of your brush to paint the spaces between the roots. Finally, apply Mix B to cover the stems.

Step 6: Mix cadmium lemon with water and paint the very tips of the center petal of the top flower with your small brush. Let it dry, and in the meantime, mix carmine with water for a light pink. Now, let's create two more mixes for the petals:

- Mix A: carmine + cobalt blue or ultramarine + water = medium purple
- Mix B: Mix 6A (above) + more cobalt blue or ultramarine + water = darker purple

Apply the cadmium lemon and water mix to the bottom semicircular edge of the petal. While it's still wet, switch to the light pink mix (carmine and water) and cover half the petal, and then switch to Mix A and finish covering the petal. Make sure to preserve a small yellow tip in the middle of the top area of the petal. Repeat this process for the other two flowers.

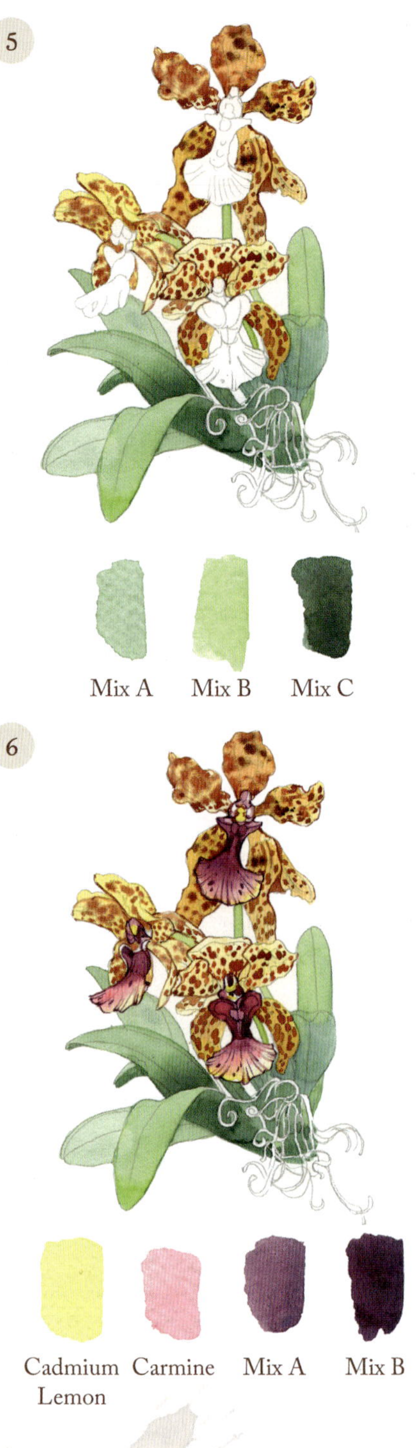

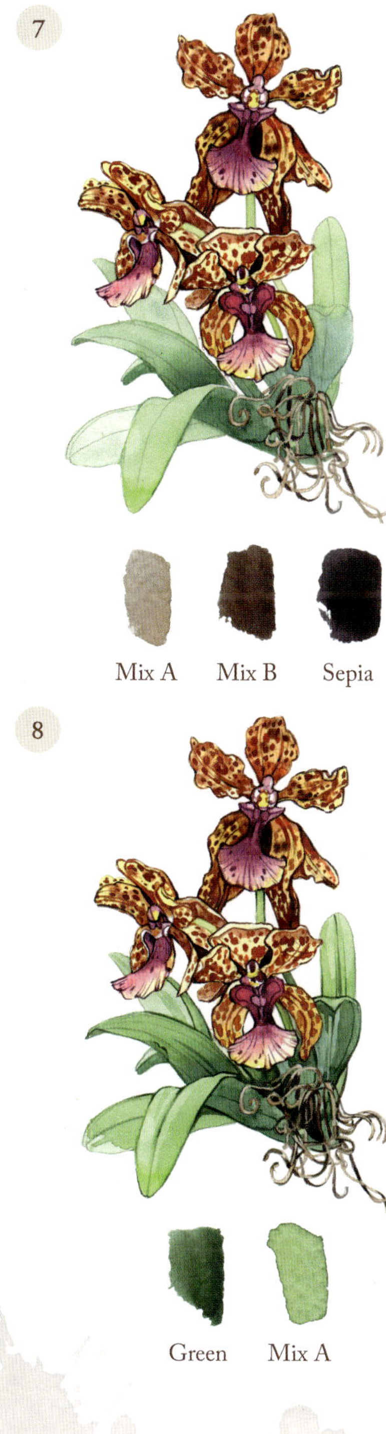

When the first flower dries, use Mix B to darken the thinner top area of the petal, darken the outline a bit, accentuate the folds of the petal on the lower side, and add some details to the tip of the petal. Add some small spots on the lower part of the petal for more texture and interest. Repeat for the remaining flowers.

Step 7: Apply Mix 4A to the darkest areas of the spotted petals; create even more spot texture by making crisp marks with the tip of your small brush. Then, mix some colors for the roots:

- Mix A: ochre + sepia + water = light, watery brown

- Mix B: sepia + carmine + indigo + water = dark brown-purple

Use Mix A to cover all the roots with the tip of your small brush. Once dry, darken the roots that are behind the others with some sepia mixed with water. Once completely dry, use Mix B to accentuate some of the darkest parts of the roots, especially where they intersect. You can also use this dark color to refine the outline of the petals in certain areas. Just make sure to use very thin lines and avoid making the outlines uniform, as this might make your flowers look flat.

Step 8: Combine green with water for a medium green. Then, mix another green:

- Mix A: green + cadmium lemon + water = light yellow-green

Apply Mix A to the back leaves, stems, and center line near the borders of the front leaves, leaving the center of the leaves lighter. Then, use the green and water mix to darken the shadow areas of the front leaves and the stems. Add a thin outline to the stems. Finally, add Mix 7B between the leaves in the root area to accentuate some final details of the roots. After that, you're done!

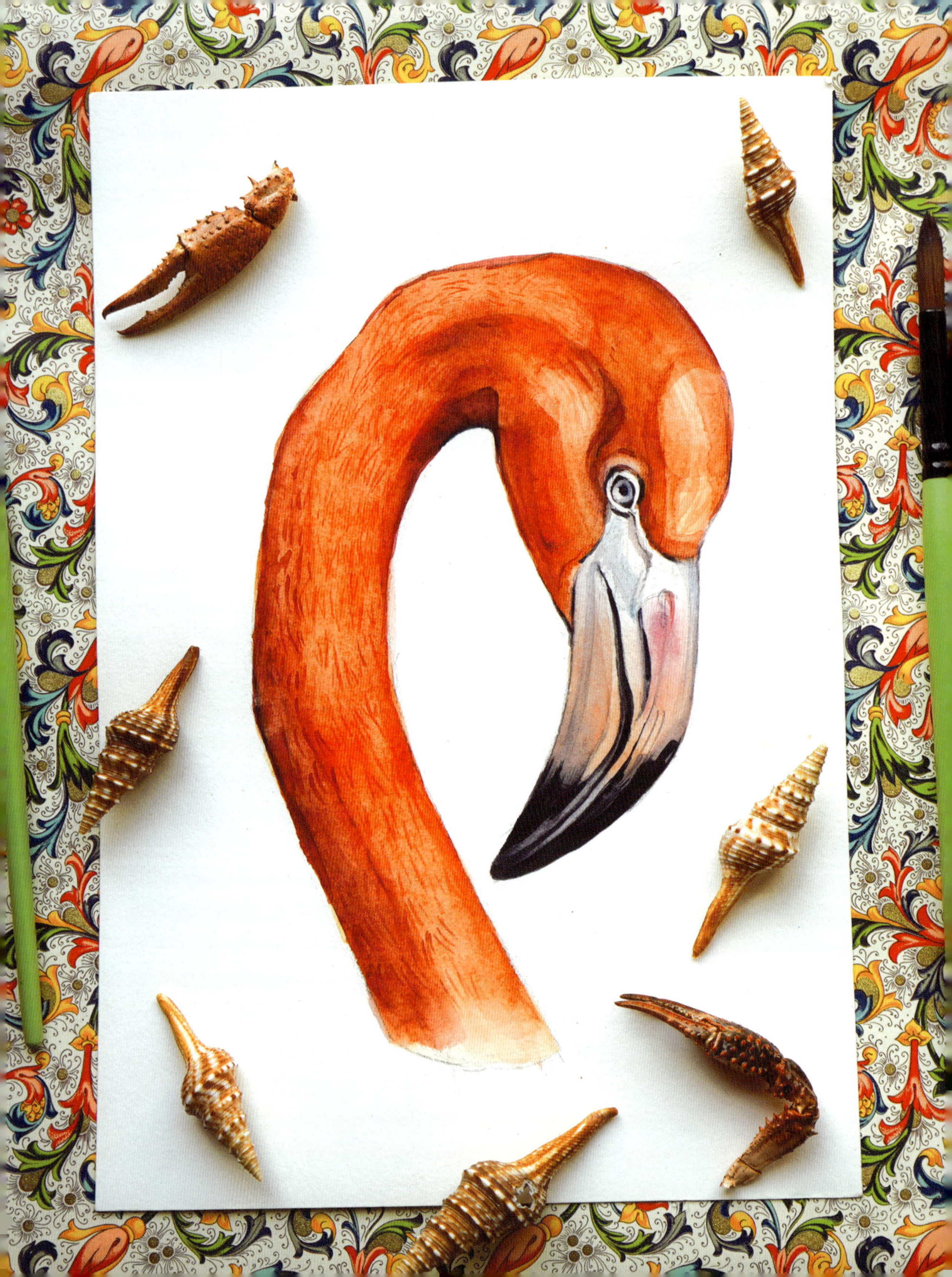

Flamingo

Continuing our adventure, we'll journey to the highlands of South America, including the awe-inspiring Salar de Uyuni, the world's largest salt flat in Bolivia. Although it may seem barren at first, this stark landscape is actually home to resilient and beautiful creatures, such as the flamingo. In this tutorial, we'll focus on painting the flamingo's head, allowing you to practice short feather techniques and the intricate color transitions of its distinctive beak. You'll also master realistic shading as you capture the beak's complex shape. Let's get started!

Colors Needed

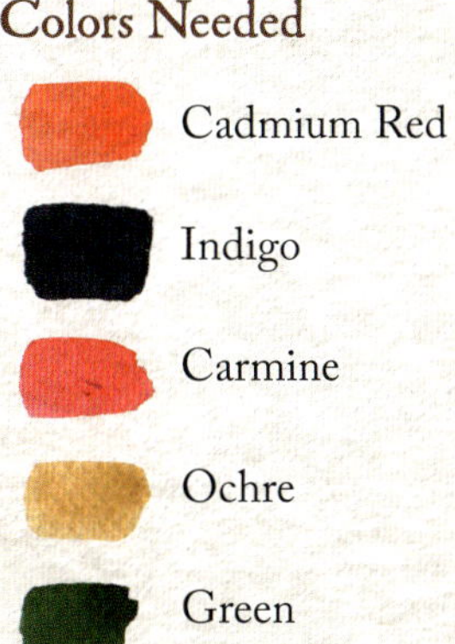

Cadmium Red

Indigo

Carmine

Ochre

Green

Suggested Paper Orientation: Vertical

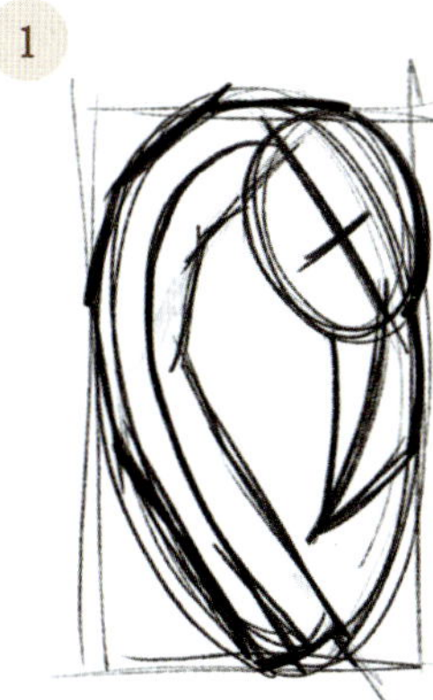

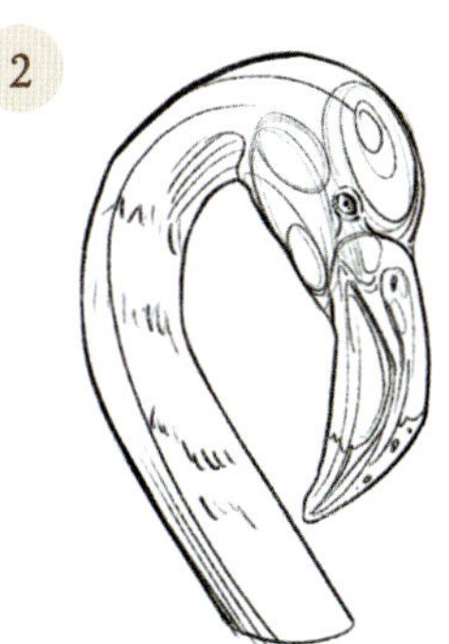

Step 1: Draw a tall rectangle. Next, fit an inclined oval inside. The left side of this oval represents the left side of the neck. Add a smaller oval in the top right corner of the main oval to represent the head. Add a cross in the middle of this oval, which will help us place the eye in the next step. Create a line that shows the direction of the beak.

Outline the beak by connecting the tip of the beak to the head with a straight line on the left side. For the right side of the beak, trace a line parallel to the left side until you reach the midpoint. Stop there, and then change the direction of the line to connect it to the tip of the beak. You should end up with an irregular triangular beak.

Next, to capture the movement of the head and neck, draw a curved line parallel to the left side of the main oval and connect it with the center line of the head. This line represents the center of the neck. Then, outline the right side of the neck by adding a line parallel to the one you just created.

Step 2: Draw a small circle at the intersection of the cross to represent the eye. Add a semicircle connecting the beak to the head.

(Step 2 continued)

Divide the base of the beak into three equal parts. Add a little circle on the top right part of the beak to show the nostril and create a curvy line in the middle of the beak to represent the beak opening. Add some zigzag lines to divide the lower third of the beak from the rest. This is the division between the pink part of the beak and its black tip. Draw a small circle inside the eye circle and add a point in the middle for the pupil. Add any last details to the head, beak, and neck, such as the feather texture.

Step 3: We will start by mixing a general light color for the beak and will mix other colors in the following steps.

- Mix A: a touch of cadmium red + a bit of indigo + a lot of water = light warm gray
- Mix B: Mix 3A (above) + more cadmium red + more indigo = dark warm gray

Apply Mix A to the entire surface of the beak and the eye with a medium brush. Avoid touching the feathery head and neck. Without waiting for this to dry, apply Mix B to the left side of the beak. Create a soft transition between the light gray and the darker gray to show a light-and-shadow effect on the beak. Then, while you're waiting for this to dry, apply Mix A to the inner part of the eye. While it's still wet, apply Mix B to the upper and lower corners of the eye. This will make the eye look more alive and three-dimensional.

Step 4: While the first layer in the beak is drying, create your beak mixes. Mix carmine with water for a bright medium pink. Then, create:

- Mix A: cadmium red + ochre + water = pink

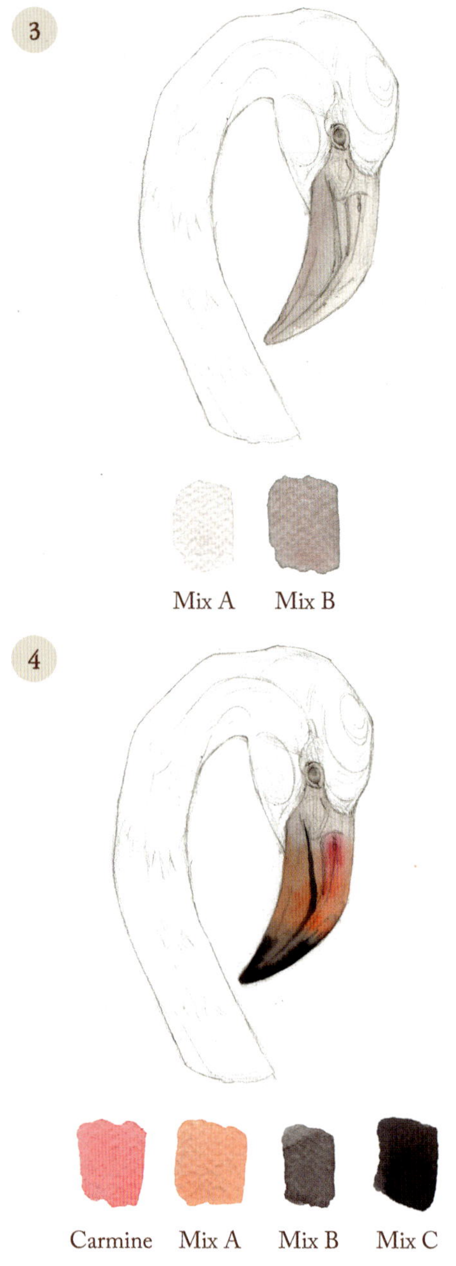

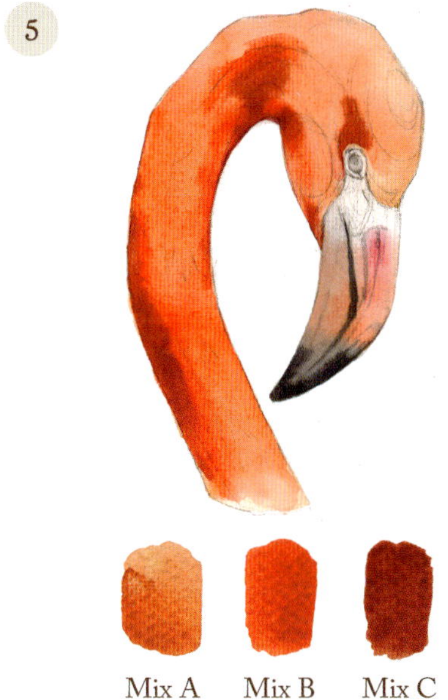

Mix A   Mix B   Mix C

The next two mixes will be for the dark tip of the beak.

- Mix B: indigo + carmine + a touch of green + water = dark, neutral gray (on the bluish side—so if it turns out too red, neutralize it with a touch of indigo and green)
- Mix C: same as Mix 4B (above) but with more pigment = darker, neutral gray

Before applying this layer, make sure that the previous one is completely dry. While we will be using the wet-on-wet technique (page 17) to color the beak, we don't want to muddy the layer we just painted in Step 3. Load your medium brush with water and cover the top area of the beak with water, avoiding the eye. Once you've reached one-third of the way from the top, while the water is still wet, add Mix A to the lower three-quarters of the beak, gradually bringing Mix A toward the tip. While this is still wet, apply the carmine and water mix to the right side of the beak where you see transition between the white and the pink.

While the wash is still wet, apply Mix B to the lower one-third of the beak. It should blend seamlessly with the previous pink. If Mix B starts to bloom too much and heavily affects the pink, wash your brush in clean water, dry it with a paper towel, and pull Mix B down where you originally applied it. Repeat this action as needed.

After that, while the watercolor is still wet, apply Mix C to the tip of the beak (approximately one-third of the whole length of the beak). Add the mouth opening line using the same mix but in an even darker version. You can obtain this by adding more indigo to your mix. Then, apply the carmine and water mix to the upper right side of the beak, in the nostril area, and smooth the edge.

Step 5: Let's mix some colors for the feathers. We will need several shades of pink, starting with the lightest one:

- Mix A: ochre + cadmium red + water = warm medium red
- Mix B: same as Mix 5A (above) but with more pigment = medium saturated red
- Mix C: same as Mix 5B (above) + more carmine = dark saturated red

With your large or medium brush, apply Mix A to the remaining part of the bird, avoiding the eye and the beak. Make sure that the color remains wet while you're working to create a uniform wash with no visible brushstrokes. Wait for this layer to dry.

Apply Mix B around the eye, on the left side of the head, and on the left side of the neck. Smooth the edges for a seamless transition. Then, take Mix C and apply it to the upper side of the neck where the head transitions into the neck and to the left side of the neck. Smooth out the edges like you did before.

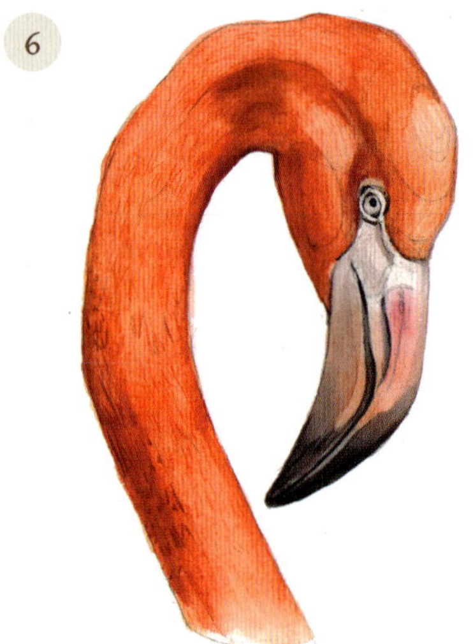

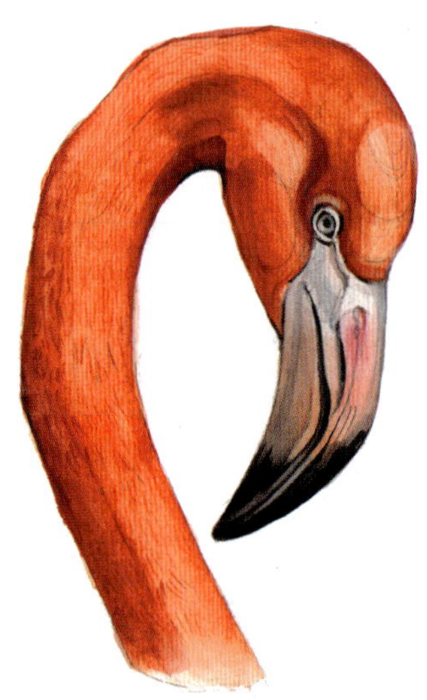

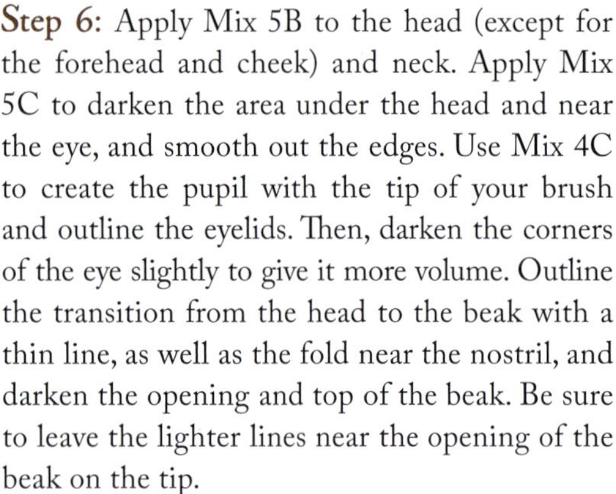

Step 6: Apply Mix 5B to the head (except for the forehead and cheek) and neck. Apply Mix 5C to darken the area under the head and near the eye, and smooth out the edges. Use Mix 4C to create the pupil with the tip of your brush and outline the eyelids. Then, darken the corners of the eye slightly to give it more volume. Outline the transition from the head to the beak with a thin line, as well as the fold near the nostril, and darken the opening and top of the beak. Be sure to leave the lighter lines near the opening of the beak on the tip.

With your small brush, add feather details to the neck and head using Mix 5B. Use thin, short strokes across the entire surface of the neck and head, following the natural shape and movement of the bird.

Step 7: Use your medium brush and Mix 5C to deepen the shadow where the head transitions into the neck and darken the area near the eye. Enhance the highlight on the neck and head, but make sure it's not uniform, as a solid tone could make the bird look flat. Use Mix 4C to darken the beak's tip further while leaving the part near the opening lighter. Add some clean water to the top area of the eyeball; this will activate the dark color of the pupil, creating a shadow in that area and giving the eye a more three-dimensional look. Once the area dries, restore the pupil using Mix 4C. Your painting is complete!

Alpaca

Alpacas are adorable, fluffy mammals often mistaken for their larger cousins, llamas. Native to the Andes, these gentle creatures are known for their soft, luxurious fleece, which is highly prized for its warmth and durability. Alpacas graze peacefully in high-altitude meadows, living in herds and producing some of the finest natural fibers in the world. In this tutorial, you'll discover how to create the soft textures of alpaca fleece, blend warm earth tones for their gentle features, and add fine details to bring these charming animals to life.

Colors Needed

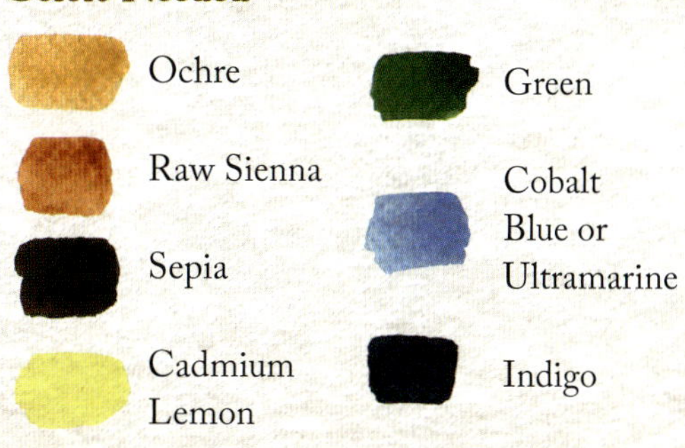

- Ochre
- Raw Sienna
- Sepia
- Cadmium Lemon
- Green
- Cobalt Blue or Ultramarine
- Indigo

Suggested Paper Orientation: Vertical

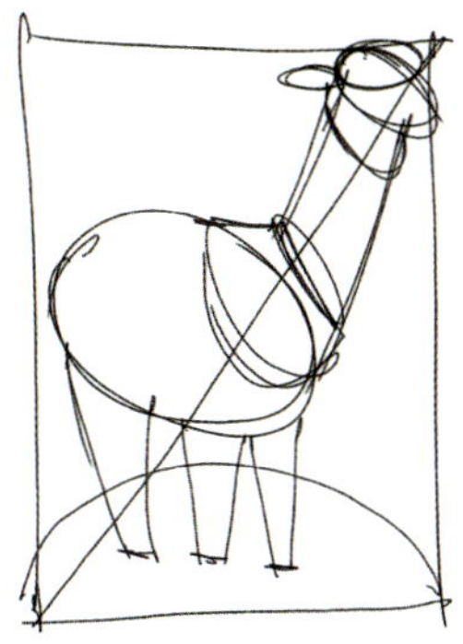

Step 1: Draw a vertical rectangle. Draw a diagonal line from the lower-left corner to the upper-right corner that will represent the general movement and direction of the alpaca's neck. Outline a semicircle on the lower part of the rectangle to show the ground. Outline the body with a horizontal oval in the middle of the rectangle, closer to the left side. For the legs, draw three long, thin cylinders. (The back legs will be represented by a single cylinder.) Create the neck using a shortened cylinder for the base and a longer cylinder for the neck itself. Then, outline the head with a small horizontal oval, and attach an even smaller oval to the left for the ear. Sketch the fur under the head with a semicircle, and add the bangs with another oval on top of the head oval.

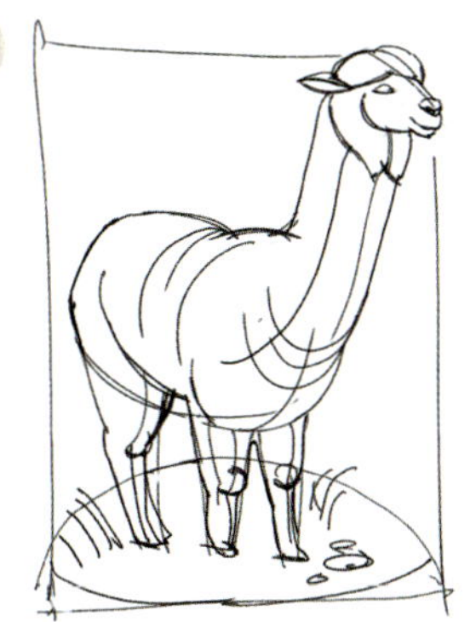

Step 2: Make the chest, back, and neck more voluminous and defined. Add small ovals for the ankles on each leg, and then draw a vertical line on each leg to represent the center line. Outline the shape of the legs with curvy lines to create a more organic, natural look. Add vertical lines along the neck to suggest its natural movement, which will also help in defining light and shadow areas when painting.

(Step 2 continued)

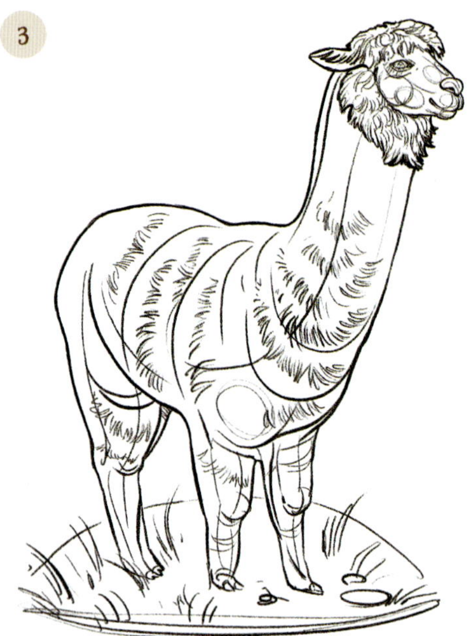

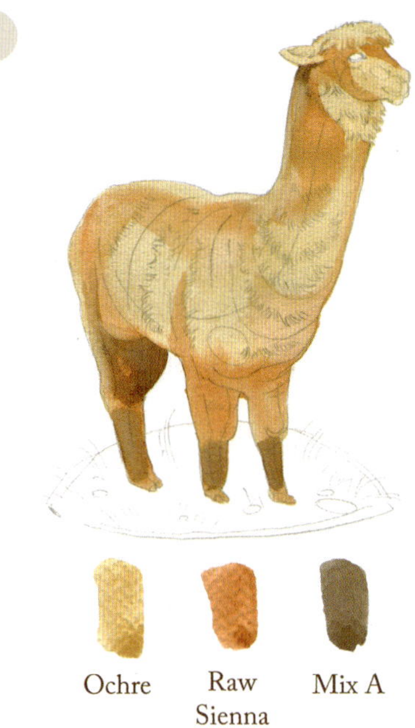

Use curved, semicircular lines to emphasize the shapes of the body and chest. Define the line of the belly, then move on to adding facial features. Draw a line to guide the nose direction, round out the cheeks, add a mouth line, and create the nose with a small oval. Add thickness to the ear with a horizontal line, and divide the bangs and the fur under the head into two sections, giving them a more defined look with pointy tips. Lastly, add details to the grass and outline a few rocks with small circles or ovals.

Step 3: Erase all the previous guide lines and focus on defining the final outline. Use short zigzag strokes to create the fur texture on the neck, body, and legs, letting the direction of the lines follow the alpaca's anatomy. Refine the facial features with ovals to emphasize the roundness of the cheeks and muzzle, and add details to the eyes and nose. Outline the fur on the bangs and the area under the head, adding texture to the tip of the ear as well. Use short wavy strokes to make the outer outline of these areas bolder. Finally, add more grass, and you can proceed with the painting process.

Step 4: The first color we will use is a light yellow mix you get by combining ochre and water. Create a bright orangey mix by combining raw sienna and water. Then, create another mix:

- Mix A: sepia + raw sienna + water = brown

Cover the entire surface of the alpaca with the ochre and water mix, avoiding the eye and the grass. Start from the top and gradually move down until you reach the tips of the toes. Then, while this layer is still wet, apply the raw sienna and water mix to the legs, the top side of the back, the left side of the neck, and some areas of the face—especially under the bangs and on the left side of the face. While this layer is still wet, apply Mix A to the lower part of the front legs and almost all of the back leg. Add some of this color under the ear as well. Wait for this layer to dry.

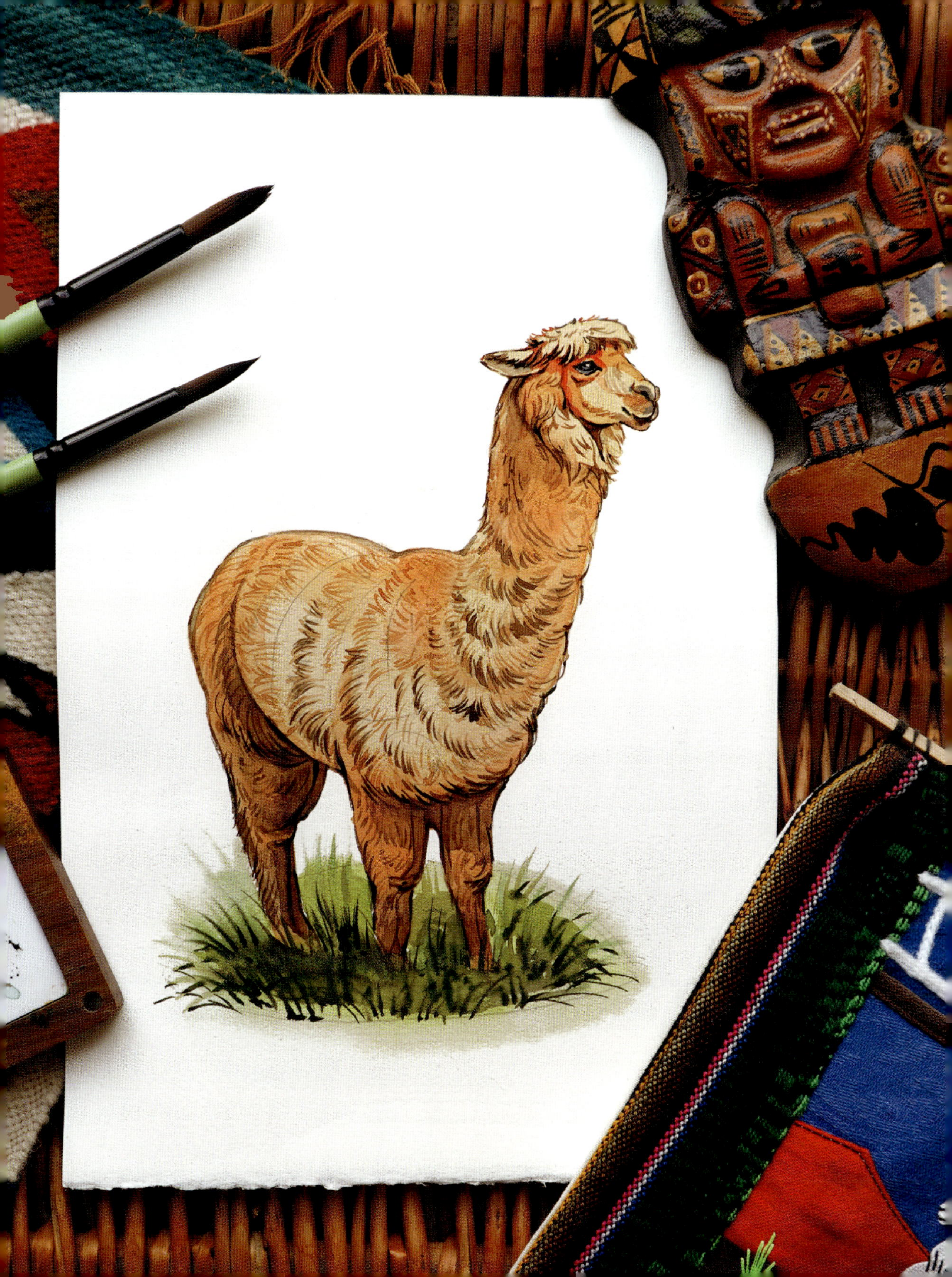

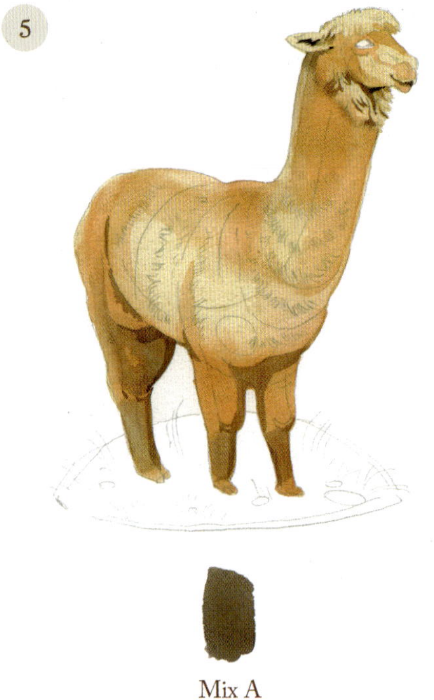

Mix A

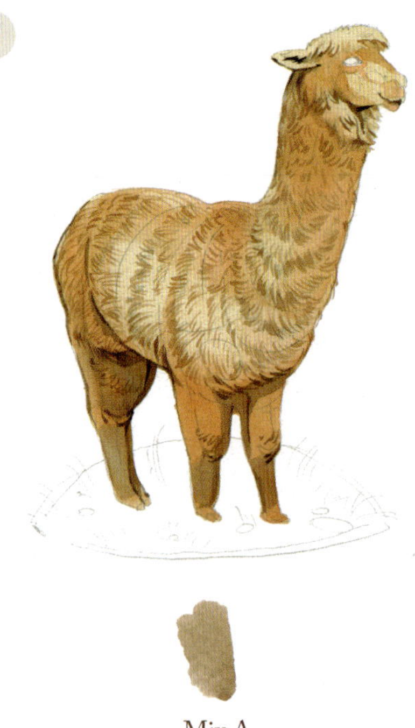

Mix A

Step 5: Apply the raw sienna and water mix from the previous step to the entire surface of the neck, back, and legs. Then, use a clean, dry brush to smooth the edges for a seamless transition. Add the same color to the muzzle with your smaller brush, and apply more under the bangs. Wait for this layer to dry.

Meanwhile, use Mix 4A to darken the left side of the right front leg, the right side of the front left leg, and the back leg that's partially hidden (to the right of the fully visible leg). Use the same color to darken the transition between the chest and the legs and between the belly and the back leg with wavy strokes. There's no need to smooth these edges. Finally, create a new mix:

- Mix A: raw sienna + sepia + water = medium brown

Use this to accentuate facial features such as the open mouth, the fur under the face, and the inside ear area. Wait for this layer to dry.

Step 6: Create a new mix:

- Mix A: raw sienna + sepia + water = light brown

Using a small brush, use this mix to paint short zigzag strokes following the natural shape and direction of the fur on the body; your drawing will guide you. Add the same fur texture under the head and for the bangs. Slightly outline the left side with thin lines for more definition. Then, using shorter, curvy lines, create the outline on the right side of the neck. The neck is fluffy, so a wavy outline will enhance this effect. Finally, use Mix 5A to add texture to areas on the legs, such as the knees and the transition between the body and legs.

Once the legs are dry, use Mix 6A and the dark sepia and water mix to add fur texture on the legs. Use the dark sepia color to emphasize the ankles and make the outline of the legs more defined.

Step 8: Refresh your water container, as we'll use the wet-on-wet technique (page 17) and clean water is essential. Then, mix these grass shades:

- Mix A: cadmium lemon + ochre + a touch of green + water = vibrant yellow-green
- Mix B: green + sepia + a small amount of water = dark, earthy green

Use a large brush—ideally a mop brush—to cover the grass and surrounding area with clean water. Ensure the paper is evenly damp without puddles—we want it damp, not soaking wet. Without delay, apply Mix A across the grass area. Then, switch to green mixed with water, using thin, curved vertical strokes to outline the grass. If the color spreads too much, wait briefly for the paper to dry slightly before trying again. After creating one layer of grass, use Mix B to add foreground grass. By now, the paper should be almost dry, so the darker color won't spread as much. You can also extend the grass texture slightly over the alpaca's feet to integrate it with its surroundings, making the composition look more cohesive, natural, and realistic.

Mix cobalt blue or ultramarine with water for a light blue, and with a small brush, paint the eye, leaving the tiny highlight unpainted. While this dries, create a very dark mix, such as indigo with minimal water, to complete the eye, outlining the pupil and shading the inner area. Use this dark mix to accentuate the facial details, like the nose and mouth.

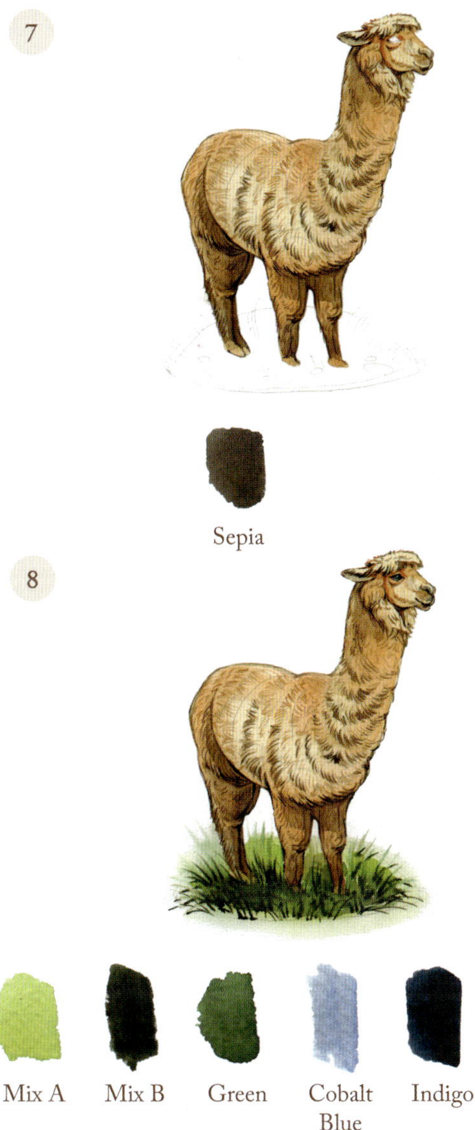

Sepia

Mix A   Mix B   Green   Cobalt Blue   Indigo

Step 7: Apply Mix 5A to the legs (except for the ankles) and the transition between the belly and the back legs. While this dries, create a dark brown color (sepia with a small amount of water). Outline the mouth and nostrils and add shading under the chin, inside the ear, and along the lower edge of the bangs. Then, add more fur texture to the body. Concentrate the darkest fur in the center of the neck and the lower part of the body, using short, wavy strokes for a natural effect.

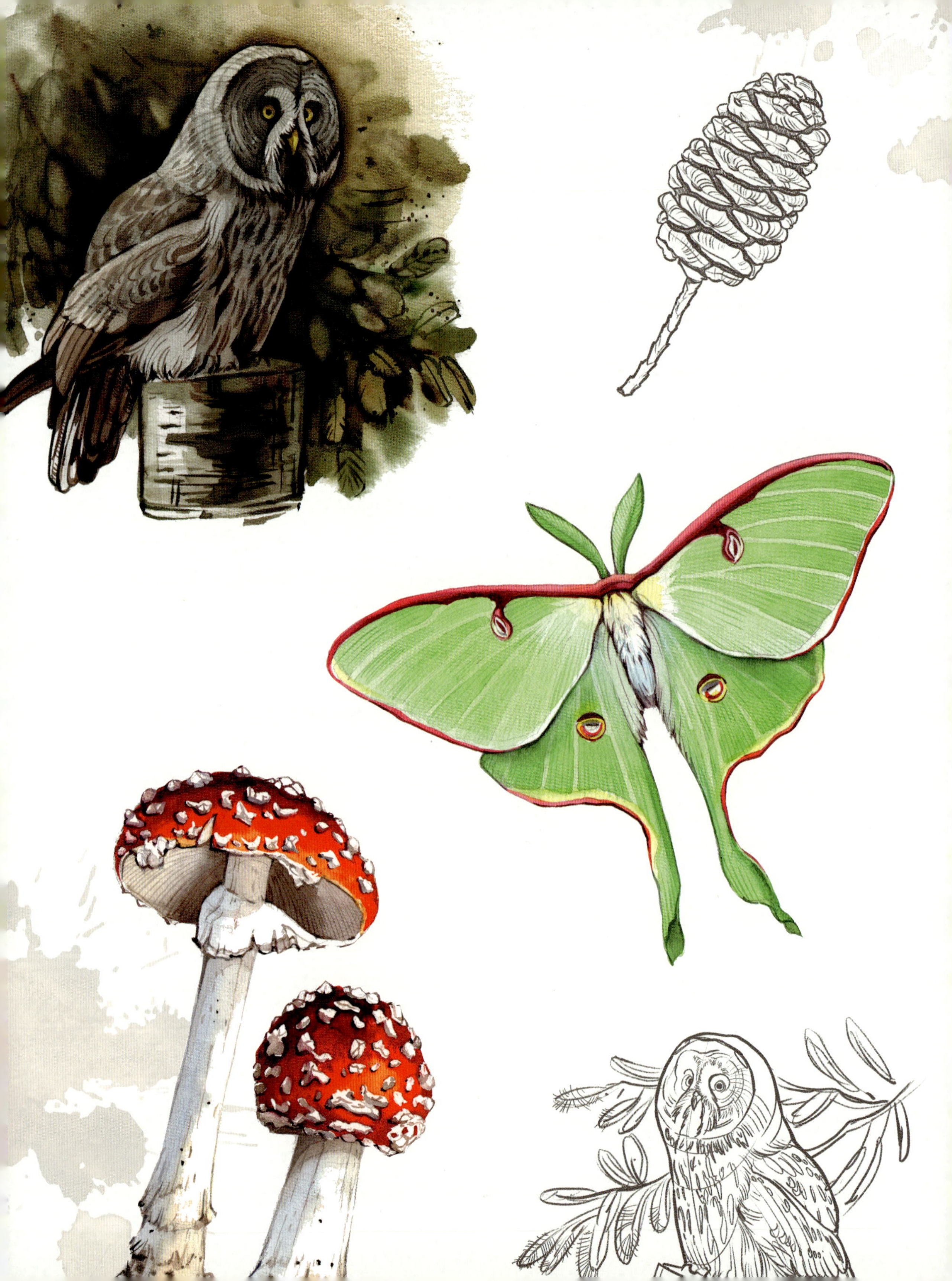

North America
Nature Across National Parks

This vast continent is where the concept of the national park was established in 1872, and it is home to countless animal, plant, and fungus species. Among them is the Fly Agaric Mushroom (page 55), famous for its vibrant appearance and its association with shamanic rituals. In this tutorial, you'll learn how to use masking fluid to capture the white dots on its red cap.

No exploration of North American nature would be complete without the giant sequoia. These towering trees, some of the largest living organisms on Earth, can reach impressive heights. The Giant Sequoia Cone (page 65), though small in comparison, contains the seeds that will eventually grow into these giants—a testament to the power of nature's cycles.

Another species endemic to North America is the beautiful Canada Lily (page 60), which blooms in June with elegant nodding flowers. Known for its medicinal uses by Native Americans, the Canada lily was often used in poultices to treat wounds and as a tonic for health.

In the animal kingdom, North America also boasts a variety of endemic species, including the Bald Eagle (page 75). This majestic bird, a symbol of the United States, is also found in Canada and Northern Mexico and is the only eagle native to North America. Its powerful wingspan and keen eyesight make it an awe-inspiring subject for artists.

Speaking of remarkable birds, we also have the Great Gray Owl (page 79), the largest owl species by length. This bird's large facial disc helps channel sound directly to its ears, allowing it to hear prey even under the snow. Its ability to rotate its head 270 degrees, and its silent flight, make it an exceptional predator. In Native American culture, owls are often seen as messengers from the spirit world. I first encountered a Great Gray Owl through the iconic *Twin Peaks* TV series, and I've been captivated by them ever since.

And finally, we turn to one of North America's most stunning insects: the Luna Moth (page 69). With its lime-green wings and false eyespots, this moth uses its unique features to ward off predators. The Luna moth has a short adult life—lasting only about a week, during which its only purpose is to mate and continue its species. This fascinating creature will be an exciting subject, especially with its ethereal, translucent wings.

Each of these incredible species is a window into the natural world of North America. Ready to explore and paint these wonders? Grab your art supplies and let's get started!

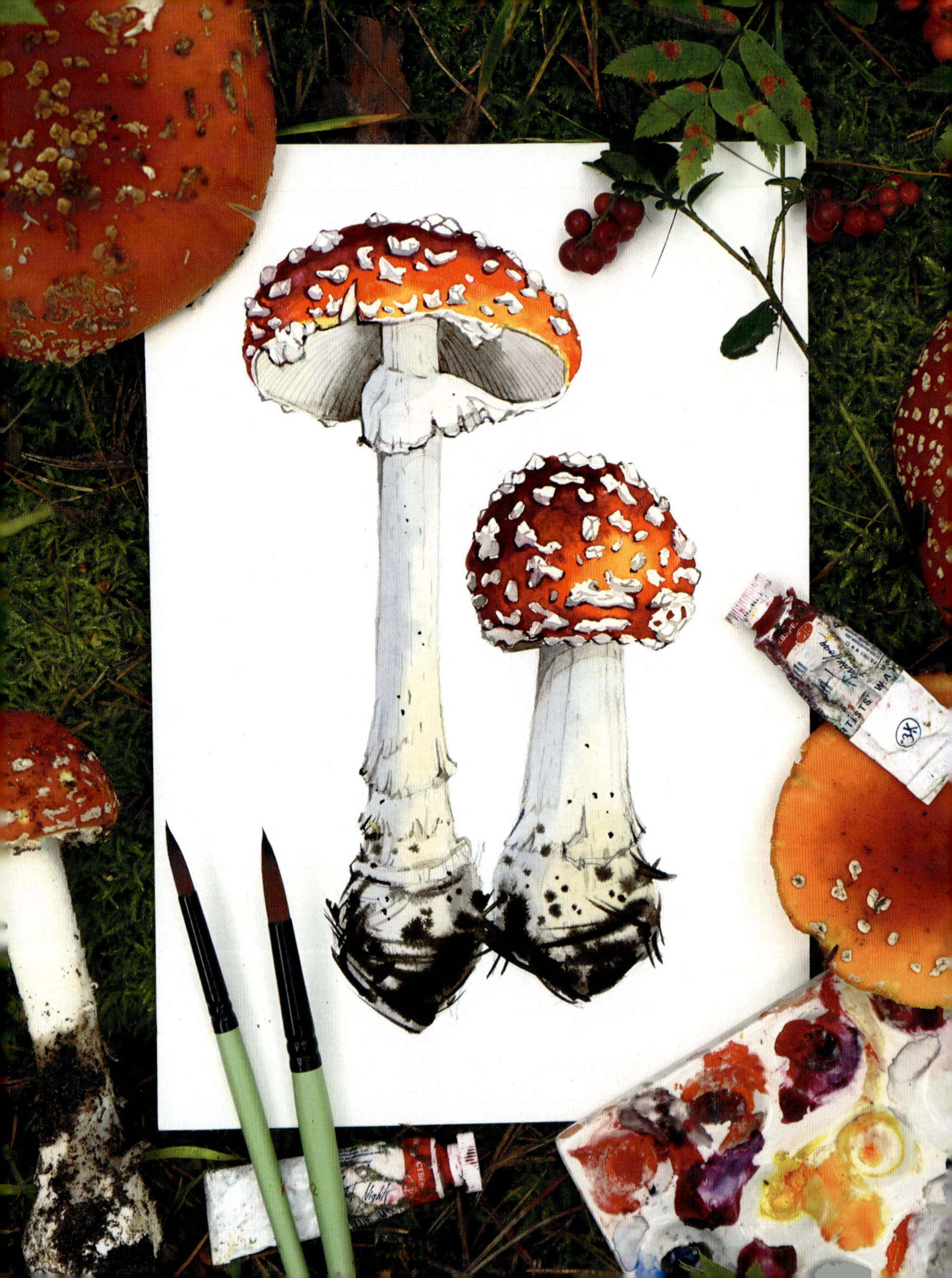

Fly Agaric Mushroom

The fly agaric, with its striking red cap and white spots, is one of the most iconic mushrooms in the world. Known for its hallucinogenic properties, this mushroom is often featured in folklore and fairy tales, adding a touch of mystery to its allure. In this lesson, you'll learn how to paint this colorful mushroom realistically while also practicing the use of masking fluid to protect specific areas of your painting. The white spots on the cap offer the perfect opportunity to master this technique and create a clean, crisp effect without the need for white paint.

Colors Needed

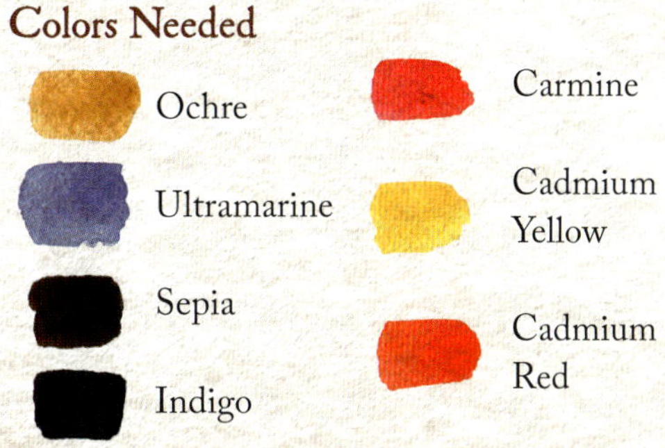

Suggested Paper Orientation: Vertical

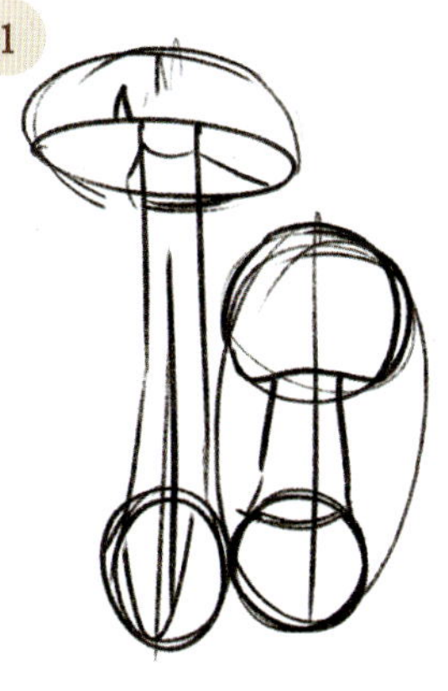

Step 1: Draw two vertical center lines for the mushrooms: one tall on the left side and one shorter on the right. Sketch an oval for the right mushroom. Then, sketch the caps of the mushrooms with a horizontally oriented oval for the left mushroom and a circle for the right one. Indicate a small break in the cap of the left mushroom with a small triangle. Add thickness to the stalks of each mushroom, making the stalk of the left mushroom thinner than the one on the right. Create a horizontal oval inside the left mushroom's cap to define the area under the cap. Finally, outline the lower bulbous parts of both mushrooms with circles.

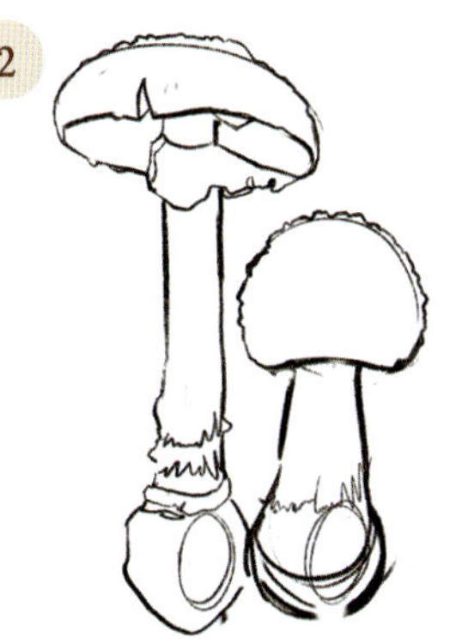

Step 2: Refine the outlines of the stalks and caps. On the left mushroom, refine the break in the cap and define the shape of the partial veil that is attached to the cap on the right side. Then, refine the shape of the bulbous part on both mushrooms and make zigzag lines on top of them to show the remains of the lower partial veil.

Step 3: Add zigzag, hairy lines to the lower part of the stalks. Sketch the end of the bulbous part of the left mushroom more clearly with two parallel lines, and give it a more pointed tip. Include random lines and dots to imitate pieces of ground and pine needles. Add parallel lines to the stalks to separate the shadow areas from the light areas. Give the partial veil attached to the cap a more defined look with an irregular lower edge. Draw white spots on the caps, ensuring they vary in size and shape. To show the three-dimensionality of the white spots, place some along the outlines of the caps so they appear as little bumps. Add parallel lines to represent gills under the left cap.

Step 4: Apply masking fluid (page 12) to the white spots on the caps using an old brush or a toothpick. Let it dry completely before starting the painting process. This may take 15 to 30 minutes, depending on the thickness of the layer and the temperature in your room. The milky white color of the fluid will turn more green-yellow. If you want to be extra sure that the fluid is completely dry, touch it with your finger; it should leave no wet stain, but you will feel a slightly sticky surface.

Step 5: Mix ochre with water for a light yellow. Then, create two mixes:

- Mix A: ultramarine + a touch of sepia + water = medium blue-gray
- Mix B: sepia + indigo + carmine + water = warm dark brown

Apply the ochre and water mix to the right half of the left mushroom stalk. Begin at the top of the stalk and gradually bring the color lower, covering the partial veil attached to the cap. Once you reach the end of the bulbous part, while this color is still wet, switch to Mix A and apply it to the remaining left part of the stem. You should achieve a color blend from yellow to blue, helping to distinguish the left shadow area from the right

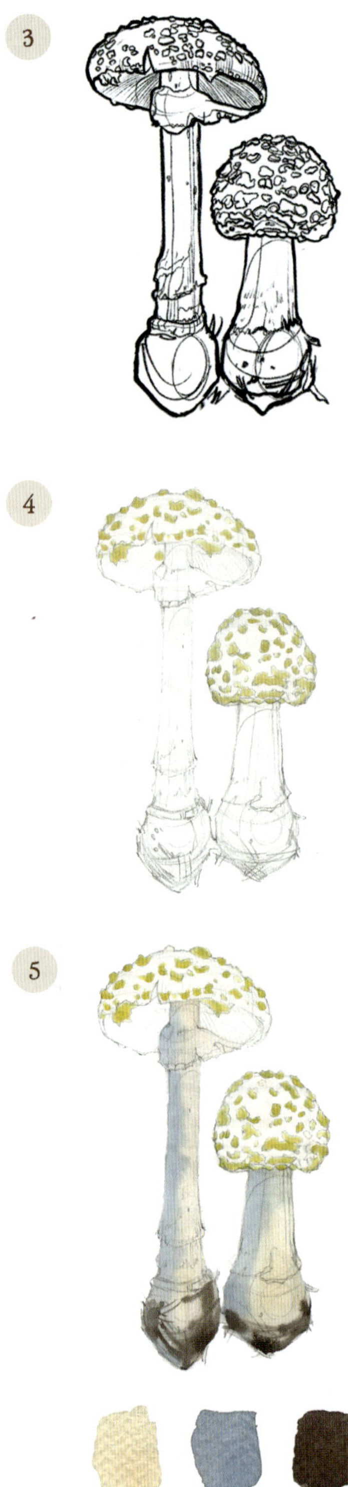

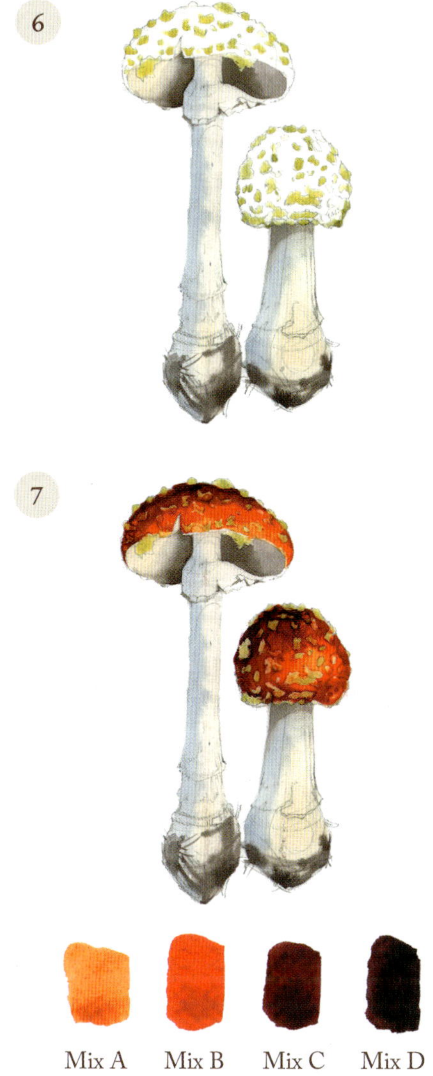

light area. While this layer is still wet, switch to Mix B and apply it to some parts of the bulbous part of the mushroom. Use long irregular strokes to imitate mud and some pine needles attached to the bulbous part that was pulled out of the ground. Then, proceed with the same steps on the right mushroom. Wait for this layer to dry.

Step 6: Apply the ochre and water mix from the previous step to the left side of the under-cap area. Once you reach approximately halfway, switch to Mix 5B and finish covering the remaining area until you reach the left border of the stem. Use the same method to create a color graduation from yellow to brown on the right side of the under-cap area. Create a circular shape under the right mushroom cap and the upper part of its stalk to outline a shadow. Smooth the lower edge of this color for a seamless blend with the previous color layer. Let this dry.

Step 7: Mix the color for the caps of the mushrooms:

- Mix A: cadmium yellow + cadmium red + a bit of water = bright orange

- Mix B: cadmium red + carmine + a bit of water = saturated red

- Mix C: cadmium red + carmine + a touch of indigo + a bit of water = rich dark red-purple

- Mix D: carmine + indigo + water = dark purple

Apply Mix A to the lower border of the left mushroom cap. Leave a thin white line between the under-cap and where you apply the color. Use Mix A to cover one-third of the lower right part of the mushroom. Avoid the triangular break. Then, while this color is still wet, switch to Mix B and cover two-thirds of the surface of the cap. Then, while the paint is still wet, use Mix C to cover the remaining portion of the surface. While this layer is still wet, apply Mix D to the top of the upper edge of the cap and make this dark color seamlessly blend in with the rest of the color surface. Switch to Mix B to paint the far right part of the cap to give it an even more three-dimensional look. Repeat the same process for the right mushroom. Wait for this layer to dry.

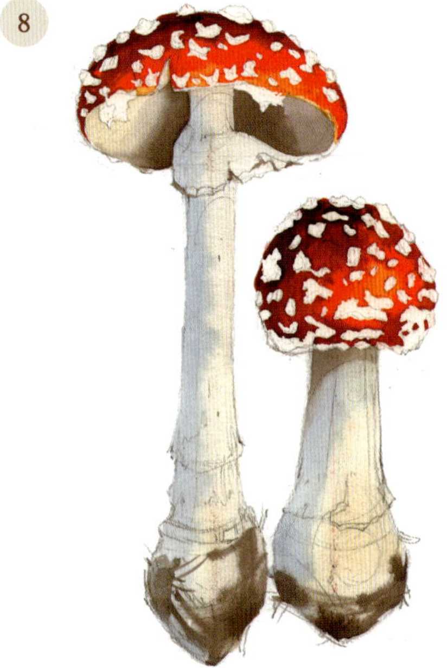

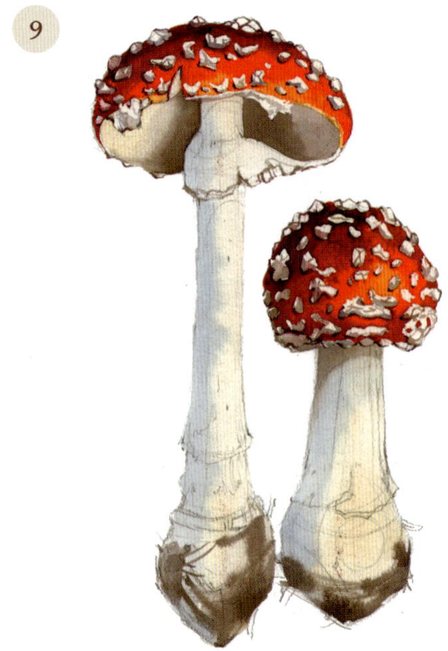

Step 8: Remove the masking fluid. The easiest way to do this is to use the tip of a toothpick to grab the edge of a spot, then pull it off with your fingers or continue using the toothpick to peel it away. You can also use your finger to rub against the spots for removal, but be careful not to do this too close to the edges, as the paint covering the masking fluid may smudge and stain the white background around the mushrooms. Repeat this process until all the masking fluid has been removed.

Step 9: Use Mix 5A to add details to the white spots. Cover some of the spots on the left sides entirely with this color, as they will be in the shadow area. Then, using the very tip of your small brush, add some shadow to the lower part of the spots in the middle and on the right sides. Additionally, use thin lines to create texture on the larger spots to give them a more three-dimensional look. Add a bit more sepia to Mix 5A to darken it, and use this to create outlines for the spots on the right sides of the mushrooms. Once you're done, use Mix 7D to add a small cast shadow under the spots on the left sides.

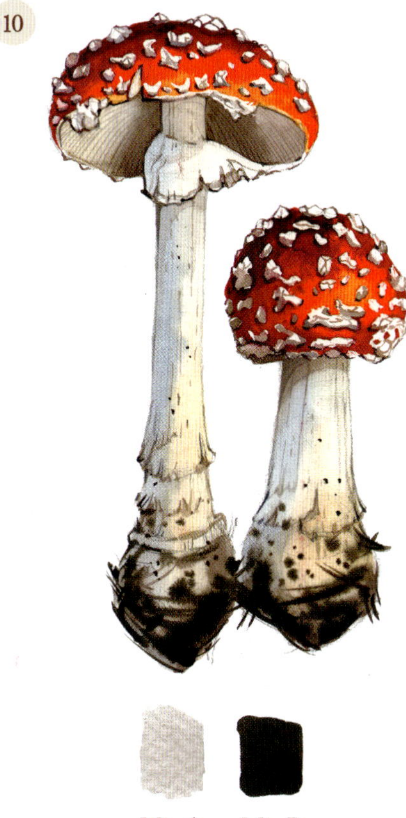

Mix A   Mix B

Step 10: Apply the ochre and water mix from Step 5 to the lower right part of the stalks. This will add a warm hue and saturation to these areas. Smooth the edges for seamless blending if needed. Then, create a new mix:

- Mix A: sepia + some ultramarine + water = light gray

Use Mix A to darken the small upper portion of the stalk of the left mushroom under the cap. Next, use the same color and the tip of your smallest brush to paint the gills under the cap of the left mushroom. Ensure your lines are very thin and parallel. Then, add the final touches to the stalks by painting thin, zigzag lines to indicate the remains of the partial veil on top of the bulbous part. Add some final touches to the partial veil of the left mushroom, making its lower outline more defined.

Now, let's mix the last color:

- Mix B: sepia + indigo + water = very dark color, close to black

We will use Mix B to add the final touches to the bulbous parts of the mushrooms and to create the effect of the ground attached to the mushrooms using the wet-on-wet technique (page 17). Take a medium or large brush and cover half of the stalks with clean water until you reach the tip of the bulbous area. While the surface is still wet, use a smaller brush and Mix B to add lines, dots, and texture to the bulbous part. The color will start to bloom, so allow it to do its work. This part of the painting process is quite intuitive, so it's up to you to decide when to stop. Make sure not to overwork the bulbous part and ensure that some of the white surface on it is still visible. This will guarantee a more realistic effect, so don't simply cover everything with this mix. As a final touch, use the tip of your brush to add a couple of tiny dots to the stalks for specks of dirt to accentuate the outline in some areas of your painting, such as the lower edge of the partial veil or the break on the cap of the mushroom. That's it! Your painting is now complete.

Canada Lily

Standing tall in quiet woodlands and vibrant meadows, the Canada lily is a graceful reminder of nature's artistry. Found across eastern North America, this wildflower enchants with its elegant trumpet-shaped blooms, which range from golden yellow to fiery orange and are often sprinkled with delicate speckles. Reaching up to 4 feet (1.2 meters) in height, it attracts a host of pollinators, including hummingbirds and butterflies, making it an essential part of its ecosystem. Here, you'll refine your skills in creating realistic botanical subjects, focusing on capturing the lily's intricate petal patterns and subtle color transitions while practicing light and shadow techniques on softly curved surfaces.

Colors Needed

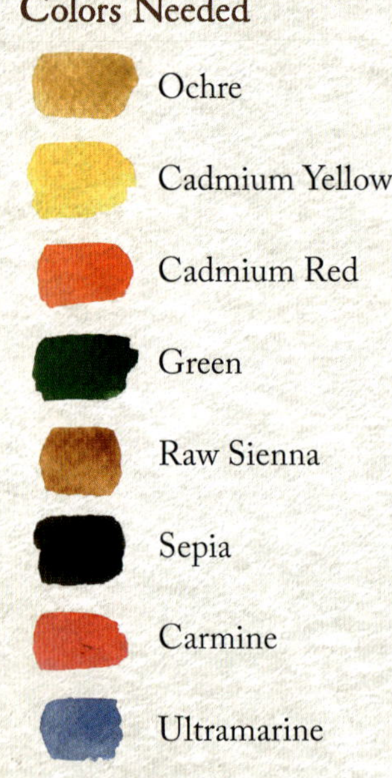

- Ochre
- Cadmium Yellow
- Cadmium Red
- Green
- Raw Sienna
- Sepia
- Carmine
- Ultramarine

Suggested Paper Orientation: Vertical

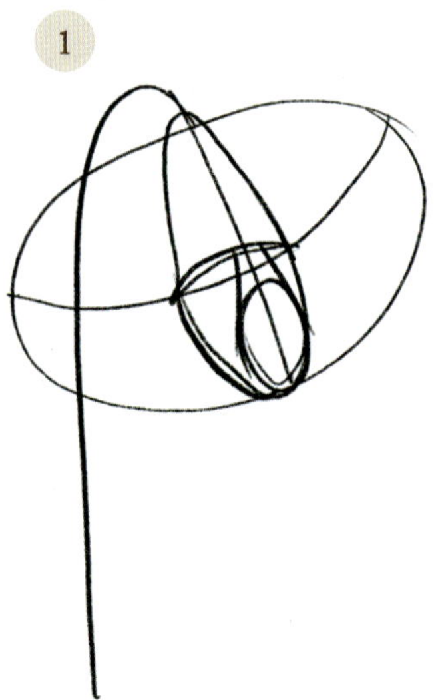

Step 1: Sketch a vertical line on the left side of your sheet of paper; let the top portion of this line curve down and to the right. Then, draw an oval slightly lower than the top of this line, with the right end a bit higher than the left. This oval will represent the entire surface of the bloom. Divide the oval into two parts horizontally with a long curved line that will help to begin outlining the petals and separate the outer area from the inner area. Next, place a smaller, thin oval perpendicularly in the middle of the main oval. Divide it in half with a short curvy line. This will help to visually separate the inside area of the flower from the base of the flower. Draw an even smaller oval at the end of the lower portion of the perpendicular oval; this will represent the clusters of stamens (anthers). Connect it to the other half of the perpendicular oval using two curved lines to represent the cluster of stamens.

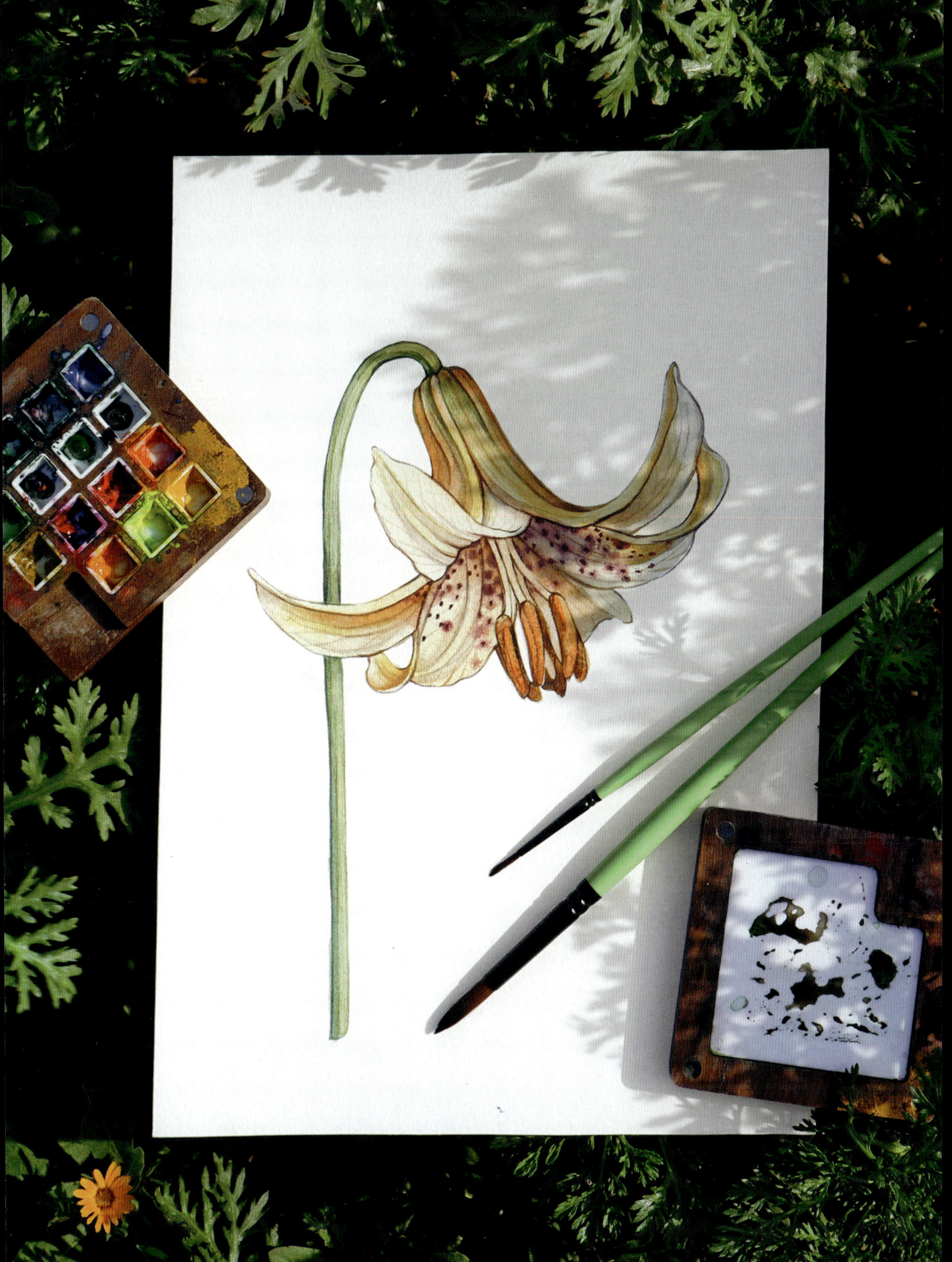

Step 2: Add thickness to the stem by drawing another parallel line alongside it. Then, begin outlining the individual petals with smooth, curved lines. Pay attention to the direction of the petals, ensuring they face different ways depending on their positions. Next, use long parallel lines to create individual stamens. Do the same with the pistil cluster, but use long, thin ovals.

Step 3: Erase any remaining guide lines and add the final details to the flower. Start by refining the shape of the petals, giving each one a center line, and adding texture to the inside of the petals near the stamens with tiny circles and dots. Add some long lines to emphasize the shape of the base of the bloom, and also apply these lines to the petals, following their natural curves. These will help define light and shadow on the petals. Draw a long line along the entire length of the stem to separate the light and shadow areas. Finally, add the finishing details to the stamens and pistils, and now you're ready to move on to the painting process!

Step 4: Mix ochre with water, and with a medium brush, apply this light color to the entire surface of the bloom, avoiding the gaps between petals. While this color is still wet, add some pure cadmium yellow (with almost no water) to certain parts of the petals. Next, create a mix:

- Mix A: cadmium yellow + cadmium red + water = red-orange

Apply Mix A to the shadow areas at the base of the flower (near the stem) and to some areas of the petals. Then, create a mix for the stem:

- Mix B: cadmium yellow + a touch of green + water = light green

Apply Mix B to the whole surface of the stem uniformly, leaving a thin line between the bloom and the stem if the bloom is still wet to prevent colors from mixing. Wait for this layer to dry.

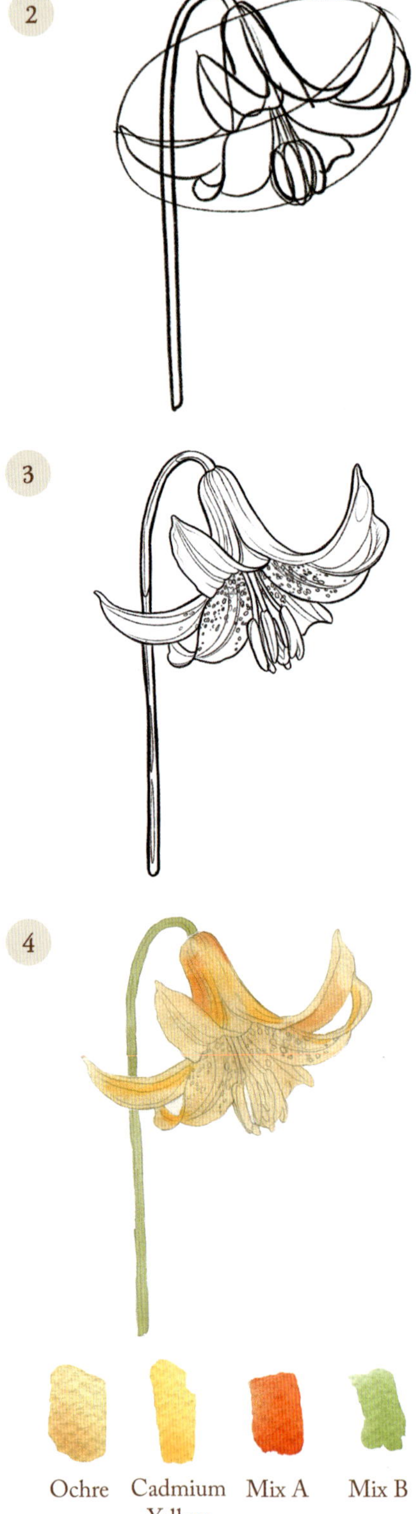

Ochre Cadmium Yellow Mix A Mix B

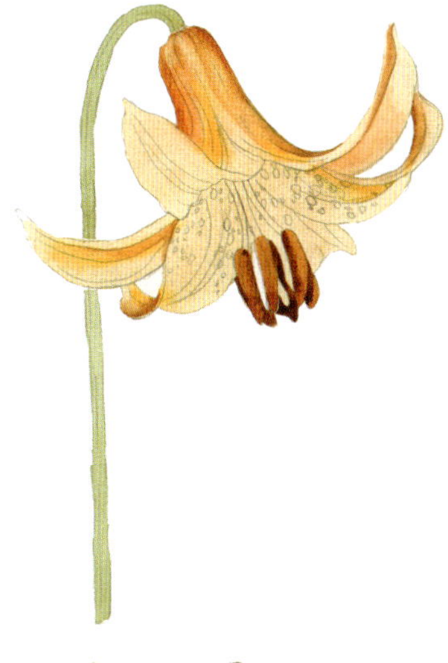

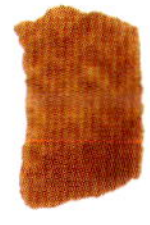 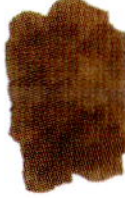

Mix A   Mix B

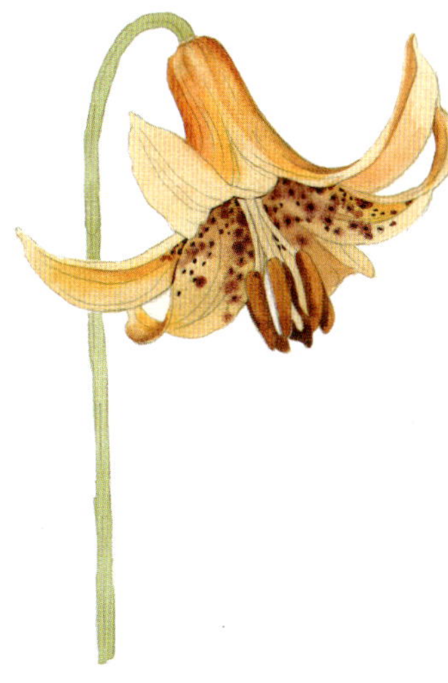

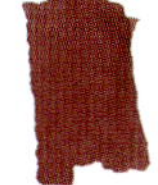 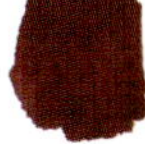

Mix A   Mix B

Step 5: Create these color mixes:

- Mix A: raw sienna + cadmium yellow + water = bright orange
- Mix B: raw sienna + sepia + water = brown

Apply Mix A to the tips of the stamens (anthers) of the lily. Next, apply Mix B to the left shadow areas of each anther and to the anthers positioned behind. Apply Mix A to the right and left sides of the base of the bloom, smoothing the edges for a seamless transition. Add the same color to the shadow areas of the petals and smooth the edges. Allow this layer to dry completely.

Step 6: Now, create two dark mixes using the same colors but in different proportions:

- Mix A: more carmine + sepia + a bit of water = burgundy
- Mix B: Mix 6A (above) + more sepia + almost no water = dark red-brown

Apply the ochre with water from Step 4 to the whole surface of the inside petals. While still wet, add a touch of Mix 5A to the areas near the borders of the upper petals. Allow this layer to sit until the paper is almost dry. Then, use Mix A to create the spots on the petals. The color spots should have fuzzy edges because the paper is still slightly wet. It's important to catch the moment when the paper is drying but not completely dry. If the paper is too dry, you'll only have dark spots with sharp edges and no fuzziness, which won't help achieve the natural, organic look we want. So, try to find that perfect balance before applying the spots. To test, you can add one spot and observe how it behaves before proceeding. Once the fuzzy spots are completely dry, apply Mix B to the center of some of the spots for more contrast. Create additional tiny dark spots on the already dried surface using this color. Use the same Mix B and the very tip of your brush to create a very thin outline between some inside and outside petals.

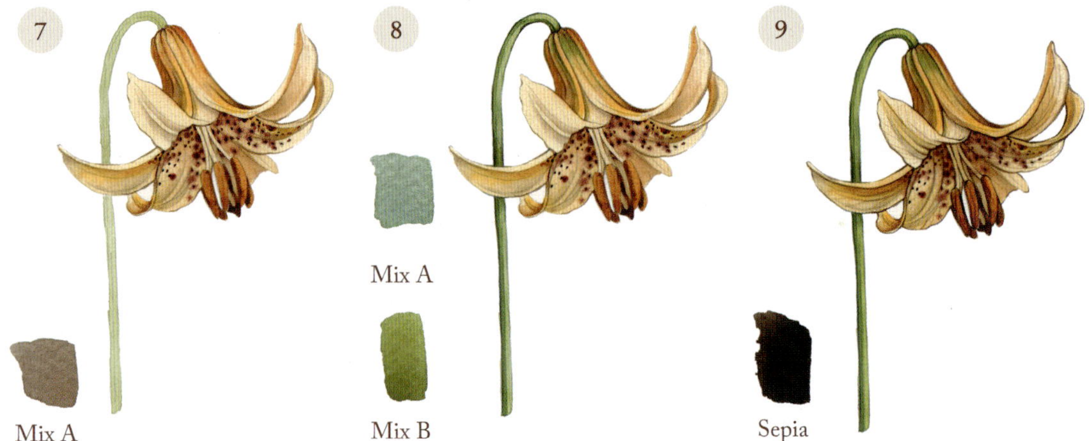

Step 7: Create a new mix:

- Mix A: raw sienna + sepia + water = light brown

Use Mix A to create lines at the base of the bloom, starting from where the bloom is attached to the stem. These lines will emphasize the natural shape of the bloom and help define the individual petals. Vary your strokes—for example, begin with larger strokes on the left side of the bloom, as this is the shadow area. Then, use the very tip of your brush to add thin lines to outline the petals. With the same thin lines, make the outline of some of the stand-alone petals a bit more defined, but as usual, ensure that it's not too dark or uniform. Use the same color to add shadows to each petal, especially in areas where you see natural folds. While this layer is drying, you can add details to the stem.

Step 8: Create two green mixes for the stem:

- Mix A: cadmium yellow + ultramarine + water = light blue green
- Mix B: Mix 8A (above) + green = medium green

Apply Mix A to the shadow areas of the stem, especially on the left side and the upper portion where the stem connects with the bloom.

While this is still wet, introduce Mix B to emphasize some shadow areas even more, and add it to where one of the petals intersects with the stem, as there will be a shadow cast by the petal on top of the stem. Smooth out the edges if needed. Use the same mix and the very tip of your brush to create lines in some parts of the stem, especially on the left side. If needed, you can darken this color during the painting process by adding more green and ultramarine to it. Next, let's introduce some green to the bloom as well. Apply Mix A to the base of the bloom while avoiding the yellow lines. Smooth out this stroke using our usual method: Rinse your brush in clean water, dry it with a paper towel, and gently go over the edge to blend it with the rest of the paper surface.

Step 9: Apply cadmium yellow mixed with water (from Step 4) to some parts of the front and back petals for more vibrancy. Then, apply it over the entire stem for more warmth and saturation. Apply a mix of sepia with a touch of water to create outlines on some petals and especially on the stamens. Next, dilute Mix 7A to make it even lighter. Use the tip of your small brush to create tiny, wavy veins that extend from the center to the edges of the biggest petals. Your painting is now complete!

Giant Sequoia Cone

This cone may be small, but it holds the potential to give birth to one of the most majestic living organisms on Earth: the giant sequoia tree. Native to California's Sierra Nevada mountains, these trees can reach over 300 feet (91 meters) in height, making them some of the tallest and oldest living things on the planet. Despite its towering size, its cones are relatively small, typically measuring 2 to 3 inches (5 to 8 centimeters) in length. It's a powerful reminder that even the smallest things can lead to something immense. In this tutorial, you'll refine your skills in drawing and painting a realistic botanical subject. We'll focus on capturing the cone's intricate details while practicing light and shadow, especially on round objects divided into sections.

Colors Needed

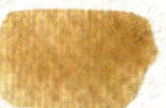 Ochre

 Sepia

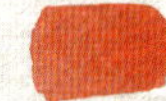 Cadmium Red

Suggested Paper Orientation: Vertical

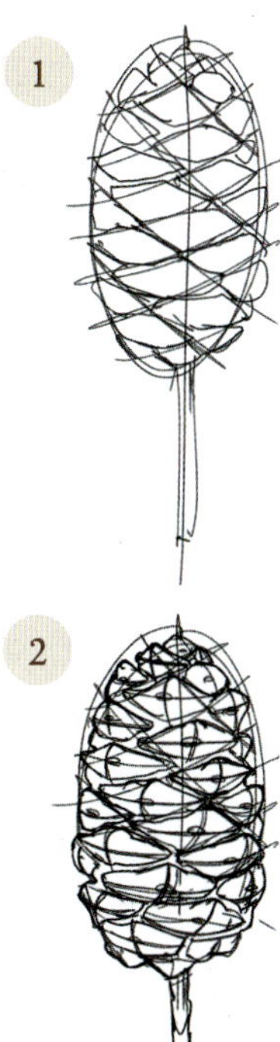

Step 1: Sketch a vertical line in the middle of your paper. Then, place an oval over the line, making sure it takes up a bit more than half of the line's height. The oval's height should be about twice its width. This oval is the cone, while the remaining part of the line is the stem. Give the stem some thickness with two parallel lines close to the center line. Then, draw a grid of diagonal guide lines on the cone. One set of lines should go from the bottom left to the top right and the other set should go in the opposite direction. Use the guide lines to outline the individual scales of the cone, rounding their tips.

Step 2: Give each scale a curved center line. Keep in mind the foreshortening effect and the fact that the cone is round when viewed from the top. This means the center line on the center scales will be in the middle, but as you move to the outer scales, the line will shift to the left on the left scales and to the right on the right scales. Add tiny ovals in the middle of each scale to outline its center. Make each scale look even more realistic by defining the outline more clearly (it should be curvy, not completely straight) and giving them bolder outlines. Finally, add some details to the stem using semicircles that go across its surface.

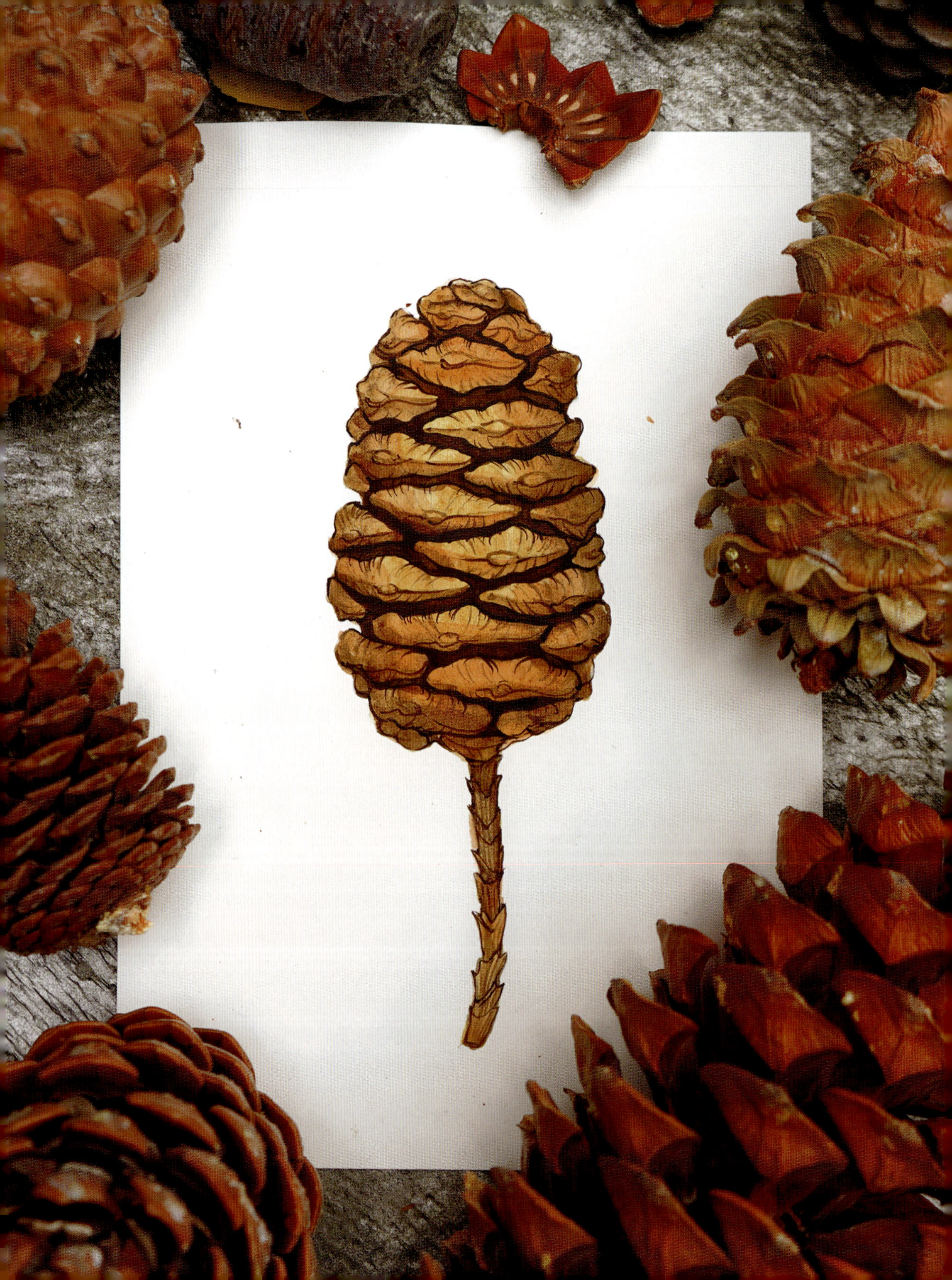

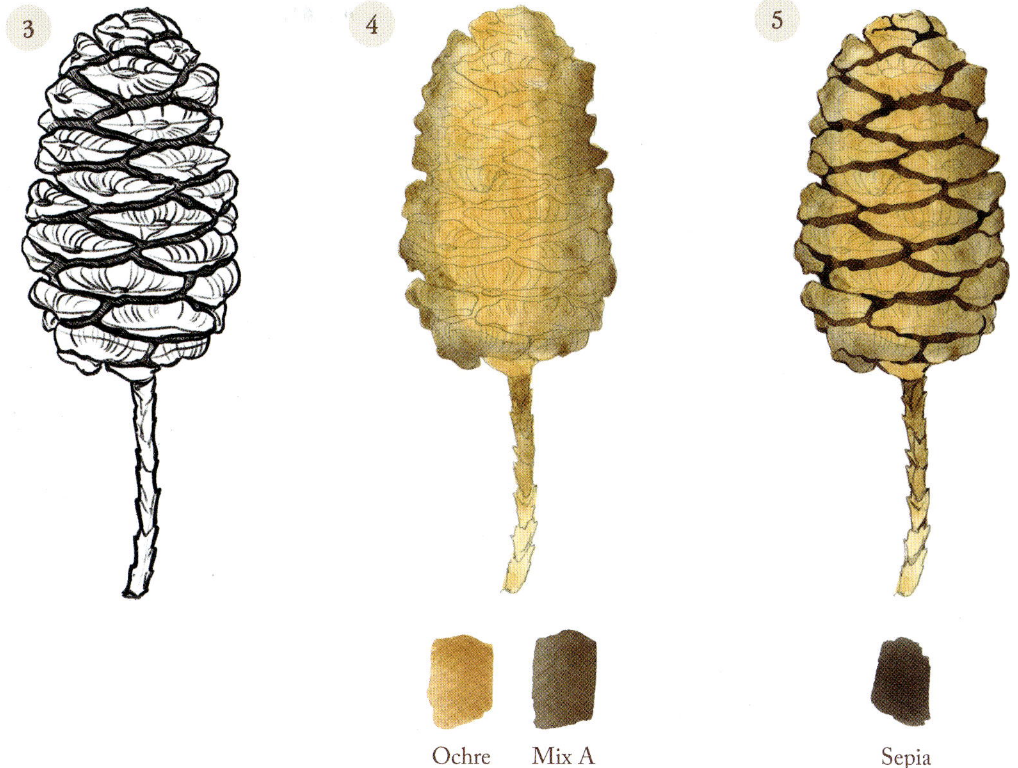

Step 3: Erase the main guiding oval and focus on adding final details. Darken the spaces between scales and add final touches by drawing long horizontal lines dividing each scale into two parts. Also, add some short, curvy vertical lines to emphasize the bumpy shape of the scales and give them more texture. Define the outline of the stem more clearly and add more details to it using short lines. Now, your drawing is ready!

Step 4: Combine ochre with water for a watery medium brown mix. Make sure you have a good quantity of this color, as we will need quite a lot of it. Then, make a new mix:

- Mix A: sepia + a touch of cadmium red + water = light watery brown

Paint the whole surface of the cone with the ochre and water mix. Your goal is to create a wash without visible brushstrokes. Start from the top of the cone and gradually pull the color down until you reach the tip of the branch (peduncle). Then, while this first color is still wet, apply Mix A to the extreme left and right parts of the cone. Smooth out the edges if needed. You should end up with darker edges and a lighter center, which will help you achieve a more three-dimensional effect. Apply Mix A to the upper part of the branch, making sure to leave the last section of cone untouched. Let this layer dry before proceeding.

Step 5: Mix sepia with water and apply this to the areas between the scales of the cone. Use the tip of your medium or small brush for precision. Then, create outlines in some areas of the cone. Use the same mix to underline the prickle by adding thin lines. Allow this layer to dry.

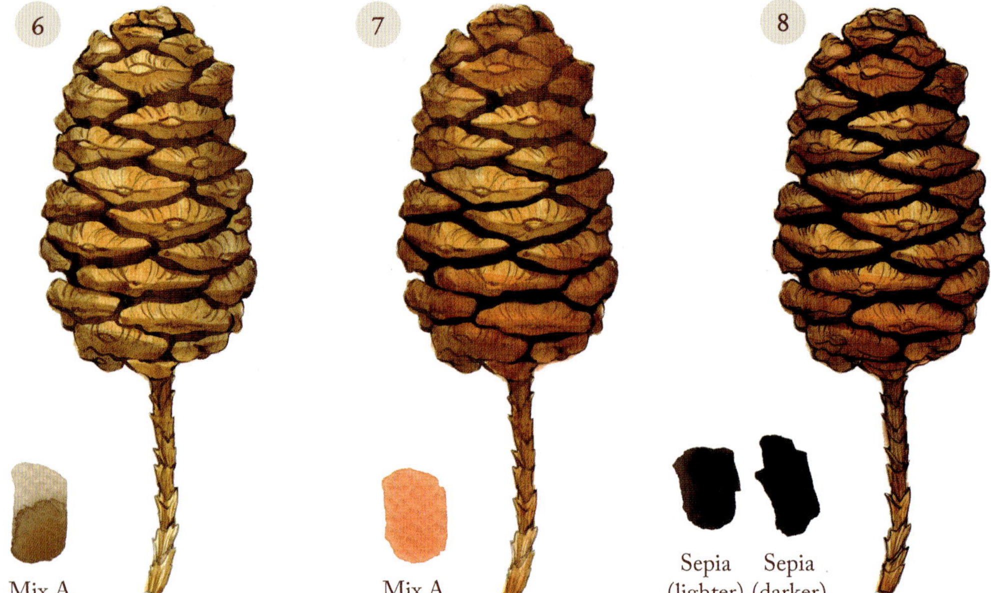

Step 6: Use the sepia and water mix from Step 5 to outline the prickles (the little round part in the middle of each scale) with a small horizontal oval. Then, create a new mix:

- Mix A: ochre + sepia + water = light, watery brown

Apply this color to the lower half of each scale. Use thin lines and the very tip of your brush to create folds on the upper and lower parts of some scales—especially the larger ones. Wait for this layer to dry.

Step 7: Let's make a new mix:

- Mix A: ochre + cadmium red + water = watery orange

Apply Mix A to the left and right sides of the cone, leaving the center oval part untouched. This will give the cone an additional reddish hue, accentuate light and shadow, and help unify the surface of the painting. Use Mix 4A to outline the tiny ovals in the middle of the larger scales that represent the prickles. Do so with the very tip of your brush, ensuring your lines are very thin. Then, apply the sepia and water mix from Step 5 that you used between the scales to darken the empty spaces between the center scales even more.

Step 8: Continue darkening the spaces between the scales and adding even more details to the cone. First, take Mix 7A and cover the lower halves of the scales with it. Let them dry completely.

Mix a very dark color by combining sepia with very little water. Use this color to paint the remaining spaces between the scales. Then, mix sepia with almost no water at all. This should be the darkest color we've mixed so far in this tutorial. Use it to outline each individual scale, create the outline on the cone (make sure it interrupts in some areas), and also to add final touches to the upper and lower halves of the scales. To do this, use the very tip of your small brush and create small folds on the scales of the cone. Use the same method to outline the small oval centers of the scales more clearly. Add some additional details to the peduncle by using thin, short lines. Your painting is complete.

Luna Moth

The Luna moth is a fascinating creature, known for its stunning green wings and eyelike spots that serve to confuse predators. Despite its beauty, this moth only lives for about a week, during which time it doesn't feed but focuses solely on reproduction. This short lifespan makes capturing its delicate features all the more special. In this tutorial, you'll learn how to paint its soft, almost ethereal wings and the fine, hairlike texture of its body. You'll also explore the challenge of painting subtle details without getting overwhelmed by complex patterns.

Colors Needed

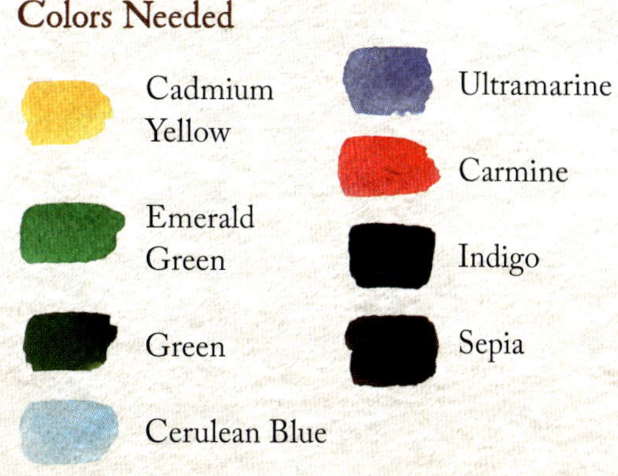

- Cadmium Yellow
- Emerald Green
- Green
- Cerulean Blue
- Ultramarine
- Carmine
- Indigo
- Sepia

Suggested Paper Orientation: Horizontal

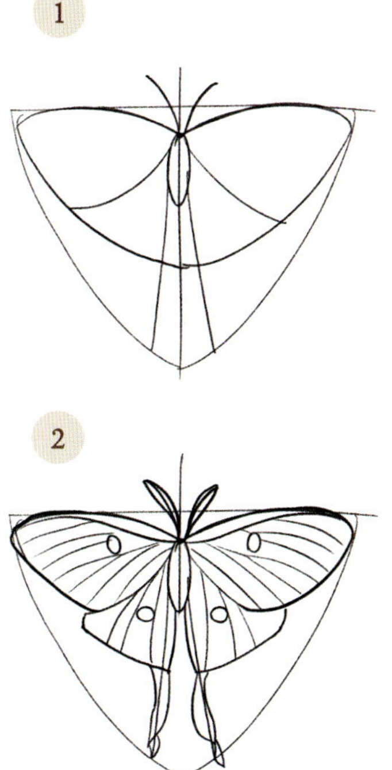

Step 1: Draw a straight vertical line down the middle of your paper. Sketch a triangle with the line in the center. The triangle's base should be at the top, and the sides should be slightly rounded. The flat base of the triangle will be your guide line for the wings. Create a thin oval just below the base to represent the body. Draw two antennae with curved lines going in different directions. Connect the top of the body with the edges of the triangle's base using curvy lines. This will form the top outline of the wings. Connect the tips of the wings together with a semicircle. Separate the upper wings from the lower wings with semicircular lines starting from the top of the body. Finally, draw two curvy lines starting from the lower side of the moth's body and ending to the left and to the right of the tip of the main triangle. These lines will help place the tails.

Step 2: Add some thickness to the antennae. Create a top border for the wings with a line parallel to the outline but slightly lower on each wing. From this line, create the veins that spread across the wings until they reach the lower border. Then, define the shape of the lower wings and add veins. Next, add some small ovals to the top and bottom wings. The ovals on the top wings should be placed vertically, while the ovals on the bottom should be placed horizontally. Finally, add some details to the tails using wavy lines.

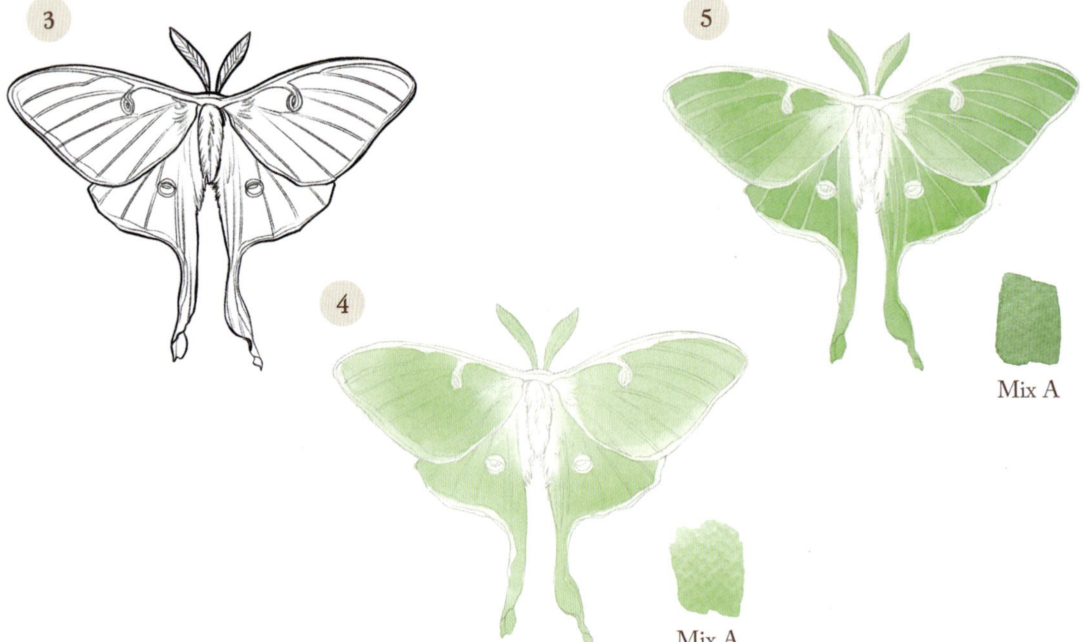

Step 3: Erase the guide lines and add the final details. Start by refining and bolding the outline. Then, give the veins thickness by adding a parallel line to each vein. Add final details to the antennae with short, tiny lines that radiate from the center toward each side. Add details to the ovals on the wings, making them resemble eyes. Add some hairy texture to the body and the inner side of the lower wings, next to the body. It's time to start painting!

Step 4: Let's mix a base tone for our moth:

- Mix A: cadmium yellow + emerald green + a lot of water = light green

Apply this mix to one side of the moth with a medium or large brush. If you're right-handed, start from the left side; if you're left-handed, start from the right. This way you won't accidentally smudge the paint with your hand. Avoid the eye pattern and the border on the top and right side of the wing. Once you've covered approximately two-thirds of the right wing, switch to clean water

and blend the color until you reach the body. Repeat this process on all the wings. Don't forget to cover the antennae as well. Wait for this layer to dry.

Step 5: Mix another green color:

- Mix A: Mix 4A (cadmium yellow + emerald green + a lot of water) + a touch of green = green

Use this color to cover all parts of the wings except for the areas you left untouched in the previous step and the veins. Where the wings overlap, make sure the two lowest sections of the upper wings are lighter than the others. You can achieve this by diluting the mix with more water. Also, be careful to preserve the white body and the lighter areas of the upper wings close to the body. You can do this by lifting some of the color from those areas with a clean, dry brush while it's still wet. Then, cover the left half of the left antenna and the right half of the right antenna with this mix. Wait for this layer to dry.

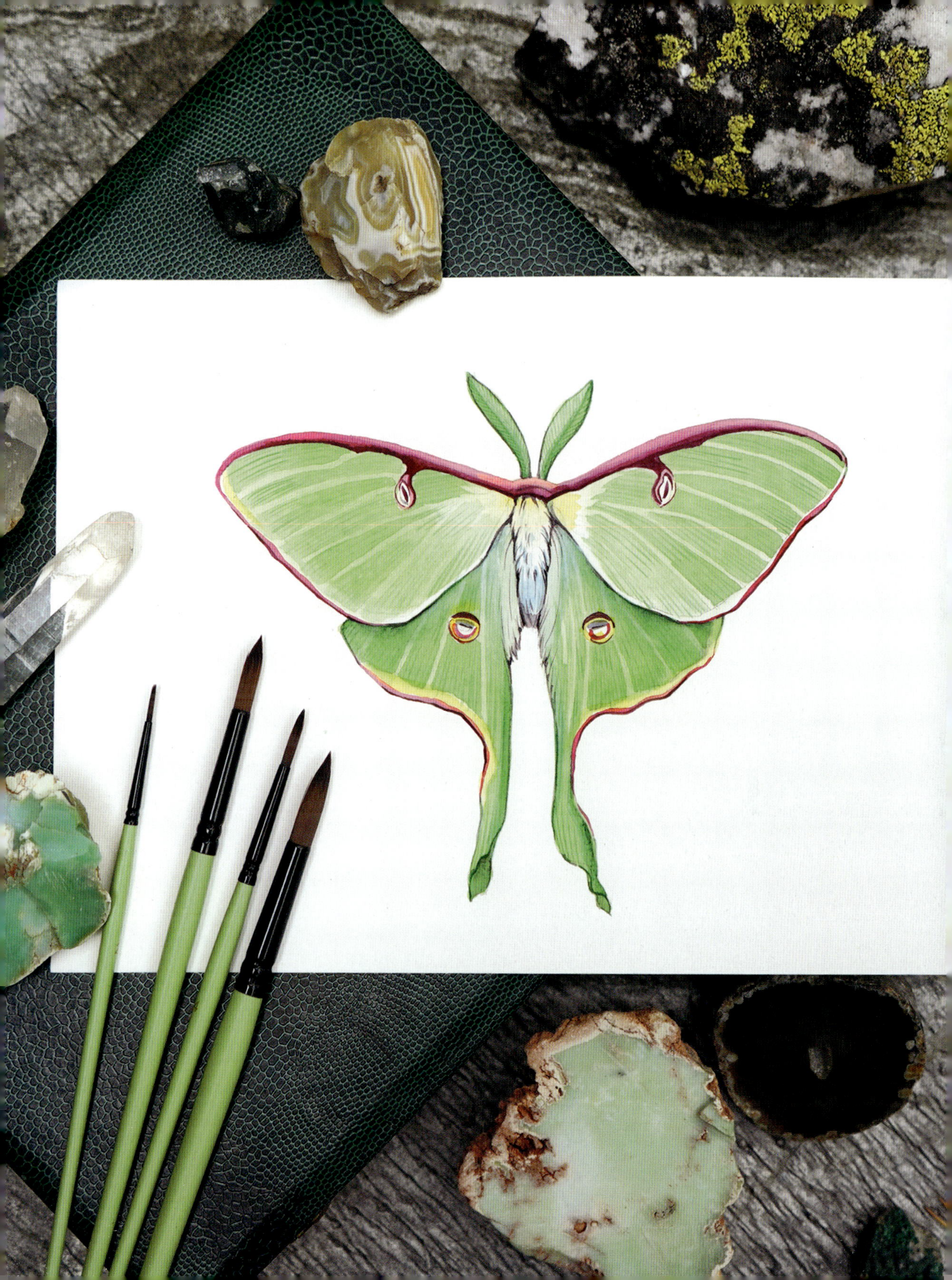

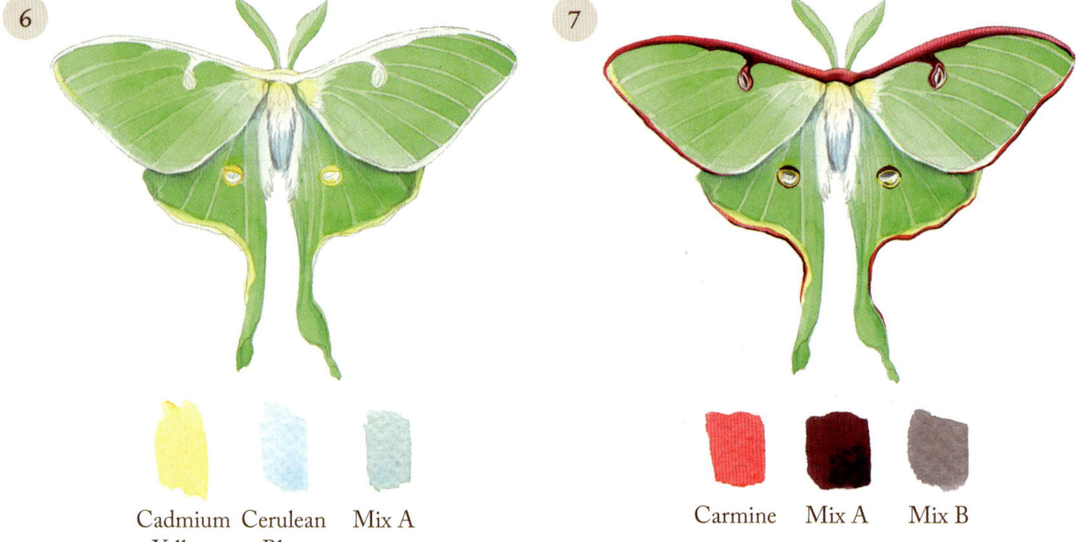

Step 6: Apply cadmium yellow mixed with water to the lower border of the lower wings. Also, apply this color to the fake eyes on the lower wings, but make sure to leave the center of the eyes white. Add the same color to the base of the upper wings and smooth the edges for a seamless transition. Next, combine cerulean blue with water, and apply it to the lower part of the body, smoothing the edges. Then, create a new mix:

- Mix A: cerulean blue + a touch of ultramarine + water = light blue

Use this mix to better define the base of the lower wings and create the shadow cast from the top wings onto the lower wings. To do this, apply a stroke of Mix A under the upper wings, and while the color is still wet, smooth the transition with a clean, dry brush. Repeat this process on both sides. Use the same color to darken the long parts of the lower wings in the shadowed areas. As a result, the lower wings should appear darker than the upper wings.

Step 7: Start by mixing a vibrant pink color by combining carmine with water. Then, create another mix:

- Mix A: carmine + indigo or ultramarine + water = dark purple

Apply the carmine and water mix to the lower borders of the wings, making sure this color follows the natural outline of the moth. Apply the same color to the costal margin (the top of the top wings) and use it to outline the top fake eyes, leaving the center oval untouched.

Once dry, take Mix A, and with the very tip of your small brush, apply it as a fine line beneath the carmine and water mix you placed on the lower wings. On the top part, apply Mix A to cover the lower half of the pink area, then smooth out the edge by washing your brush, drying it with a paper towel, and gently going over the edge to blend. Then, use Mix A to add more details to the top fake eyes by making the right outline of the left eye and the left outline of the right eye more visible. Add a thin oval in the center using the same color. Use a very thin line to outline the lower fake eyes and make the top outline bolder.

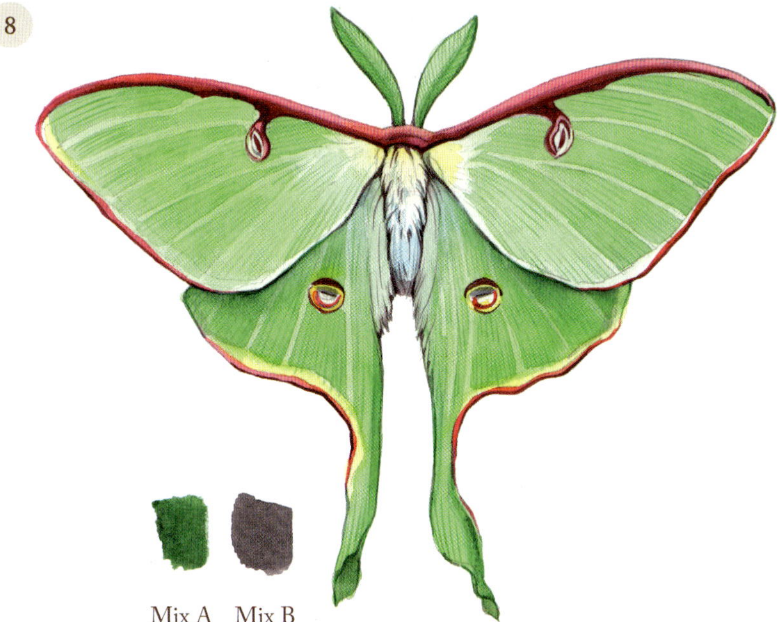

Then, create a new mix:

- Mix B: carmine + ultramarine + sepia + water = gray

Use Mix B to create thin ovals in the center of the eyespots. Be sure to leave some white in the middle.

Step 8: Use Mix 5A to create thin, short lines that follow the natural direction of the wings. These lines will represent the hairy texture of the wings. Use the same color and technique on the antennae, creating fine lines that go from the center of the antenna to its sides. If needed, visually unite the surface of each antenna by using your small brush and clean water. This will make the lines on the antennae appear a bit fuzzier.

Next, use Mix 5A to outline the folds on the long parts of the lower wings. After that, create a new mix:

- Mix A: Mix 5A (cadmium yellow + emerald green + a touch of green + a lot of water) + a touch more emerald green + more green = green

Use this to better define the long parts of the lower wings and outline the antennae, making sure the outline is very thin.

Then, create a new color:

- Mix B: Mix 7B (carmine + ultramarine + sepia + water) + more ultramarine + more sepia = dark gray

Use Mix B to create the hairy texture on the body and the lower wings that connect to the body. Use short, curved strokes to imitate fur. Add a couple of strokes to the middle of the body as well to accentuate the hairy look even more. You're done!

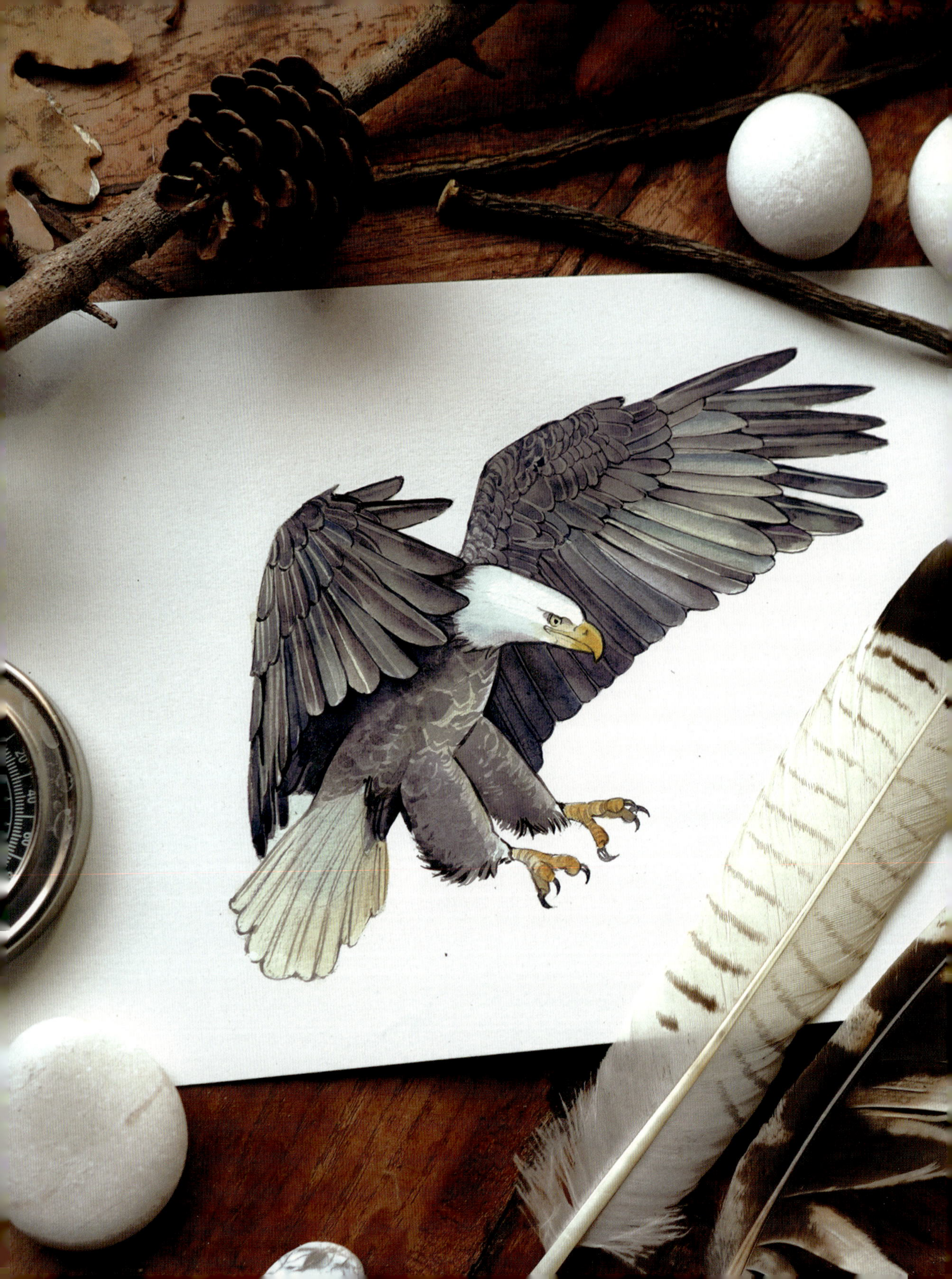

Bald Eagle

The bald eagle, a symbol of strength and freedom, is one of North America's most majestic birds. Found particularly in the United States, Canada, and northern Mexico, bald eagles are known for their impressive wingspan and powerful flight. In this lesson, you will have a unique opportunity to represent a bird in motion, capturing the fluidity of flight and the position of various feathers. You'll learn how the movement of the bird influences the arrangement and orientation of its feathers. Additionally, I will guide you in incorporating subtle colors into the feathers, enriching your painting and giving it depth and interest.

Colors Needed

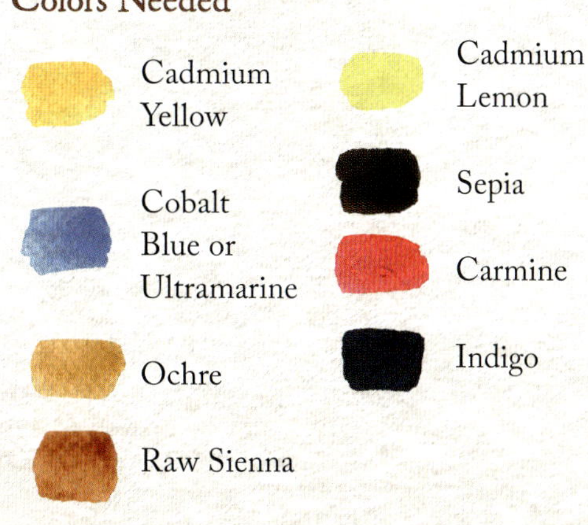

Suggested Paper Orientation: Horizontal

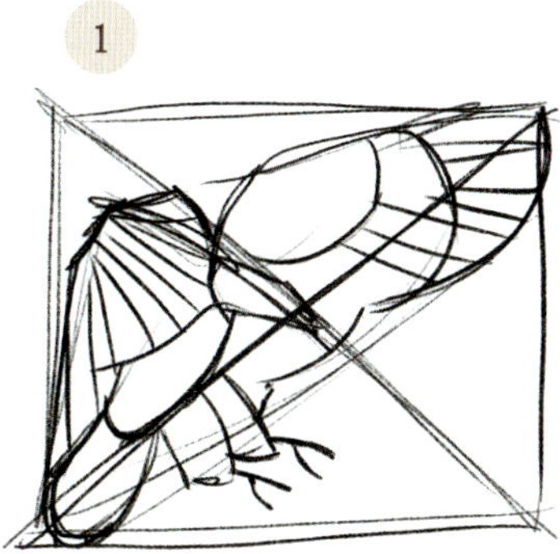

Step 1: Sketch a rectangle that's slightly larger than its height. Draw two diagonal lines connecting the opposite corners. One line will represent the movement of the head and the other will represent the movement of the tail and the wing. Outline the wings with rough semicircular shapes for now, and then use long lines to begin outlining the individual feathers. Outline the body and tail with two ovals, and use a triangle to roughly outline the neck and head. Finally, outline the legs with two oval-shaped forms and attach two "Y" shapes at the bottom to represent the feet.

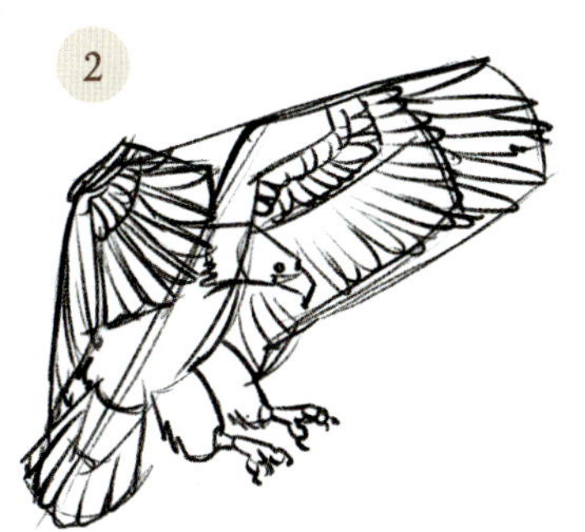

Step 2: Erase the main rectangle and focus on defining the feathers. There are three levels of feathers on each wing, with the size of the feathers gradually decreasing from the bottom to the top. The feathers in the lowest layer should be longer, more pointed, and spaced farther apart. The feathers in the second layer are smaller and more rounded. The feathers in the top layer should be the shortest and most rounded. Detail the feathers on the tail. Then, define the shape of the head more clearly and add a beak and an eye. Give some realism to the legs by adding zigzag lines to imitate the feather texture on the left sides of the legs. Finally, add details to the feet.

Step 3: Erase the remaining guide lines. Draw a center line on some of the feathers and make the outlines of the individual feathers bolder, especially for the larger ones. Add details to the feathers in the third layer using small, short, circular strokes. Do the same on both wings. Then, add a similar texture to the body and legs as you did with the small feathers. Add more lines to highlight the direction of the tail feathers. Draw lines that imitate feathers on the head and refine the details and shape of the head and beak. Add talons, and once you're finished with these details, you can start painting!

Step 4: Create a light watery yellow mix by combining cadmium yellow and water. Then, mix cobalt blue or ultramarine with water to obtain a light watery blue mix. Apply the light yellow mix to the top of the right wing. When you reach halfway down—where the head, chest, and leg start—switch to the light blue mix and finish covering the wing. You should have a nice color blend from yellow to blue. Let this dry.

Apply the light yellow mix to the entire left wing and the tail. Let these areas dry before proceeding. Then, apply the same mix to the belly and the right side of the legs. While the color is still wet, switch to the light blue mix and continue covering the legs and body area. Create a new mix:

- Mix A: ochre + raw sienna + water = light warm yellow

Apply this color to the eagle's feet. Then, mix cadmium lemon with water and apply this to the beak. Let everything dry.

Step 5: Mix these colors for the feathers:

- Mix A: cobalt blue or ultramarine + a touch of sepia + water = medium blue

- Mix B: cobalt blue or ultramarine + carmine + sepia + water = gray-purple

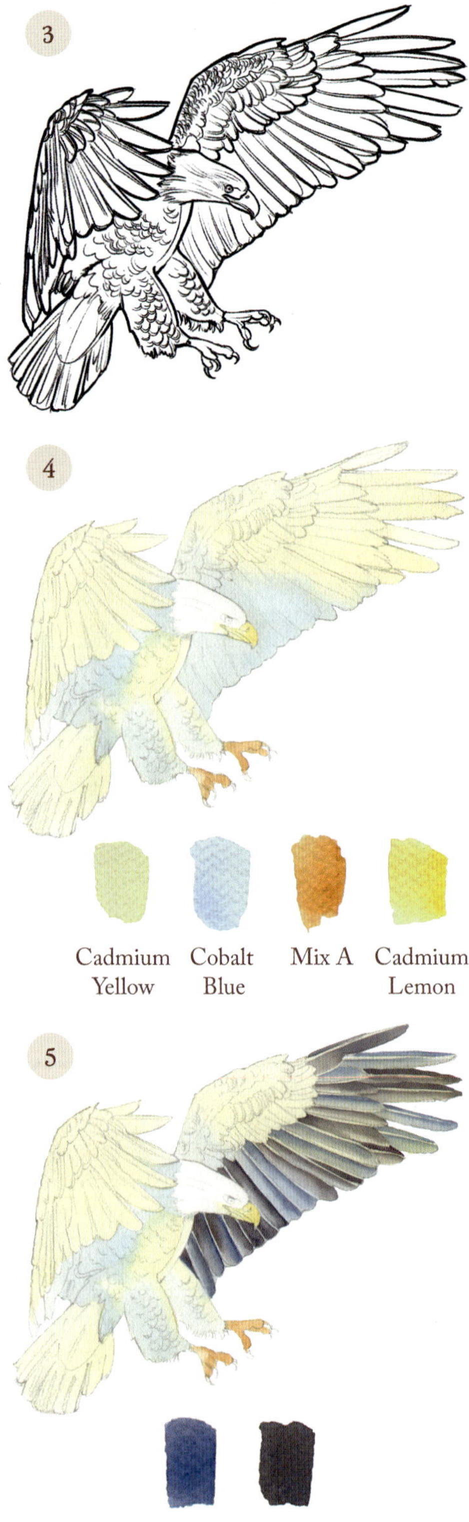

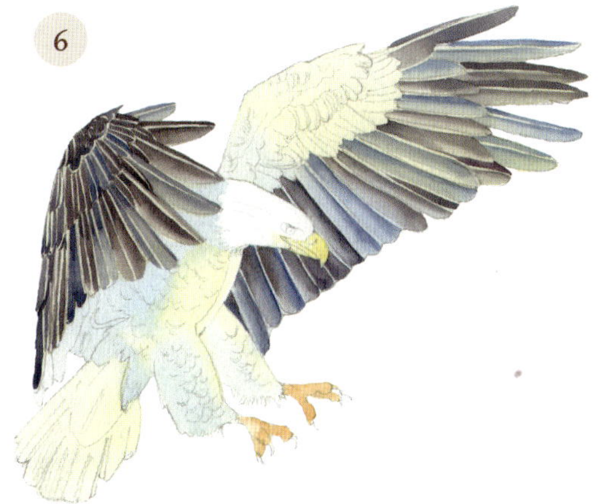

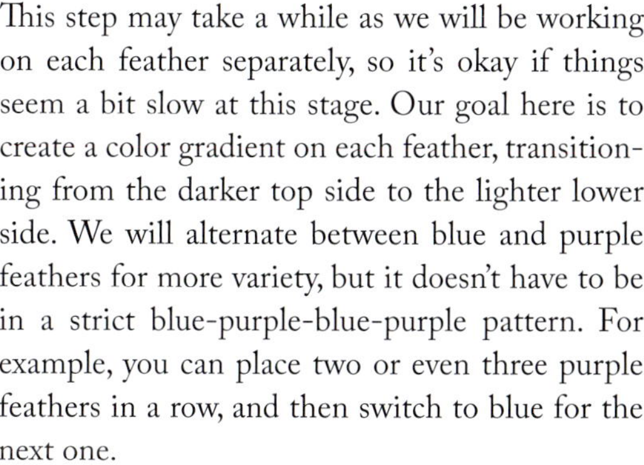

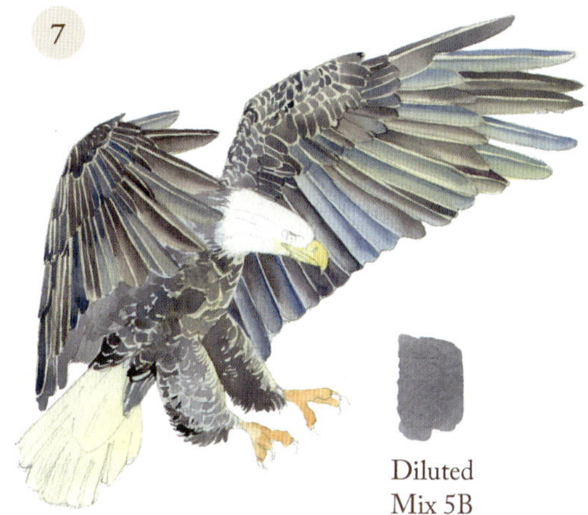

Diluted
Mix 5B

This step may take a while as we will be working on each feather separately, so it's okay if things seem a bit slow at this stage. Our goal here is to create a color gradient on each feather, transitioning from the darker top side to the lighter lower side. We will alternate between blue and purple feathers for more variety, but it doesn't have to be in a strict blue-purple-blue-purple pattern. For example, you can place two or even three purple feathers in a row, and then switch to blue for the next one.

Start with the top feather on the right wing. Make a thin line of Mix A or B with a small brush. (I started with B.) Then, leave a thin line of dry paper that will represent the middle part of the feather. Take the color you were using and create a thin line under the dry area. While the line of color is still wet, rinse your brush, dry it with a paper towel, and smooth the edge to create a transition from the darker top to the lighter lower part. When the first feather is done, proceed with the remaining ones using the same method and switching between the A and B mixes.

Step 6: Use the same colors and method from the previous step to paint the lower-level feathers on the left wing. Then, proceed with the top feathers of the same left wing. Use the same procedure as before, but there's no need to blend these feathers, as they are too small. Simply cover both parts of each feather with color and leave the thin center line untouched.

Step 7: Use Mix 5B diluted with water to paint the small top feathers of the right wing. Leave a thin layer of dry paper between the individual feathers that resemble scales. Continue to use the diluted mix to paint the feathers on the body and legs. Wait for this layer to dry.

Step 8: At this stage, our painting looks quite scattered, with too much contrast between the feathers, making it hard to see the general shapes of the bird. In this step, we will unify these surfaces to make them look more harmonious while still preserving the intricate details. With a medium brush, gently cover the entire surface of the feathers on the body and wings with clean water. Avoid rubbing the brush too hard against the paper to prevent disturbing the layers we've already applied.

(Step 8 continued)

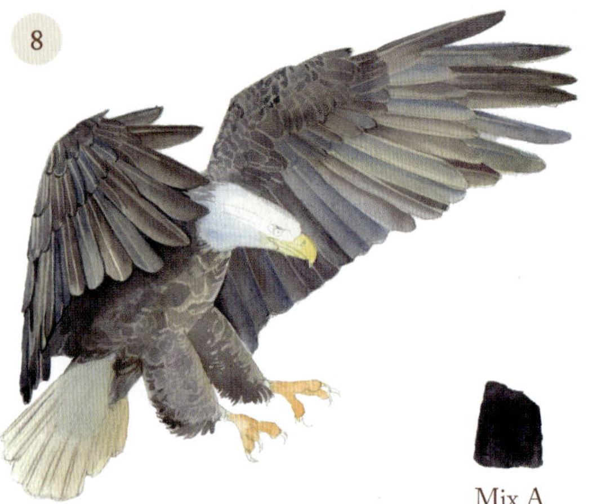

Mix A

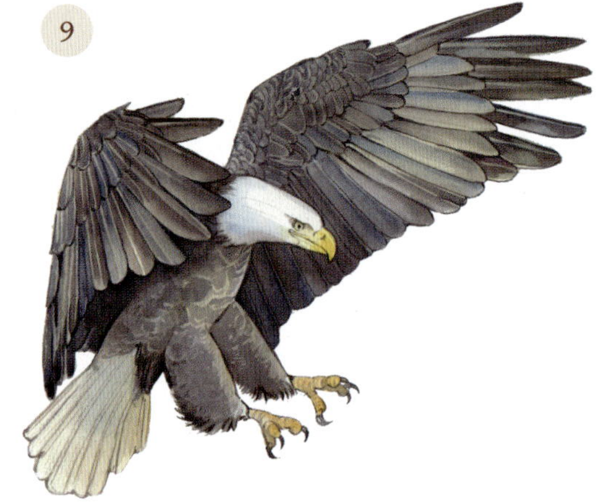

As a result, the white feather lines will still be visible but will appear more natural, realistic, and integrated with the entire surface of the wing. Let the water dry completely.

To add contrast to the body and the left wing, mix a new color:

- Mix A: indigo + carmine + sepia + water = dark purple (should be the darkest purple we've used so far)

Apply this color to the body under the wing and smooth the edges. Use the tip of your brush with the same color to add details to the wing, outlining some of the larger individual feathers with thin lines. Finally, use the light yellow and blue mixes from Step 4 to add color to the tail. Start by covering the tip of the tail with the yellow mix, then switch to the light blue mix when you reach halfway down the tail. While the tail is drying, use the light blue mix to add a shadow to the lower side of the eagle's head, and smooth the edges. Once the tail has dried, use Mix 5B to make long, thin lines that better outline the individual feathers.

Step 9: Add even more contrast to the bird by working on the shadow areas. Use Mix 5B and a small brush to darken the lowest feathers on the right wing, focusing on their tips and bases. Use the same color to darken the area under the head. After that, using the same 5B mix, create the outline on the tail and the individual feathers of the tail. Then, use Mix 8A to outline some of the individual feathers on the right wing.

Next, outline the legs of the bird, paint the talons, and outline the head using Mix 8A. Add some shadow under the eyebrow area using the diluted Mix 5B from Step 7. Afterward, add cadmium yellow diluted with water (from Step 4) to the eye, and make the tip of the beak more saturated using the same color. Use the diluted Mix 5B from Step 7 to outline the texture on the feet with thin, short, curved strokes across each individual toe and the top part of the feet. Then, use the same color with very thin strokes to outline the mouth, beak, and nostril.

Make sure the yellow on the eye is completely dry before doing this last step. With the very tip of your small brush, apply Mix 8A or any dark, almost black color to the center of the eye for a pupil. That's it! Your eagle is complete.

Great Gray Owl

The great gray owl is a symbol of wisdom and mystery, often representing intuition and the secrets of the forest. Native to the dense boreal and coniferous forests of North America, Scandinavia, and Siberia, these majestic birds thrive in cold, remote habitats. In this tutorial, you'll learn how to depict the owl's intricate feather patterns and textures with precision. You'll also practice creating an optional abstract background inspired by its habitat.

Colors Needed

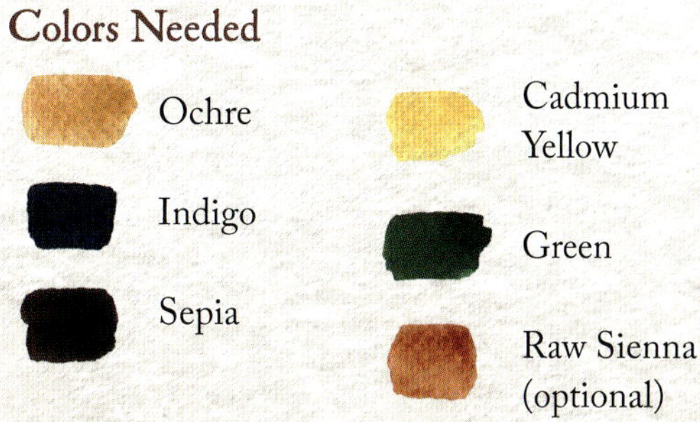

Suggested Paper Orientation: Vertical

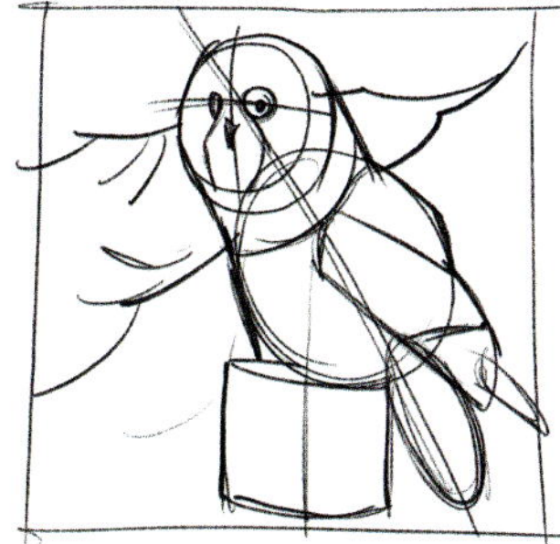

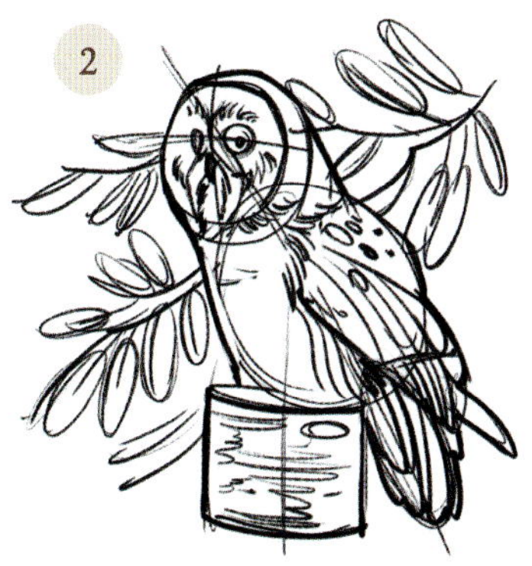

Step 1: Draw a square in the middle of your paper. Create a diagonal line one-third of the way from the left of the top to one-fifth of the way from the right of the bottom. This line will represent the general direction and movement of the bird. Next, create a short vertical line in the center of the lower side of the main square—this is the center line for the log. Give the log thickness by adding sides to it, making it look almost like a square.

Outline the owl using simple geometric shapes. Start with an oval on top of the log, leaning a bit more toward its right side. This is the body. Attach a smaller circle to it toward the left for the head. Sketch the tail with an even smaller thin, long oval and the wing with a similar but slightly bigger oval. Add wavy lines behind the owl to imitate the branches behind it. Start connecting the different body parts together with smooth lines. Add one horizontal line and one vertical line to the center of the face to help position the eyes. Draw two circles close to the center of the face; the one on the left should be more oval-like because the owl's head is turning. Then, add the eyes within those circles.

Step 2: Define the facial features better and add some feather texture to the head using small zigzag strokes. Outline individual feathers on the wing and tail with long, parallel lines. Add small circles to the right side of the owl to begin outlining the texture. Add some texture to the log using long and short curvy horizontal lines and circles. Finally, start outlining the branches in the background with thin ovals.

Step 3: Erase any distracting guide lines and focus on adding the final details to the owl, the log, and the background, if you want to include it. Finalize the feather texture on the body using shorts strokes, tiny spots, and dots. Then, add even more details to the wing and tail, and refine the outline of the owl. Add some wood texture to the log with more horizontal strokes and dots. Refine the facial features and add final touches to the background, if desired, and after that, we can start painting.

Step 4: Let's start by defining the light and shadow areas of the owl. Mix ochre with water. You should have more water than pigment in this mix, resulting in a very light yellow. Then, create the following mix:

- Mix A: indigo + sepia + water (more water than pigment) = light watery blue-gray

Also, combine sepia with water to obtain a brown color that is significantly darker than the previous ones.

Apply the ochre and water mix to approximately one-quarter of the right side of the owl. Then, switch to Mix A and continue covering the surface of the owl and the log. Avoid the beak, the area near the beak, the small area on top of the right wing, and the highlights on the right side of the log. If you accidentally cover these areas, you can quickly correct it by blotting the area with a paper towel. This trick will only work if the color is still wet, though. Let this dry for just a little bit—but not completely.

Try to capture the moment when the paper is still damp and start creating the feather texture on the back and belly using short ragged strokes with the sepia and water mix. To create this effect your brush should be almost dry. When you're done with the feather texture, wait until the first layer is completely dry before adding the sepia and water mix to the tail, leaving some feathers on the right part of the tail untouched.

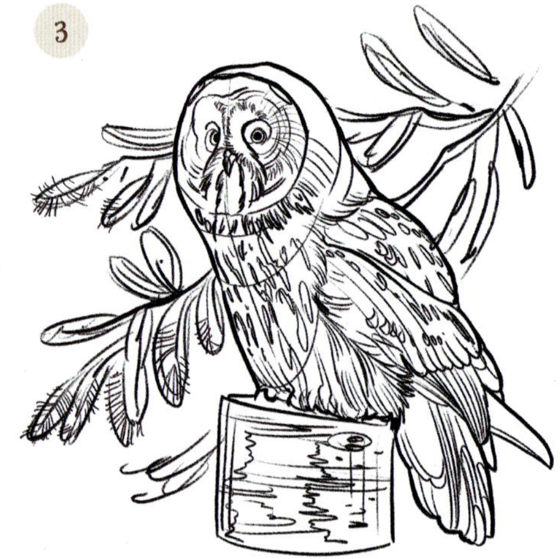

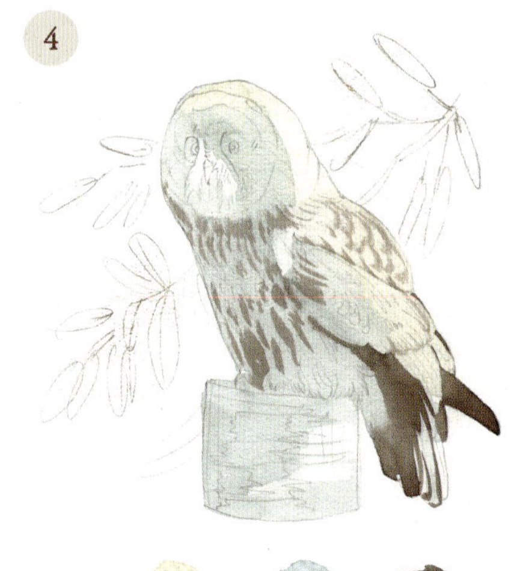

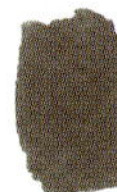

Ochre   Mix A   Sepia

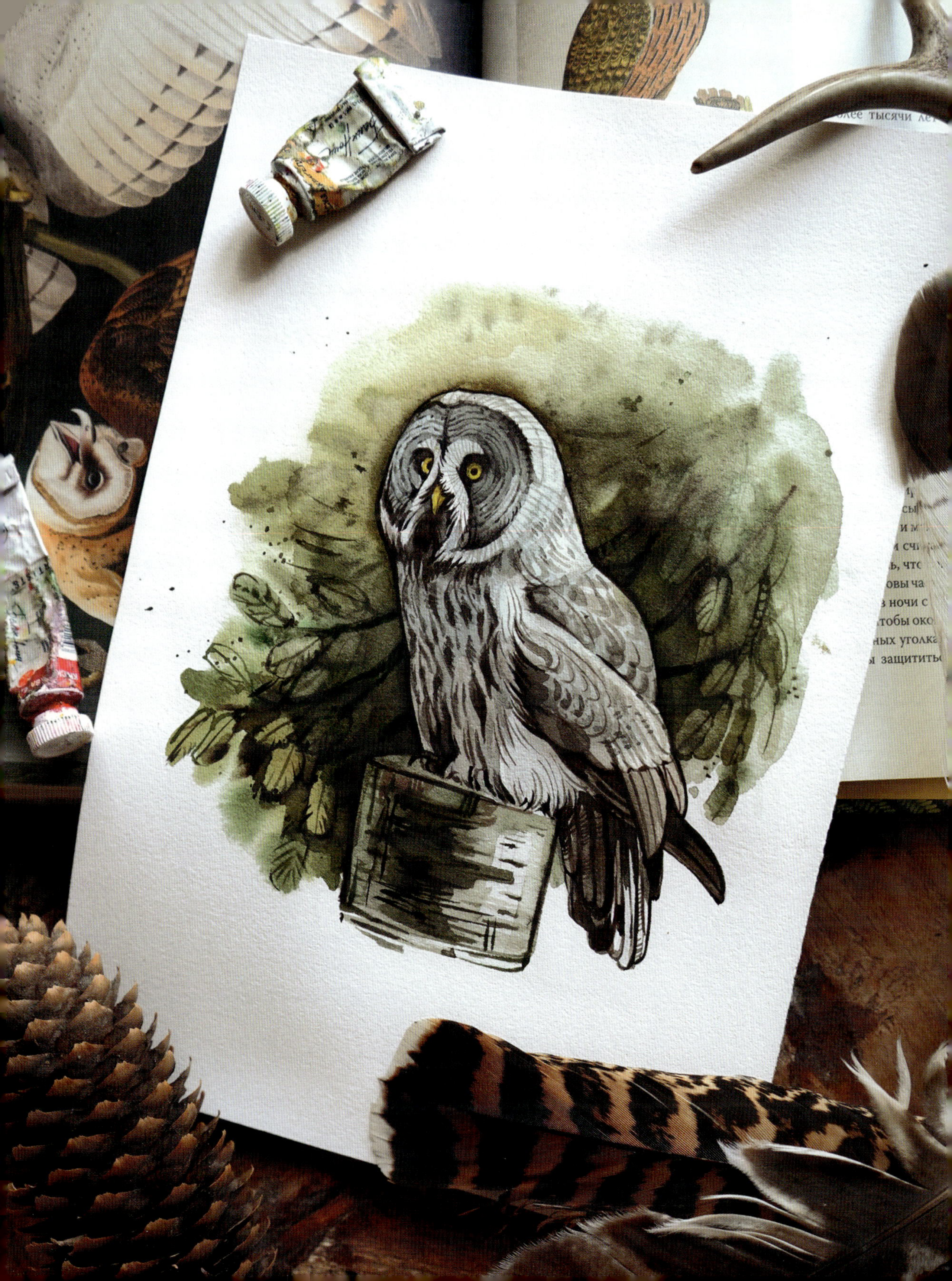

Step 5: Darken the shadow areas on the owl using Mix 4A. With your small brush, darken the areas around the eyes but not the eyes themselves. Leave the pieces of feathers between the eyes light, with just a center line separating them. Next, darken the area under the beak and add some texture to the face with very thin strokes that go from the center of the face to the edges in a circular way. Add Mix 4A to the chest, the back, and the left side of the wing. Also, paint some horizontal strokes for the log. As a last step, restore any pencil lines on the tail and the tip of the wing that you may have lost during the painting process. Use the sepia and water mix from Step 4 to add thin, short lines for some texture on the left side of the wing. Also, paint the outline on the right part of the owl so it's more visible, but not uniform.

Step 6: Cover the eyes and the beak with cadmium yellow diluted with a bit of water. Then, use Mix 4A to darken some areas of the face even more, such as the forehead, the left side of the face, and the border between the face and the head on the right side. Next, mix a new color:

- Mix A: sepia + indigo + water = dark gray

Use the tip of your small brush and Mix A to add some details to the face. Outline the eyes and add contrast around and under the beak, around the facial disc, at the beginning of the neck, and in the area between the legs, as well as the wing and tail. Use strokes appropriate to the area you're painting—for example, use small, short strokes on the face, longer strokes at the base of the wing, and long strokes to outline the feathers of the wing and tail.

Step 7: Combining colors already on your palette to add the finishing details in your painting can help unify the piece. First, combine Mix 4A with the sepia and water mix from Step 4. Use it to darken the belly and the facial disc. While these areas are drying, use the sepia and water mix from Step 4 to darken the tail and the tip of the wing. Darken the base of the wing using thick strokes and the same sepia and water mix. Switch to the 4A and sepia mix to add texture to the wing and back with short round strokes, lines, and dots. For the belly, create a similar texture with Mix 6A, making sure the strokes are vertical. Paint hairline strokes to outline the soft feathers of the feet next to the wing with short, thin, wavy strokes. Use the same type of strokes to better outline the base of the wing.

Once the facial disc has dried, use Mix 6A to darken the area around the yellow eyes and smooth the edges. Then, darken the borders of the facial disc. Create a very dark mix for the pupils:

- Mix A: sepia + indigo + almost no water = almost black

Use this mix to add pupils with the very tip of your small brush. Outline the beak from all sides and highlight the fur texture around it. Also create a circular texture on the facial disc by forming concentric circles starting from the eyes and extending to the border of the facial disc. Finally, outline the center line on the forehead of the bird.

Step 8: For the trunk, create this new color:

- Mix A: green + sepia + water = light green

Add Mix A to the left side of the trunk, leaving the right third untouched. While the green color is still wet, add some horizontal lines to the center of the green area using Mix 6A. Then, add thin, short horizontal strokes to the entire surface of the trunk. Make sure these strokes are shorter on the right side and longer on the left. Also, add the outline to the trunk using the same color.

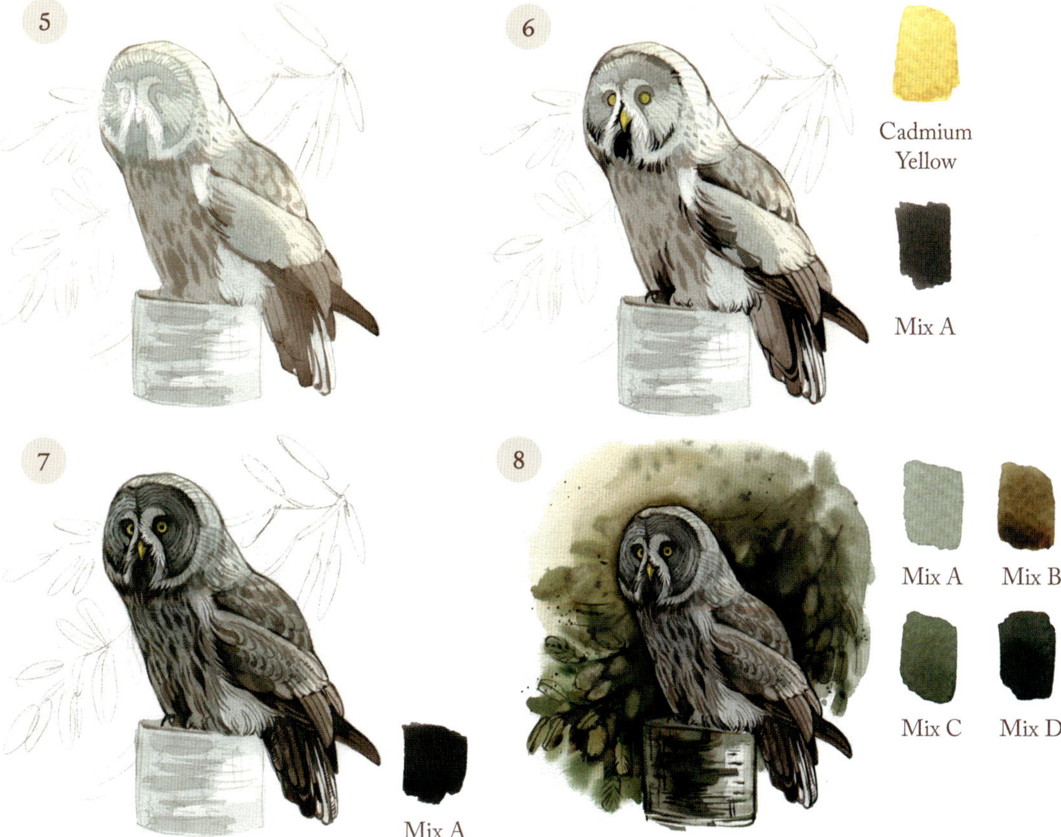

If you want to paint the background, create some color mixes for it:

- Mix B: raw sienna + green + water = medium brown-orange
- Mix C: green + sepia + water = medium muted green
- Mix D: same as Mix 8C (above) but with more pigment and less water = dark, muted green

Make sure you have a good amount of all these mixes. Keep in mind that there is no single correct way to paint the background, so be creative about it and don't worry if it turns out differently from what you expected.

Use a large brush or a big soft mop brush with a pointy tip if you have one to cover the entire surface of the paper around the owl and the trunk with water—coming close but not touching them. Apply Mix B with the same brush to cover the dry space and get right next to the subject.

Apply Mix C to some areas of the background, especially behind the back of the bird and in front of its belly. Then, use Mix D to outline some branches of the pine tree. You can also add some splashes for a more expressive look. To create them, load your brush with color and hit it against your finger, protecting the owl with your other hand or a piece of paper while doing so. Don't get carried away with the details, as we still want the bird to be the main focus. Once everything feels right, your owl painting is ready.

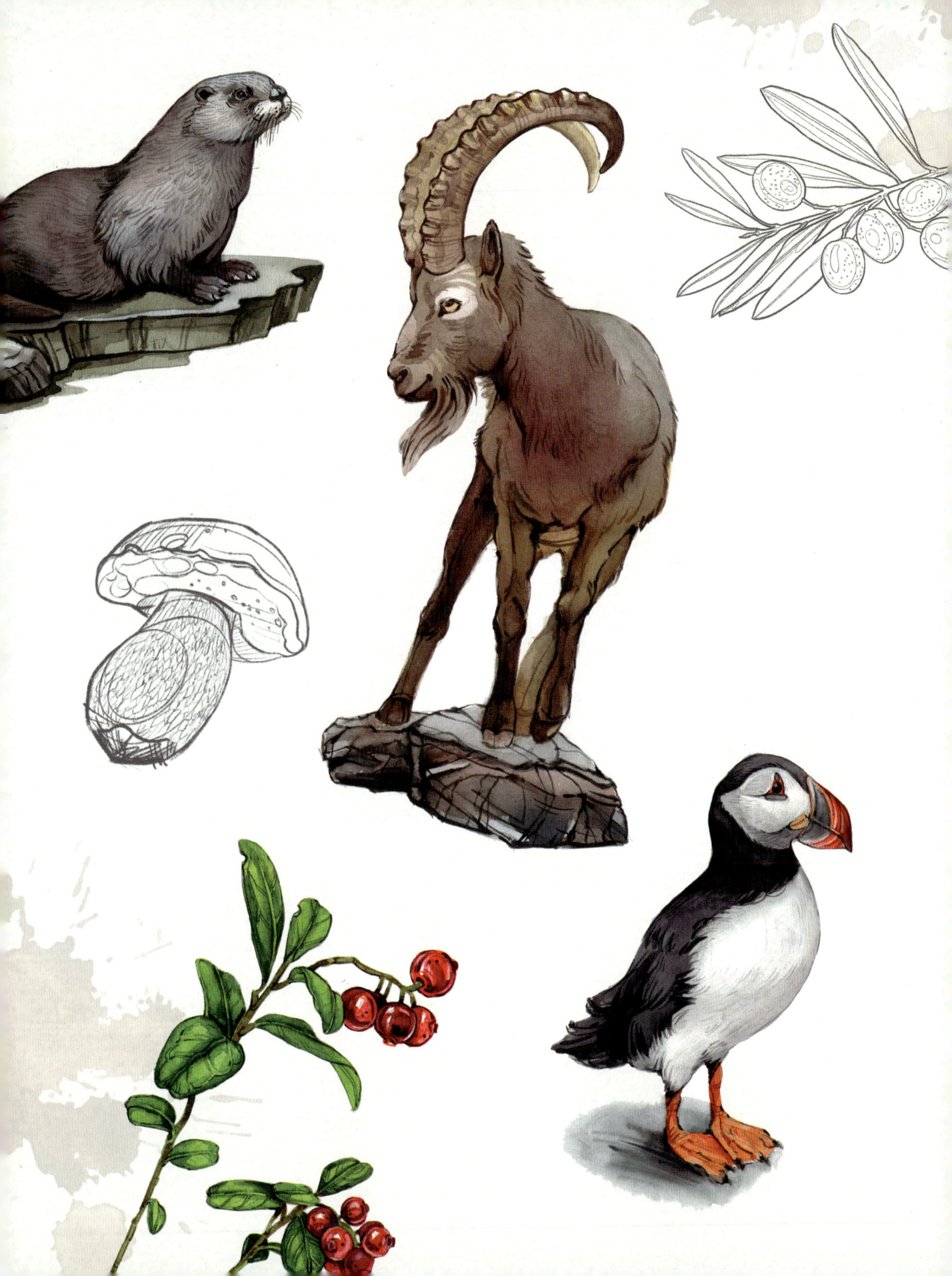

Europe
From Northern Lights to the Mediterranean Breeze

Welcome to a small continent packed with many ecosystems that coexist to create a vast natural mosaic. Parts of Europe are situated in the Nordic hemisphere, where the colorful Northern Lights shine above a three-month-long night. The northernmost part of Europe is home to one of the most curious and charming Nordic birds: the Atlantic Puffin (page 95). These extravagant birds live in colonies on cliffs and are characterized by their huge, colorful beaks, which serve to attract mates.

Farther east, the Ural Mountains in Russia form the geographical border between East and West. This is my birthplace, where my passion for nature began. Cranberries (page 91) are one of the common edible berries where I lived, and I remember picking them as a little girl. Another tasty wonder we'll paint is the Porcini Mushroom (page 111), the "king of mushrooms." As a passionate mushroom hunter, there is no greater joy than stumbling upon some in the forest.

Other European countries have also been home to me throughout my life, such as France and Italy. These countries are home to the River Otter (page 100), a mammal that lives in the pure waters of mountain rivers. The Alps, the highest mountain range of South-Central Europe, unite Italy, Switzerland, and France and are home for the Alpine Ibex Goat (page 105). The horns of this mountain goat are incredibly large in relation to its head and body and are used to conduct fierce combats with male rivals during mating season.

Europe is also known for the bright hues of the Mediterranean Sea. The southernmost point of Europe is only 9 miles (14 kilometers) from Africa, with the Strait of Gibraltar sitting between Point Marroquí in Spain and Point Cires in Morocco. No surprise that the climate and nature here are drastically different from those of Northern Europe. The hot weather allows for the growth of one of the longest-living plants in the world: the olive tree. Though it's hard to estimate their exact age, the oldest living olive trees are located on the island of Crete in Greece and in Sardinia in Italy, with the oldest reaching an estimated age of 4,000 years. Olive trees are not only famous for their longevity, but also for what can be obtained from their fruit: precious olive oil—often called liquid gold. Italy, the country that I currently call home, and especially its southern regions, where I live, are famous for it.

Europe is strikingly diverse from north to south and from west to east. This continent is especially dear to me due to my personal story, and I can't wait to share its beauties with you through watercolor painting. Let's get started!

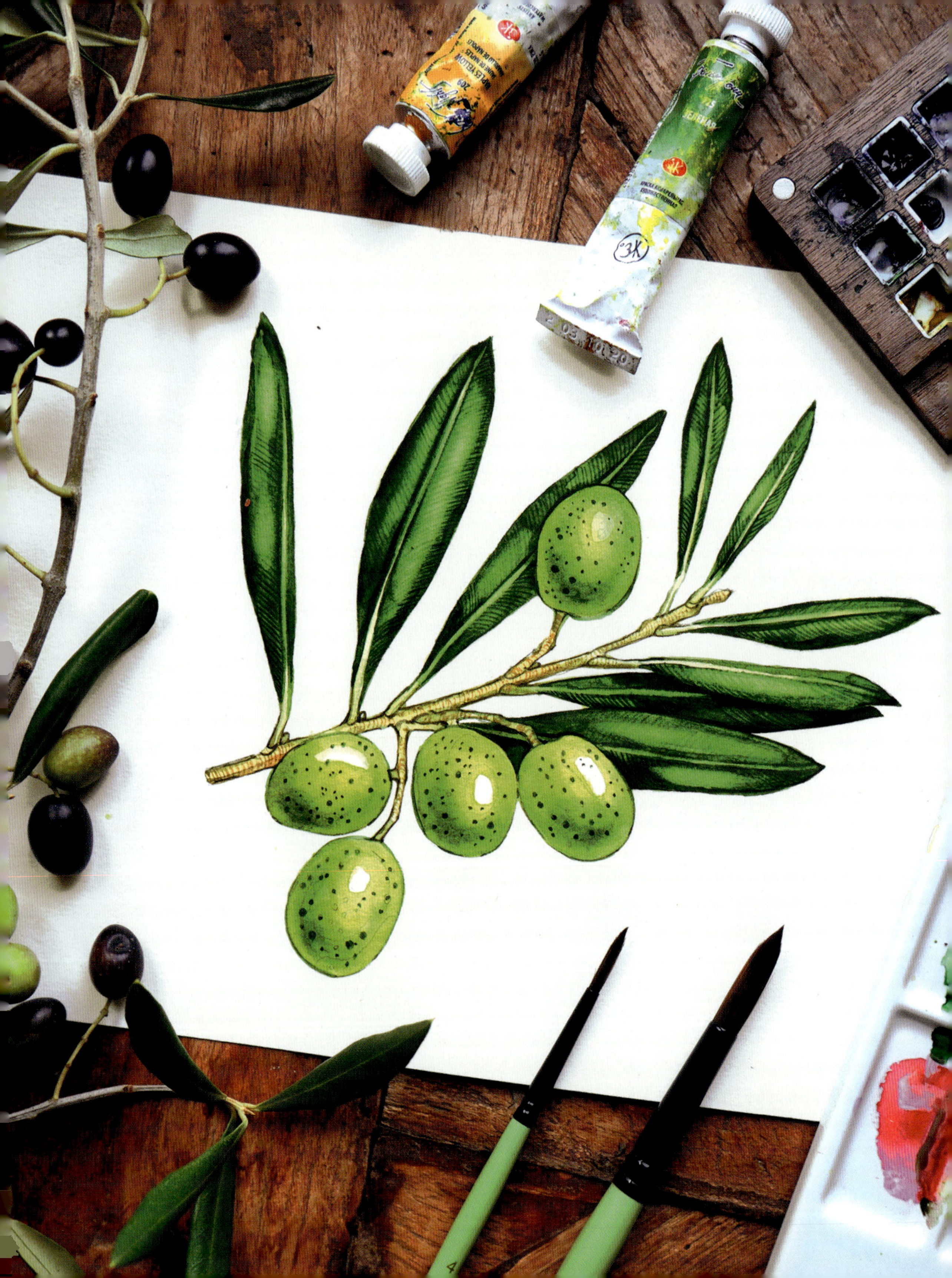

Olives

Olives have been part of Mediterranean life for thousands of years. Ancient civilizations, such the Greeks and Romans, used olives in a variety of ways. Olive oil, which is extracted from the fruit, was considered a sacred substance and used for everything from cooking to religious rituals. Olives and their oil were so essential that olive trees were often seen as symbols of peace, prosperity, and longevity. In this tutorial, you'll practice how light and shadow interact on round objects and explore different techniques for painting the olives' skin texture in a limited color palette of greens and yellows.

Colors Needed

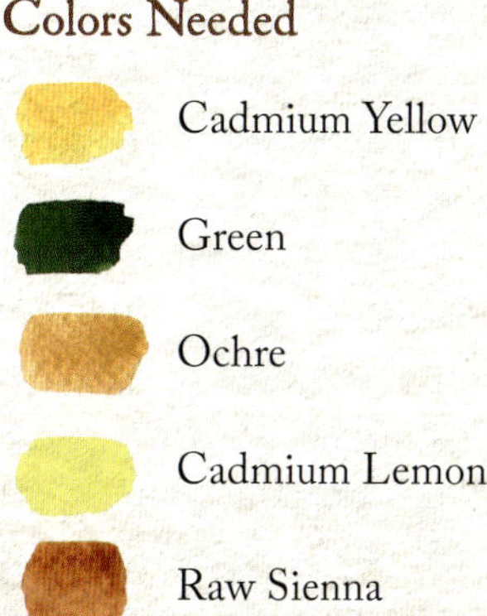

Cadmium Yellow

Green

Ochre

Cadmium Lemon

Raw Sienna

Suggested Paper Orientation: Horizontal

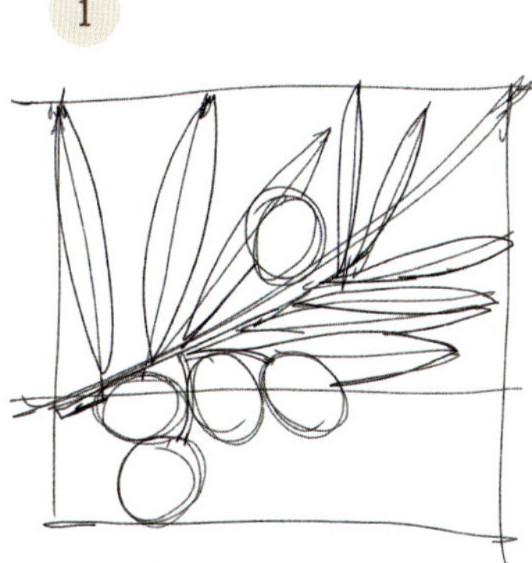

Step 1: Draw a square that represents the whole surface of your painting. Draw a horizontal line cutting off the lower third of the square. This line will indicate the beginning of the branch and help us place the three lower olives. Place three ovals symbolizing olives in a row: the first laying horizontally and the two others inclining toward the left. Then, place a fourth oval right under the first and second olives. The group of olives should be closer to the left edge of the square than to the right. After that, start outlining the leaves. First, give the leaves a direction using a center line. Begin with the two larger leaves on the left side of the square; the first starts from the top left corner and ends where the first olive begins. The second leaf starts from the middle of the second olive and reaches one-third of the way to the top side of the square. Then, place the last stand-alone olive with an oval a bit higher than the center of the main square. Next, add a third leaf that starts near the second one and extends to the left, hiding behind the stand-alone olive. Finally, add two smaller upper leaves to the right of the stand-alone olive and three laying horizontally under the branch—to the right of the fourth olive. Then, give the leaves a more defined shape by adding pointed oval shapes to the sides.

Step 2: Erase your guide lines, and let's keep work-ing on the leaves. Give them a more realistic shape by making the sides pointier and thinning the area that connects the leaves to the stem. Add thickness to the stem with a parallel line next to the center line. Use two parallel lines close together to outline the smaller stems that connect each olive to the main branch. Make the stems connecting the stand-alone olive and the lowest olive curvy. Then, define the shape of the olives better and add some details by outlining the highlight with small ovals on the right side of each olive. Additionally, use curvy lines to visually separate the shadow areas from the light areas on each olive.

Step 3: Finish the leaves: Smooth out the lines of the outlines to create a smoother transition between the pointy lines. Add thickness to the center veins by adding a line parallel to the main line. Add one long line that follows the shape of the leaf on the left and the right sides of each leaf to visually separate the light and shadow areas. Give the branch a more refined look by enhancing the transitions between the leaves and the branch, and do the same for the smaller stems connecting the individual olives to the main branch. Finally, add some finishing touches to the olives. Smooth their outlines and add texture using tiny dots. The drawing is ready!

Step 4: Create this light green color that we will use as the base tone for the olives:

- Mix A: cadmium yellow + green + water = light yellow-green

Apply this uniformly to all the leaves, except for the stems. Paint the olives as well. Start with the first olive, covering it with the same color, but be sure to leave a white circle in the highlight area. Then, while the color on the olive is still wet, smooth out the edges with a clean, dry brush. You should achieve a gradient from a light center to darker edges. Repeat with the remaining olives.

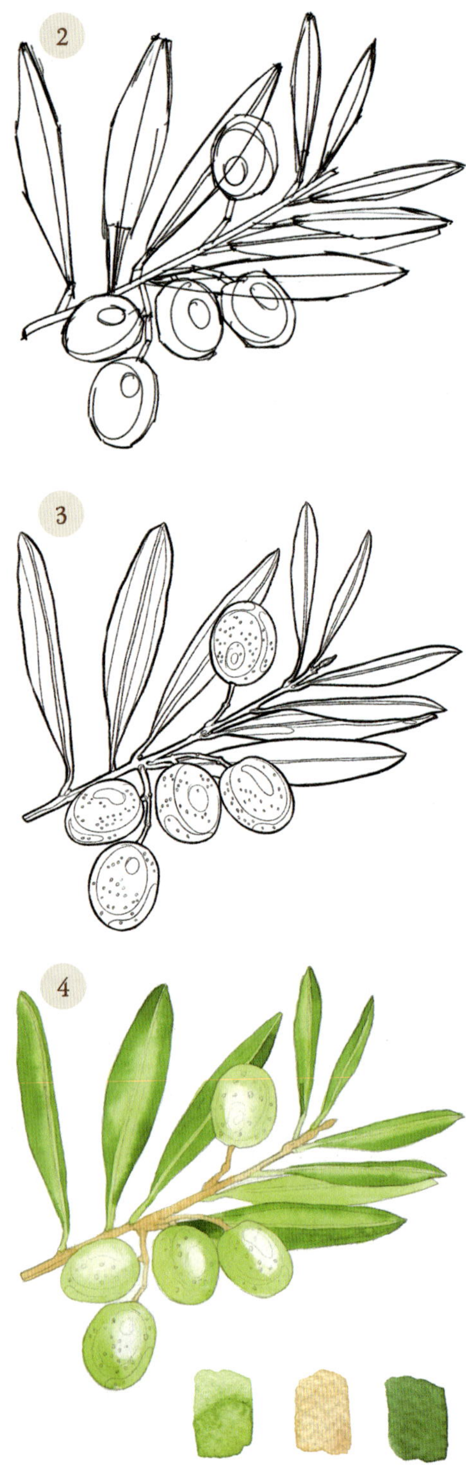

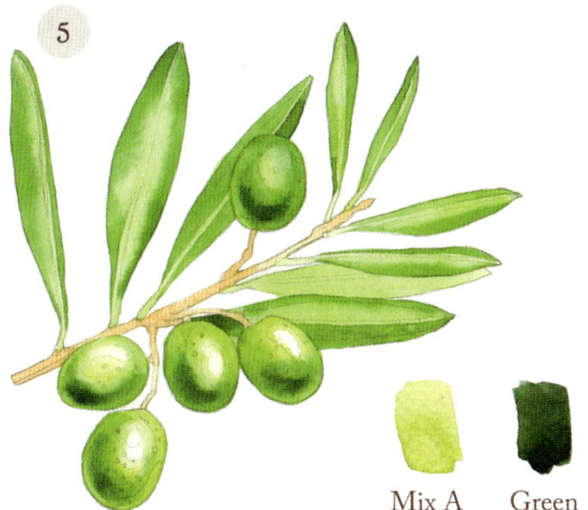

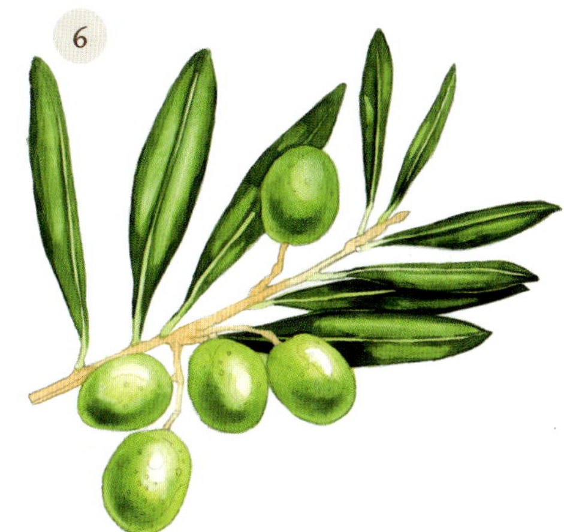

Then, combine ochre with water for a light yellow and apply it to the main stem and the smaller stems of the individual olives. Wait for this layer to dry.

Next, let's create a darker green mix for the leaves:

- Mix B: Mix 4A (previous page) + more green = yellow-green

Cover the top leaf except for the center vein with water. Paint the left side of the leaf with Mix B. You should get a gradient that is darker near the edge and lighter near the center vein. Repeat this step on all the leaves except for the one behind the top olive (just cover both sides with green without a gradient, leaving the center line untouched). Also, leave the leaf that is behind all others on the lower side completely untouched for now.

Step 5: Create a new mix:

- Mix A: cadmium lemon + a touch of green + water = vibrant yellow

Also, combine green with a touch of water to create the darkest green we've used so far in this tutorial.

Apply Mix A to the entire surface of the first olive, except for the small highlight. While still wet, smooth the color near the highlight to blend with the yellow; if it affects the highlight too much, lift it where needed using a clean, dry brush. Then, apply Mix 4B to the remaining part of the olive. With a clean, dry brush, lift some paint from the reflective area on the extreme left side of the olive. This will help make the olive look more three-dimensional. Next, apply the green and water mix to the middle of the shadow area on the left side while this layer is still wet. Smooth out the edges if needed. If the area has already dried, you can still apply the green and water mix, but remember to smooth out the edges to avoid hard lines. Repeat on the remaining olives.

Step 6: To darken the leaves, we will use the green and water mix from Step 5 and a slightly darker version of Mix 4B (simply add more green to it). Apply a thin line of the green and water mix near the center veins of the leaves, and then smooth out the edges for a seamless transition, avoiding the center vein. Paint the edges of each leaf and smooth them out. The leaves should be darker near the center vein and near the edges and lighter in the center of each half. This makes them appear three-dimensional.

(Step 6 continued)

Apply the darker Mix 4B to add even more shadow near the edges of the leaves and along the center veins of some leaves. Also, use this color to darken the top area of the top leaf that is behind the olive. Darken the leaf on the lower side that is behind all the others and the leaf that is behind the two lower olives.

Step 7: To increase the saturation of the olives, use Mix 5A to cover the entire surface of all the olives, making sure to leave an even smaller highlight untouched this time. There's no need to smooth the edges. Next, with a clean, wet brush, go over the center leaves to activate the green around the veins and make them less bright, helping to unite the leaves and make them look more realistic.

Darken the tips and bases of the leaves using the darker Mix 4B, and then smooth out the edges. Use the green and water mix with almost no water from Step 5, and with the very tip of your small brush, create texture in the leaves using lines that go from the center of the leaf toward its sides. If you're struggling to make your lines thin and even, practice on a spare piece of paper beforehand or simply skip this last step and leave your leaves as they are. If you decide to add the line texture, as a final touch, lift off some paint from the highlight of the leaves using a clean, dry brush. Then, use the same green and water mix to make the outlines of the olives more visible, ensuring the outline is very thin, not too dark, and not uniform; otherwise, it will make your olives look flat.

Step 8: Mix a new color for the stem:

- Mix A: raw sienna + green + water = light muted green

Cover the right side of the main and smaller stems with Mix A. Let dry completely. With the tip of your small brush, apply the green and water mix from Step 5 to place tiny spots of slightly different sizes on the surface of the olives. Ensure you place

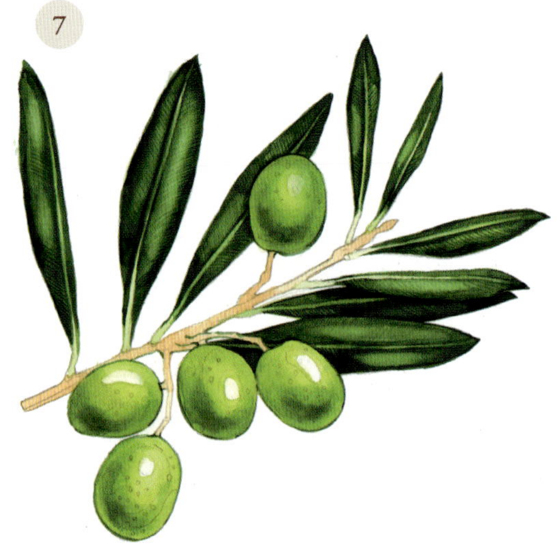

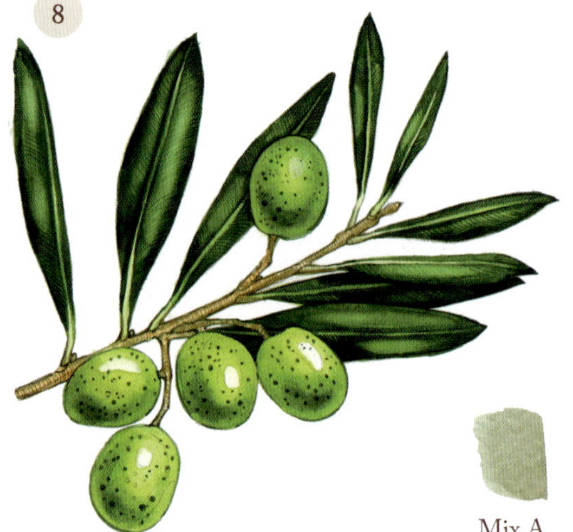

Mix A

the larger spots in the shadow areas and the tiniest ones in the light areas. Aim for an approximately equal number of spots on each olive.

Use the same color to make the outline of the stem a bit more visible by painting very thin lines created with the tip of your brush. As a final step, add more pigment to Mix A and use short circular lines to add texture to the main stem and a bit to the individual olive stems. After that, your painting will be complete.

Cranberries

Cranberries hold a special place in my heart, as they remind me of picking them with my parents and grandmothers in the woods. Known for their bright red color and tart flavor, cranberries have been used for centuries in traditional remedies, beverages, and dishes, especially in Northern Europe. In this tutorial, you'll learn how to paint small leaves with precision and create volume and a shiny effect on the small surface of the berries.

Colors Needed

Cadmium Yellow

Green

Carmine

Raw Sienna

Sepia

Cobalt Blue or Ultramarine

Ruby (or mix cadmium red and carmine)

Indigo

Suggested Paper Orientation: Vertical

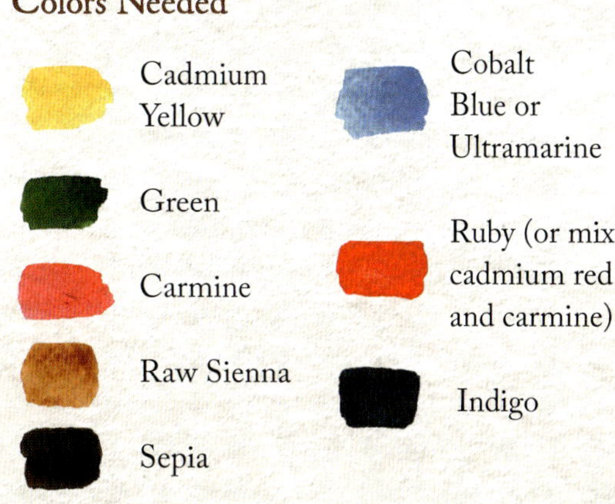

Step 1: Draw a rectangle approximately two and a half times as tall as its width. Draw vertical lines for the stems. Outline the top part of the berry clusters with ovals; sketch a larger oval for the left plant and a smaller oval for the right plant. Then, add a curvy, almost horizontal line near the top of the left plant to indicate the curve from which the berries hang. Sketch the individual berries on the left plant with four small circles. Next, outline the leaves facing different directions using ovals. Outline the berries and the leaves within the smaller oval of the right plant you've previously sketched. Finally, start adding smaller leaves to the rest of the plants beneath the petals.

Step 2: Erase unnecessary guide lines. Divide the largest leaves into two parts and outline the folded leaves, showing bits of the leaves that are visible from the other side. Then, outline the small stems that attach the berries of the left plant to the main stem. Add highlights to the berries with tiny circles.

Step 3: For the inside of the leaves, add center and thinner lateral veins. Add details to the surface of the stems, incorporating small irregularities and bumps for a more natural and organic look.

(Step 3 continued)

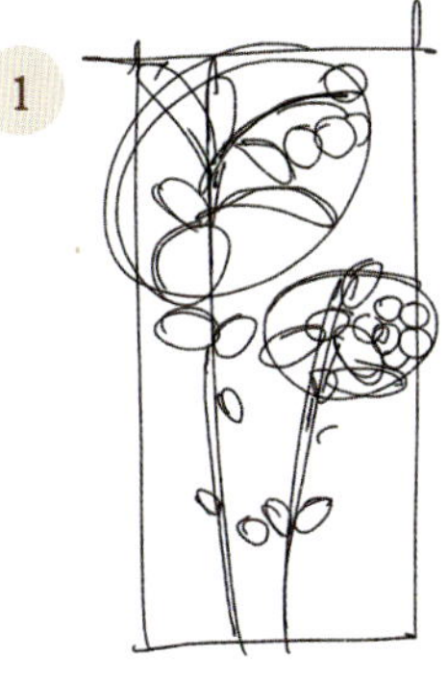

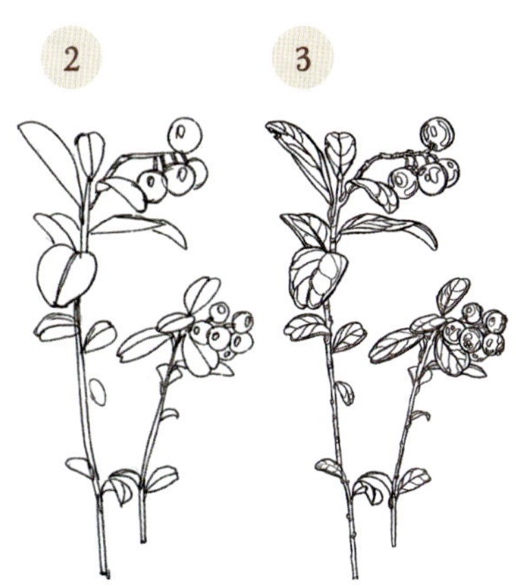

Add tiny horizontal lines for more texture and interest. Do this on both plants, and finally, add the last details to the berries using lines and ovals that emphasize the natural round shape of the berries, which will help us place light and shadow more accurately during the painting process. When you're satisfied with your drawing, get ready for painting!

Step 4: This step will be simple to execute but will require a bit of patience. Create this color mix:

- Mix A: cadmium yellow + green + water = light green

Also, mix carmine with water to obtain a light pink. With the tip of your small brush, add Mix A to the tips of the stems of the cranberries. Begin from the lower portion of the first berry and gradually work your way up the stems without interrupting, letting the color dry as you want to create a uniform wash with no visible brushstrokes. Once you reach the leaves, use the body of your brush or switch to a bigger brush. Cover the entire surface of the leaves and stems. Let the green near the berries dry completely before painting the berries uniformly with the carmine and water mix (except for the highlights).

Step 5: Create two colors to darken the stems of the cranberries:

- Mix A: raw sienna + a touch of sepia + water = light brown
- Mix B: raw sienna + sepia + a touch of green + water = darker brown-green

Paint the stems with Mix A, making sure to avoid the leaves. Then, while this color is still wet, introduce Mix B near the leaves. This area will be darker due to the shadow cast by the leaves.

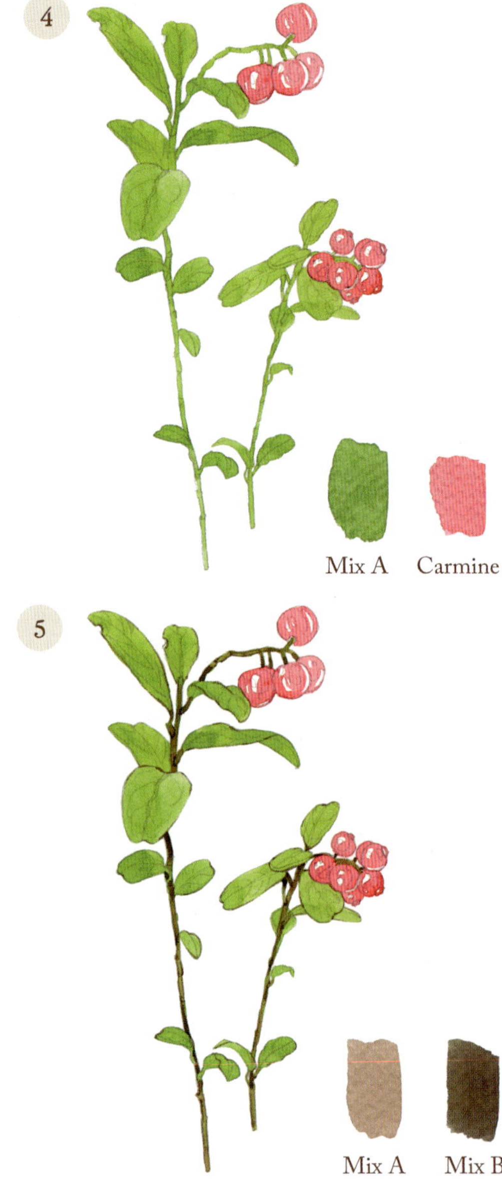

Do the same thing near the berries. You can also use Mix B to make the outlines of the stems and leaves a bit more visible. Just make sure these outlines are very thin and irregular—otherwise, your painting may start to look too flat.

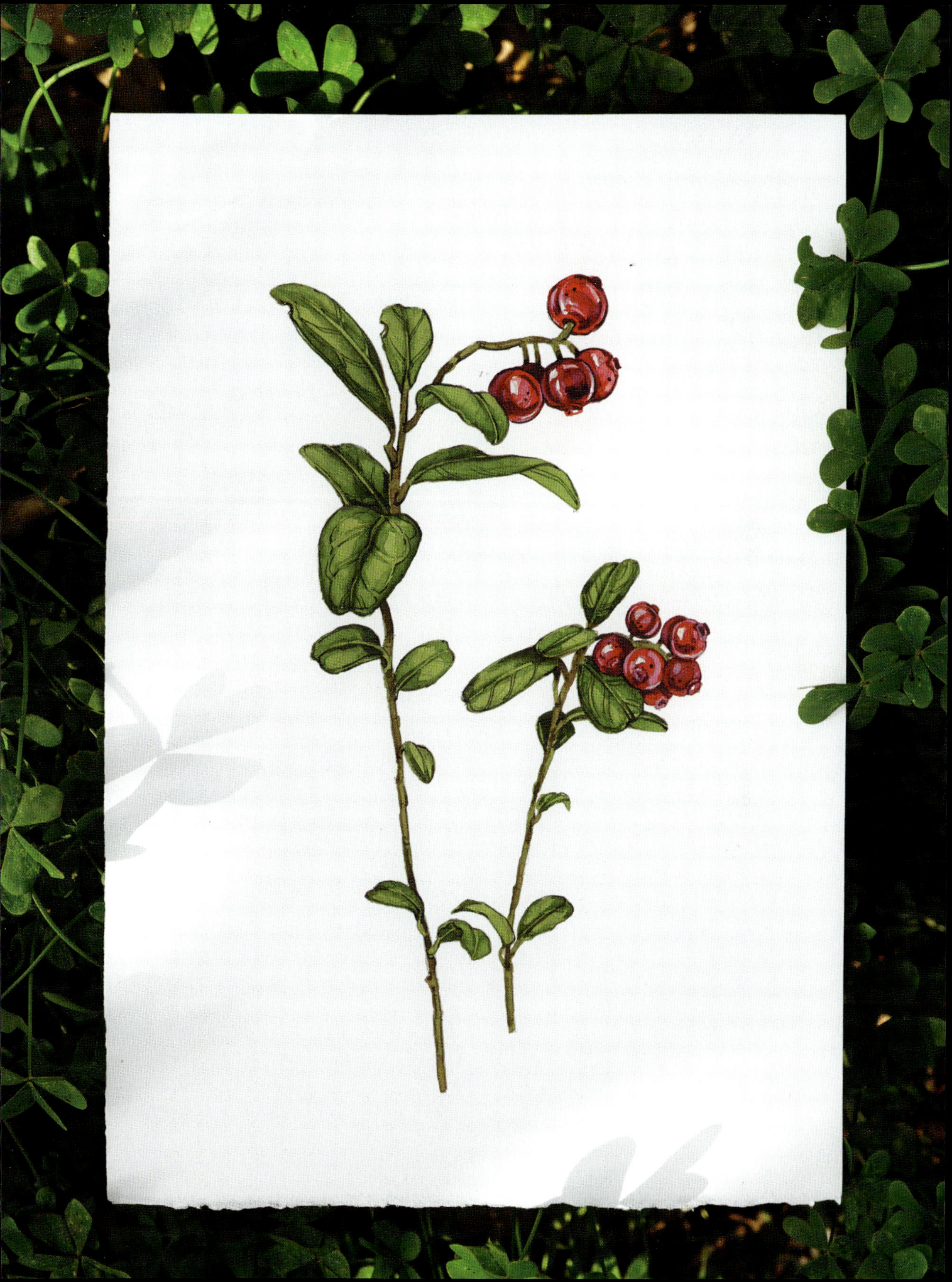

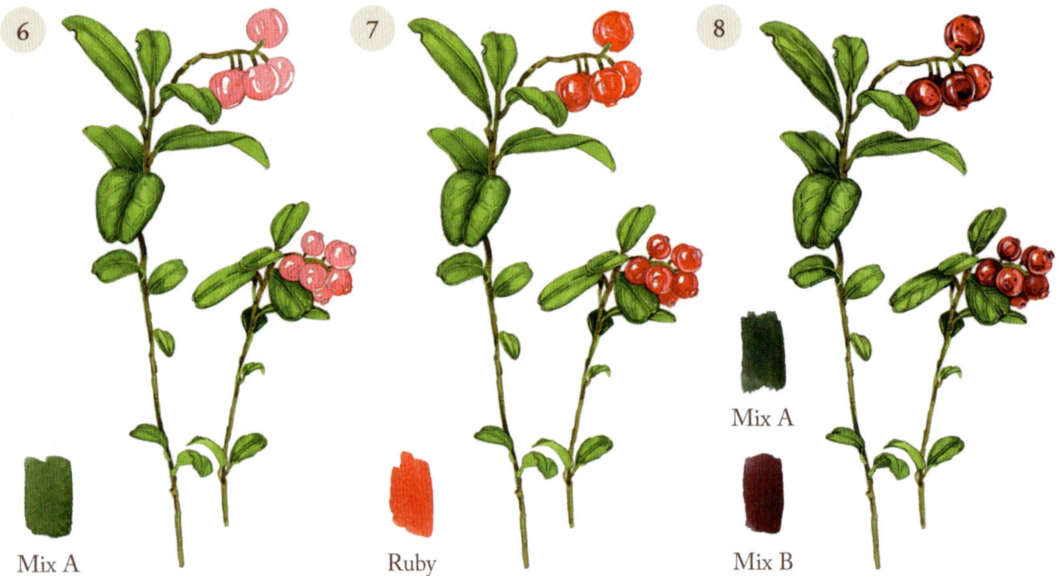

Step 6: To add realism and shadows to the leaves, create this new color:

- Mix A: green + cobalt blue or ultramarine + water = medium-dark green

The light will be concentrated in the middle of each part of the leaf, while the shadows will be near the center veins, on the lower part of the leaves, and near the borders. Apply Mix A accordingly, always smoothing out the edges for a seamless transition. Proceed gradually on all of the leaves using the same method. Then, add texture and veins to the larger leaves using the same color and the tip of your brush. The trick here is to leave the veins lighter and paint around them, just as you did with the center veins.

Step 7: In this step, you will add more saturation and details to the berries. Mix ruby and water to get a saturated pink. If you don't have ruby, you can create a similar color by mixing cadmium red and carmine. Apply this color to the shadow areas of the berries, making sure to leave the highlights untouched and to keep some pink areas free as

well, especially in the reflective areas, to emphasize the shiny look of the berries. Also, keep in mind that the berries in the back should be darker than the berries in front of because those behind are more in shadow.

Step 8: To finish up, we will need two new colors:

- Mix A: indigo + green + a touch of water = dark green-blue
- Mix B: carmine + some indigo + water = dark purple

Use Mix A to add the final details to the leaves. Highlight the outline of some leaves, and use this color to make the center and lateral veins on the larger leaves more visible. Darken the outlines of the stems in certain areas as well.

With Mix B, darken the core shadows (on the opposite side from the highlight) on each berry, and darken some of the back berries completely, as they are in shadow. Add texture with tiny lines to enhance the shiny effect, and incorporate tiny dots to add even more interest to the surface of the berries. After that, your painting will be ready.

Atlantic Puffin

The Atlantic puffin is a charming and colorful seabird known for its vibrant beak and striking appearance. Found along the coasts of the North Atlantic, these birds are excellent swimmers, diving for fish with impressive agility. Despite their small size, puffins are hardy and thrive in harsh, rocky environments, often nesting in burrows. In this tutorial, you will learn how to paint this charismatic bird, focusing on techniques for painting white feathers, adding texture to plumage, and learning how to depict black without using pure black paint.

Colors Needed

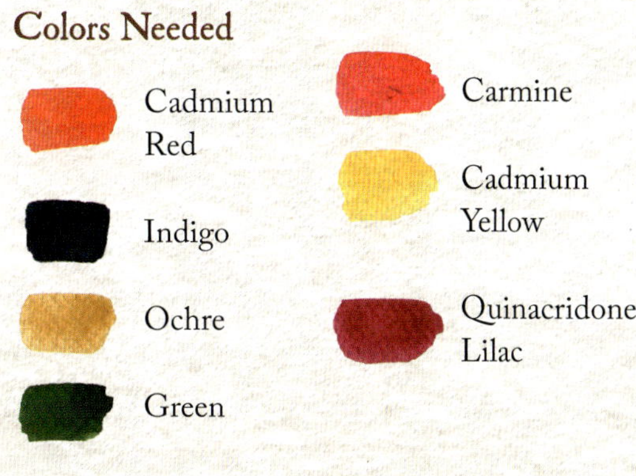

Suggested Paper Orientation: Vertical

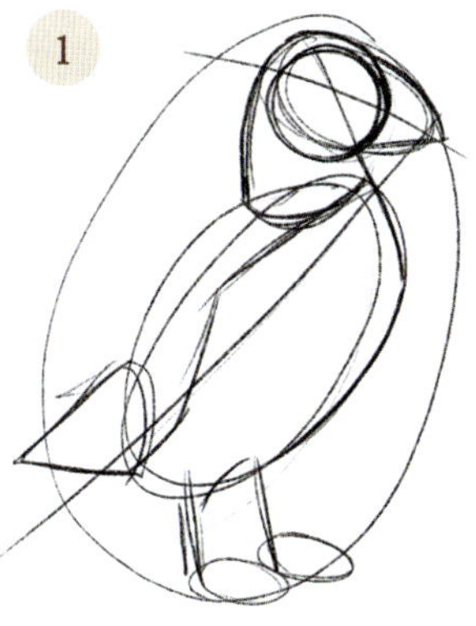

Step 1: Draw an oval. Add a center line to define the general direction of the body. Position the oval for the body and a smaller horizontal oval for the head. Add a horizontal line to show the direction of the neck. From the lower part of the body oval, draw two perpendicular lines to represent the legs. Finally, outline the feet with two horizontal ovals.

Add a tail using a triangle and another triangle for the beak. Place a circle to represent the face. Create the neck by connecting the head circle to the body.

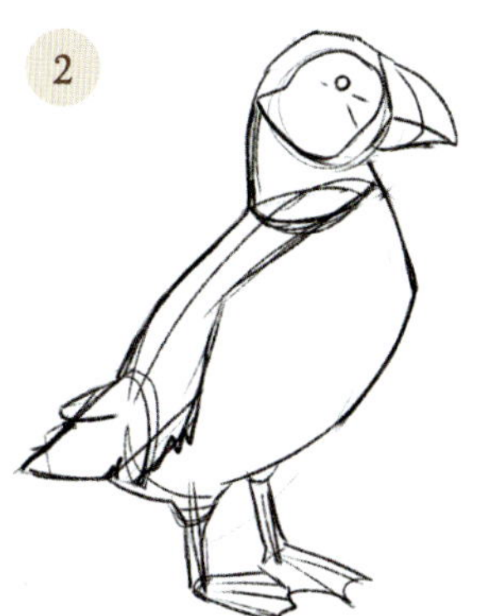

Step 2: Begin to refine the shape of the body. Use a zigzag line to separate the black side of the body from the white side. Make the chest slightly pointy. Place a circle for the eye in the center of the head. Outline the base of the beak and refine its shape. Add details to the feathers and the tail, and outline the wing. Thicken the legs and define the shape of the feet more clearly. Then, draw triangles for the toes.

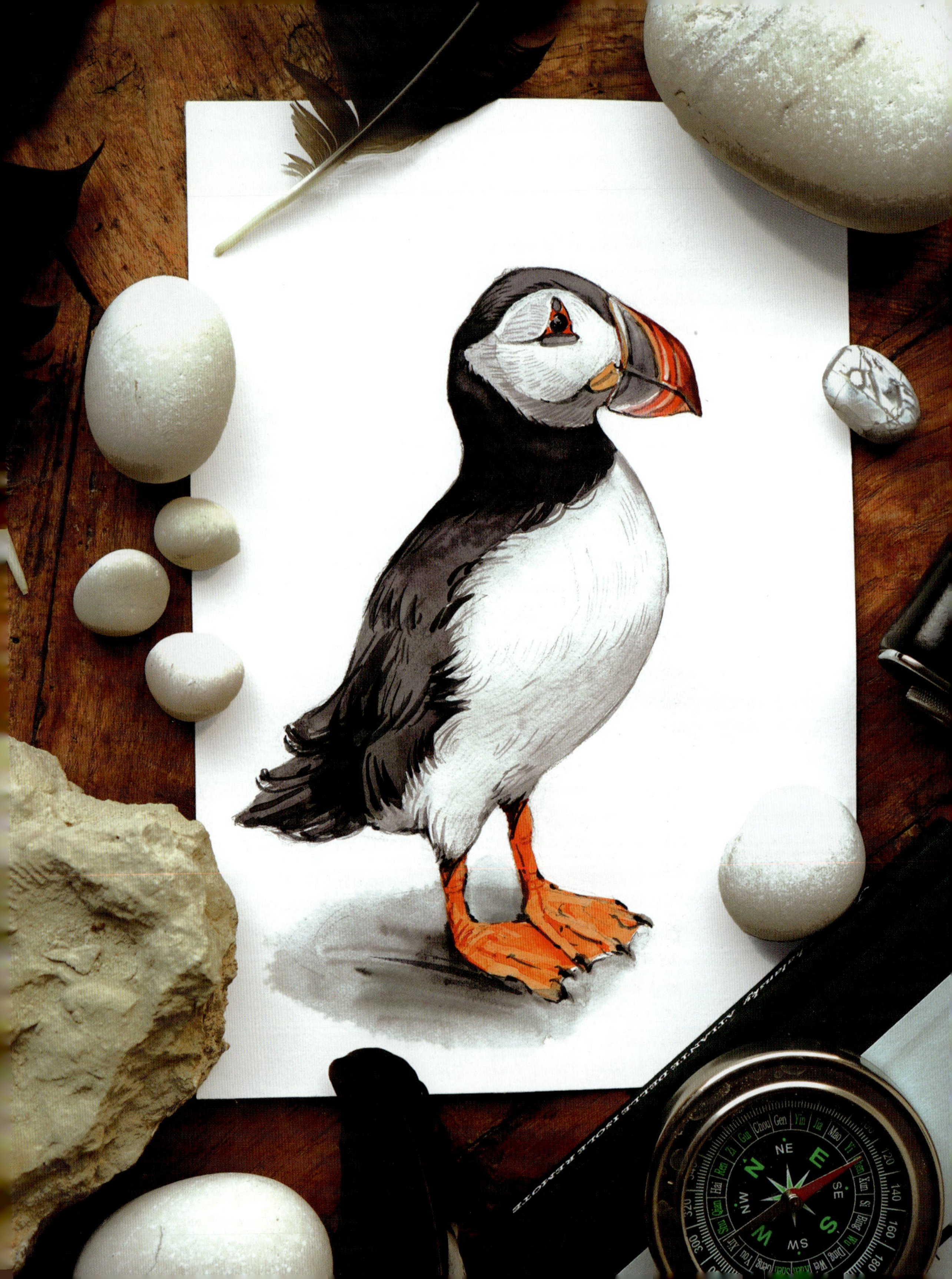

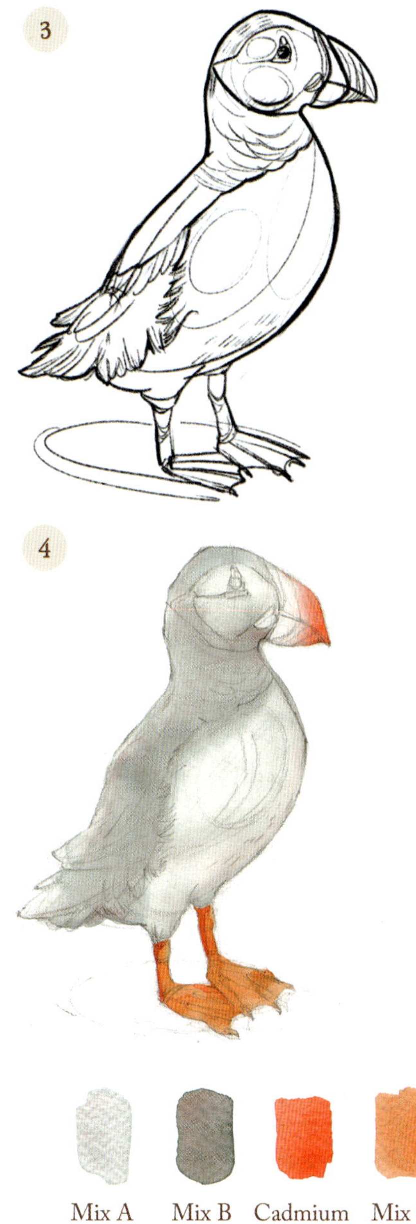

details to the eye and eye ornament, and include the roseate patch (a brightly colored fleshy area around the base of the beak, extending toward the cheeks). Add some feathers around the neck, and then add final details to the feet by outlining the individual toes; don't forget the nails. Outline the ankles with two small ovals to give the legs a more realistic appearance. Add more details to the feathers of the tail and wing. Finally, add a drop shadow oval on the left side of the puffin.

Step 4: Mix these two grays:

- Mix A: cadmium red + indigo + ochre + green + water = gray
- Mix B: same as 4A (above) but with more pigment and less water = medium gray

Cover the puffin with water, avoiding the beak, the eye, the roseate patch, and the legs. While the surface is wet, apply Mix A to the extreme right side of the bird. Then, apply Mix B to the left side, avoiding the belly, the chest, and the area near the eye.

While this layer dries, mix cadmium red with water for a bright red that we will use for the beak and feet. Then, mix another color for the same body parts:

- Mix C: cadmium yellow + cadmium red + water = medium orange

Apply Mix C to the legs and feet. If the previous layer has dried completely, you can paint directly. If it's still wet, make sure to leave a thin white line that separates the upper side of the legs from the lower parts, and then paint the legs. We do this to prevent the colors from mixing. Next, cover one-third of the beak—starting at the tip—with the cadmium red and water mix. Smooth out the edge to create a seamless transition from white to red. Using the same color, add shadow to the left sides of the feet, covering about one-third of the legs, and add a bit more of the cadmium red and water mix to the area

Step 3: Finish the drawing by smoothing and refining the outline. Erase any guide lines that you no longer need. Add some lines to the beak to represent the red markings. Place an irregular triangle around the eye to represent the eye ornament, a typical trait of Atlantic puffins. Add more

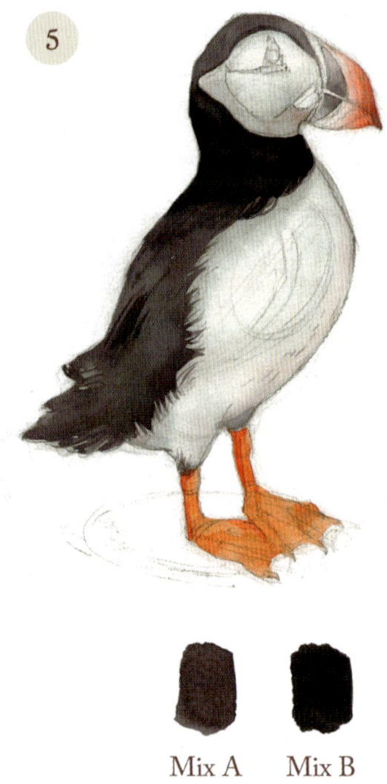

Mix A   Mix B

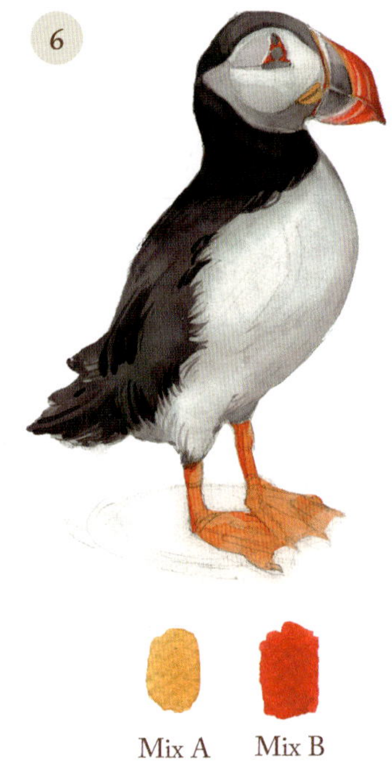

Mix A   Mix B

where the legs meet the white feathers.

Step 5: Mix these two darker colors:

- Mix A: carmine + indigo + a touch of green + water = dark purplish-gray

- Mix B: Mix 5A (above) + more carmine + more indigo = dark, almost black purple

Apply Mix A to the upper side of the head and the left part of the body. Once you reach the area where the dark feathers meet the white ones, use the tip of your brush and short, thin, irregular strokes to create texture by mimicking fur.

Continue filling the dark area with Mix A until you reach the tip of the tail. While the previous color is still wet, introduce Mix B to the neck. If your layer has already dried, you can still add Mix B, but you still need to smooth the lower edge with a clean, dry brush. With the tip of your brush loaded with Mix B, create lines imitating the feather texture on the tail and near the wing.

Add a thin line that divides the black top part of the head from the white face.

Dip your brush in clean water, remove the excess water with a paper towel, and smooth the edge. Apply Mix A to the base of the feet and the beak. On the beak, leave a thin white line in the middle, apply the gray near the beak opening, and then continue painting with water to create a color gradient from dark gray to light gray on that portion of the beak. Allow this layer to dry.

Step 6: Darken the belly on the right side by using Mix 4A, and then smooth the edge. Add the same color where the legs emerge from the body. For the face, apply the same mix to the lower side of the cheek and smooth that edge. Apply it near the eye, especially on the left side. Apply Mix 4B to the lower side of the face, beneath the yellow roseate patch. Create this mix:

- Mix A: cadmium yellow + a touch of cadmium red + water = yellow-orange

Use Mix A to cover the roseate patch and add lines to the upper side of the beak.

Then, create a new mix:

- Mix B: cadmium red + carmine + water = intense red

With a small brush, apply Mix B to the eye ornament and the beak, adding three lines to the top side and two lines to the bottom side. Also, paint the tip of the beak. Smooth the edges of the lines and connect them near the top and bottom edges. Use Mix 5B to create some feather texture on the tail, the lower portion of the body, and the neck. Apply the same color to the lower part of the dark area on the head and blend it with the rest of the dark head. Add a gray line to the yellow area with Mix 4B, and then paint the eye and the base of the legs to create fur texture.

Step 7: Mix a new color to darken some parts of the feet:

- Mix A: quinacridone lilac + carmine + water = muted medium red

Use this color and a small brush to add the final details to the beak and legs, and add more saturation to the tip of the beak. Then, paint thin lines to outline the toes. Use Mix 4B to create texture on the bird's face and on the white part of the body. Use dry brushing (page 18) and very thin strokes with the tip of your small brush. Make sure to place the strokes in a way that emphasizes the natural shape of different parts of the puffin.

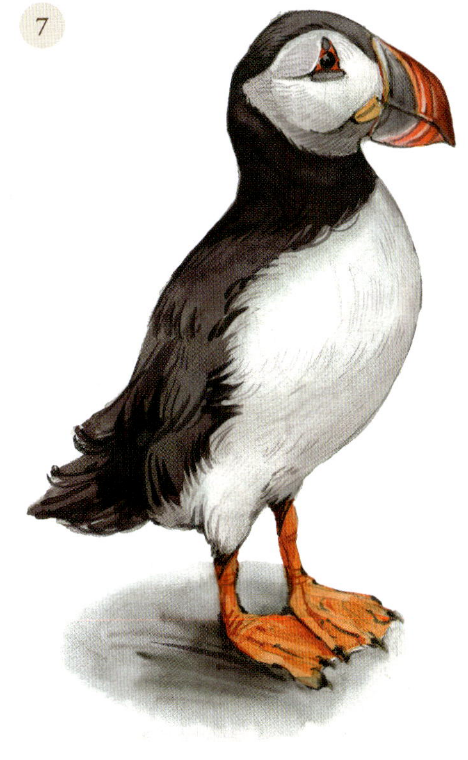

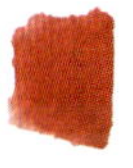

Mix A

Use your small brush and Mix 5B to paint the final outline and finer details on the beak. Paint the eye, leaving a lighter highlight. Use this same color and small, thin strokes where the legs meet the white body. Add details to the feet of the bird, outlining the nails with the dark 5B mix. As a final step, create the shadow cast by the bird. Apply Mix 4B to the left side of the puffin, then smooth out the edges with a clean, dry brush. Do the same on the right side of the feet, and while this layer is still wet, use Mix 5A to add some lines in the middle of the gray shadow area we just created near the left foot. And you have completed the painting.

River Otter

River otters are playful and agile creatures often found along rivers, lakes, and marshes, where they swim gracefully and hunt for fish. Known for their thick, waterproof fur, they thrive in both cold and temperate climates. Did you know river otters use rocks not just for lounging but also to crack open shellfish or play games? Their curious and energetic behavior makes them a fascinating subject. In this tutorial, you'll refine your ability to use color blending and layering to achieve smooth transitions and build depth in natural subjects. You'll also practice incorporating additional elements like rocks and the ground, enhancing the realism and storytelling in your painting.

Colors Needed

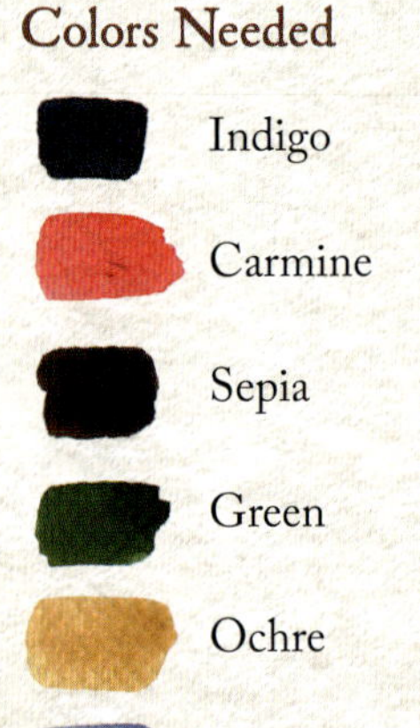

Indigo

Carmine

Sepia

Green

Ochre

Cobalt Blue

Suggested Paper Orientation: Horizontal

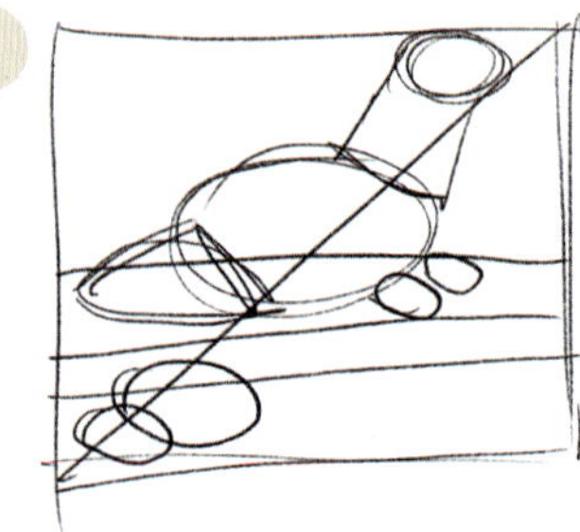

Step 1: Draw a rectangle that's slightly wider than it is tall. Draw a diagonal line from the lower left corner to the top right corner, and then divide the rectangle into two equal parts horizontally. This line will represent the top edge of the rock platform. Next, divide the lower half of the rectangle into two equal parts horizontally, helping to define the platform's position in the next step. Create an oval in the middle of the main rectangle to represent the body, then attach a triangular-shaped tail and a cylindrical neck. Attach a small horizontal oval to the neck cylinder for the head, and then sketch the paws with two small ovals on the bottom right of the body oval. Finally, outline one smaller and one bigger rock, positioned in the lower left corner of the main rectangle.

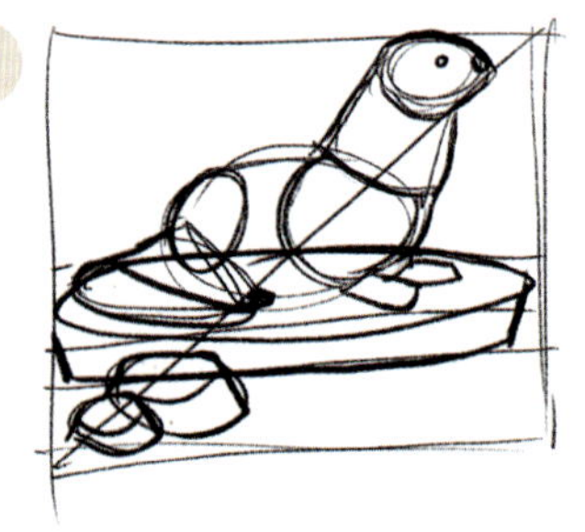

Step 2: Add a line from the right corner of the tail triangle, where it intersects with the diagonal line, to around one-third of the way from the left side. Create an oval for the chest area (to help position the legs) and one near the tail, outlining the back. Define the paws by making them more rectangular. Connect all the geometrical

(Step 2 continued)

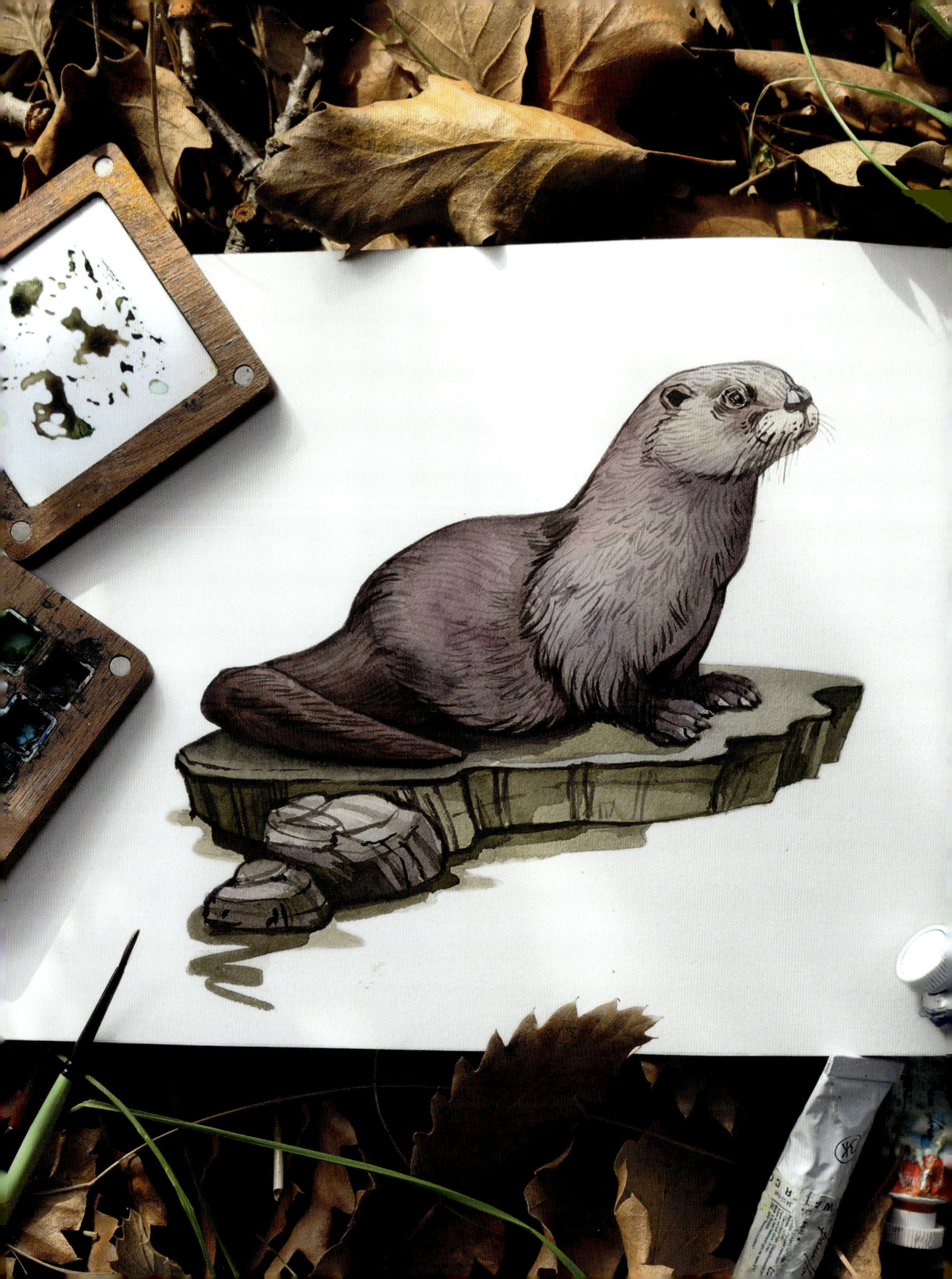

shapes with smooth lines to define the outline of the otter, then add the nose and eye. Finally, define the placement of the platform by positioning it in the top half of the lower half of the rectangle. Make the back edge more rounded, add a line representing the front edge, and give the rocks thickness by drawing curvy horizontal lines parallel to the lower edge of the rocks.

Step 3: Add the belly line and include more details on the face such as a small ear, a cheek, a circular area around the eye, and whiskers. Then, add fingers to the hands and create breaks on the edge of the platform with short vertical lines on the right side. Refine the shape of the platform, especially the right portion where the breaks are. Add some lines to the sides of the stone to indicate shadow. Outline the shadow cast by the stone and the platform using a wavy line.

Step 4: At this stage, erase all guide lines and focus on adding the final details. Refine the shape of the head and work on the facial features. Give the nose a triangular shape, define the eye better, and add a muzzle and more whiskers. Create fur texture for the body by adding short zigzag lines that follow its shape. Add lines to the side of the platform to outline the shadow in that area, then add details and texture to the rocks and define the shadow shape better. After that, you can proceed with painting!

Step 5: Create these three color mixes for the otter:

- Mix A: indigo + carmine + water = light watery purple

- Mix B: same as Mix 5A (above) but with more pigment and less water + a touch of sepia = darker medium purple

- Mix C: same as Mix 5B (above) but with even more pigment (especially sepia) and less water = darkest purple-brown

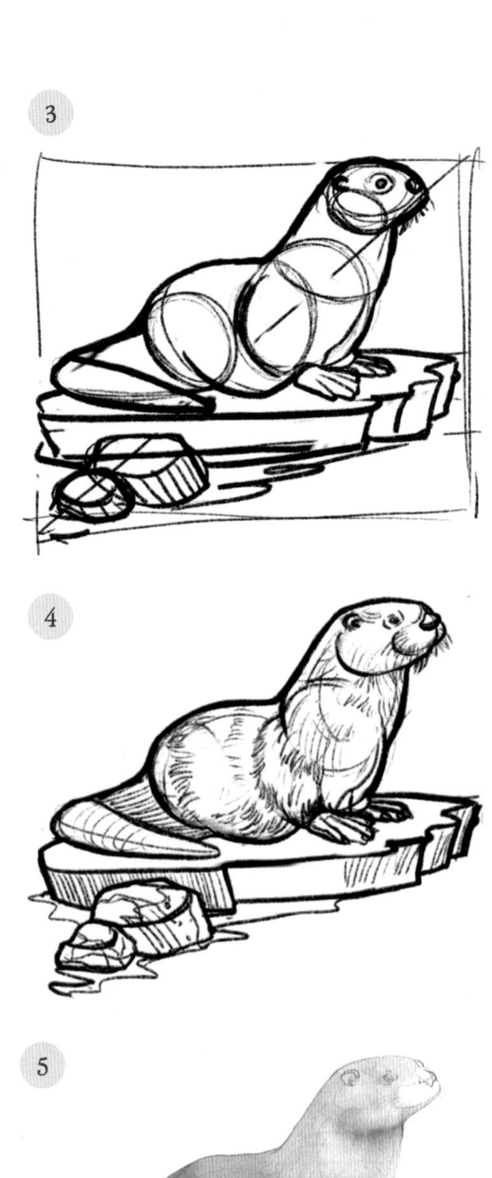

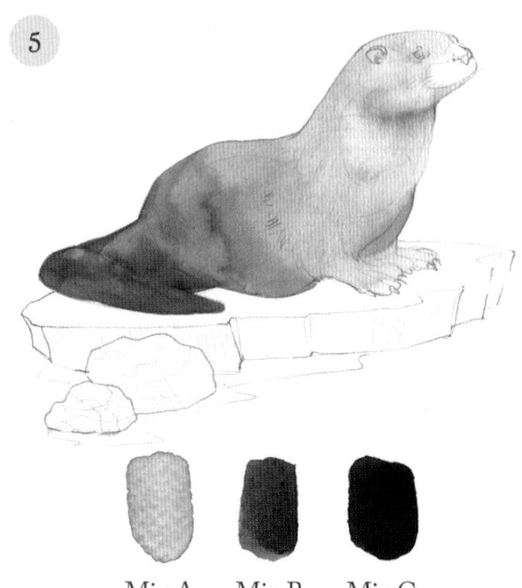

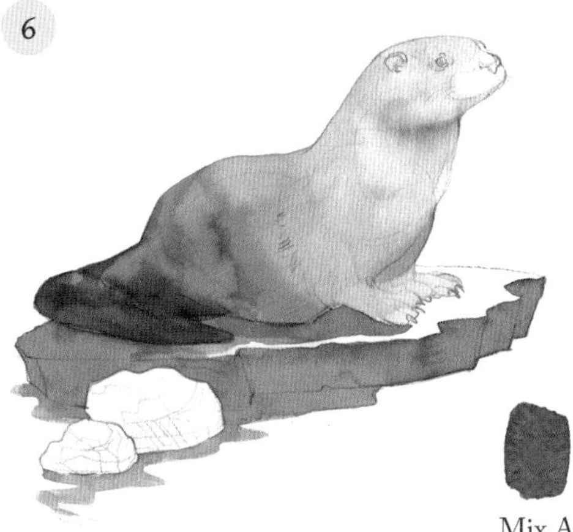

Mix A

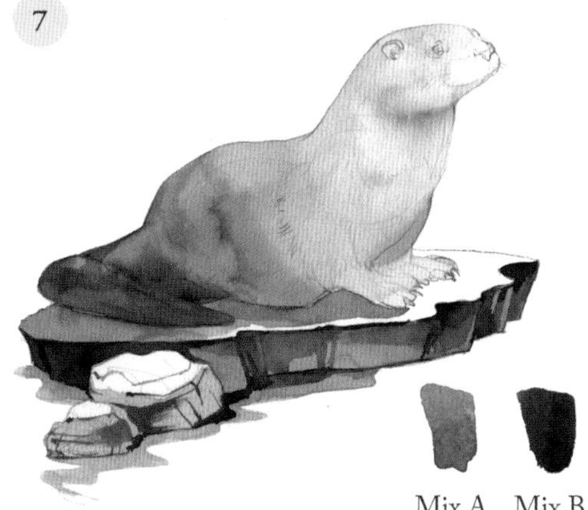

Mix A   Mix B

Get ready to work without interruption until the end of this step. Start by applying Mix A to the right part of the otter, then, once you have painted approximatively one-third of the body, switch to Mix B and paint until you reach the start of the tail. Then, without letting the surface dry, switch to Mix C and paint to the end of the tail. You should have a uniform wash with no visible brushstrokes. If the layer is still wet, use Mix B to apply it to the neck under the head and to the top part of the right leg. The color should seamlessly blend into the previously created layer. If the layer has already dried, work wet-on-dry (page 16) and smooth the edges well.

Step 6: In this step, we will add the first layer of color to the platform. Create a new mix:

- Mix A: sepia + green + ochre + some water = medium muddy green

Starting from the right side of the platform, apply Mix A to the edge, and then continue covering the edge until you reach the rocks. Continue painting the platform, this time applying the color to the edge and top on the left side of the platform. Also, cover the area in the middle under the otter, but make sure to leave an uncovered white line between this shadow and the edge you already covered. Finally, add the shadow near the rocks.

Step 7: Create these two mixes to add shadows to the rocks and darken the side of the platform:

- Mix A: cobalt + carmine + water = medium-light purple
- Mix B: green + carmine + sepia + water = dark, muddy green

Apply Mix A to the lower half of both rocks and let it dry. Apply Mix B to the left side of the platform and in the folds on the right side. Accentuate the shadows cast by the platform as well. Once the stones are dry, apply Mix B to parts of their lower halves, enhancing the texture of the rocks with long, thin lines made using the tip of your brush.

Step 8: Now, let's add volume to the otter's body and increase contrast. Use Mix 5A under the head and along the left and right sides of the neck. Smooth the edges with a clean, damp brush for a soft transition. Use Mix 5B to add shadow to the otter's right leg and the left side of its left leg. With Mix 5A and the tip of your brush, create fur for the left leg. Finally, use Mix 5C to darken the tail, especially the lower half where the tail bends. Paint the left paw and add fine details to the left side of the leg using the tip of your brush and Mix 5C.

Step 9: Combine cobalt with water for a light blue. Then, create two mixes:

- Mix A: carmine + cobalt + water = light pinkish-purple
- Mix B: indigo + carmine + sepia + a touch of water = dark, almost black

Apply the light blue mix to the forehead and the left leg, smoothing the edges for a seamless look. Add Mix A to the body and the area under the head as well as under the eye. Smooth the edges. Use Mix B to create fur on the otter and outline its fingers. Strengthen the lower outline of the otter's body, as well as the outline of the platform. With Mix B and a medium or small brush, create the shadow cast by the otter on the platform, softening the shadow's edges for a blended effect.

Step 10: Use the light blue cobalt and water mix from the previous step to paint the top right side of the platform. Add a touch of sepia to Mix 9A to make it slightly gray, and use it to enhance the texture of the otter's body and head. With Mix 5C, paint the otter's eye, ear, nose, and whiskers. Use this mix to refine the paws, outline the nails, and add final details to the platform and rocks. And you're done!

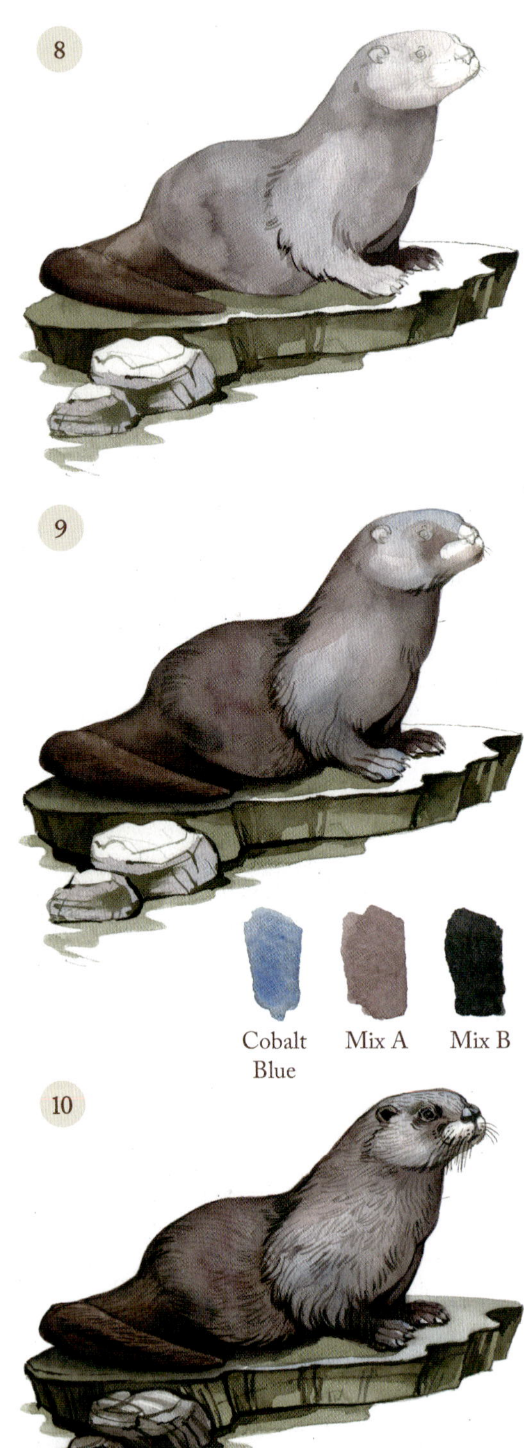

Alpine Ibex Goat

The ibex, with its impressive curved horns and rugged appearance, is a true survivor of the steep cliffs and rocky terrain of mountainous regions. Known for its agility and strength, the ibex can scale near-vertical rock faces with ease, making it a symbol of resilience in the animal kingdom. In this tutorial, you'll learn how to paint this magnificent mammal by breaking down the process into manageable steps, making it both exciting and achievable. By mastering the techniques for painting the ibex, you'll be equipped to tackle other similar animals with confidence and skill.

Colors Needed

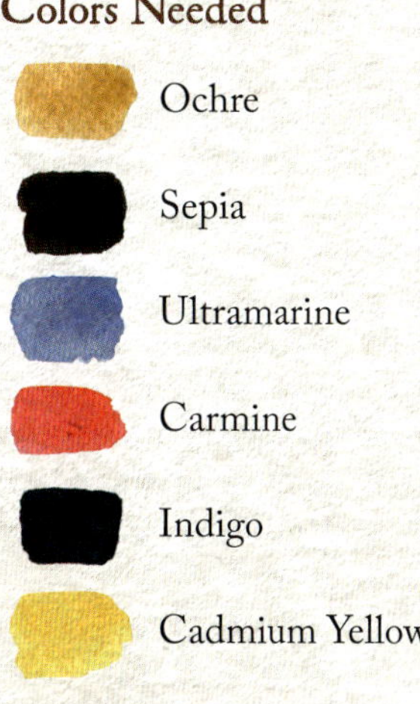

Ochre

Sepia

Ultramarine

Carmine

Indigo

Cadmium Yellow

Suggested Paper Orientation: Vertical

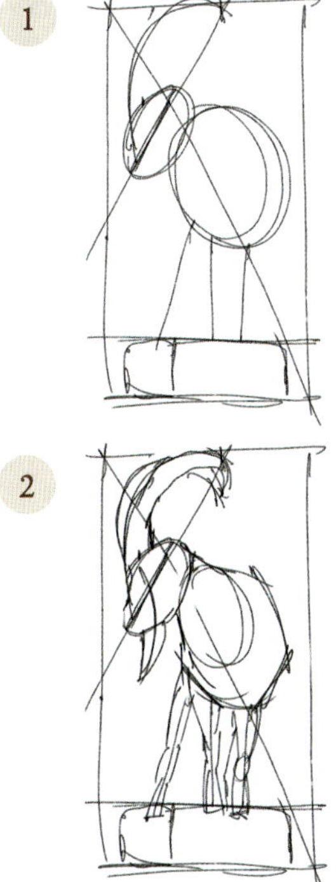

Step 1: Draw a rectangle that's twice as tall as it is wide. Divide the main rectangle using a diagonal line from the top left corner to the lower right corner. Outline the body with a big oval and the head with a smaller oval. Then, create a semicircle at the top center of the main rectangle. For the rocks, create a horizontal guiding line on the lower portion of the main rectangle. The width of the rocks should be smaller than the width of the main rectangle, so define the left and right edges with two vertical lines. Then, add a vertical line that separates the rocks into two pieces. Add two parallel lines that start under the oval of the body and reach the top of the rocks for legs. Then, add a third (back) leg with a diagonal line that goes from the oval of the body to the left side of the rocks.

Step 2: Give the body a more realistic shape using lines that create sharper, more defined contours. Connect the body with the head and outline the beard with a curvy triangle. Add thickness to the horns, ensuring the second horn is positioned behind the first. Separate the chest from the neck with an oval that extends from the head.

(Step 2 continued)

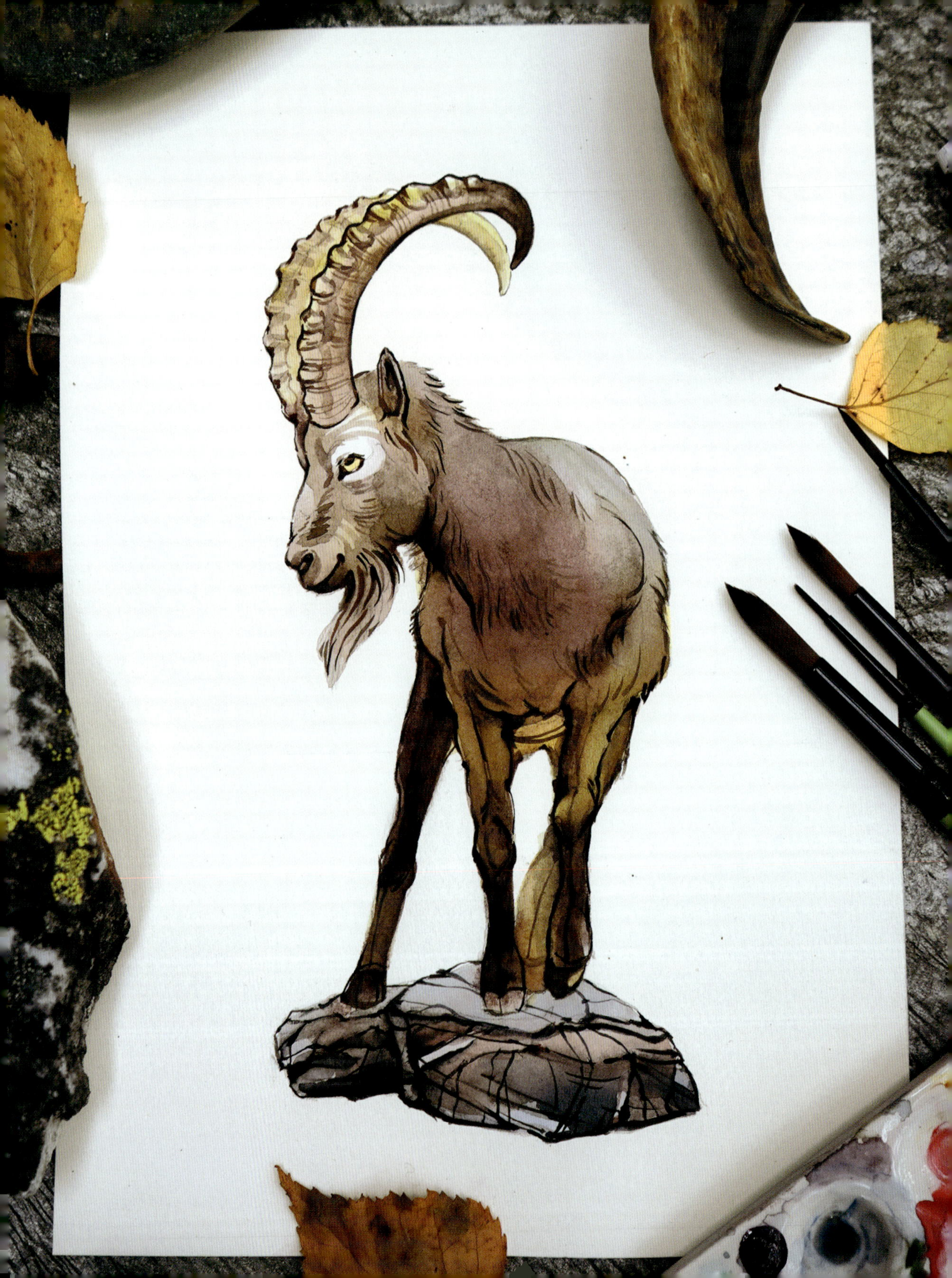

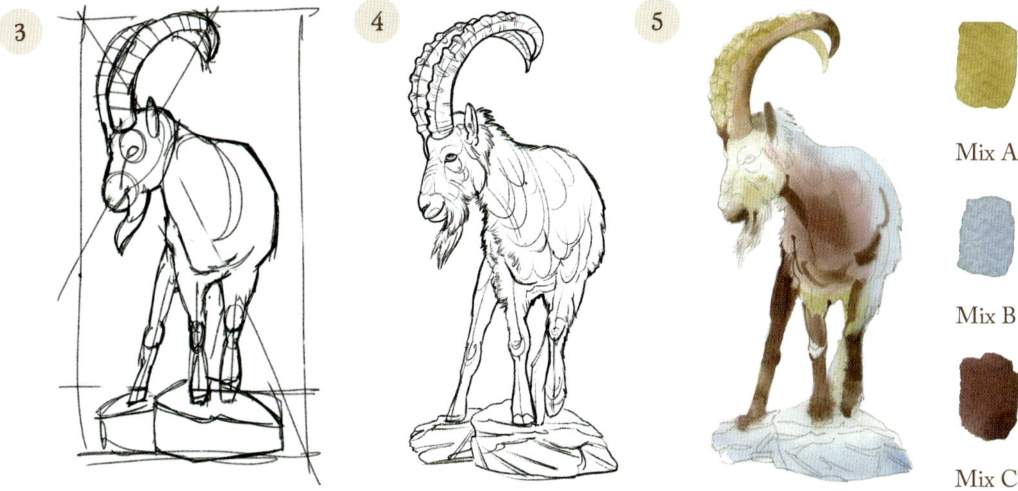

Then, add thickness to the legs, but instead of simply drawing parallel lines, keep the musculature in mind. First, create two circles in the middle of the legs for ankles. Then, connect the ankles to the body with two lines. The legs should be thicker at the top and thinner near the ankles. Connect the ankles to the hooves, making the hooves larger than the area where the legs meet the ankles. Separate the hooves from the legs with short, horizontal lines. Outline the fourth leg, which is positioned between the two front legs, with a simple line for now.

Step 3: Make the outline of the body, head, and legs of the goat more defined and accurate. Add some short vertical lines across both horns that follow the natural direction of each horn. Draw a circle beneath the front horn to outline the area around the eye. Outline the eye with a small horizontal oval placed slightly lower than the center of the main eye area circle.

After that, outline the snout with a circle and add a line for the mouth. Draw the separation between the bridge of the nose and the cheek with a line that extends from the eye toward the mouth. Outline the ear with a thin oval to the right of the horns. Lastly, separate the rocks into two pieces, and outline the back and front edges of the rocks with curvy lines.

Step 4: Remove the guide lines you no longer need. Add fur texture to the body, front legs, and where the neck transitions into the head and beard using short zigzag strokes. Define the facial features more clearly by adding a nose and giving the ear a more realistic appearance. Create round bumps on the horns and underline the texture of the horns with the lines going across their surface. Add final details to the legs and the rocks. It's time to paint!

Step 5: We will start painting using the wet-on-wet technique (page 17). Make sure to work quickly during this step without interruption. First, let's mix the colors we will be using:

- Mix A: ochre + a touch of sepia + water = medium beige

- Mix B: ultramarine + a touch of sepia + water = medium-light bluish-gray

- Mix C: sepia + carmine + a touch of indigo + water = medium-dark, saturated Bordeaux wine color

(Step 5 continued)

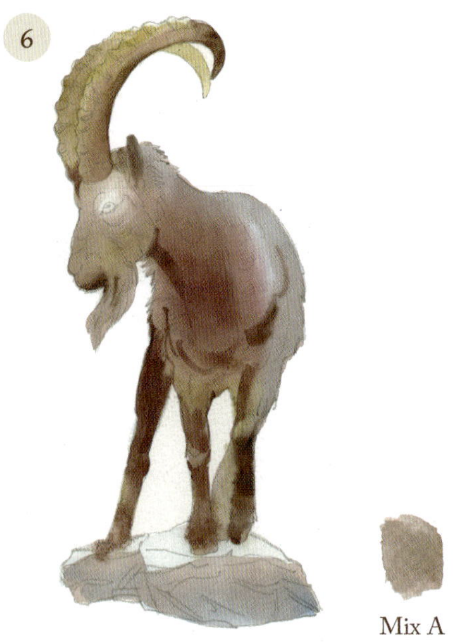

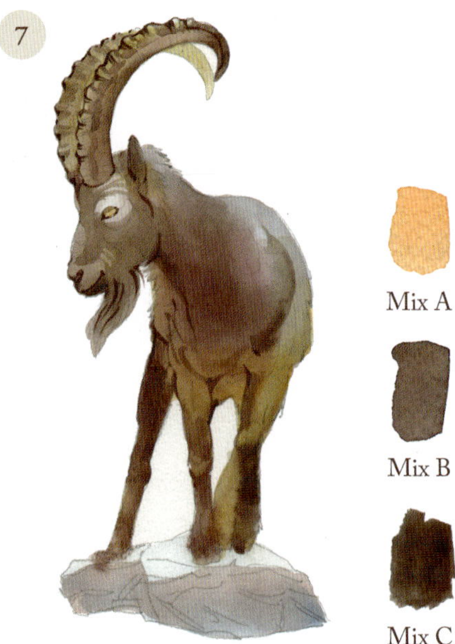

Cover the entire surface of the goat with clean water. Apply Mix A to the horns, the lower part of the face, and the visible part of the belly. While this layer is still wet, apply Mix B to the right side of the goat and to the rocks. Then, apply Mix C to the base of the back horn, the right side front horn, the ear, the neck line, the two front legs and the left back leg, and the jaw, and finally add some curvy lines to the chest. The final leg should be covered with Mix B. All these colors should blend slightly but still remain distinct. Don't worry if things look a bit messy; we will refine the details in the next steps. For now, let this layer dry.

Step 6: Create a new mix:

- Mix A: Mix 5C (sepia + carmine + a touch of indigo + water) + more water = diluted Bordeaux wine color

Apply Mix A to the head and body, but avoid the horns. Now, lift off the color with a clean, dry brush from the eye areas and from the right side of the goat, as we want some of the blue color to show through this new layer. Use the same color

to cover the lower part of the rocks. Then, apply the same color to the right part of the front horn and smooth out the edge. Then, apply the same color base on the back horn and smooth the transition. Let this dry completely.

Step 7: Now, let's add some details to the goat's face. First, we will introduce a warm hue to the goat to make the fur look richer and more interesting:

- Mix A: cadmium yellow + a touch of carmine + water = light orange
- Mix B: sepia + carmine + water = medium warm brown

Apply Mix A to the horns and the legs, and also color the eyes. Let this dry a bit, and while it's damp, apply Mix B to the right part of the front horn. Then, outline the features of the face by darkening the cheek and the area under the eye. Darken the ear. Create some texture on the left wavy part of the horns with this color. Also, add some of this color to the neck to darken that area.

Create a new mix:

- Mix C: same as Mix B but with more pigment and less water = saturated warm brown

Use Mix C and the tip of your small brush to underline the texture of the horns on the left side by using short, thin, vertical lines that will help visually separate the sections of the horns from one another. Make sure the front horn is more detailed. Then, use the same color to outline the ear, eye, mouth, and nose using very thin lines from the tip of your small brush. Finally, add a few wavy strokes to the beard to start outlining the curls.

Step 8: Use Mix 7B to add even more details to the horns by painting thin, horizontal lines. Then, paint tiny, thin strokes on the face in the area that separates the nose from the rest of the face. Add some wavy strokes under the ear and use the same technique to start creating the fur texture on the neck and the beginning of the chest.

Use Mix 7C to darken some areas of the goat. Start by darkening the tip of the front horn, then smooth out the edge. Darken the left back leg and the lower portion of the front legs under the knee, starting from the areas under the knee. Make sure to leave the knees light and keep the hooves lighter as well, especially on the right side. Using the tip of your brush, darken the features of the face such as the eyes, nose, and ear with very thin lines. Create a few darker waves on the beard and the areas that separate the face from the neck, and add some details to the legs by outlining the middle line of each leg with a very thin line. Paint a couple of wavy strokes where the legs transition into the body, and add a few horizontal lines to accentuate the belly. Darken the outline of the goat in some areas, especially on the right side and on the front horn. Make sure to use thin, irregular, interrupting lines while doing so.

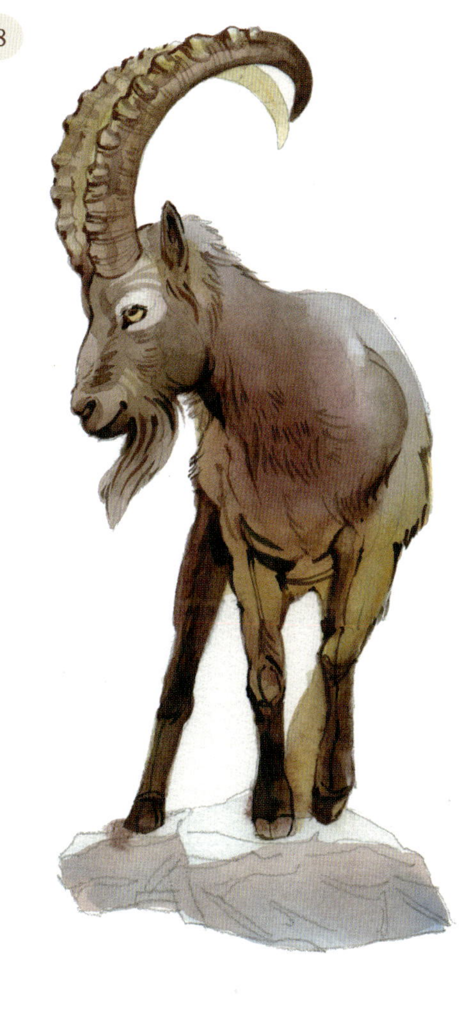

Step 9: Apply Mix 6A to the neck, chest, and legs, avoiding the face and the belly. Smooth out the edge of the right side of the body, as we want the extreme right part to be a bit lighter. Then, slightly darken the left side of the back horn. Add a final outline to the left side of the front horn using the very tip of your brush and Mix 7C, or just use sepia with a touch of water. Make sure this line is very thin. You can also darken the outline of the back horn a bit, but ensure that it remains lighter and thinner than the outline of the front horn. Use the same color and technique to add final details to the fur on the neck and the beard, and to make the outline of the front legs bolder.

Now, let's add more details and realism to the rocks. We will use a mix of existing brown hues you already have on your palette and combine them with some cooler hues:

- Mix A: ultramarine + sepia + water = light blue-gray
- Mix B: same as Mix 9A (above) but with more pigment and less water = darker blue

Cover the top side of the rocks with Mix A. Add some of this color to the lower side of the rock as well. Then, apply Mix 7C to the center of the rocks. While Mix 7C is still wet, take the darker Mix B and add it to the lower parts of the rock. This will allow the two colors to blend together slightly, helping to imitate the rock texture. Repeat these steps if needed, especially if the external part of the rocks is still too bright. Leave the rocks to dry completely before adding the darkest details. We will need a new color for that:

- Mix C: sepia + indigo + water = very dark, almost black gray

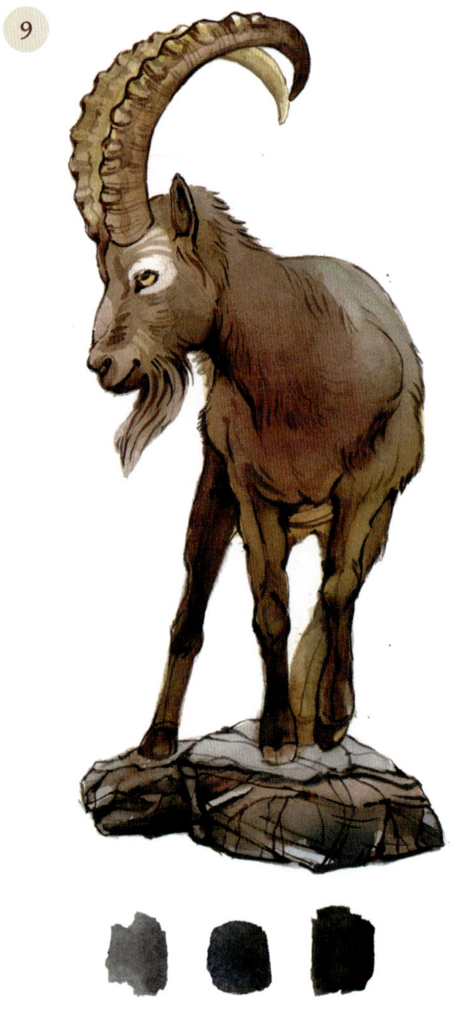

Mix A   Mix B   Mix C

Using the very tip of your small brush, create the outline of the rocks and imitate cracks with Mix C. You can do so by drawing long, thin, horizontal lines and upside-down "Y" shapes to make the cracks look even more realistic. The process of working on the rocks is quite intuitive, so yours will turn out differently than mine, and that's okay. Once you feel happy with the texture of the rocks, your painting is complete.

Porcini Mushroom

The porcini mushroom, a prized delicacy in many cuisines, is known for its rich flavor and meaty texture. Found in forests across Europe and North America, this mushroom thrives in the wild, often growing in symbiosis with certain trees. In this tutorial, you'll learn how to paint this unique mushroom realistically, focusing on the various textures that make it stand out. You'll also discover the best techniques for representing the different parts of the mushroom and how to add charm and spontaneity by incorporating pieces of grass and mud, making it look as though it's just been pulled from earth.

Colors Needed

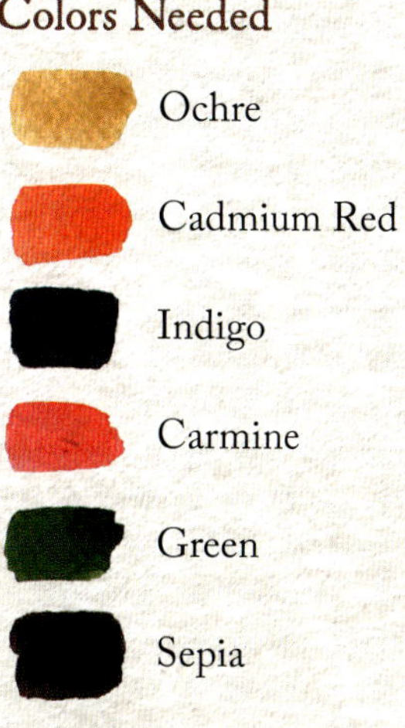

Ochre

Cadmium Red

Indigo

Carmine

Green

Sepia

Suggested Paper Orientation: Vertical

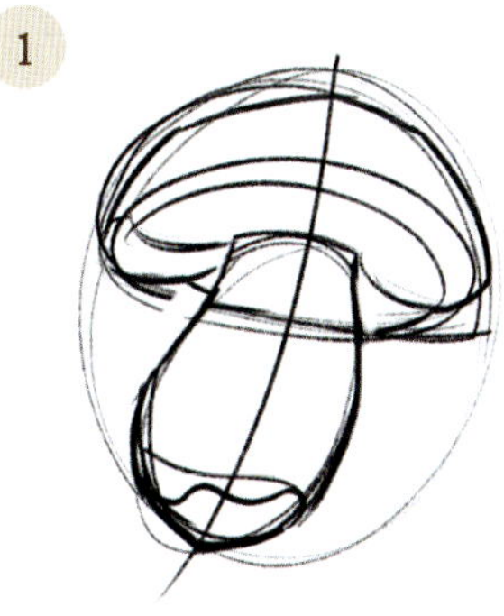

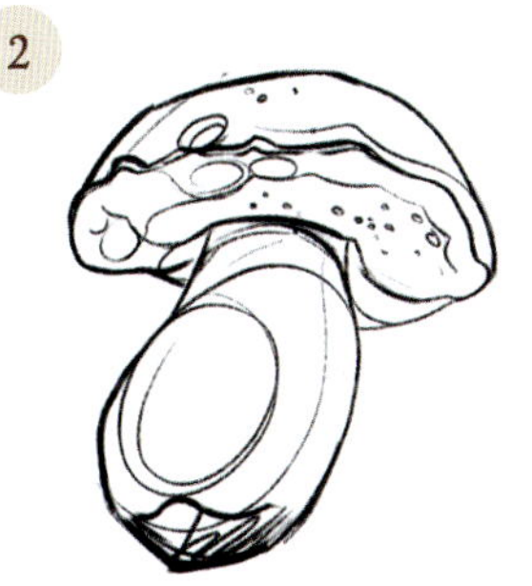

Step 1: Draw a large oval for the whole mushroom. Then, draw an oval inside the top part of the large oval for the cap. Draw a curved line from the center of the main oval to the bottom—a little to the left of center—this will correspond to the stalk, also known as the stipe. Inside the cap area, add another oval to separate the external part of the cap from the underside of the cap (the pore surface). Draw a circle at the lower end of the stipe to indicate that it is thicker than the upper part. Define where the stipe ends with a horizontal line. Next, divide the pore surface into light and shadow areas using a curved line. Add a parallel line below the main line that divides the pore surface from the external part of the cap. This way, we have identified three main values of the pore surface: light, mid-tone, and shadow. Start giving the outline of the cap a more realistic appearance by making the shape slightly more organic and irregular.

Step 2: Erase guide lines. Draw a small oval at the base of the stipe to indicate where the mud is attached. Add a circle to the left side of the thicker part of the stipe to highlight its volume. Next, begin adding some characteristic elements and irregularities to the cap and the pore surface. You can do this by placing some ovals on the left side of the cap and pore surface.

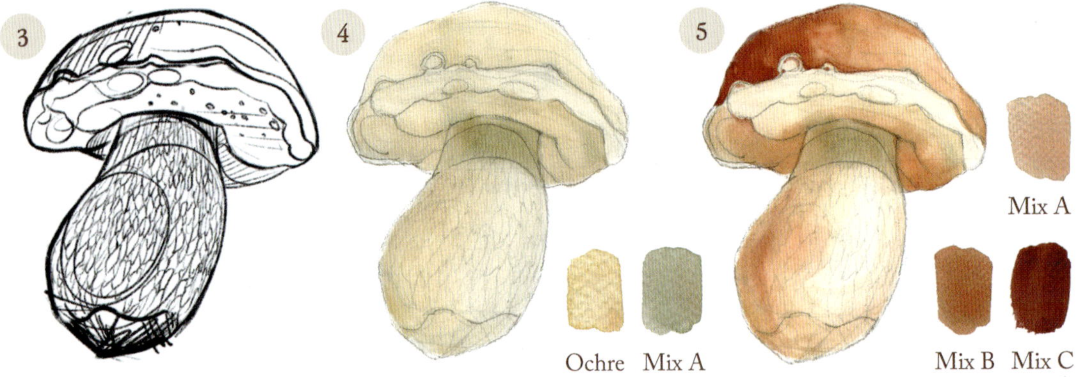

Step 3: Transform the straight lines dividing the pore surface into organic, wavy lines. Refine the shape of the stipe further and start adding some texture to it. There is a weblike texture on the stipe. To create this, beginning at the bulbous part of the stipe, sketch long, irregular rhombuses. Make sure to place the larger rhombuses in the center and gradually make them smaller and thinner as you reach the tip of the stipe and its sides.

Step 4: Create a light watery beige mix by combining ochre and water. Then, create a new mix:

- Mix A: ochre + cadmium red + indigo + water = medium brown-beige with a greenish hue

Cover the entire mushroom with the ochre and water mix. Let dry completely. Next, apply the same color everywhere except the light area of the pore surface and the right side of the stipe. While this layer is still wet, smooth out the edges on the stipe. Then, while this layer is still wet, apply Mix A to the stipe under the cap and on the left side of the stipe. If this color starts to affect the surrounding areas too much, push it back to where you originally applied it with a clean, dry brush. Let this dry completely.

Step 5: Now, we'll create three warm brown color mixes using the same colors as in Mix 4A but in different proportions:

- Mix A: ochre + cadmium red + a tiny touch of indigo + water = light brown-orange
- Mix B: same as Mix 5A (above) but with more ochre and cadmium and less water = warm brown-red
- Mix C: same as Mix 5B (above) but with more indigo and even less water = dark brown

Use Mix A to cover the brown part of the cap by creating a wash with no visible brushstrokes, avoiding the lighter under-cap and the imperfections on the surface of the cap. Then, using the same color, apply it to the back side of the under-cap, the upper portion of the stipe where it connects with the cap, and the left side of the stipe until you reach the tip. After you reach the tip, continue applying the same color to the lower right part of the stipe. Smooth out the edge for a seamless transition with a clean, dry brush.

Now, cover the under-cap with water, but make sure not to touch the brown cap; leave a line of dry paper between the water you are applying to the under-cap and the cap that is still wet from the previous color. While still wet, apply Mix B to the back area of the under-cap. Smooth the transition even more if needed.

(Step 5 continued)

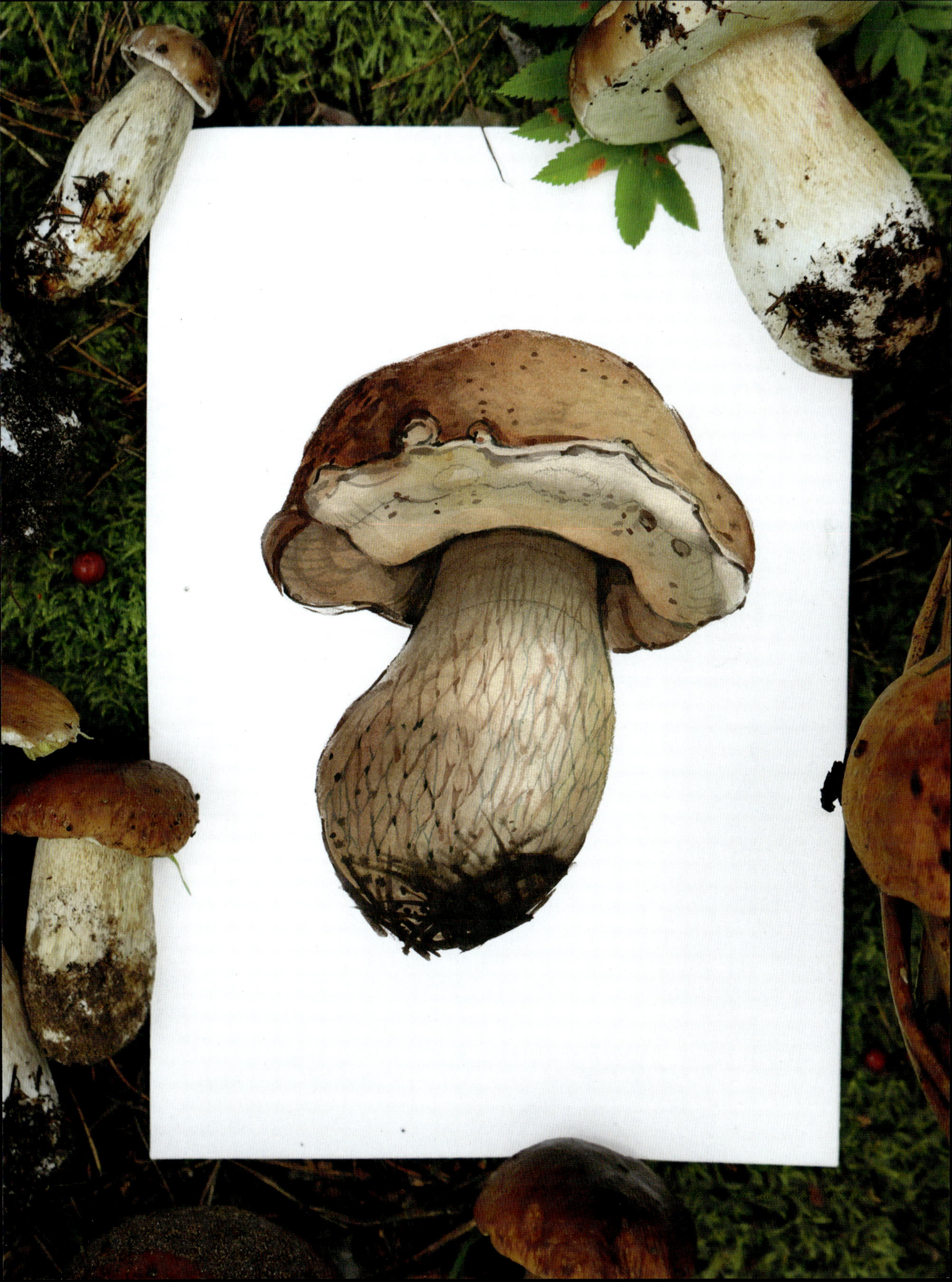

Apply Mix C to the left half of the cap. If the cap is still wet, the new color will blend seamlessly. If the color on the cap has already dried, you will need to smooth the edges for a seamless transition with a clean, dry brush. Use the same color and the tip of your brush to add details to the imperfections on the cap. Then, apply Mix C to the left, thick part of the stipe, which is the shadow area. Smooth out the edges of this stroke for a seamless transition.

Step 6: In this step, we will darken the under-cap and the stipe while adding a cooler hue to our mushroom. Let's start by creating a new mix using equal amounts of three colors:

- Mix A: indigo + ochre + cadmium red + water = natural medium gray

Cover the under-cap and the whole stipe with clean water. While the paper is still wet, apply Mix A to the under-cap, as well as to the left and right parts of the stipe. Make sure to leave a lighter oval on the right side of the mushroom. If the gray affects it, lift it using a clean, dry brush.

Apply Mix 5C to the left side of the cap using the wet-on-dry technique (page 16). To create the texture of the cap, use short strokes. Let them dry. Make sure that the spots are larger closer to the edge and smaller closer to the center. Then, dilute Mix 5C with water, and use it to add spots to the center of the cap and its right side. Then, darken the back side of the under-cap. Smooth out the edges in that area for a seamless transition. Next, cover the whole stipe with clean water. Let it dry for a moment so that the color we will apply to the damp area doesn't bloom too much. You need to find that perfect moment when the paper is drying but not completely dry. Once there, use Mix 5C and the tip of your brush to create the web texture on the stipe. Wait for this to dry completely before proceeding.

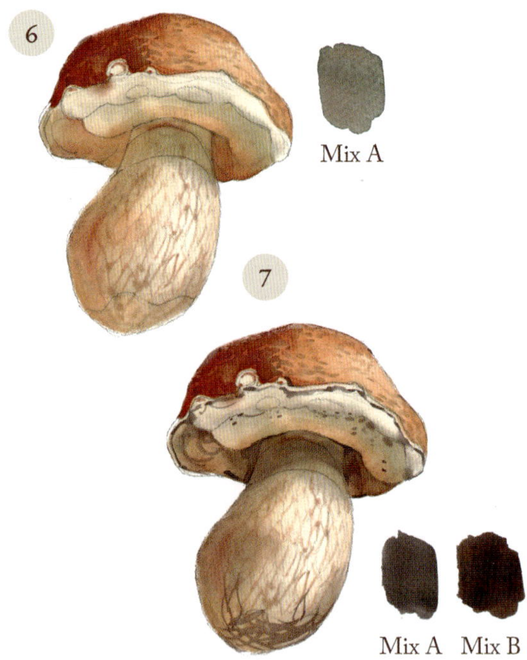

Step 7: Create two mixes:

- Mix A: indigo + carmine + ochre + a touch of green + some water = medium cool purplish-gray
- Mix B: same as Mix 7A (above) but with more pigment and less water = dark purplish-gray

Using the wet-on-dry technique, apply Mix A to the upper portion of the stipe, as well as to the back part of the under-cap. Add a touch of this color to the left side of the upper part of the stipe and to the left side of the thicker part; smooth out the edges. Add the same color to the under-cap area where you see the border with the lighter front part. Smooth the edge as you did previously.

Now, let's visually separate the cap from the under-cap. Take the same color and, using the tip of your brush, create an irregular line under the cap that follows its natural shape. Continue this line onto the back part of the under-cap. Don't smooth the edges this time; leave the line crisp.

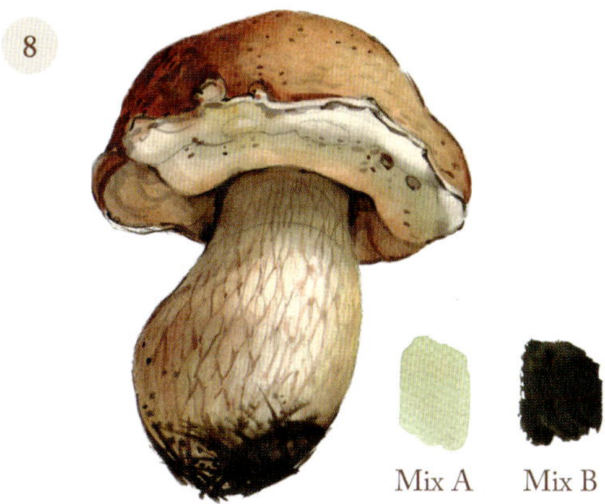

Mix A   Mix B

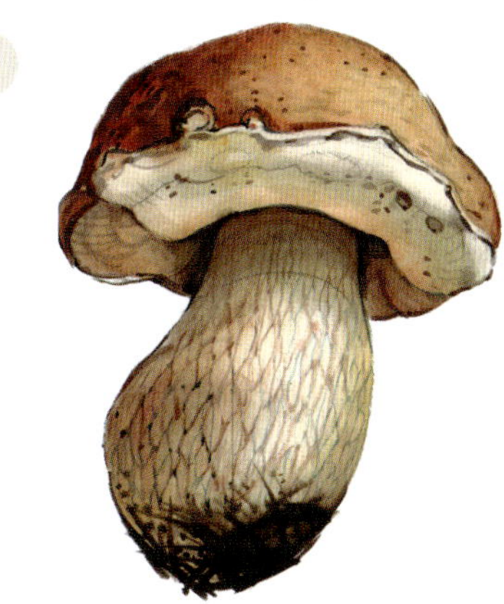

Then, apply Mix B to the left and right areas of the under-cap close to the stipe. Switch to Mix A and add strokes, lines, and dots to the under-cap to create more texture. Finally, use Mix B to enhance the texture of the lower part of the stipe and begin to create the impression of mud attached to the lower part of it.

Step 8: Create a new mix:

- Mix A: green + ochre + a good amount of water (more water than pigment) = light yellowish-green

Apply Mix A to the right part of the under-cap, the right part of the stipe, and part of the cap. Because the color is light and translucent, it will add a subtle additional hue to our painting and enhance its interest. Since the color is light, there's no need to smooth the edges.

Next, create a very dark color to paint the mud attached to the lower part of the stipe:

- Mix B: green + indigo + sepia + a tiny touch of water = dark, almost black color

Cover the lower half of the stipe with clean water. While still wet, use Mix B to add texture to the lower part of the stipe using irregular lines and dots. There will be some blooming because you are applying the dark color to a wet surface, but the color will not expand too much because of the high concentration of pigment. Use a diluted version of Mix B to add additional details to the edge where the cap meets the under-cap and to darken the back side of the under-cap where it meets the stipe.

Then, use Mix 7B to add additional texture to the left part of the cap, using the same short strokes and dots. This time, smooth some of these strokes. Next, use the same mix to underline the web texture on the stipe with the tip of your brush. Use the same color to create texture with dots and lines on the cap and the under-cap. Finally, use Mix 8B to darken the back side of the under-cap near the left and right sides of the stipe to emphasize the shadow concentrated in this area.

Step 9: Use Mix 6A to create additional textures on the under-cap by adding tiny lines that showcase the natural curves of that area. Underline the web texture of the stipe. Next, use Mix 8B and the very tip of your brush to add final touches, such as some dots on the cap, the under-cap, and the left side of the web texture on the stipe. Use the same color to further accentuate the outline of the cap, to create a darker outline on the left part of the stipe, and to outline the area where the stipe meets the cap. If needed, create additional texture to imitate the grass and mud on the lower part of the stipe. After this, your mushroom is ready!

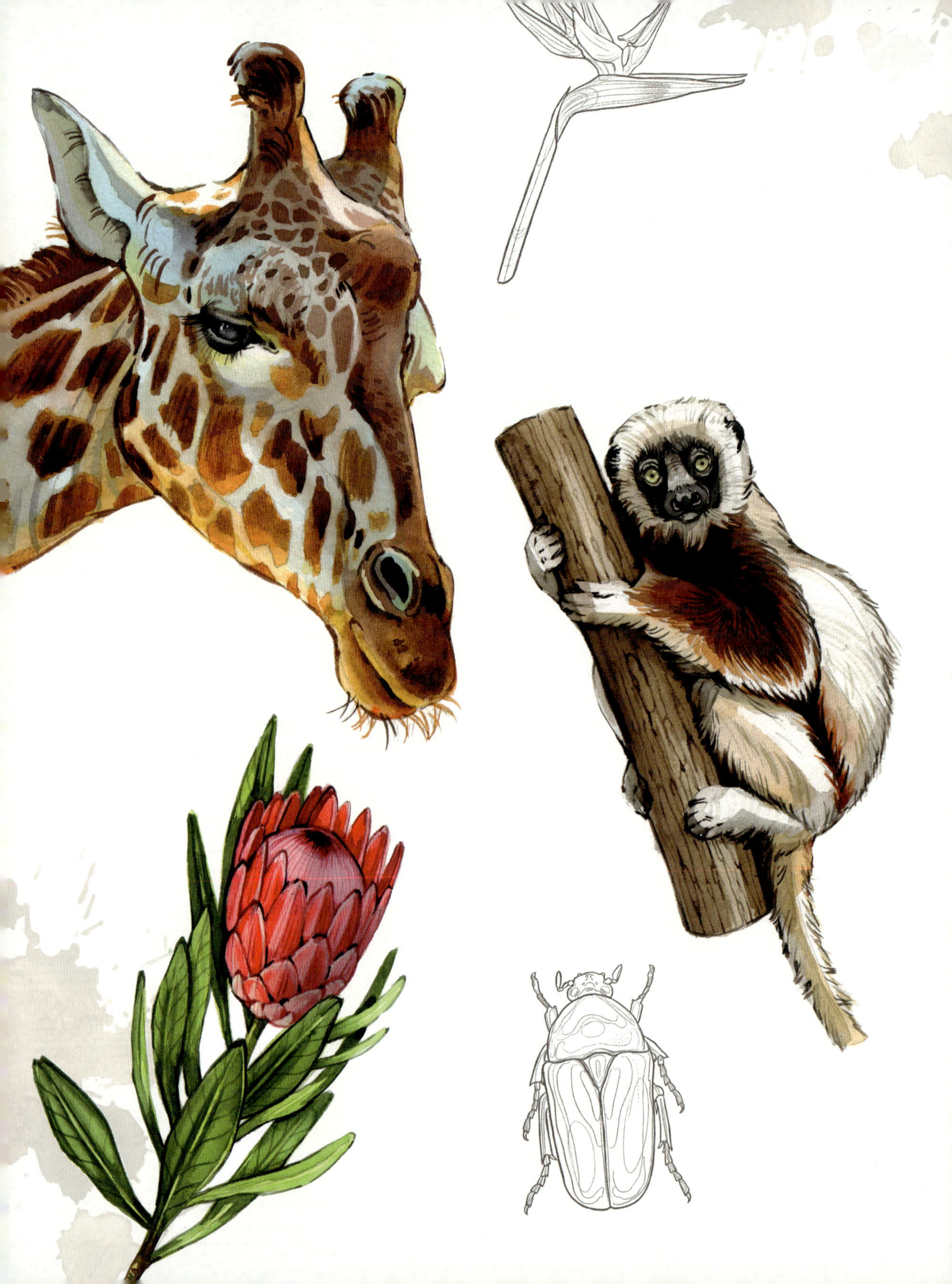

Africa
Origins and Biodiversity

Welcome to Africa, a continent of extraordinary contrast and wild beauty! Often called the cradle of humanity, Africa is where life on Earth began and where nature continues to astound. Home to a rich cultural tapestry, from vibrant cities in South Africa to the pyramids of Egypt, Africa is a place where history, culture, and tradition are ever-present. The continent is home to more than 1,500 languages, and each region has its own story to tell.

From the vast, arid expanse of the Sahara Desert to the lush, verdant jungles of Central Africa, this continent is also home to some of the most incredible landscapes and diverse ecosystems you can imagine. The Sahara, stretching across 11 countries, is the world's largest hot desert, offering a surreal landscape of endless dunes and ancient, rugged plateaus. Despite its harsh conditions, it supports a surprising range of life, from resilient desert plants to unique animals adapted to the extreme environment.

More of Africa's true magic lies in its extraordinary biodiversity, and nowhere is this more evident than on the island of Madagascar. Did you know that up to 90 percent of Madagascar's wildlife can't be found anywhere else on Earth? Madagascar's isolation has given rise to some of the most fascinating creatures. The Coquerel's Sifaka (page 139) is one of the most iconic species, known for its charming, acrobatic movements as it leaps between trees in the forest.

As we venture into the heart of Africa, we'll encounter the magnificent Giraffe (page 134), an iconic symbol of Africa's savannahs. Did you know that each giraffe's coat pattern is like a fingerprint, entirely unique? Their towering height allows them to browse the treetops for fresh leaves, giving them access to food other animals can't reach and making them one of Africa's most remarkable animals.

No African journey would be complete without a splash of color, and we'll find that in the stunning Bird of Paradise Flower (page 119), Protea (page 122), and the remarkable African Jewel Beetle (page 129). The exotic bird of paradise flower is a striking masterpiece—its vivid orange and blue petals resemble the vibrant plumage of a bird in flight. The protea is the oldest flowering plant genus on Earth—dating back 300 million years! With its iridescent, gem-like shell, this flower is another true marvel of nature. Its colors change when you look at it from different angles.

Get ready to unleash your creativity and paint some of the world's most extraordinary animals and plants. It's going to be an unforgettable artistic adventure!

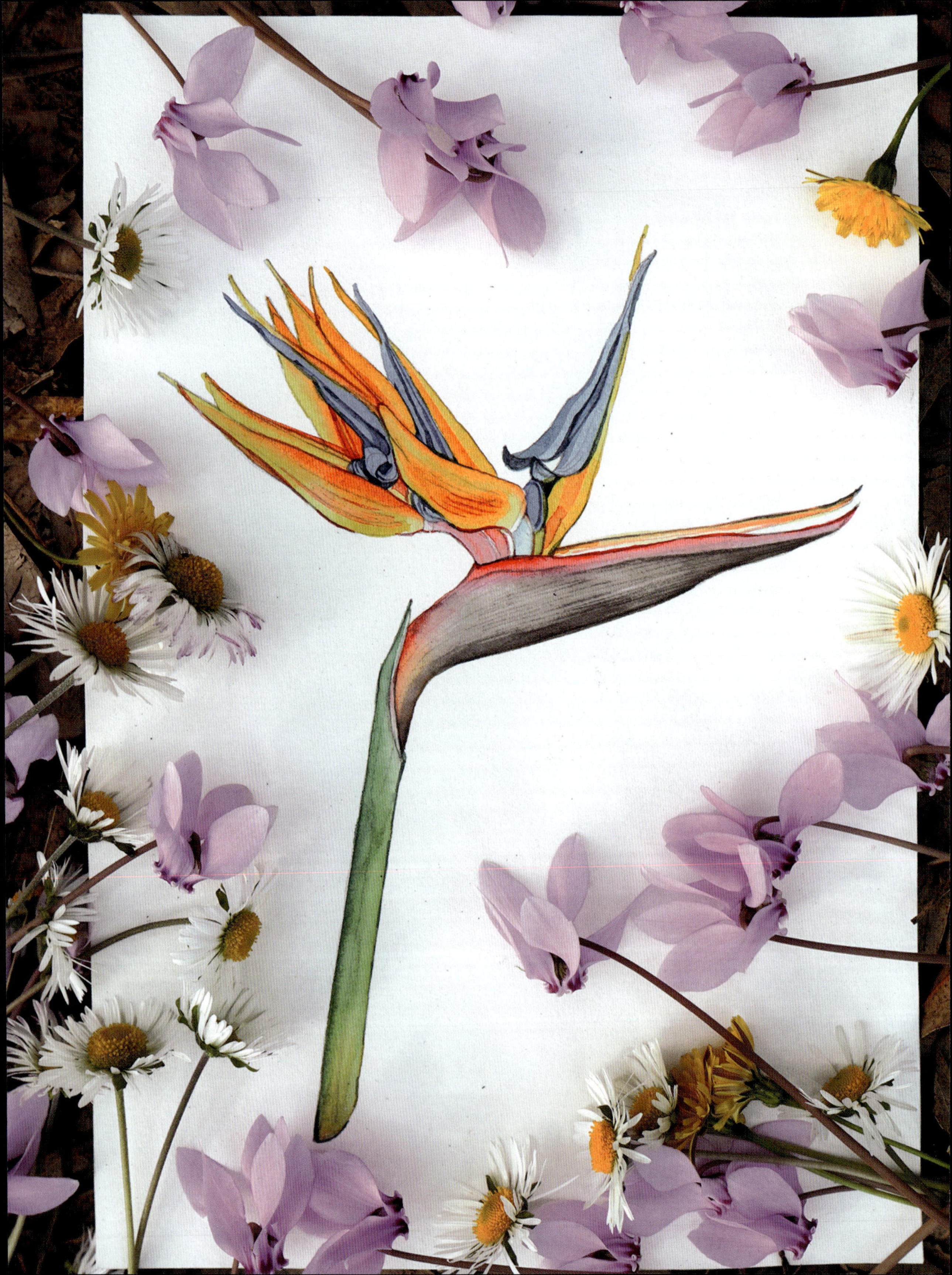

Bird of Paradise Flower

Known for its vibrant colors and striking shape, this plant symbolizes exotic beauty and freedom. In this tutorial, you will learn how to paint multicolored subjects without colors mixing together or looking muddy. The key is to work on the different parts of the flower separately, allowing each color to shine. This tutorial will also give you the perfect opportunity to practice soft gradient techniques, creating smooth transitions between hues while keeping the vibrancy intact.

Colors Needed

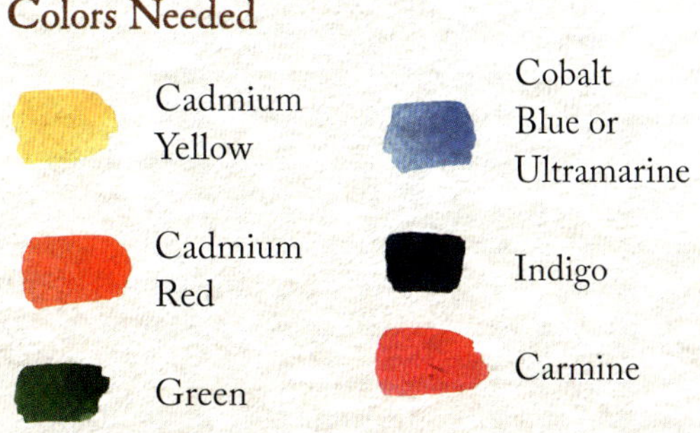

Suggested Paper Orientation: Vertical

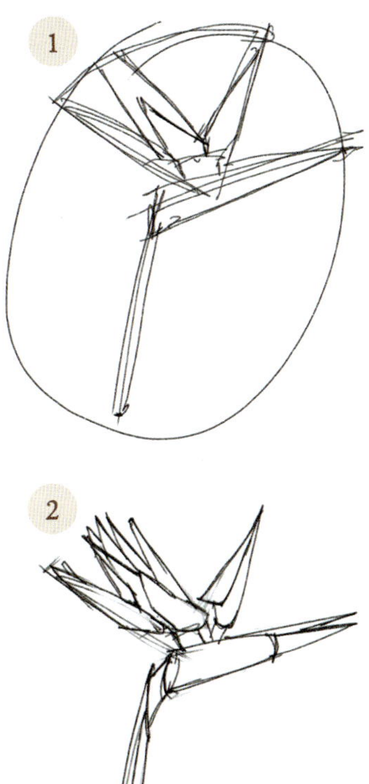

Step 1: Draw an oval leaning slightly to the right. Draw a vertical line starting around the middle of the bottom of the oval up to just past the center. Add a parallel line for thickness. This is the stem. From the top of the stem, draw a line to the right, reaching the side of the oval and creating an angle slightly bigger than 90 degrees. Then, add a line starting from the end of the line you just created and connect it with the stem, lower than the original line, creating a thin triangle. This is the body. For the petals, sketch two lines coming from one-third of the way from the base of the body—one to the left and one to the right, reaching the top of the oval, creating a shape similar to a triangle. Transform these two lines into two thin triangles using a similar method to the one we used for the body. These two triangles will be two petals. Then, add two lines starting from the same point as the two triangles that go up slightly to the left. Finally, add a smaller triangle in the middle, between the two main triangular petals.

Step 2: Attach the body of the flower to the stem with two parallel lines. Add a small triangular petal on top of the body. Then, give the petals a more defined shape. The part that connects the petals with the head should be thin, so you can create it with two parallel lines. Make the lower portion of the petal (the part on top of the thin connection) more rounded. The petals should appear thicker on the lower side and thinner at the tips.

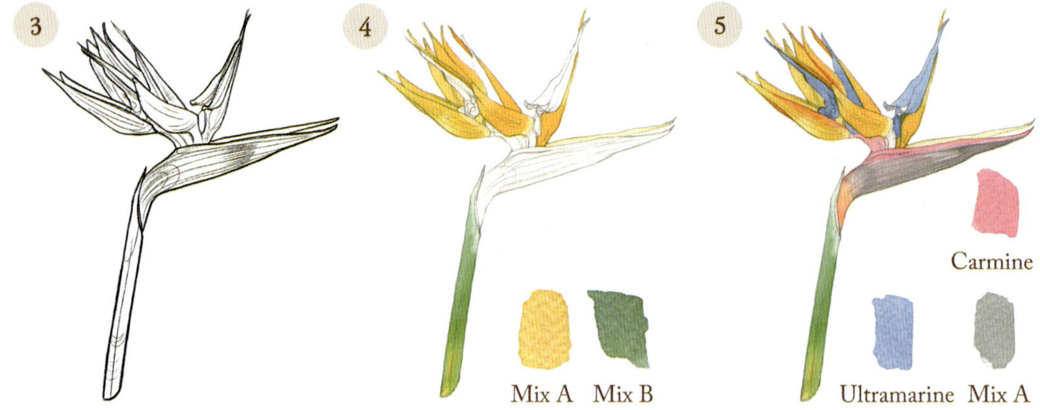

Step 3: Add a vertical line along the entire length of the stem to separate light and shadow areas. Then, using long, thin lines and following the direction of the head of the flower, add texture. Use shorter, rounded strokes to create texture on the lower portion of the petals to emphasize their roundness, and apply thin lines to the tips to highlight their sharpness. Define the shape of each individual petal and make the outline bolder. After that, you can proceed to the painting process.

Step 4: Let's start by painting the yellow petals of the flower. Create this mix:

- Mix A: cadmium yellow + a tiny touch of cadmium red + water = saturated warm yellow

Apply Mix A to the yellow petals, being careful not to accidentally cover any blue petals, which you should leave white for now. Next, add this color to the yellow area of the stand-alone petal on the right side.

Now, let's paint the stem of the flower using this mix:

- Mix B: green + any blue (cobalt blue, ultramarine, or indigo) + water = bluish-green

Paint the lower part of the stem with Mix A.

Once you get about one-quarter of the way up, switch to Mix B and continue with it until you're three-quarters to the top. After that, switch to water for the top quarter. While this layer is still wet, apply Mix B to the extreme left and right sides of the lower portion of the stem, allowing the yellow color to remain only in the center of that area. This will help create volume.

Step 5: We'll create a few simple mixes for the other petals and the body of the flower. Combine carmine and water for a vibrant pink. Then, for a medium blue, combine ultramarine or cobalt blue with water. After that, create this mix:

- Mix A: green + indigo + carmine + water = gray-purple

Apply the carmine and water to the upper side of the beak-like part of the flower, and then smooth the edge with a clean, dry brush. Use the same color to add some shadows to a few yellow petals. Next, use the ultramarine and water mix to cover the remaining blue petals.

Apply Mix 4A to the area where the stem ends and the body of the flower begins. Smooth out the edges, and then apply the carmine and water mix to the line separating the stem and body. Apply Mix A to the beak-like body, starting from the tip. Continue to the left, then blend the gray with the pink-yellow portion of the body. Wait for this layer to dry.

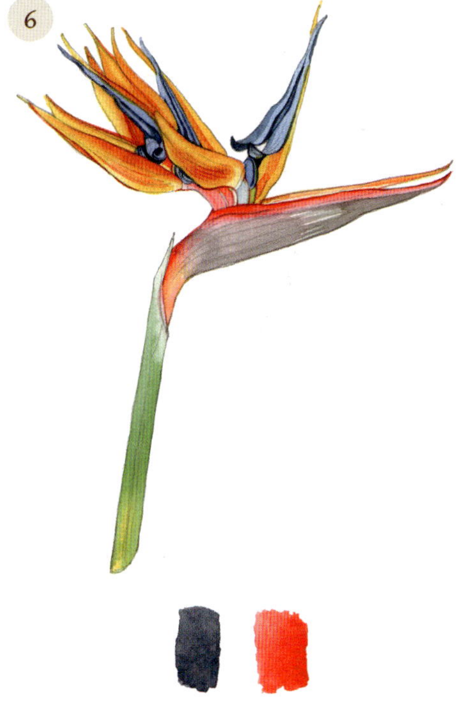

Step 6: Combine indigo with water for a saturated medium blue. Then, create this mix:

- Mix A: cadmium yellow + cadmium red + water = medium orange

With the indigo and water mix, paint long, thin lines across the surface of the blue petals. Pay attention to the folds and small details. Then, do the same thing with Mix A and the yellow petals. Smooth out the strokes and leave the lines with crisp edges on the thinner petals.

Create a more saturated version of carmine and water from Step 5 (more carmine and less water) to add some fullness to the upper border of the beak-like part of the flower. Smooth out the edges, then use this color to better outline some of the yellow petals.

Step 7: Create this new mix:

- Mix A: same as Mix 5A (green + indigo + carmine + water) but with more pigment and less water = dark gray-purple

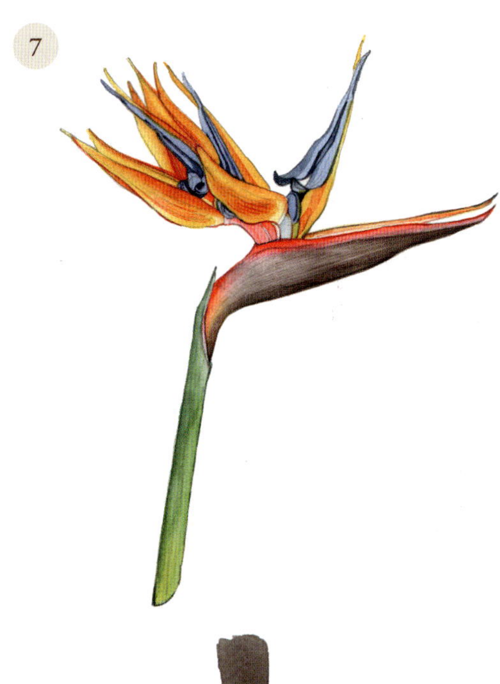

Apply Mix 5A to the body while avoiding the red and yellow parts, then smooth the edges. While still wet, apply Mix A to the lower side and the right tip. Let the darker color blend into the lighter one for a smooth transition. We need to add more detail to this part of the flower, but on a dry surface, so while the area we just painted is drying, let's finish the stem. Apply Mix 4B to the left side of the stem, then smooth out the edge.

Create long horizontal parallel lines on the body with the tip of your brush loaded with Mix A. Practice your lines on a spare sheet first, as these should be very thin and even. Finally, use the same mix to paint the outline of the stem so it is more visible in some areas, especially on the left side, and add this color to the tips of the beak. After that, you're done.

Protea

The protea, native to South Africa, is a symbol of resilience and beauty with its bold, intricate petals and unique structure. Known as the sugarbush, this stunning blossom comes in a variety of shapes and colors, often resembling a crown. In this tutorial, you'll learn how to use layering techniques to create a realistic effect in a stress-free way. It's the perfect opportunity to practice painting complex structures, delicate leaves, and soft gradients that bring the protea's vibrant beauty to life.

Colors Needed

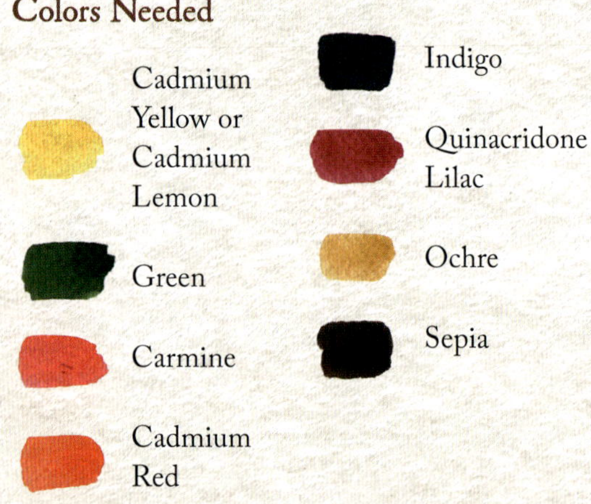

- Cadmium Yellow or Cadmium Lemon
- Green
- Carmine
- Cadmium Red
- Indigo
- Quinacridone Lilac
- Ochre
- Sepia

Suggested Paper Orientation: Vertical

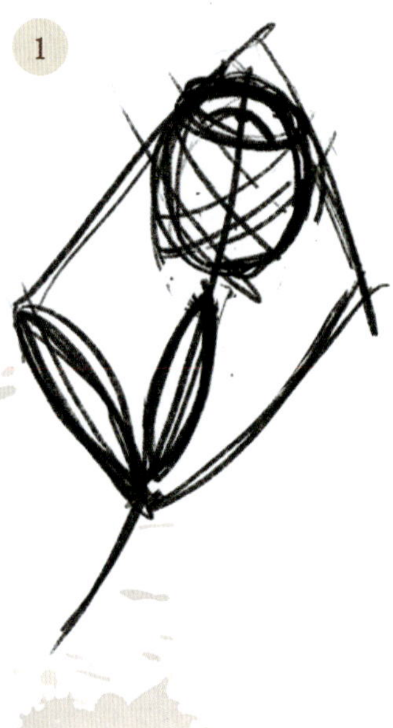

Step 1: Draw a slightly curved guide line from the top right to the lower left. Draw a shape resembling a rhombus or rectangle. Make sure its upper corner aligns with the beginning of the line, while the lower corner meets the line, leaving approximately one-third of the line extending beyond the shape. This one-third will represent the stem. Outline the head of the flower with an oval, positioning it at the top of the rhombus. On the upper side of the flower, draw a pointed top to depict the inner part of the flower.

Draw a grid in the flower head to guide you in the second step when outlining the petals. To do this, create four parallel lines with a curved motion from the top right to the lower left corner and another set of four lines going in the opposite direction. This should create a grid of horizontally oriented rhombuses. Then, outline the leaves using simple shapes, like long, thin ovals. Begin with the two largest leaves, both of which grow from the lower corner of the rhombus. The first leaf will align with the lower left side of the rhombus, while the second will be positioned along the center line, ending nearly where the flower head begins.

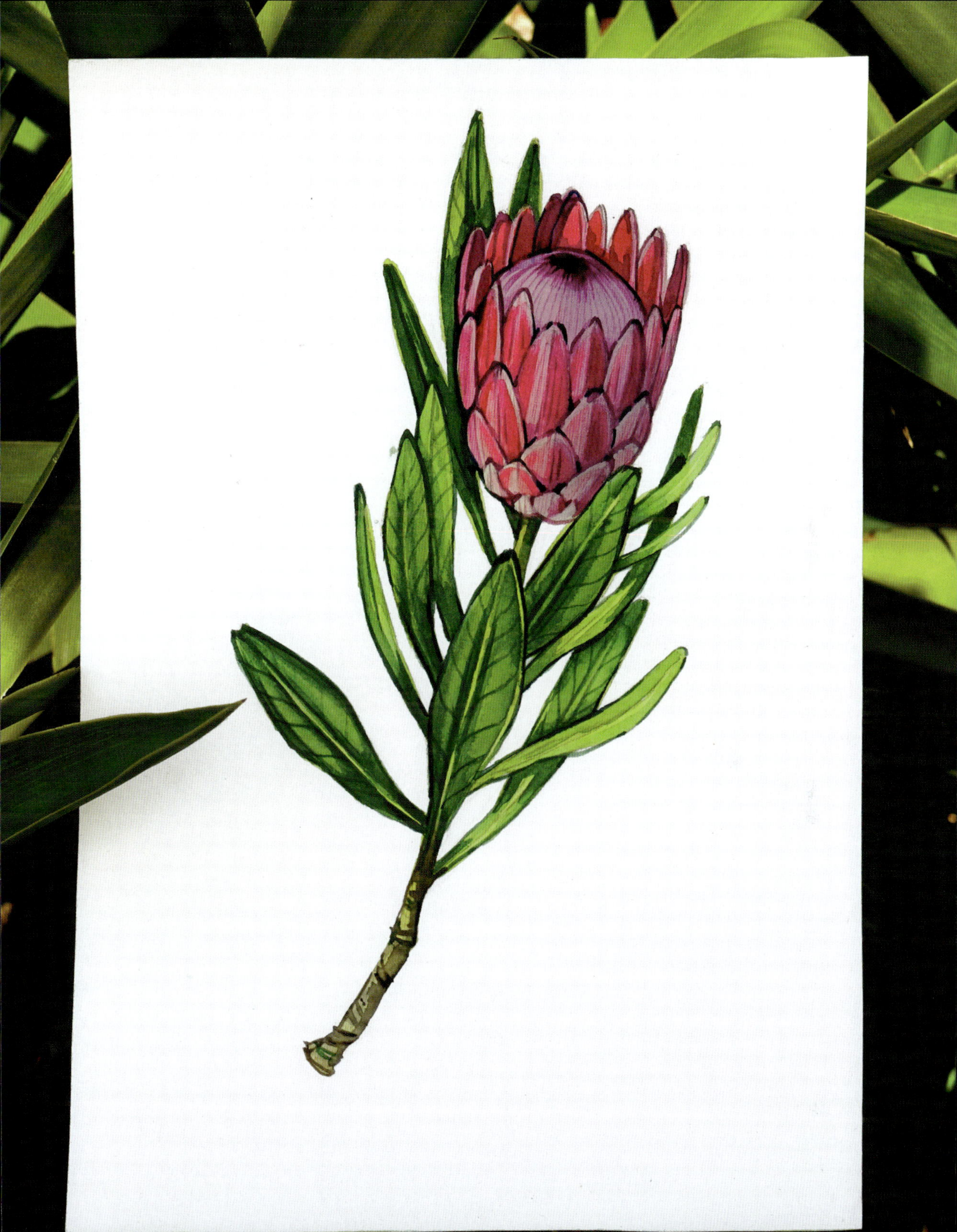

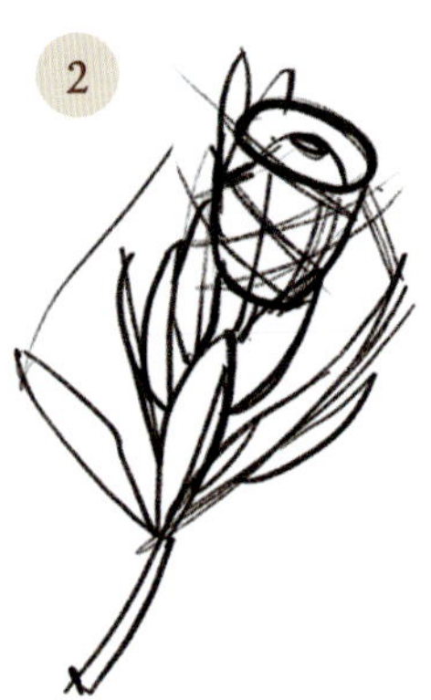

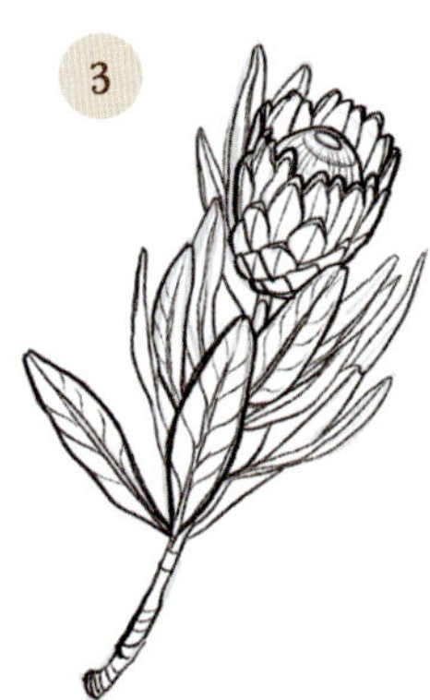

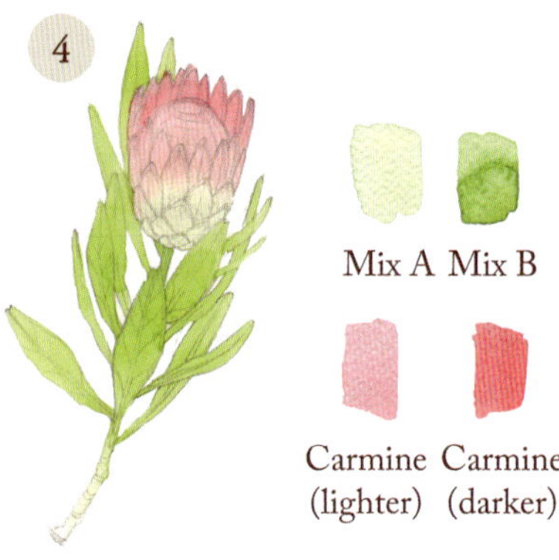

Step 2: Outline additional leaves, ensuring that some are positioned behind others. Add a few leaves behind the head of the flower as well; this will help create depth. Make sure the leaves extend in slightly different directions for an organic and spontaneous look. Then, add center lines to some of the larger leaves, making sure each line aligns with the direction of the leaf. These represent the main veins. Then, add some thickness to the stem where it's visible—at the top, where it attaches to the head of the flower, and beneath the leaves.

Step 3: Add detail to the head of the flower, using our grid structure as a base. The tips of the rhombuses will represent the top edges of the petals. Add some smaller petals between the larger ones on the top row; these should be thinner and taller than the petals below. Each layer should be smaller than the one beneath it, so the lowest petals should be the smallest. Add petals to the top layer that extend behind the flower, and then add a center line to the front petals, similar to what you did with the leaves in the previous step.

Add final touches like short horizontal lines on the lower part of the stem and some curving parallel lines from the top layer of the front petals to the point at the flower's center. Add thickness to the largest front petals by drawing a line parallel to the petal top, slightly lower. The petal tips are white, and this line will help separate the white tips from the rest of the petal while painting.

Finally, add side veins to the largest leaves. Now, we can move on to the painting process.

Step 4: Here, we will be using a layering technique to create a realistic effect and subtle blending on the leaves and the flower. Let's start with the leaves. Create these two mixes:

- Mix A: cadmium yellow or cadmium lemon + green + water = light watery green
- Mix B: same as Mix 4A (above) but with more pigment and less water = medium green

Starting from the top, apply Mix B to the whole surface of the leaves and the stem uniformly. Once you reach the part of the stem with no leaves, switch to Mix A to make this area lighter. Let everything dry.

Then, create two simple pink mixes, one watery pink made of carmine and water, and a second darker, more vibrant pink with less water and more pigment.

To create a blend, use Mix A for the base of the flower. Once you reach one-third of the way up, switch to the lighter pink mix, and then once you're two-thirds of the way up, switch to the darker pink mix. Then, while this layer is still wet, lift some color from the round center portion of the flower by washing your brush, drying it with a paper towel, and gently lifting excess color. Wait for this to dry.

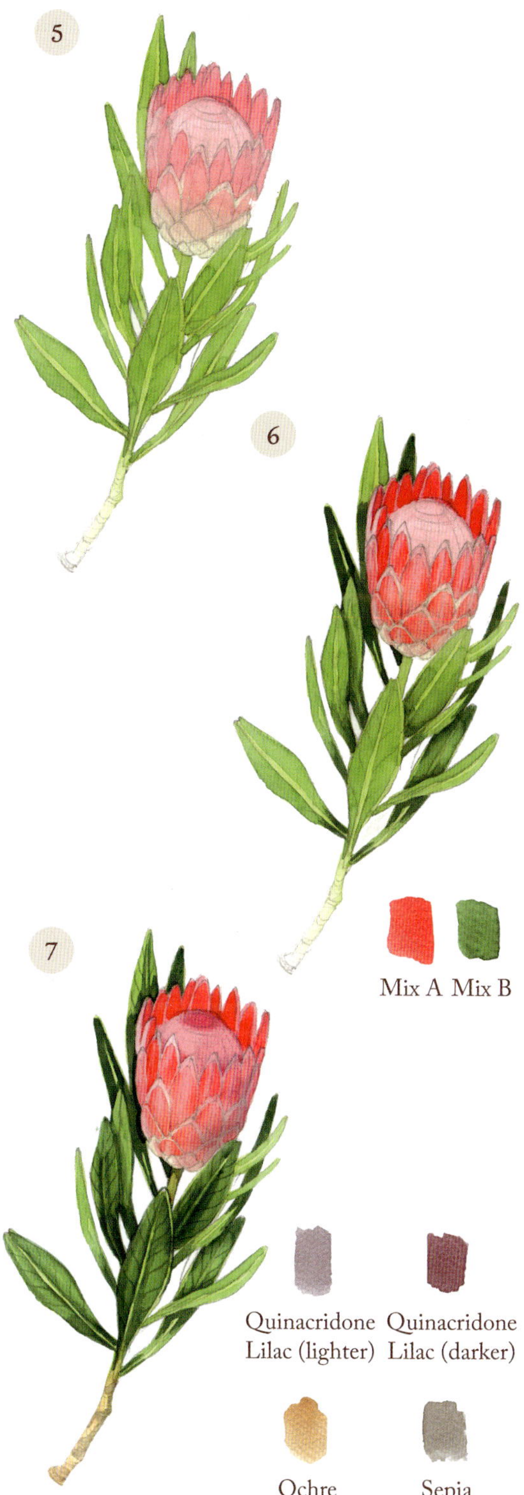

Step 5: Cover the front petals with the darker carmine and water mix from the previous step, avoiding the tips. As you reach the lower petals, switch to water. Cover all the back petals evenly with Mix 4B. Then, cover the front leaves with the same mix, but avoid the center vein.

Step 6: Create a new mix:

- Mix A: cadmium red + carmine + water = red

Cover individual petals with water, and then apply Mix A to the left and right sides of the petals, leaving the tips untouched. Smooth the centers if needed. For the smaller petals, just apply the color to the left and right sides and smooth the center without adding water first. Then, create a new mix for the leaves:

- Mix B: green + indigo + water = light blue-green

Use Mix B to darken the leaves in the background or where they intersect with other leaves. Smooth the edges as needed, and keep the veins light. Wait for this layer to dry.

Step 7: While the leaves dry, we'll move to the blossom. Focus on the round, internal part of the blossom that has remained untouched until now. Create two simple mixes: quinacridone lilac with lots of water for a light shade and lots of quinacridone lilac with only a little bit of water for a dark shade.

Apply the light quinacridone lilac mix to the entire surface of the round area. While this layer is still wet, apply the darker quinacridone lilac mix to the top of the area in a circular manner and around the front petals. If the color starts to spread too much, clean the affected area with a clean, dry brush.

(Step 7 continued)

While this section dries, shift focus back to the leaves. Use Mix 6B and your medium or small brush to apply this color near the center vein of the first large leaf of your choice, and then, as quickly as possible, smooth the edge with a clean, dry brush. Next, apply the color around the edges of the same leaf and soften the edges. This should create a leaf that is darker near the center vein, lighter in the middle, and darker again around the edges. Repeat this for all the large leaves.

Then, use Mix 6B to add some intersections of the leaves to enhance depth, and use it to cast a shadow from the blossom on the upper part of the stem. Now, let's create a light yellow mix for the stem by combining ochre with water. Apply this color to the portion of the stem near the blossom and to the lower, wider section of the stem. While doing this, the leaves should have dried fully, so switch to your smallest brush, and using a thin line of Mix 6B, outline smaller lateral veins on all the large leaves. Then, return to painting the blossom, which should now be dry.

Take the light quinacridone lilac mix and apply it to the entire right part of the flower. Once you reach the center, and while the paint is still wet, switch to water to complete the wash. This light wash will create general volume. As a final step, mix a light brown by combining sepia and water. Apply it to the right side of the lower stem. Smooth the edge and use thin lines to add texture to the stem using the same color.

Step 8: Mix a new color:

- Mix A: carmine + cadmium red + water = pink-red

Apply Mix A to the right side of each front petal, except for the tips of the large petals and the smallest lower petals. Use the same color to outline the individual front petals. While this dries, let's head back to the leaves.

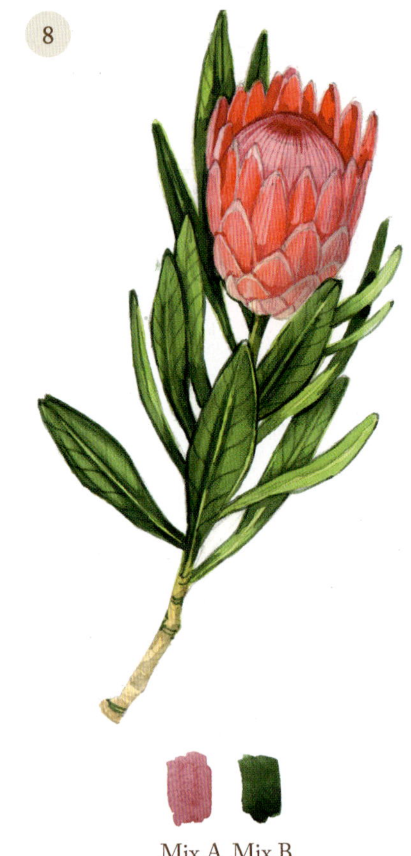

Mix A Mix B

Darken some of the back leaves even more with Mix 6B, adding volume to the leaves by following the technique from the previous step. Use this color to darken the right side of the lower portion of the stem and to add texture to the same part of the stem using thin horizontal lines. Next, create a new mix:

- Mix B: green + indigo + water = dark green

Use Mix B to create thin outlines on some of the leaves, ensuring the outline is thin and interrupted in some areas. Then, return to the blossom. Use Mix A to add texture to the flower petals and to the round inner part. To do this, use the dry brushing technique (page 18) with very thin lines, making sure there's almost no water on your brush and that the lines are as fine as possible.

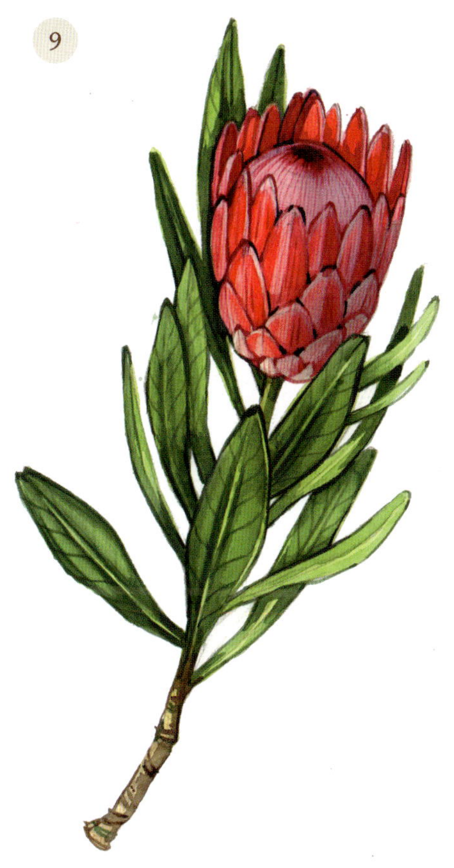

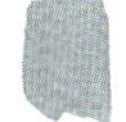 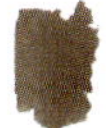 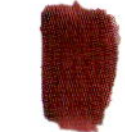

Indigo Sepia Mix A

Step 9: Before adding final details to the blossom, create a light blue mix by combining indigo and water. Apply it to the entire right side of the blossom. Once you reach the center of the flower, and while the color is still wet, switch to clean water to cover the remaining left part of the blossom. This wash will reinforce the light and shadow effect on the flower, making it appear even more three-dimensional. While this layer dries, let's add the final touches to the leaves and stem.

Create a simple mix of sepia and water for a dark brown. Use this for final stem details. Then, using Mix 8A, enhance the dark lines in certain areas of the leaves, with extra attention paid to the front leaves. Make sure the darkest leaves are those behind the blossom. Add extra texture to the stem with the same color or by adding a bit more pigment.

Now, it's time to add the final touches to the blossom. Increase the saturation of the flower using Mix 8A. Apply this color to the left and right sides of some petals, and smooth the edges if needed. Then, create a new mix:

- Mix A: carmine + cadmium red + quinacridone lilac + water = dark red-purple

Use Mix A to darken the spot on the round inner part of the flower, deepen some areas of the back petals, and create a thin outline separating the round inner part from the back petals.

Then, with the very tip of your small brush, use Mix A to accentuate some of the petal edges, especially their tips, with ultra-thin lines. Make sure that these outlines are spotty rather than uniform to avoid flattening the flower; we just want to add accents to specific points. Finally, use the same color to add even more contrast to the dark spot on the round inner part. That's it! Your protea flower is ready.

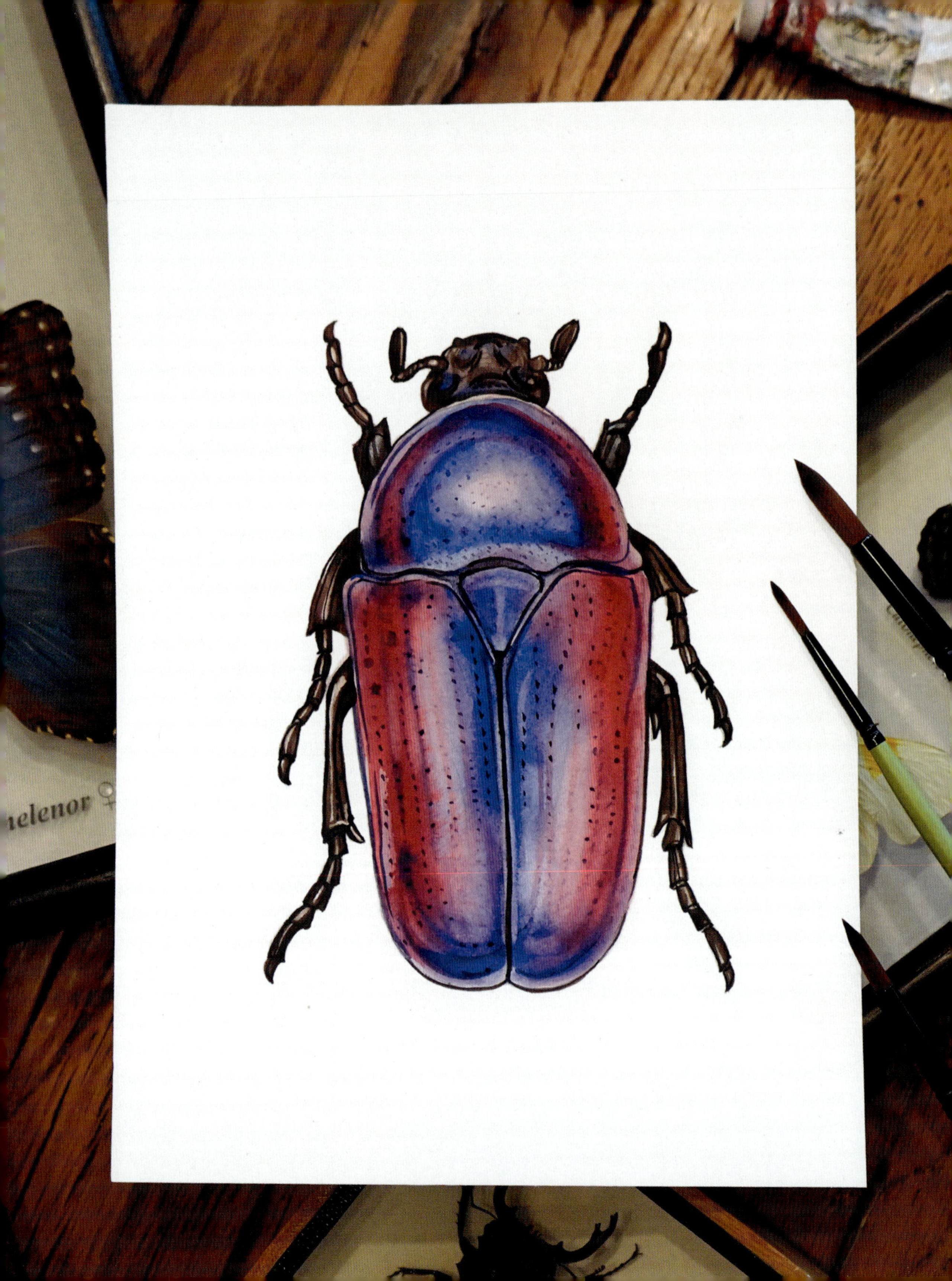

African Jewel Beetle

The African jewel beetle truly lives up to its name, dazzling with metallic hues that make it look more like a precious gem than an insect. Known for their shimmering, jewel-like exoskeletons, jewel beetles are often admired for their beauty and unique reflective properties. In this tutorial, you'll learn how to replicate the beetle's vivid purple and pink hues, capturing the iridescence that makes them so striking. With just your standard watercolor set, we'll explore how to use color gradation to mimic this shiny effect, making the beetle's surface come alive with light, without relying on special iridescent paints.

Colors Needed

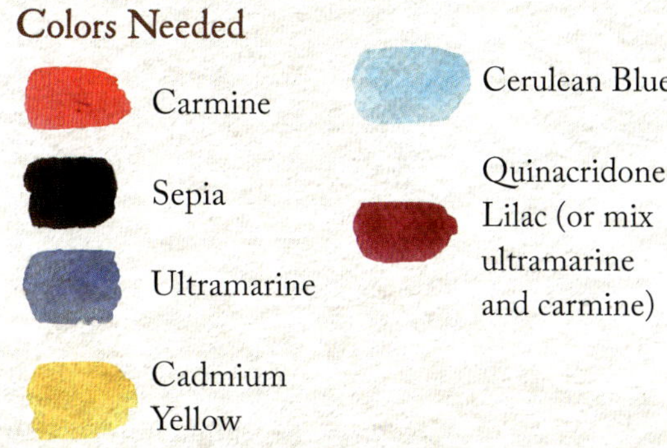

Suggested Paper Orientation: Vertical

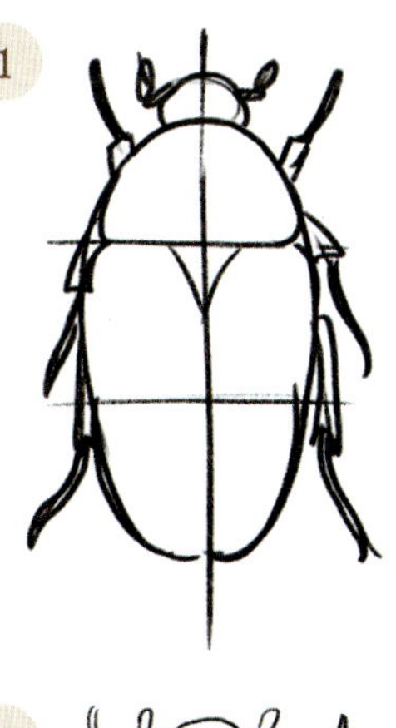

Step 1: Draw a straight vertical line in the middle of the paper. Draw an oval so that the line is in its center. The height of the oval should be about double its width. Divide the oval horizontally into two equal parts. Create a small horizontal oval at the top for the head. Add antennae on both sides. The lower two-thirds of the oval will be the main part of the body, where the wings are hidden. To make this part more realistic, create a small, curvy triangle in the middle. Then, add the legs: one pair at the top of the body facing upward and two pairs on the lower part of the body facing downward.

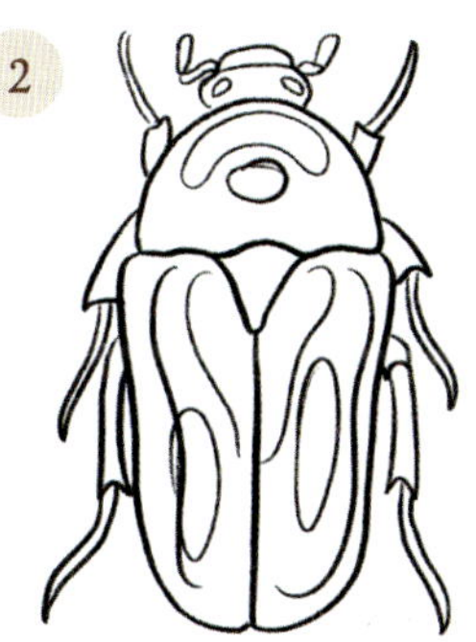

Step 2: Now for some details. Draw two ovals on the top part of the body: one larger oval at the top to represent the reflective area and another smaller one lower in the middle of that area to show the highlight. Then, create an oval on each side of the lower part of the beetle for highlights. Next, create some lines on both sides, following the natural movement of the beetle. These lines will help us apply different colors more accurately. Finally, add more details to the legs, dividing them into two parts. The upper part should be bigger and bolder than the lower part.

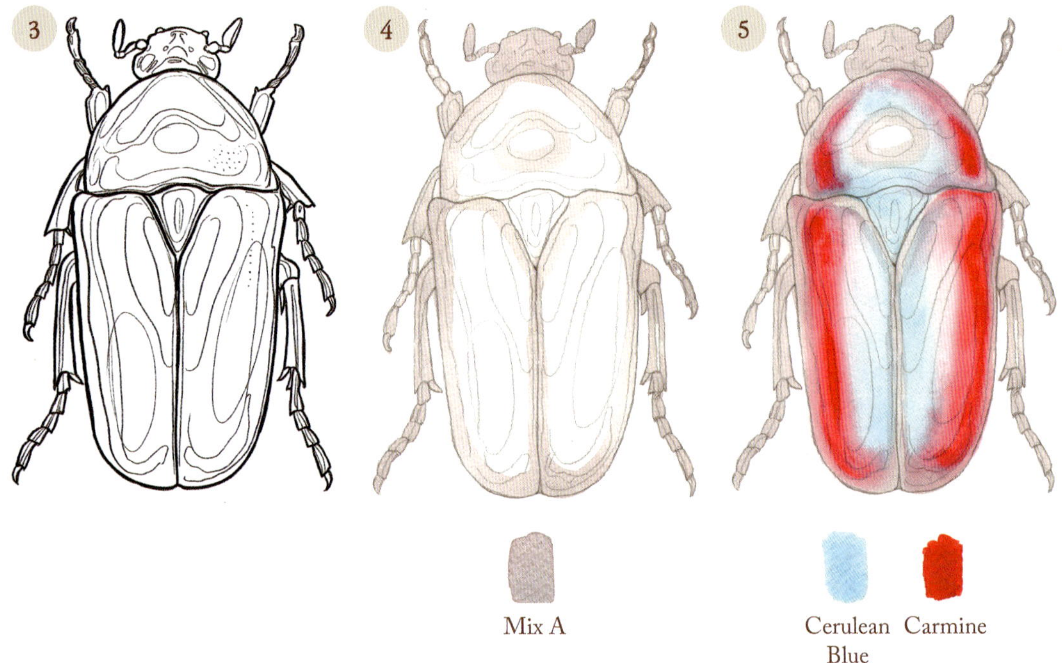

Step 3: Finalize the drawing by refining the general outline and adding more lines to the body, similar to what we did in the previous steps. Work on the structure of the legs: Divide the lower portion into sections with pointed edges. Make some lines on the legs and on each section as well. Add some ovals to the center triangle to highlight the reflective area. Add some dots on the body and head to enrich the texture, if desired. Now, let's bring this beetle to life!

Step 4: Create a light pink mix:

- Mix A: carmine + sepia + ultramarine + a touch of cadmium yellow + water = light, watery pink

Use Mix A to cover the entire head, the borders of the body, and all the legs, except for the tiny highlight of the upper and middle legs. Outline the center line and the circle around the white highlight on the upper part of the body. This light color will represent the shiny tone on the beetle.

Step 5: Mix cerulean blue with water for a light blue mix. Create a second mix by combining carmine with a touch of water to create a bright and vibrant pink. With a medium or large brush, use the cerulean and water mix to cover the top area of the body, except for the white spot in the middle. Cover the white parts on the lower part of the body. Then, while this color is still wet, apply the carmine and water mix to the left and right sides of the top and lower parts of the body. Make sure not to cover the light pink color on the sides that remained from Step 4. The vibrant pink should start to blossom and blend into the blue, which is what we want. However, we also want this color to remain in place, so if you see it spreading too much, pull it back with a clean, dry brush. Add some more of the carmine and water mix to the center of the pink area for more contrast. Wait for this layer to dry.

Step 6: Create a medium blue mix by combining ultramarine and water. We will use the wet-on-wet technique (page 17) here, working on the top, left, and right parts of the body separately. With a medium or large brush, cover the top part of the body with clean water. Cover everything, including the white spot in the middle. Then, apply the ultramarine and water mix around the white spot. Apply the cerulean blue and water mix from Step 5 to the lower edge of the upper part of the body. Let this layer dry completely before proceeding to the lower left side.

Repeat the same process on the left side, but this time add the ultramarine and water mix to the right border of this area and its lower part. If the color starts to expand too much, pull it back where you originally placed it with a clean, dry brush. Repeat the exact same process on the right part of the beetle's body, making sure to leave a thin line of dry, white paper between the left and right parts of the body. Use the same method on the remaining small area in the center of the beetle, only placing the ultramarine and water mix in the middle. Let this dry completely before proceeding.

Step 7: Mix quinacridone lilac with water. If you don't have quinacridrone lilac, you can create a similar color by mixing ultramarine and carmine. Using the same technique as in the previous step, work one beetle section at a time to add additional layers. Start by covering one of the parts of the beetle with water, then add the quinacridone lilac and water mix to the pink area. While the layer is still wet, add more of the ultramarine mix from Step 6 to the blue areas for extra saturation. Repeat these steps on all sections of the beetle.

Before this layer is completely dry, lift off some paint from the red and blue areas with a medium brush. Use circular movements to create an area of reflected light. Do the same with a thin, straight stroke on the small center area of the beetle.

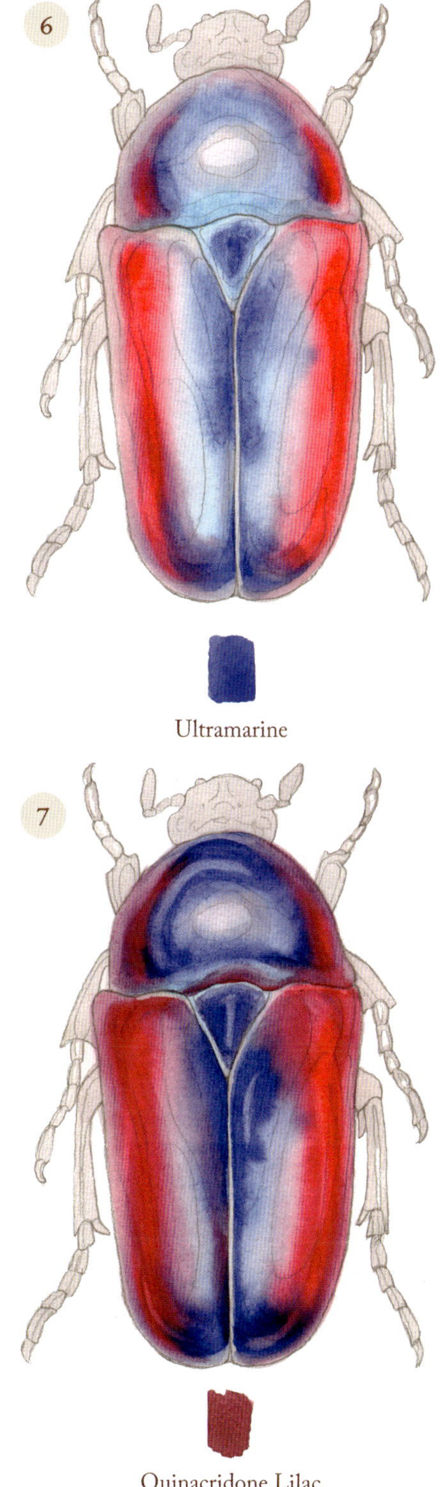

Ultramarine

Quinacridone Lilac

Step 8: Create two dark mixes for the legs of the beetle:

- Mix A: sepia + carmine + water = medium brown
- Mix B: Mix 8A (above) + more sepia + less water = brown

Use the ultramarine and water mix from Step 6 to add some blue spots to the head. Add two round spots: one on the left side of the head and one on the right. While these spots dry, apply Mix A to the legs, making sure to avoid the highlight on the small sections of the legs. Do this one leg at a time, and then add Mix B to the darkest parts of the legs, such as where one section meets another and the area closer to the body.

Next, apply Mix A to the whole surface of the head, avoiding the highlights on the antennae. Then, apply Mix B to the darkest areas to emphasize the eyes and the outline.

Step 9: Cover the entire surface of the beetle's body with clean water. This will help visually unite its parts and prepare the surface for the final layer of color. Use the carmine and water mix from Step 5 to enhance the vibrancy of the sides of the beetle and the ultramarine and water mix from Step 6 to darken the central part. At this stage, you can also cover the white line. Use the carmine and ultramarine mixes to create vertical lines that follow the natural shape of the beetle to add texture. Then, when the surface of the paper gets drier, create small random dots using the same colors across the entire surface of the body, including the lighter areas.

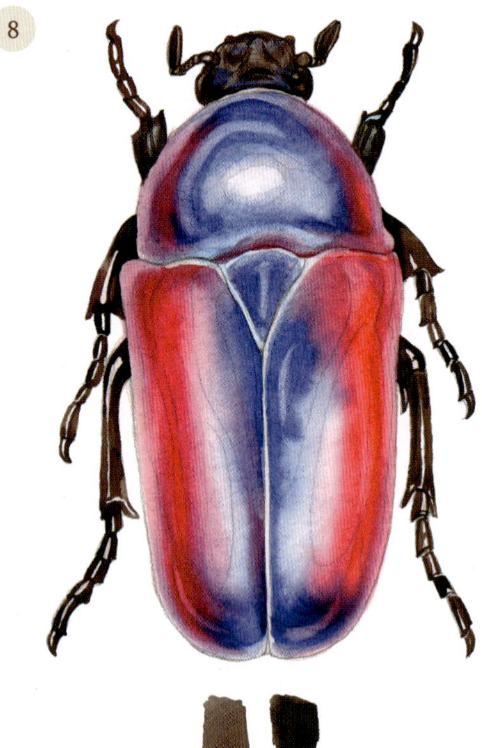

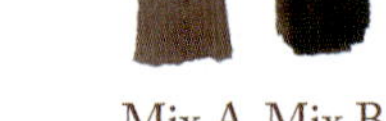

Mix A Mix B

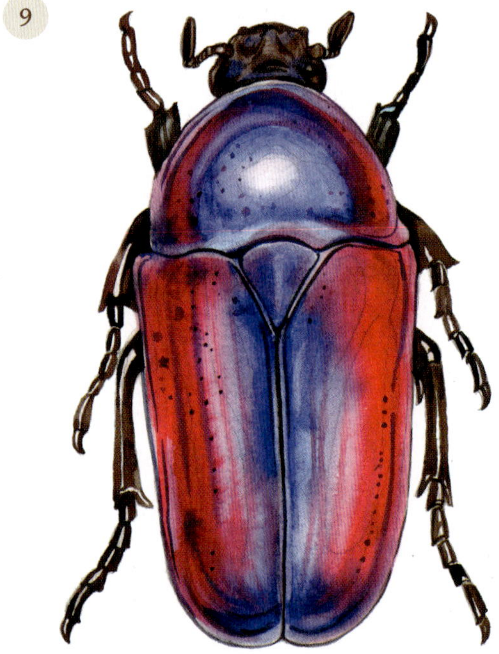

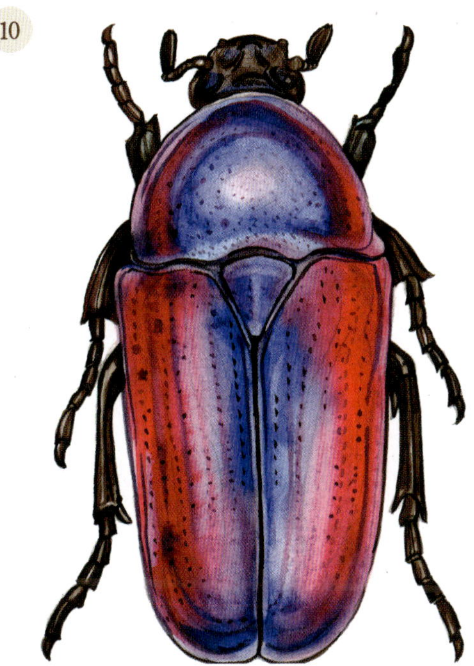

Lift some paint from the white dividing line with a clean, dry brush. Do the same from the highlight on the top area of the body, if needed. Let this layer dry, and for the final step of this stage, use Mix 8B or a similar dark, almost black color to create a long, thin line along the middle of the white line. Use the same methods and color to outline the edges of each section of the body. Create some additional dots with the same color, this time on the dry surface of the beetle. Finally, use Mix 8B and a very thin line to create an outline around the beetle. Let dry.

Step 10: Use your medium or small brush and clean water to cover the highlights on the legs. This will activate the brown on the legs and make the highlight less visible. Meanwhile, use Mix 8B or a similar dark color to add more dots across the entire surface of the beetle, this time on a dry surface. Once the legs have dried, use the same color to add texture to the sections of the legs with thin lines. These lines will also help visually separate the sections of the legs from one another. Use the same color to darken the outline of the beetle in certain areas even more. After this, your painting is done.

Giraffe

The giraffe is a true marvel. Native to sub-Saharan Africa, these gentle giants are known for their graceful movements and impressive height, which make them stand out in the savannah. Their coat pattern, unique to each individual, serves as camouflage in the wild, blending them into their environment. In this tutorial, you will learn how to seamlessly blend the giraffe's spot pattern into its skin texture, making it look natural and integrated, rather than disconnected or scattered.

Colors Needed

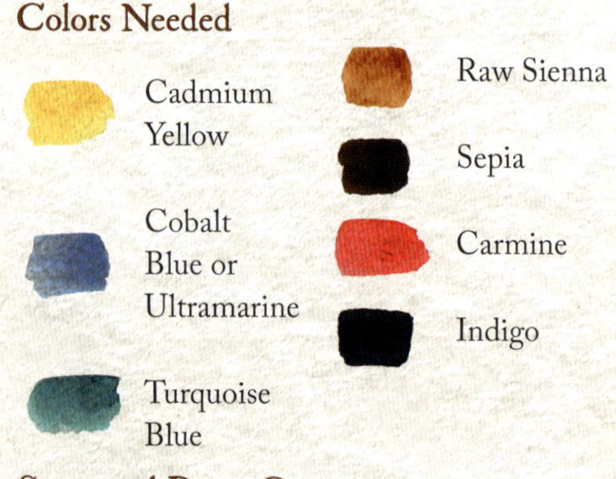

Suggested Paper Orientation: Vertical

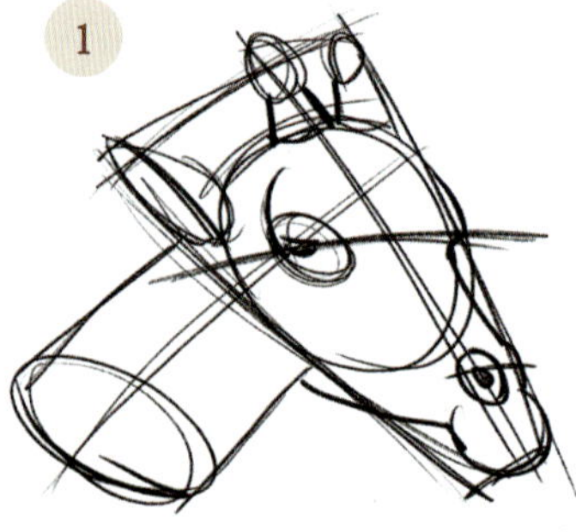

Step 1: Draw a diagonal line in the middle of your sheet of paper that goes from the lower left side to the upper right side. This will be the line of the neck. Next, give thickness to the neck by adding two parallel lines. Place an oval at the base of the neck to help visualize that the neck is round and to define its border.

Define the head with an oval on the top half of the diagonal line. The oval should be placed more toward the right of the diagonal line. Keep in mind that we are viewing the giraffe from the side, so there will be a foreshortening effect, and the left (front) side will appear larger than the right. With this in mind, create a truncated triangle, with the base representing the line of the ears and ossicones (horn-like protuberances) and the truncated tip representing the muzzle. Add a central line that is placed more toward the right side of the triangle.

Create a guide line for the eyes. Place the left eye in the middle of the left half of the oval of the head, and place the right eye on the same line, but position it along the right edge of the oval. Create a similar guide line for the nostrils. Place the left nostril aligned with the middle line of the head and the right nostril aligned with the right outline of the triangle. Outline the muzzle with an oval, then outline the ear using a triangle. Then, add thickness to the ear by drawing a line in the middle, parallel to the right side. Finally, outline the ossicones with two small truncated triangles with circles in their tips.

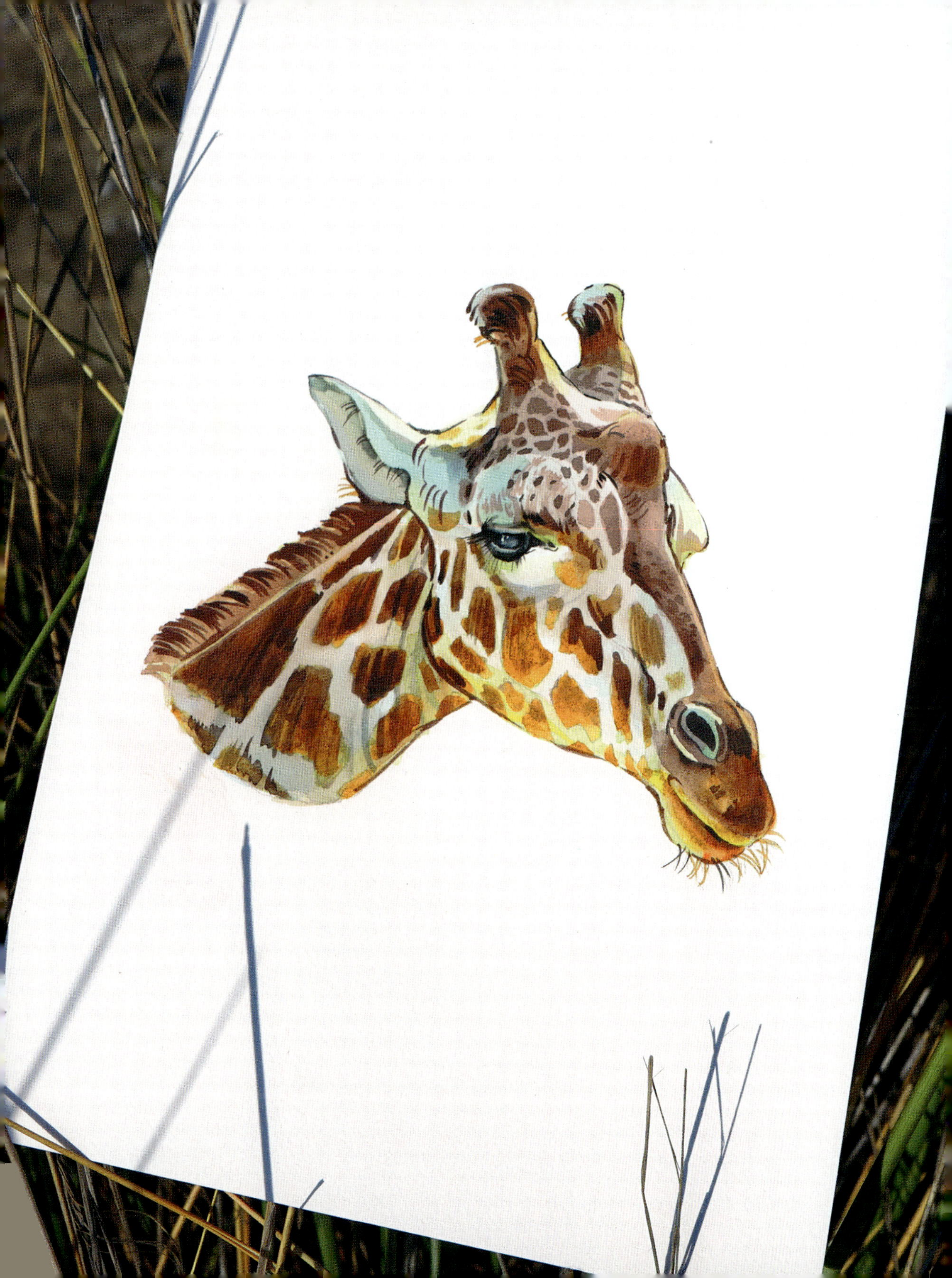

Step 2: Define the shape of the giraffe's head more clearly by outlining the jawline, the mouth, and the nose bridge. Outline the mane with short, almost horizontal strokes. Sketch the bump on the forehead with a semicircle, then sketch the area above the eye with an oval. Add some additional details to the ear and ossicones, and add typical spot patterns to the neck and face. Make sure to vary the sizes and shapes of the spots to achieve a more realistic look.

Step 3: Remove the guide lines. Add some skin folds to the neck under the jaw using curved lines. Add more detail to the eye and continue adding spots and texture to the head and neck of the giraffe, using irregular spots on the neck and cheek, and some smaller circles and dots on the forehead and near the eye. Add some fur to the muzzle and refine the shape of the ossicones and nose. When you're satisfied with the drawing, you can move on to painting.

Step 4: Create a light yellow by combining cadmium yellow with water. Then, create this mix:

- Mix A: cobalt blue or ultramarine + turquoise blue + water = light blue

Apply the cadmium yellow and water mix to the muzzle, the mane, the lower part of the neck, some of the middle of the ear, around the nose, on the bridge of the nose, on the right eye, on top of the left eye, and on the lower spots on the jaw. Apply Mix A near the yellow areas once they have dried. Apply it to the remaining part of the ear, the ossicones, on top of the eye, around the yellow spots, and in the nostrils. At this stage, some parts of the giraffe should remain white, such as some of the spots, the forehead, and the visible eye. Wait for this layer to dry.

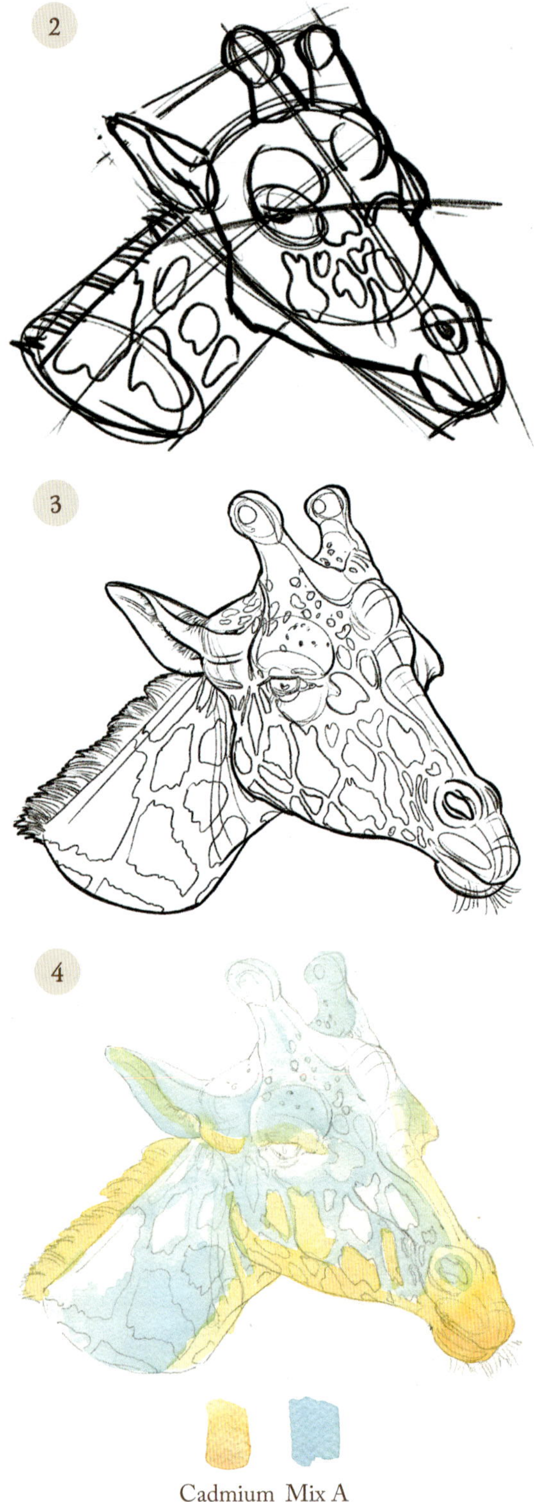

Step 5: Create a new mix:

- Mix A: cadmium yellow + raw sienna + water = vibrant orange

Apply this mix to all the spots on the jaw, neck, and the area to the right from the ear (near the left ossicone). Also, paint the lower part of the right eye, and then smooth the edge for a seamless transition. Paint the bump on the forehead, then smooth the edges with a clean, dry brush. Add this color to the middle part of the ossicones, smoothing the edges. Introduce this color to the tip of the muzzle as well, and while it's still wet, smooth the edges like you did in the other areas in this step. Add some sepia to Mix A and apply it to the lower part of the tip of the muzzle without reaching the edge, and then smooth out the edge. Wait for this layer to dry.

Step 6: Let's increase the contrast with this mix:

- Mix A: sepia + carmine + raw sienna + water = medium warm brown-red

Apply this color to the bridge of the nose, the forehead, and the ossicones. Add this color to the mane as well, but leave some thin lines of untouched dry space to imitate the hair. Add small spots on the top of the forehead and some texture above the eye using thin, short, round strokes. Darken the top of the spots on the jaw and create lines in the two spots to the left of the jaw that will be the folds of skin. Wait for this layer to dry.

Step 7: In this step, we will make the surface of the giraffe look more unified and less scattered. But before that, add more of Mix 4A to the ear, the top parts of the ossicones, and around the nostrils. When this dries, take your medium or large brush, load it with clean water, and apply it to the entire surface of the giraffe, avoiding just the eye area and the white spot on the top of the forehead.

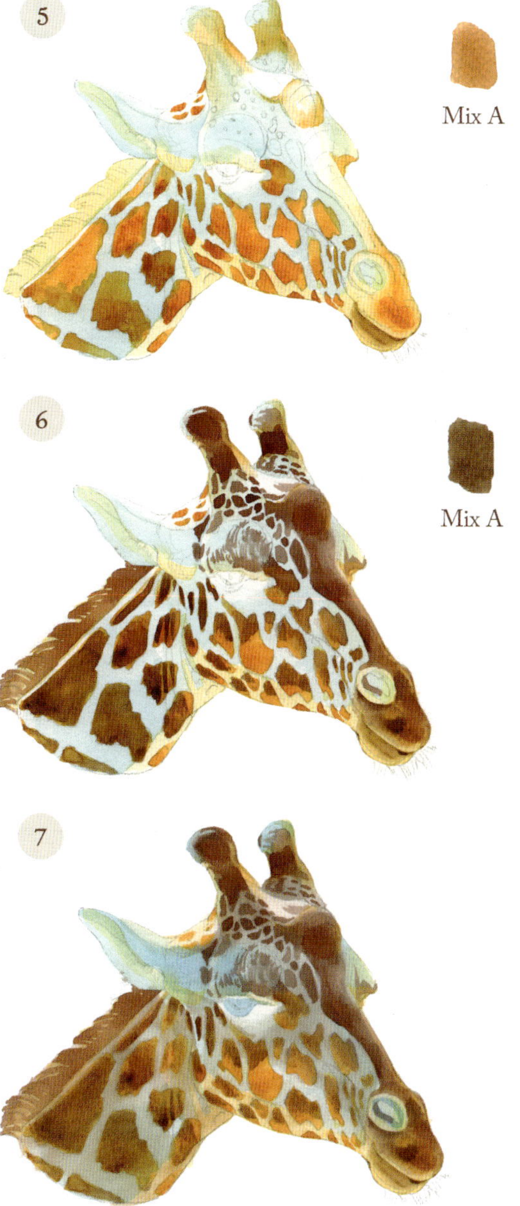

Be gentle with your brush, as you only want to reactivate the watercolor already on the paper so it unifies the surface without completely washing out the previous layers. Once you're done, wait for this layer to dry.

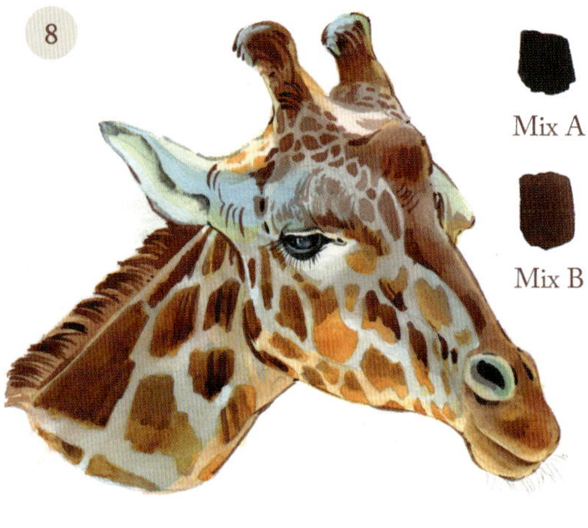 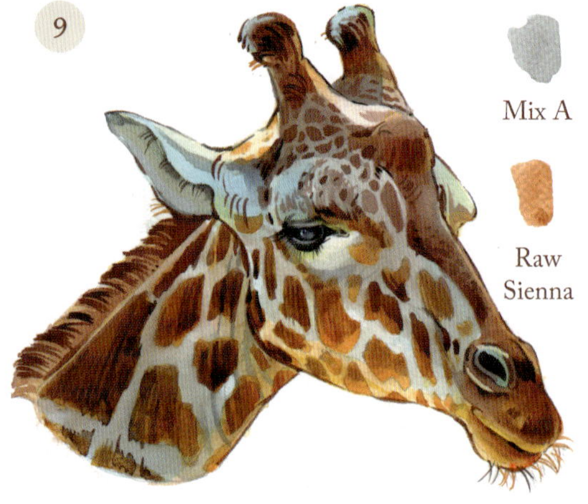

Apply Mix B to the mane with short, curvy strokes. Make the strokes denser near the ear, as they will be in shadow and darker, and space them out a bit more as you move lower. Use the same color to add details to the face, especially in the center where the bridge of the nose transitions into the jaw, as there is a shadow there. Paint thin lines to add texture to the top parts of the ossicones to imitate fur. Add similar texture to the bump on the forehead and on the ear. Darken the spots on the top side of the neck, and restore the folds in the spots where you may have lost them in previous steps. Use the same color and the tip of your brush to refine the outline of the giraffe on the neck, muzzle, and bridge of the nose.

Step 9: Create this mix:

- Mix A: sepia + any blue color + water = neutral light blue-gray

Use Mix A to darken the inside part of the ear, the white spaces between the spots on the lower part of the neck, the area above the eye, and the shadow area on the right ossicone. Also, add some shadow under the eye and forehead in the area where many spots are concentrated.

Switch to Mix 8B and add final touches to the muzzle and the area around the nostrils. Add more small spots to the area above the eye, the forehead, and the bridge of the nose. Add Mix 8B to the spots on the neck using long vertical strokes that follow the natural shape of the giraffe to outline the movement of the neck and accentuate the folds of the skin. Use short, curvy strokes to outline the tiny hairs growing out of the chin and ears. Then, use the same color to make the lower and left outlines of the jaw more visible. Add more tiny hairs growing out of the chin, but this time, use a mix of raw sienna and water. Finally, use Mix 8B to add an additional layer of saturation on the lowest part of the jaw. After that, your painting is complete!

Step 8: Here we will add contrast to the giraffe, which will really enhance the realistic effect. Create two dark mixes:

- Mix A: indigo + sepia + a touch of water = cool, almost black color (tends toward blue)
- Mix B: carmine + sepia + a touch of water = warm, almost black color (tends toward red)

Paint the eye with the tip of your brush using Mix A. Make sure to leave a highlight on the lower side of the eyelid lighter than the rest of the eye. Use the tip of your small brush and very thin strokes to paint the eyelashes. Also, darken the eye socket.

Coquerel's Sifaka

The Coquerel's sifaka, a striking lemur species native to Madagascar, has a beautiful coat of dense fur in contrasting shades of white and brown, which helps it blend into its habitat. Its diet consists mainly of leaves, flowers, and fruit, making it an important seed disperser for its ecosystem. In this tutorial, you'll learn how to depict the fur's varying textures and colors across different parts of the sifaka's body. You'll also master painting white fur without using white pigment.

Colors Needed

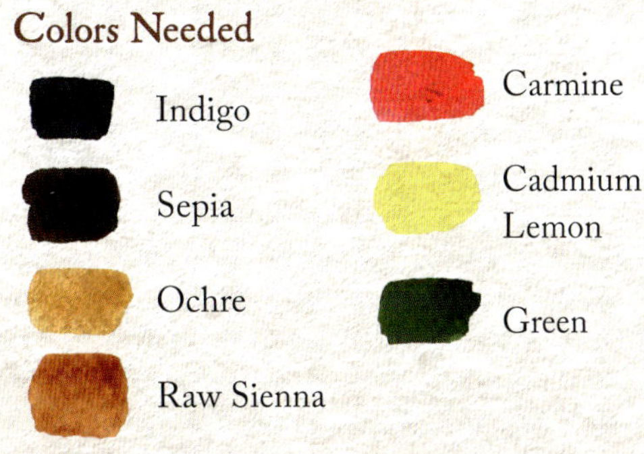

Suggested Paper Orientation: Vertical

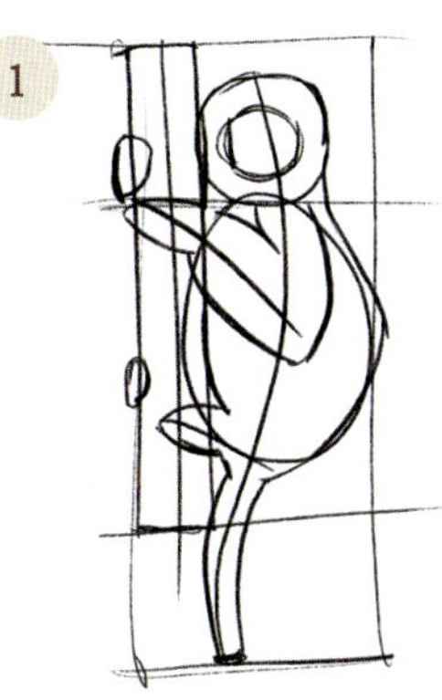

Step 1: Draw a rectangle that's three times as tall as it is wide. Draw horizontal lines to divide it into three parts, with the middle section being larger than either end. Outline the branch by drawing a line starting from the lowest guide line, extending until it reaches the top edge of the main rectangle. Add thickness to the branch by drawing lines along the sides, with the left side corresponding to the left edge of the main rectangle. Draw ovals for the body and head. Draw a smaller circle inside the head for the face. Draw a wavy line through the animal that indicates the direction and movement of the body and tail. Finish the tail at the end of the large rectangle. Make it look thicker with additional two parallel lines, and then use ovals for arms and smaller ovals for the hands and feet.

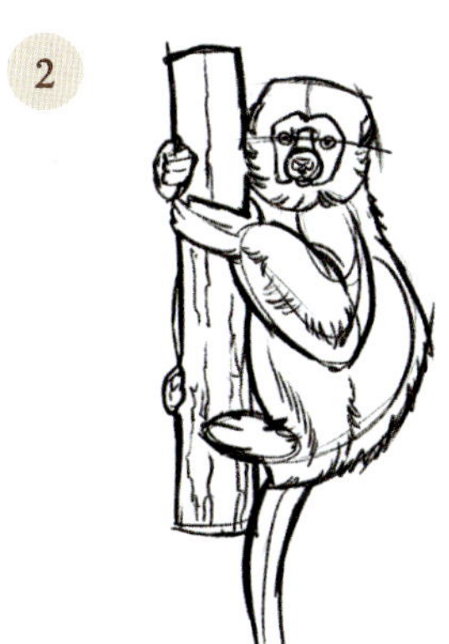

Step 2: Erase the guide lines and add a few new ones for the eye line and the middle of the face. Use these lines to outline the features of the face, especially the eyes and the nose. Define the outline of the sifaka more clearly, making sure that the shapes transition smoothly into each other. For example, instead of having just an oval back, make it more pointed by creating a break on the back with two lines. Then, begin outlining the fur. Use the same zigzag strokes for the arms, the lower part of the face, and the back to start showing fur. Give the hands and feet a more realistic look by working on the individual fingers. Start adding texture to the branch with long, thin, irregular vertical lines.

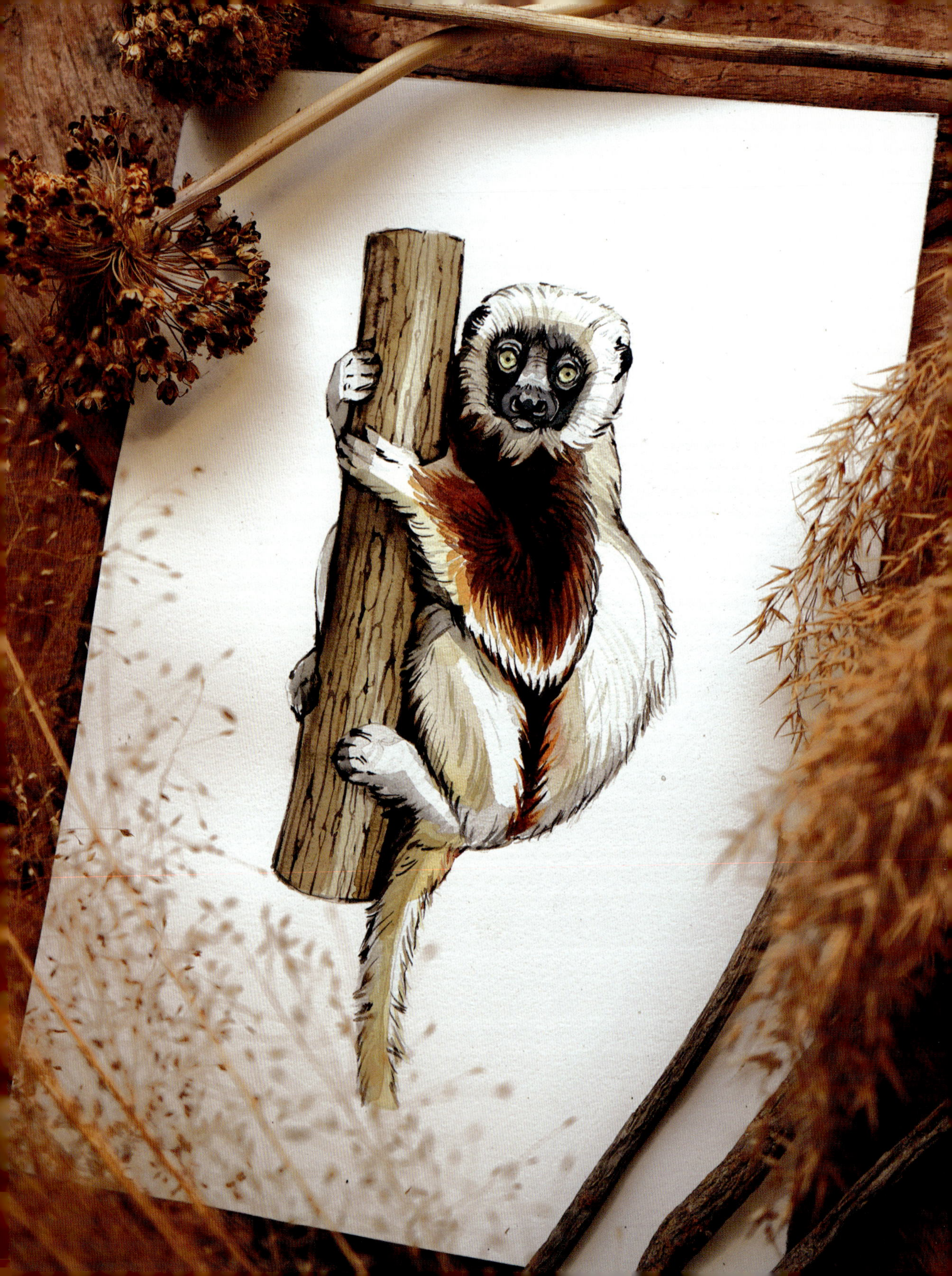

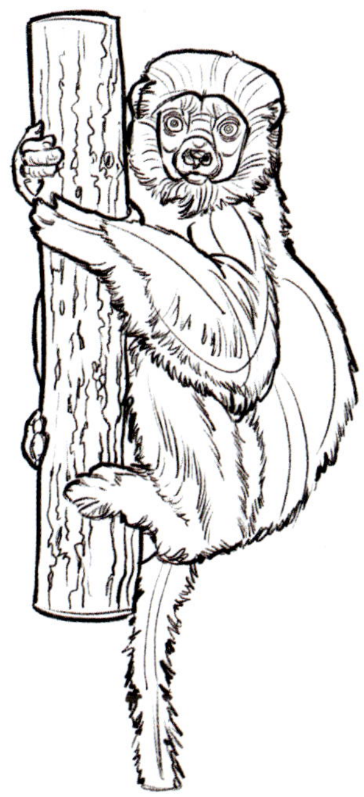

Step 3: Dedicate this stage to adding the final details to the animal and the branch. Use short strokes for more hair for different parts of the animal and the face, as well as for the tail, legs, arms, and back. Refine the facial features, darken the nostrils, add more details to the eyes—include eyelids—outline the cheeks, and add the ears. Add more details to the hands and toes, and add even more texture to the branch. You're ready to paint!

Step 4: Create three color mixes: two for the sifaka and one for the branch (ochre mixed with water for a light, watery beige).

- Mix A: indigo + sepia + a good amount of water = neutral watery light gray
- Mix B: same as Mix 4A (above) but with more pigment and less water = slightly darker gray

Apply Mix A with small individual brushstrokes to the right outline, the area under the elbow, the left side of the tail, the fur around the face, the left hand, and the tip of the right foot. Apply Mix B to the face—except for the eyes—the nostrils, the part of the nose between the eyes, the left side under the face, and under the right foot, and use it to outline some of the fur on the visible arm. Cover the whole surface of the branch with the ochre and water mix and wait for this layer to dry.

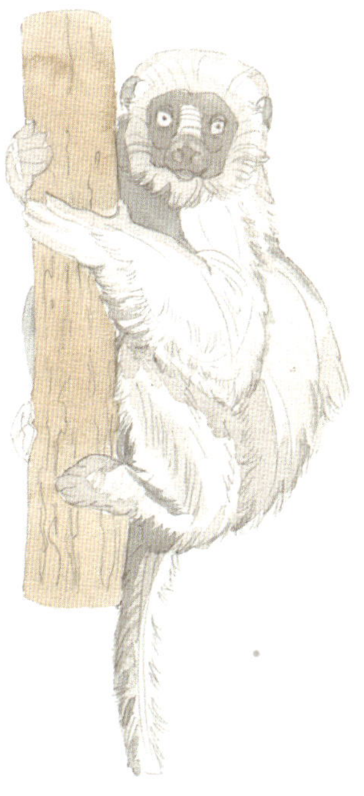

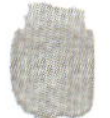

Ochre Mix A Mix B

Step 5: Combine raw sienna and water for a saturated orange. Next, mix sepia with water for a light brown. Then, create a darker variation of the same color by adding less water and more pigment. Start by covering some areas of the sifaka with the raw sienna and water mix, such as the arm. Just like in the previous step, make sure the area of this color has irregular edges to imitate fur. Use the same method you used in the last step and create strokes that are thinner at the tip and thicker in the middle. When you're done with the outline of the area, you can then cover the center of the area with this color uniformly, using the whole body of your brush. Use the same color on the thin, long area under the elbow. Wait for this layer to dry.

Use the light sepia and water mix to create shadows on the left and right parts of the branch and under the arms and feet attached to the branch. Smooth out the edges. Finally, if this raw sienna and water mix has already dried, you can apply the darker sepia and water mix to some areas of the sifaka using the same small strokes as before to imitate fur. Also apply it to the body outline, where the body touches the branch, a bit under the elbow, some in the fold of the arm, and some on the left side of the face. We will continue applying this color to other areas in the next steps, but for now, you can limit yourself to these areas.

Step 6: Apply the ochre and water mix from Step 4 to the lower part of the hand, the left part of the leg, the right side of the neck, and right on top of the face. While this color dries, mix a new color:

- Mix A: carmine + sepia + raw sienna + water = warm red-brown

Use Mix A to darken the arm even more, making sure to leave some of the orange visible near the edges. Also, apply this color to the thin, darker area under the elbow, using the same method you used on the arm. Wait for this layer to dry.

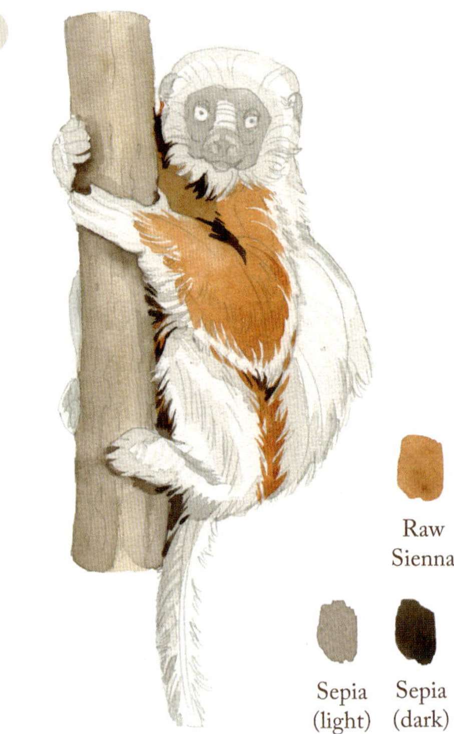

5

Raw Sienna

Sepia (light)

Sepia (dark)

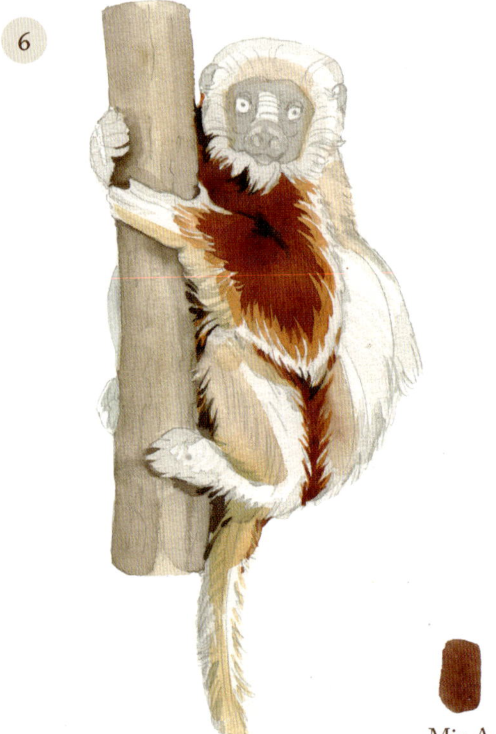

6

Mix A

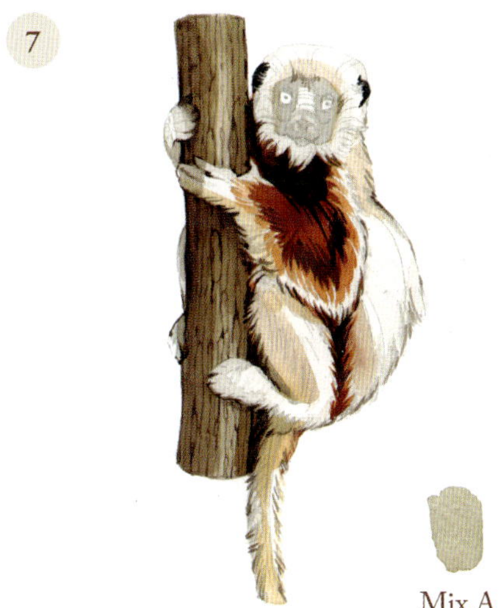

Mix A

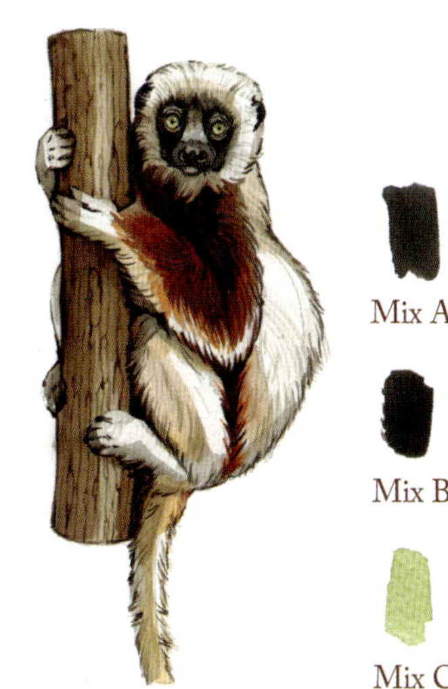

Mix A

Mix B

Mix C

Step 7: Create a new mix:

- Mix A: ochre + sepia + water = light beige

We will also need the dark sepia and water mix from Step 5. Begin by adding more value to the left and right sides of the branch using Mix A. Then, smooth out the edges so that the left side remains more illuminated while the right side stays in shadow. We will continue working on the branch later, but for now, focus on the sifaka. Use the dark sepia and water mix from Step 5 to darken the area under the neck and to add more details to the fur and outline. Use Mix A to enhance the right outline of the sifaka, and add a few details to the head and the right outline of the tail. Finally, add the dark brown sepia and water mix from Step 5 to the ears and proceed with adding texture to the branch. Use the same brown color and its variations, diluting it slightly with water or increasing the saturation by adding more sepia to the mix. Use long, thin lines to create a weblike texture that imitates the bark of the branch.

Step 8: Create two color mixes:

- Mix A: indigo + sepia + water = medium blue-gray

- Mix B: same as Mix 8A (left) but with more pigment and less water = dark blue-gray

Begin by applying Mix A to the face. Use Mix B to darken some areas, especially the outlines of the face and the areas around the cheeks. Also, use this color to define the nose and paint the eyelids. Let dry. Then, mix a yellow color for the eyes:

- Mix C: cadmium lemon + green + water = light yellow

Apply this color to the eyes. While it's drying, use Mix B to work on the hands and feet of the sifaka, making the individual fingers more defined. Use the same color to enhance the outline in some areas, applying zigzag lines as done previously.

Add outlines to the tail and some parts of the black outline. If the eyes are dry by now, use Mix B to paint the pupils. Then, create more texture on the fur of the sifaka using one of the brown or gray mixes on your palette diluted with water. Add fur texture to the head and body, always following the natural flow of the fur and placing your strokes accordingly. Add any last touches to the branch and the sifaka, and your painting will be complete!

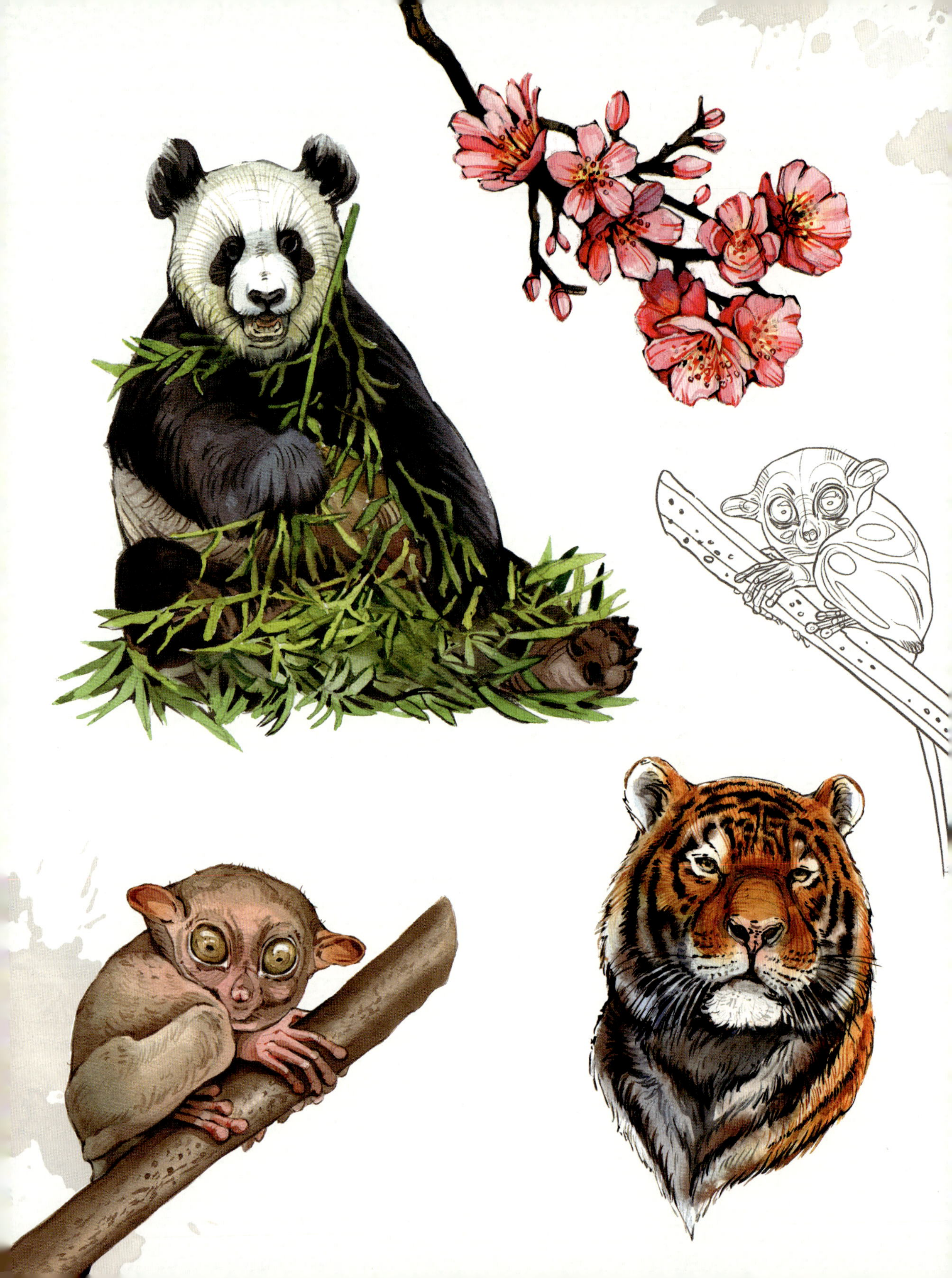

Asia
Nature's Kaleidoscope

Asia is the world's largest continent, both in terms of land area and population. From towering mountain ranges like the Himalayas to vast plateaus, endless plains, steppes, and arid deserts, Asia is the land that surprises and delights. It's a sensory feast, with vibrant landscapes, aromatic spices, and an array of tastes and scents that define this magnificent continent. One fragrance that instantly transports you to tropical islands is the sweet, heady scent of Frangipani flowers (page 172), which are often associated with the tranquil atmosphere of Bali, Indonesia.

Speaking of flowers, one bloom stands out as the embodiment of Asia's beauty and simplicity—the Sakura (page 150), or cherry blossom. Every spring, the streets and parks of Japan burst into soft pink waves of color, marking the arrival of warmer days and the renewal of life. It's a moment of deep cultural significance, symbolizing both the fleeting beauty of life and the arrival of spring.

But flowers are not the only wonders in Asia. Did you know that the banana (see Banana Bundle [page 147]), that ubiquitous fruit found in every supermarket worldwide, actually has its roots in Southeast Asia? This humble, delicious fruit has traveled far from its homeland, but it still brings the taste of Asia to tables across the world.

Asia's rich botanical diversity is mirrored in its wildlife, which boasts a range of endemic species. One of the most famous is the Giant Panda (page 160), native to China. This adorable mammal, known for its black and white fur, is the most vegetarian bear in the world, with a diet that consists almost entirely of young bamboo shoots.

In the dense forest of the Philippines, you'll find the Philippine Tarsier (page 155), the world's smallest primate. Imagine an adult tarsier fitting comfortably in the palm of your hand! These tiny creatures, which weigh no more than a handful of coins, have the largest eyes in relation to their body size of any mammal, and they can turn their enormous eyes to hunt for insects under the cover of night.

Asia is also home to a very different kind of hunter: the Amur Tiger (page 165), the northernmost species of tiger, found in the harsh winters of Eastern Russia. These magnificent creatures are adapted to survive the cold Siberian climate, with thick fur and powerful muscles. Amur tigers are solitary predators, relying on their keen senses to stalk their prey through dense forest and snowy landscapes.

This chapter promises an exciting, colorful journey through the wonders of Asia's flora and fauna. Let's dive in!

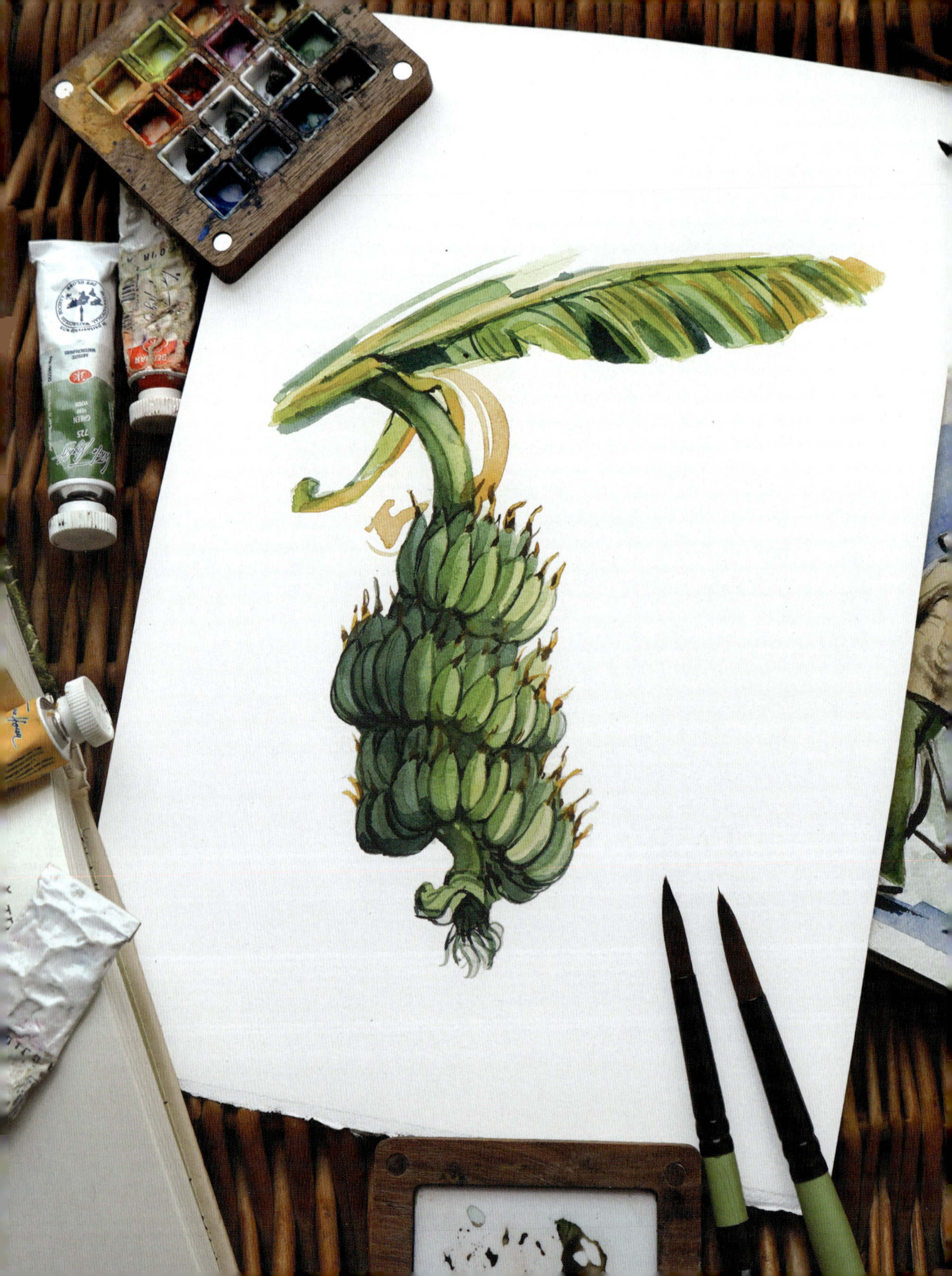

Banana Bundle

Bananas are a staple fruit with a fascinating history and cultural significance across Asia. Did you know that the banana plant isn't a tree but a giant herb? Its clusters can produce up to 20 fruits per bunch. Bananas are believed to have originated in Southeast Asia and New Guinea, and today, they thrive in tropical climates worldwide, thanks to their adaptability and economic importance. Here, you'll focus on unifying complex elements like individual bananas to create their natural arrangement. This exercise will help you master gradient techniques to create realism through light and shadow. You'll also work with a limited color palette, exploring analogous colors to achieve harmony and bring this vibrant subject to life.

Colors Needed

Cadmium Yellow

Raw Sienna

Green

Sepia

Indigo

Suggested Paper Orientation: Vertical

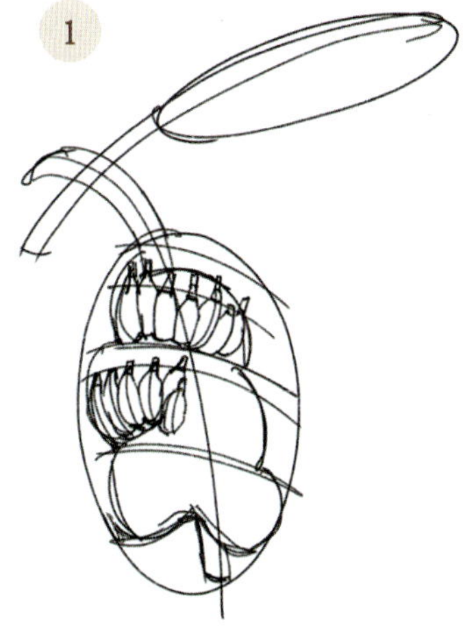

Step 1: When drawing subjects composed of multiple elements (such as various bananas), it's important to start by sketching the general shape first. Begin by drawing a curved line in the middle of your paper to indicate the overall direction of the banana bunch. Then, sketch an oval shape representing the cluster of bananas. Divide this large shape into three main sections corresponding to the three levels of bananas. Add thickness to the stem by drawing two parallel lines on both sides of the initial guide line.

Give the three levels of bananas a more defined appearance by shaping them into ovals. Make the lowest level curvy in the middle; this will help you capture its shape more realistically. To help distinguish the front bananas from those behind, add a parallel line approximately one-third of the way down each level of bananas. Start outlining the individual bananas, beginning with the top level. To sketch individual bananas, start with two vertical parallel lines, which will represent the sides of each banana. Then, add a rounded lower tip and a pointed square-looking top. Don't forget to include some bananas positioned behind the front ones.

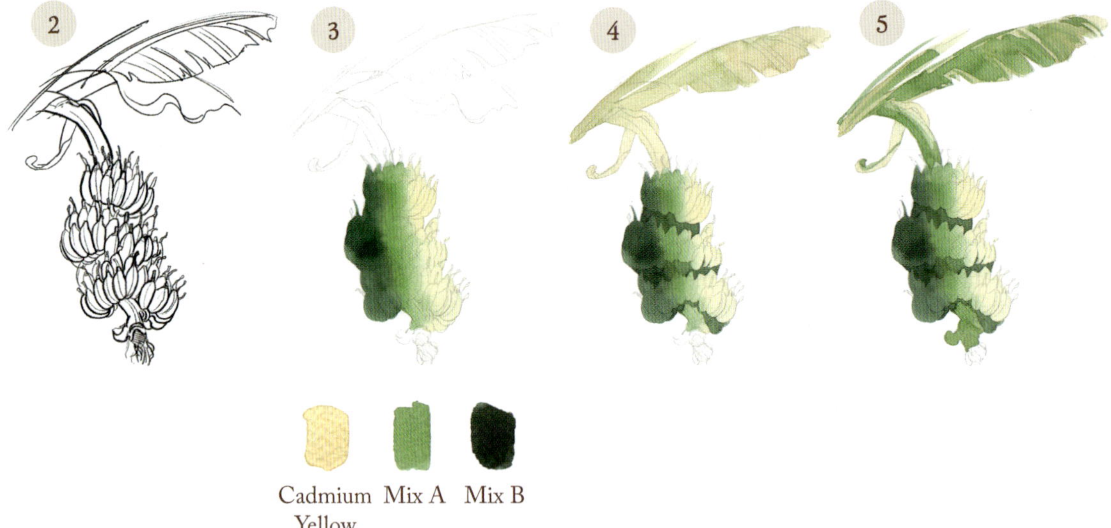

Step 2: Divide each banana with a vertical line in the middle to establish a clear distinction between light and shadow. After adding this middle line visually separating light from shadow, sketch leaves and add other details. Once complete, your drawing will be ready. If the lines are too bold, gently lighten them by rolling a kneaded eraser over the surface without fully erasing.

Step 3: Combine cadmium yellow with water (more water than pigment) for a light yellow mix. Then, create two color mixes:

- Mix A: cadmium yellow + green + water = medium green
- Mix B: green + indigo + water = darker green

We will use the gradient method to create a soft transition from light to shadow, achieving a three-dimensional look with minimal effort.

Since our light source is on the right side, apply the cadmium yellow and water mix to the right side of the banana bundle, covering approximately one-third of the drawing. Next, without letting the first color dry, apply Mix A to the left side of the bananas, covering the middle third of the drawing. Finally, while the surface is still wet, apply Mix B to the remaining part. Wait for this layer to dry.

Step 4: Apply Mix 3B between the banana layers and under the lowest layer to enhance shadows. Next, apply the cadmium yellow and water mix from the previous step to the leaves.

Step 5: As the first layer of leaves begins to dry, switch to Mix 3A for certain leaf areas. Create leaf texture by varying brushstrokes to imitate veins. Use the same color to add shadow to the left side of the stem and lower portion of the painting.

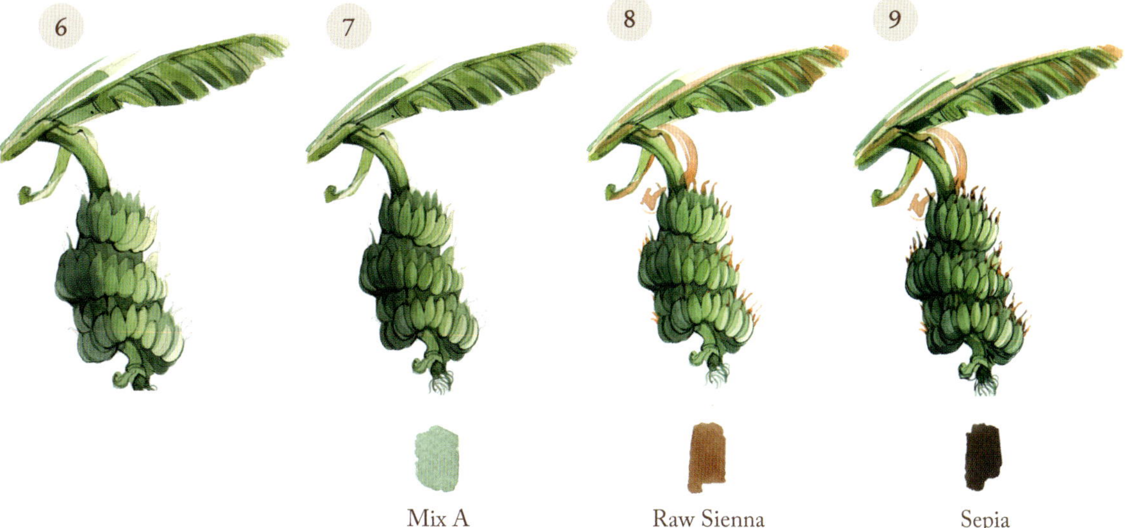

Step 6: Apply Mix 3B between banana levels and add details to the leaves and stem. Concentrate the darker strokes on the stem on the left side, as this is the shadow area.

Step 7: Mix a lighter shade of green:

- Mix A: Mix 3A (cadmium yellow + green + water) + more water = light green

Apply Mix A to the left side of each banana for contrast and volume. Then, add some hairy texture to the stem using the tip of your small brush and Mix 3B. Wait for this layer to dry.

Step 8: Mix raw sienna with water to create a medium brown-orange. Apply this color to specific areas of the leaves, and feel free to add some freehand branches or leaves for artistic effect. Use the same mix to paint dark tips on the bananas.

Step 9: Create a dark, almost black color using sepia mixed with water for the final details. Use it to add additional details to the tips of the bananas. Vary the size, shape, and direction of these details slightly to enhance the painting. With the same dark color and the tip of your brush, add some final touches such as subtly outlining certain bananas. Ensure that your strokes are thin; these final additions should enhance the overall appearance of the painting without overshadowing the main subject. That's it! Your painting is now complete.

Sakura

The sakura, or cherry blossom, is a beloved symbol of Japan, representing the fleeting beauty of life. These delicate flowers bloom in spring, transforming landscapes into pink and white wonders. The annual cherry blossom festivals, or Hanami, celebrate the beauty and transience of nature, where people gather under the blooming trees to appreciate the blossom's short-lived beauty. In this tutorial, you will learn how to represent these delicate flowers and petals realistically, while adding contrast and interest to your painting to make them truly stand out. We will focus on capturing the subtle transitions in color and light, allowing the soft, ethereal qualities of the sakura to shine through.

Colors Needed

- Carmine
- Cadmium Red
- Cadmium Yellow
- Ochre
- Sepia
- Indigo

Suggested Paper Orientation: Horizontal

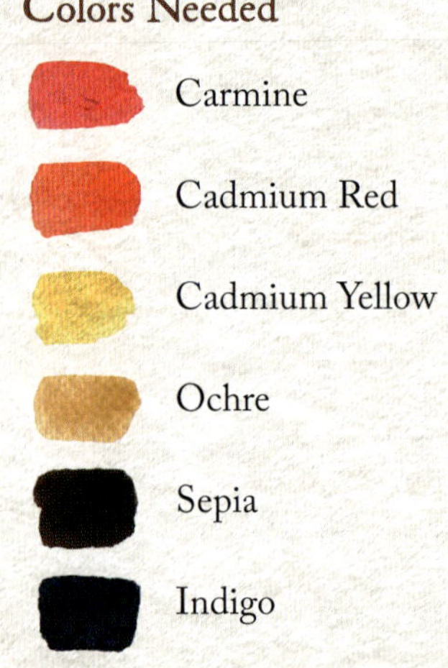

Step 1: Draw a diagonal oval. This oval will help you place the sakura branch. Add a curved line that will correspond to the general direction of the branch. Now, we will divide the flowers on the branch into three main clusters. Draw one oval close to the center of the main oval and two smaller ovals, one to the left and one to the right of its lower edge. Draw two lateral branches that start approximately in the middle of the larger internal oval and extend them in two different directions.

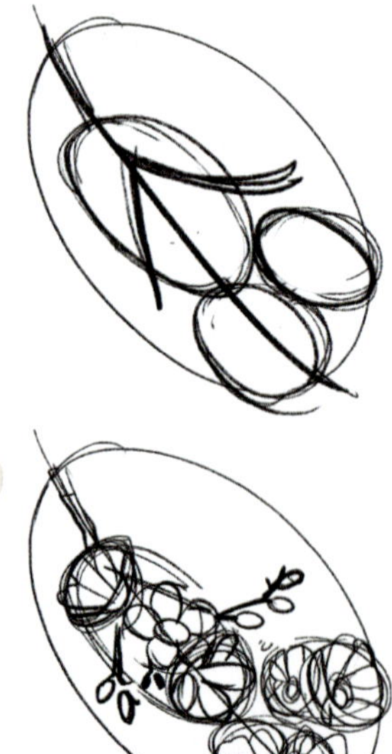

Step 2: Start defining the individual flowers on the branch. Outline three flowers on the top oval and two flowers on each of the lower ovals. Begin by drawing small ovals in the center of each flower, and then add petals around them. Add buds to the two lateral branches.

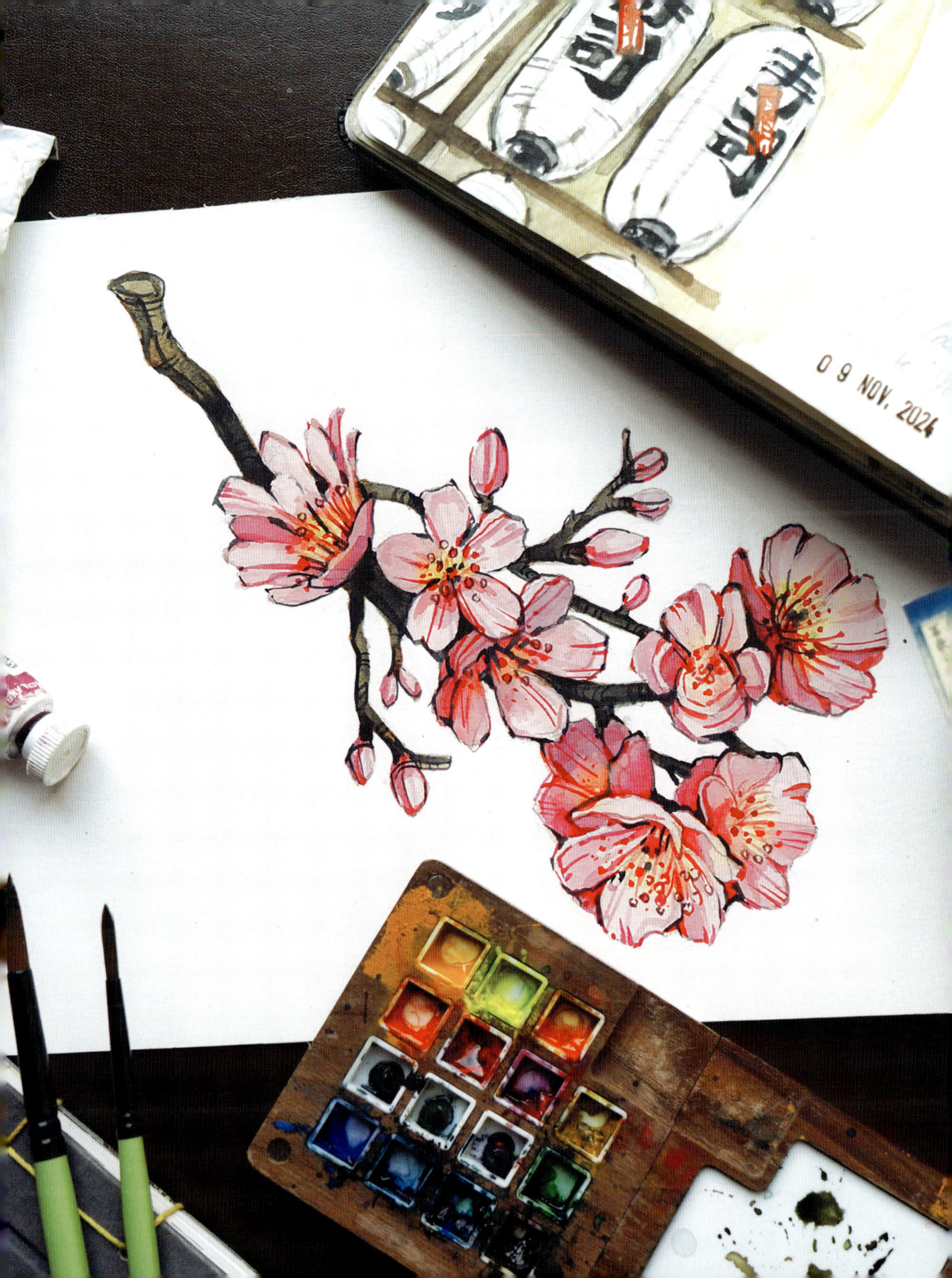

0 9 NOV. 2024

Step 3: Outline the flowers in more detail, paying attention to the shape of the petals and the direction of each flower. Add details to the branch and the flowers. Include stamens growing from the center of each flower, and add small dots to represent the tips of the stamens. Give the branch a curvier appearance and add smaller branches between the clusters of flowers. Erase your guide lines.

Step 4: Let's begin by mixing some colors for the next few steps. First, combine carmine with water to create a very light color, with more water than pigment. Then, use the same carmine and water mix but add more pigment and less water for a darker pink. Then, create the following mix:

- Mix A: carmine + cadmium red + water = medium warm red

Also, mix cadmium yellow with water for the parts of the flowers.

Use the light carmine mix to cover the flowers, leaving the centers white. While the pink is still wet, apply the cadmium yellow mix to the centers. This will allow the colors to blend, creating a soft and seamless transition between the pink and yellow. Apply the light carmine mix to some buds and branches.

Step 5: Apply the darker pink from the previous step (carmine with a little bit of water) to the petals toward the back to create volume. Use tiny lines to add shadows and detail to the stamens. Be sure to leave enough light pink and yellow areas to maintain the contrast and depth. Once dry, define the darkest shadows with a bit of Mix 4A.

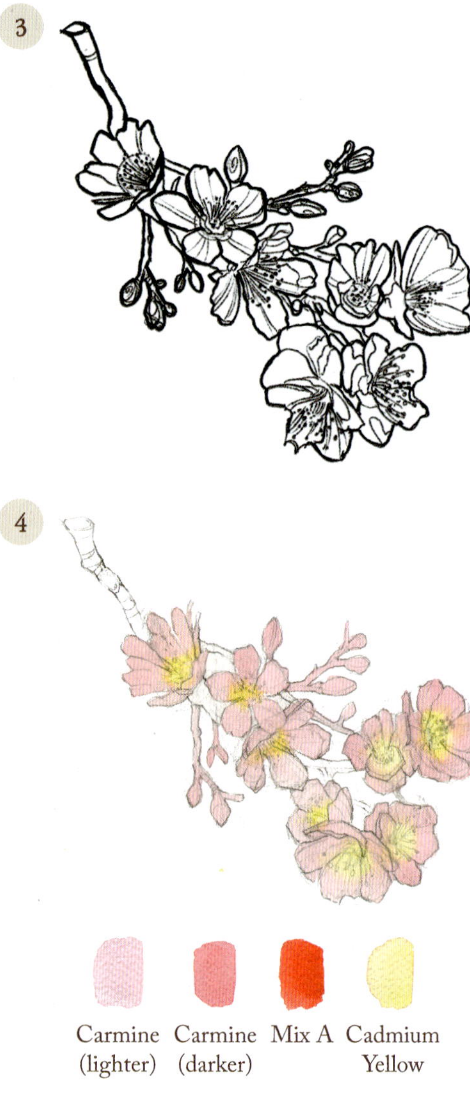

Carmine (lighter) Carmine (darker) Mix A Cadmium Yellow

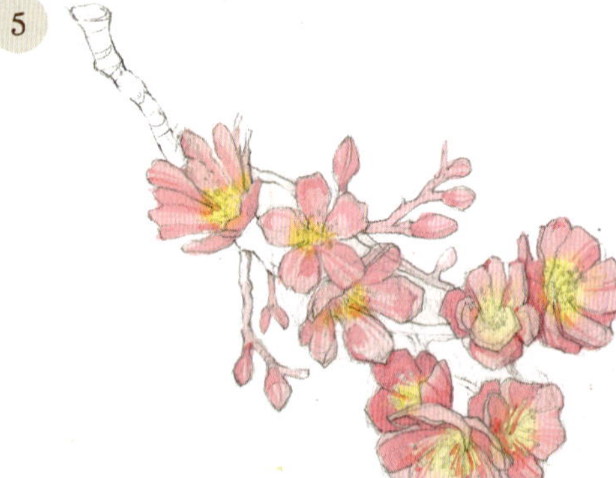

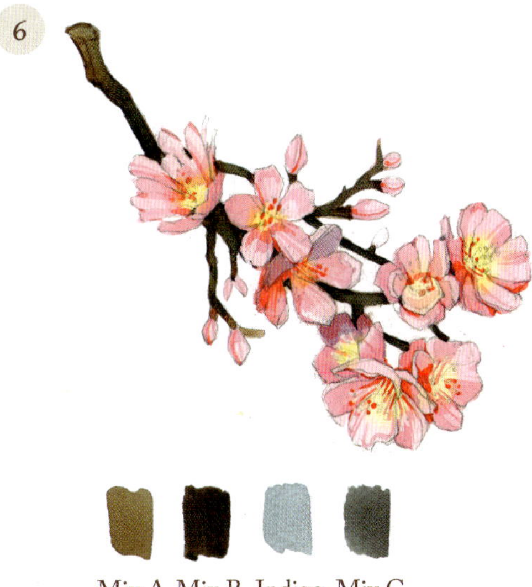

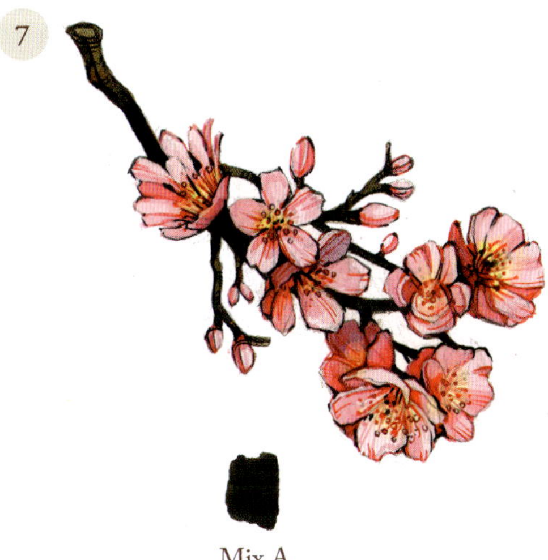

Mix A Mix B Indigo Mix C

Mix A

Step 6: Mix colors for the branch:

- Mix A: ochre + sepia + water = medium brown
- Mix B: same as Mix 6A (above) but with more pigment = dark brown

Apply Mix A to the entire branch. While it's still wet, apply Mix B to the areas where the branch intersects with flowers. Use the light carmine and water mix from Step 4 to darken and blend some of the petals, especially those that are in the back. Then, with the tip of your small brush, apply Mix 4A to areas in the center of the flowers to create a glowing effect and a darker center for contrast. Use the same color to paint the tips of the stamens, applying simple dots. Place them irregularly on all of the flowers, paying more attention to the flowers on the right. Use the same color to add a line to the buds. Then, combine indigo with water and apply it to the branch. Create a new mix:

- Mix C: indigo + sepia + water = gray

Use this new color to add darker details to the branch.

Step 7: Darken the flowers in the background with the light carmine and water mix from Step 4. With the very tip of your small brush, add thin lines and dots to the folds of the petals and the tips of the stamen using the dark carmine and water mix from Step 4. Add details to the buds and darken their lower-right sides with the light carmine and water mix from Step 4. Then, mix a new color:

- Mix A: indigo + sepia + water = very dark, almost black color

Use Mix A to darken the center of the branch, between the flowers. Use short, thin lines for texture. With the tip of your brush and using the same color, add touches of this dark color to the centers of the flowers and to their outlines. This will help visually unite the branch with the flowers. Make sure your lines are thin while doing this. Your painting is now complete!

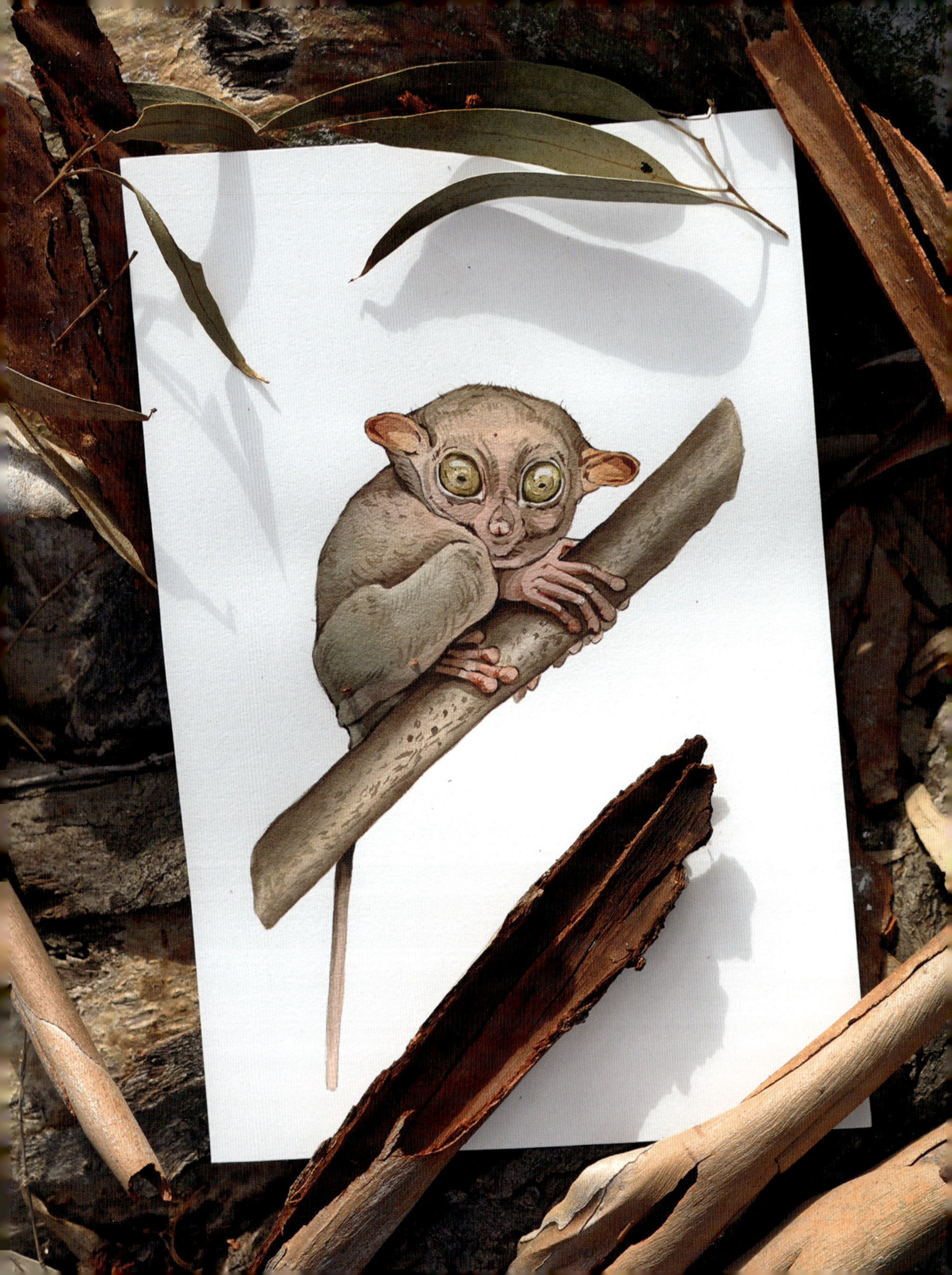

Philippine Tarsier

The tarsier is a fascinating little creature, known for its large, expressive eyes and long, delicate fingers. Despite being the smallest primate in the world, this adorable animal has a very distinct appearance that sets it apart from other monkeys. Native to Southeast Asia, tarsiers can be found in the Philippines, Borneo, and part of Sumatra, where they inhabit dense forests and rely on their excellent vision and ability to navigate their nocturnal environments. In this tutorial, you will learn how to capture these unique features realistically, with a special focus on painting the tarsier's large eyes.

Colors Needed

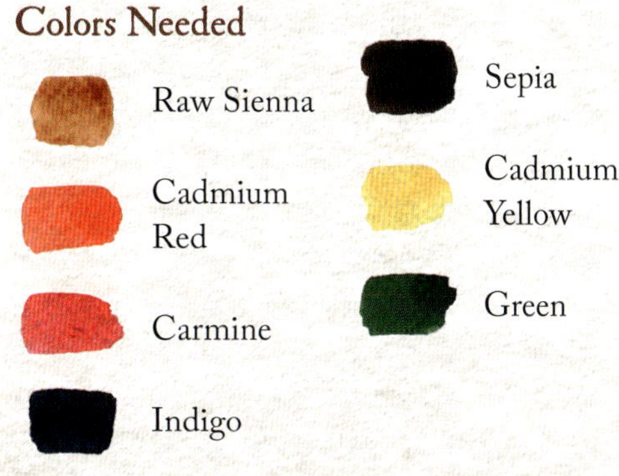

- Raw Sienna
- Sepia
- Cadmium Red
- Cadmium Yellow
- Carmine
- Green
- Indigo

Suggested Paper Orientation: Vertical

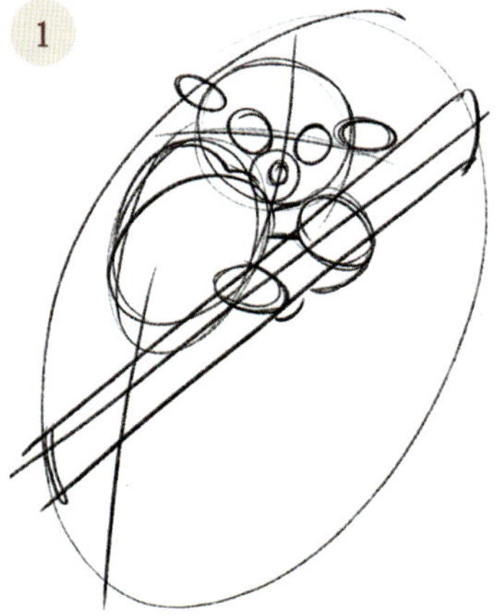

Step 1: Start by drawing an oval in the middle of your page. This oval will contain the entire animal and branch. Next, create a diagonal line dividing the oval into two parts. This line should go from the lower left corner to the top right corner. Add thickness to the line by drawing two parallel lines, one on the top and one on the bottom. You should end up with a long cylinder that will represent the branch.

Now, it's time to outline the main shapes of the tarsier. Create two ovals: one representing the body and one for the head. The body oval should be slightly bigger, and the two ovals should touch each other. Add a curved vertical line dividing the head oval into two parts. This will be the center of the face. Next, add a horizontal line in the center of the head to create a cross with the previous line, indicating the eye level. Place the ovals outlining the eyes on the horizontal line, then add an oval on the lower part of the face, with an even smaller oval inside it to represent the nose. Add two ovals for the ears: The left ear should be higher than the eye line, while the right ear should touch the eye line with its lower edge.

(Step 1 continued)

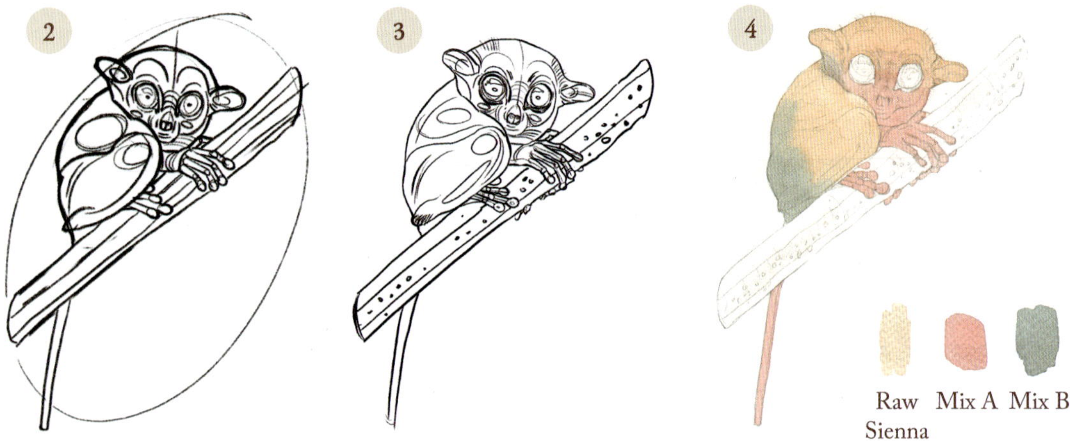

Now, let's work on defining the body better. Look at the oval of the body and create a similar oval, but imagine turning it to the right so that the top of the oval lines up to the nose. This oval will be the front leg. Outline the hand and foot with two ovals. The hand oval should be bigger, and both ovals should sit on top of the branch surface. Finally, draw a line going from the bottom of the leg oval down vertically until you reach the outline of the initial oval. This line is the tail.

Step 2: Let's now give the tarsier a more realistic appearance. Unite the head and body with an outline. Do the same for the ears. Add some lines to define the leg, and include a large oval on the body and a smaller oval on the right side of the leg. These ovals will help us place light and shadow during the painting process. Thicken the tail with two parallel lines and define the facial features more clearly. Work on the inside parts of the ears, add two small ovals on the cheeks, and refine the nose by dividing it into two parts. After that, start separating the foot and hand into individual fingers. The fingers and toes are very long, thin, and have larger round tips, so capture these features while sketching. Also add some lines to the branch to begin outlining its texture better.

Step 3: Erase the guide lines. Make the facial features even more accurate and use small lines to create the illusion of fur on the head. Enhance the realism of the eyes by outlining the highlights. Give thickness to the fingers with thin lines, and finally, add some tiny circles and dots on the branch to give it texture. After that, you can proceed with painting.

Step 4: In this step, we will give the tarsier its first color layer. Mix raw sienna with water for a watery yellow mix. Then, create two color mixes:

- Mix A: cadmium red + a touch of carmine + lots of water = light pink
- Mix B: indigo + sepia + water = light blue-gray

Apply Mix A to the tail, the fingers, and the lower part of the face. Once you've reached the lower edge of the tarsier's eyes, switch to the raw sienna and water mix and finish covering the head, avoiding the eyes. While this color is still wet, add a touch of Mix B to the left side of the head, right below the ear, to indicate shadow. After that, start covering the body from the top using the raw sienna and water mix. If the head is still wet, leave a thin line of dry paper between it and the body to prevent the colors from mixing. Once you've covered two-thirds of the body, switch to Mix B to cover the remaining third of the left part of the body. Let this layer dry completely.

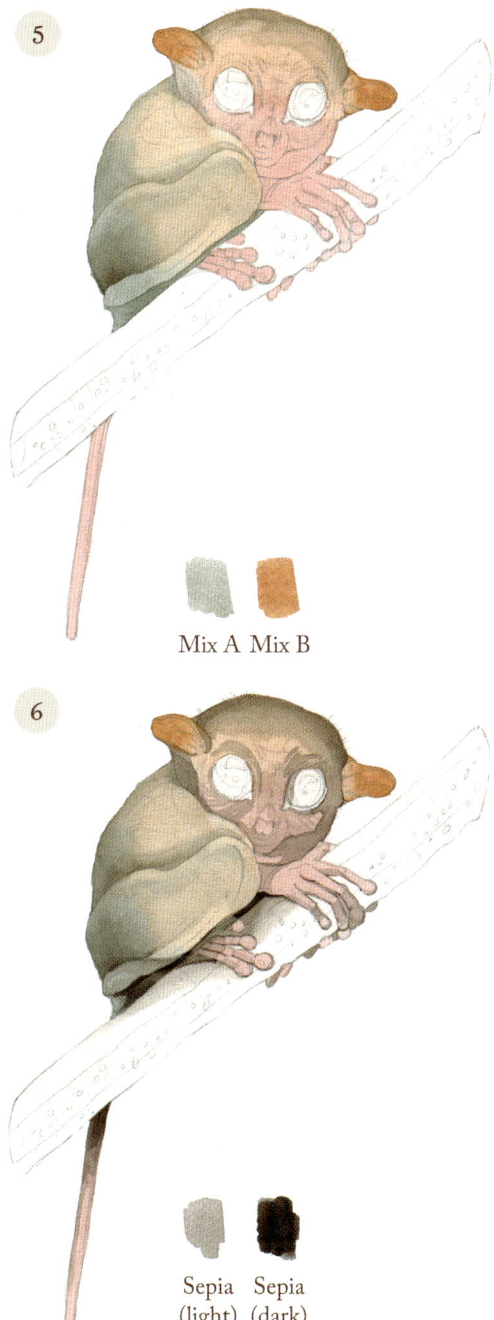

Mix A Mix B

Sepia Sepia
(light) (dark)

Step 5: Let's create two other color mixes:

- Mix A: same as Mix 4B (indigo + sepia + water) but with less indigo and more water = light brown-gray
- Mix B: raw sienna + a touch of sepia + water = saturated orange

The light is concentrated on the right side of the body, so apply Mix A to the left side and the top of the leg to create a light and shadow effect. Smooth the edges with a clean, dry brush. Then, do the same for the leg. Next, apply Mix B to the ears and smooth the edges. Let dry completely.

Step 6: Here we will better define the tarsier's face and add more contrast. Create two simple color mixes: sepia and water for a light brown and more sepia with less water for a saturated brown. Apply the light sepia mix to the shadow areas of the face, such as the right side, the top of the forehead, the area under the nose, around the eyes, and left side under the ear. Also apply this color to the last phalanges of the fingers on the top hand and to the tips of the fingers that hold the back side of the branch the tarsier is sitting on. Use the darker sepia mix to outline some individual fingers with a very thin line from the tip of your small brush. Use the same color to show the shadow between the leg and the branch. With the light sepia mix, outline the shadow cast by the tarsier onto the branch, then smooth the edge. As a final action in this step, add the darker sepia mix to the top portion of the tail and smooth the edge for a seamless transition.

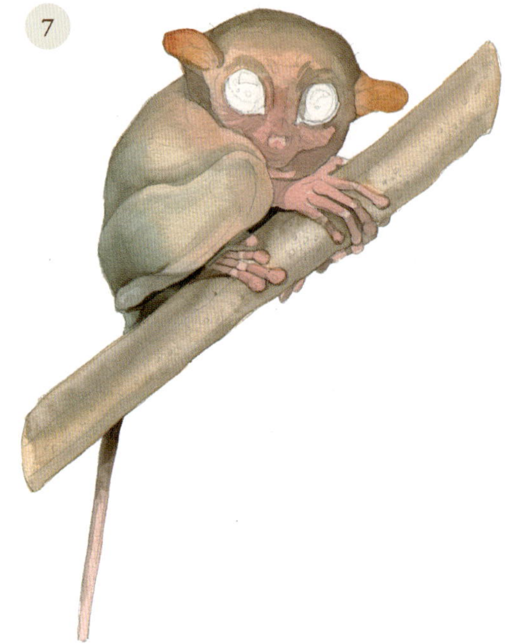

Step 7: Apply the light brown raw sienna and water mix from Step 4 to the branch. While this color is still wet, apply the light sepia mix from the previous step to the top and lower sides of the branch. As a result, you should achieve highlights in the middle of the branch and shadows on the top and bottom sides. Add Mix 4A to the lower part of the face, avoiding the nose. Use the same mix for the fingers. Additionally, apply this color to the right side of the body and smooth out this edge.

Step 8: Create two mixes for the eyes:

- Mix A: cadmium yellow + raw sienna + water = bright tan

- Mix B: raw sienna + green + water = brown-green

Use your small brush to apply Mix A to one entire eye, except for the highlight and the lower eyelid. Then, while the color is still wet, apply Mix B to the sides of the eye. As a result, the eye should start to look more three-dimensional: lighter in the middle and darker near the sides, with a white highlight. Repeat for the second eye.

Next, mix a color for darkening the ears and the nose:

- Mix C: carmine + raw sienna + sepia + water = warm brown

Use Mix C to create shadows in the ears and to outline the tip of the nose, as well as some spaces between the fingers. Then, use the dark sepia mix from Step 6 (more sepia with less water) to darken the outline of the eyes. Slightly dilute this color with water and use the tip of your brush to better outline some of the facial features of the tarsier.

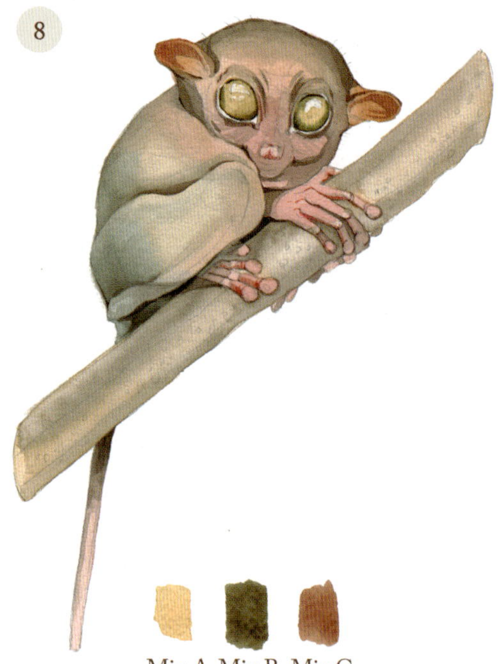

Mix A Mix B Mix C

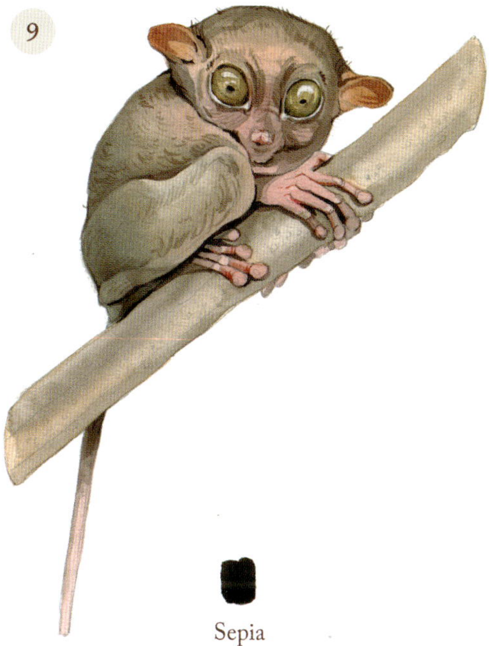

Sepia

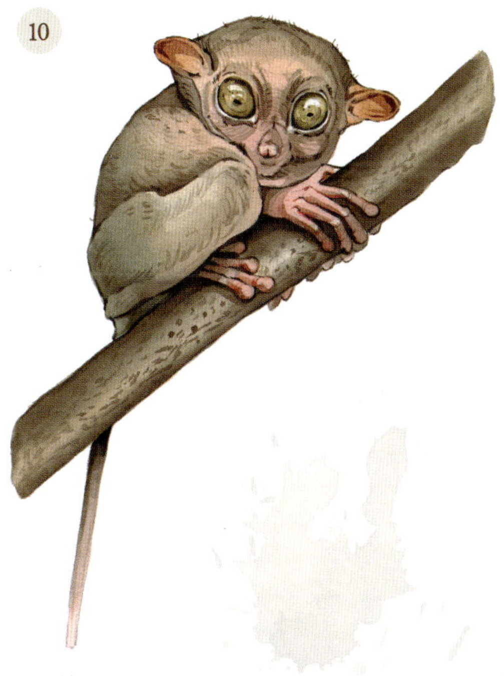

Step 9: Add pupils to the eyes using the tip of your brush and any dark color—I recommend sepia with almost no water. Use the same color to darken the outline of the body on the left side to visually separate it from the head. Use the dark sepia and water mix from Step 6 to show the shadow between the fingers, and add an outline to the lower side of the leg. Dilute this mix with just a touch of water, and apply it to the left third of the body and leg. Smooth out the edges for a seamless transition. This will help accentuate the shadow on that side of the animal. Add some dark details to the eyes and facial features using the same diluted sepia. Use it also to create fur texture on the face with short, thin strokes. Then, apply the same technique to add fur texture to the body and leg, making sure to follow the natural movement of the fur and the contours of different parts.

Step 10: Apply the same sepia from the last step (diluted with water) to the top third of the branch. Then, smooth out the edge using a clean, damp brush. Repeat this on the lower side and smooth the edge as well. This should enhance the light and shadow effect on the branch.

While the branch dries, add final touches to the head. Add some fur and details around the eyes using fine, thin strokes. Increase the saturation and contrast in the eyes by adding Mix 8B that you previously used for them to the darker areas of the eyeballs, avoiding the highlights and pupils. Darken the last segments of the hands even more using sepia diluted with water. Use the darkest color (sepia with almost no water) to add final touches to the ears, nose, and outline of the eyes. Then, use the same color to outline individual fingers more clearly, darken the spaces between the fingers, and indicate the shadow cast by the tarsier to the left of the hands. As a final step, once the branch is dry, use diluted sepia and the tip of your brush to add dots and outline the texture on the branch. Your painting is now complete!

Giant Panda

The giant panda is a beloved symbol of China, representing peace and harmony. Known for their gentle nature, these iconic creatures are native to the mountain ranges of Central China where, despite their formidable size, they spend most of their time eating bamboo shoots and leaves, which make up almost 99 percent of their diet. In this tutorial, you will not only learn how to capture the panda's gentle character but also how to paint its favorite food—bamboo shoots. This is a great opportunity to practice using masking fluid to protect certain areas of your painting, making it easier to paint around the bamboo while focusing on the panda.

Colors Needed

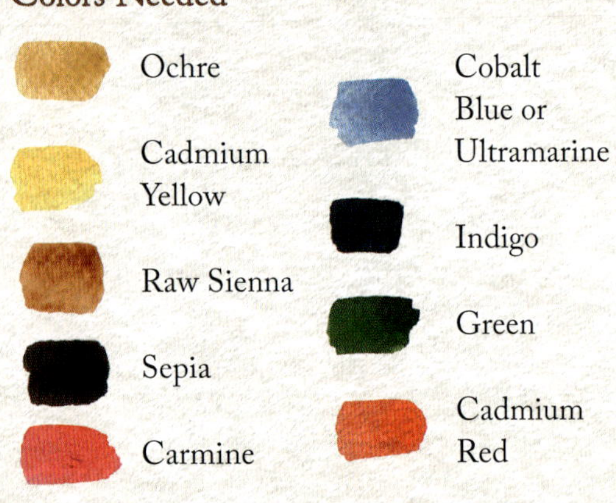

Suggested Paper Orientation: Vertical

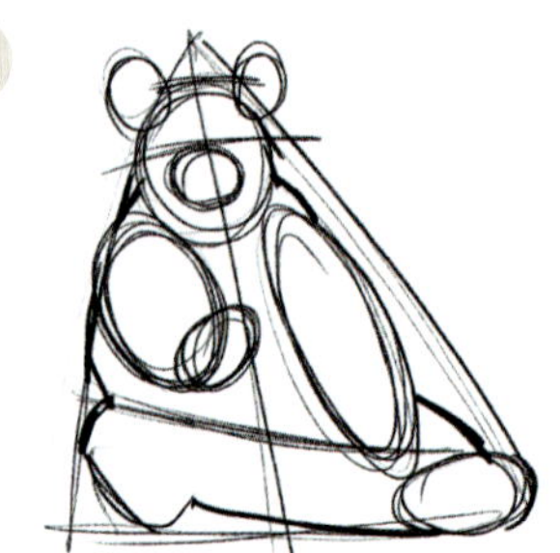

Step 1: Draw a triangle where the right line is longer than the left. This will contain the whole panda. Draw a diagonal line from its tip to the bottom center. Then, start outlining the body, head, and arms with ovals. Outline the ears, hands, feet, and nose with smaller ovals. Add a guide line that's approximately one-fifth from the bottom of the triangle to better define the placement of the feet. Draw a second line in the middle of the head that will help you define the placement of the eyes.

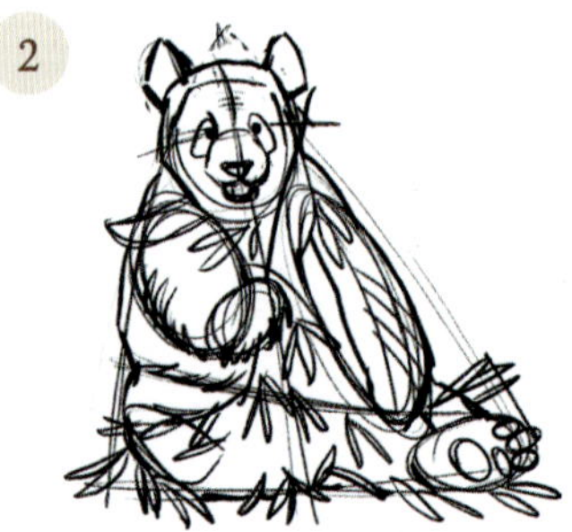

Step 2: Start defining the shape of the body, limbs, and head of the panda more clearly. Focus on defining the facial features, starting with the eyes, nose, chin, and cheeks. Outline the black spots around the eyes and define the eye holes. Make the ears pointier. Start sketching bamboo leaves and the branch that the panda is holding. Sketch the leaves that cover the lower side of the panda's body using thin, pointy ovals. Also, outline the leaves attached to the branch the panda is holding. Finally, add some details to the right foot.

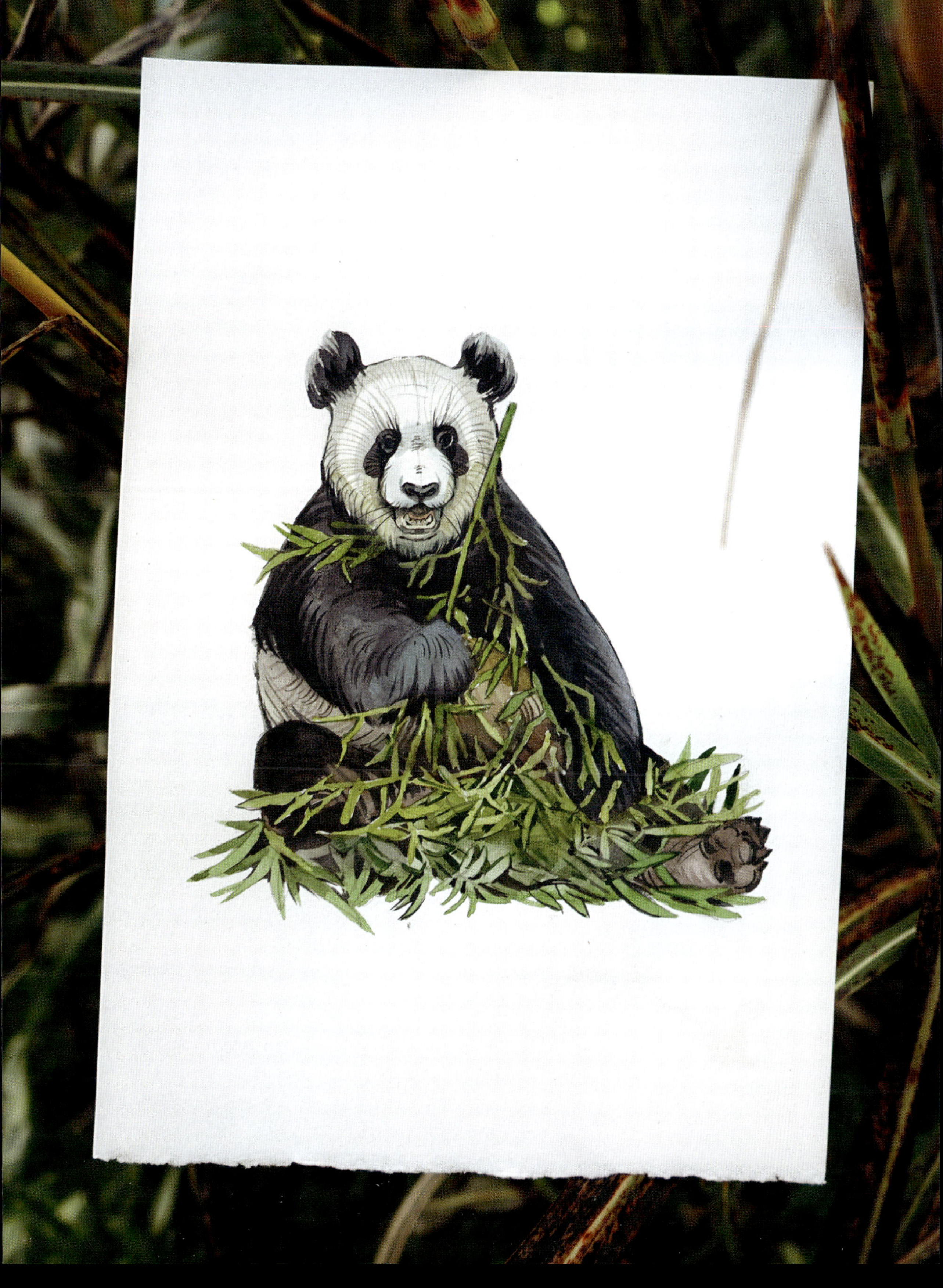

Step 3: Erase any unnecessary guide lines and the main triangle. Refine the facial features. Add a line to the nose, outline the nostril, add a furry edge to the ears, create an open mouth, and draw the teeth. Add details to the arms with long strokes across their surfaces to imitate fur. Add a zigzag to the edge of the left side of the panda's bent arm and give the left hand a more defined look. After that, add more details to the bamboo and include additional leaves. Once you've finished these details, let's start painting!

Step 4: Apply masking fluid (page 12) to any bamboo stems and leaves on the panda's body so that we can paint the panda without worrying about accidentally covering the leaves. If you don't have masking fluid, simply avoid the leaves while painting and paint around them. This will make the painting process a bit longer and more tedious, but it's doable. Apply the masking fluid with an old brush with a decently sharp tip or just a toothpick. After you've applied the masking fluid, let it dry for 10 to 15 minutes. You can proceed to the next step when the masking fluid turns yellow-green and nothing remains on your fingers if you touch its surface.

Step 5: Let's create some color mixes:

- Mix A: ochre + cadmium yellow + water = watery light yellow
- Mix B: raw sienna + sepia + water = medium brown
- Mix C: sepia + carmine + water = darker red-brown
- Mix D: cobalt blue or ultramarine + a touch of sepia + water = medium blue
- Mix E: indigo + sepia + carmine + water (more pigment than water) = dark blue-purple

Apply Mix A to the sides and top of the head, as well as to the jaw and sides of the cheeks.

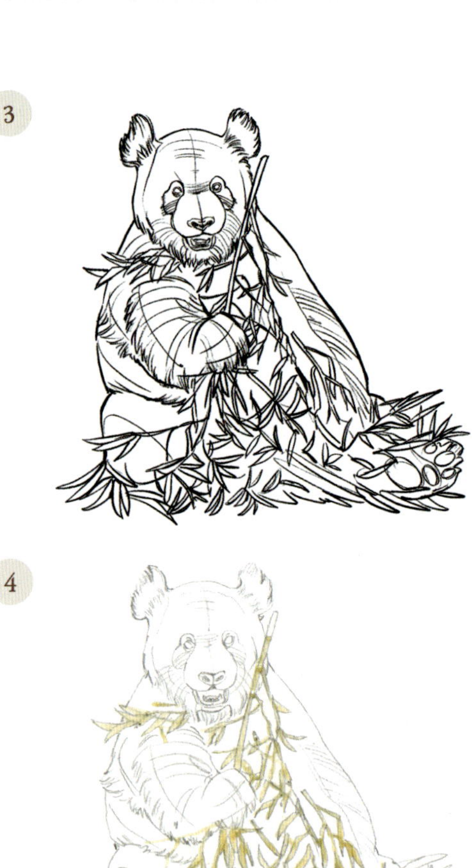

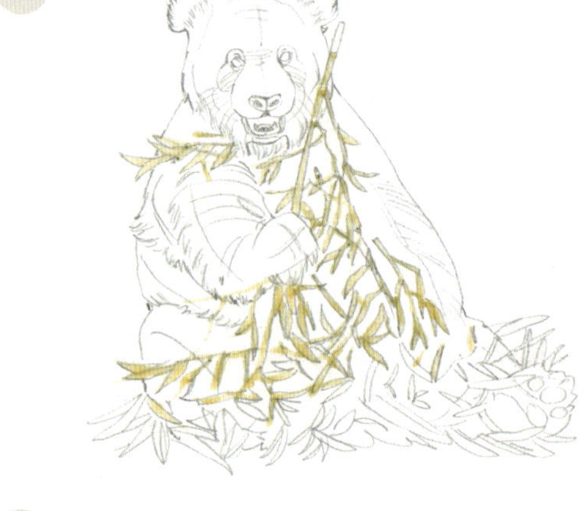

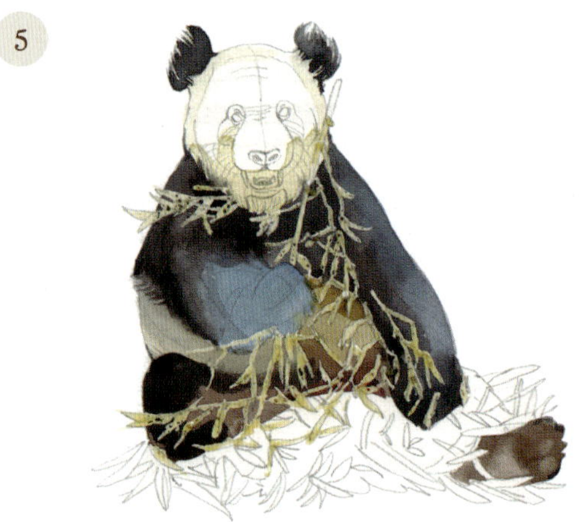

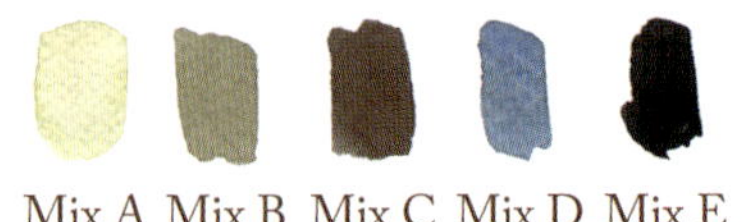

Mix A Mix B Mix C Mix D Mix E

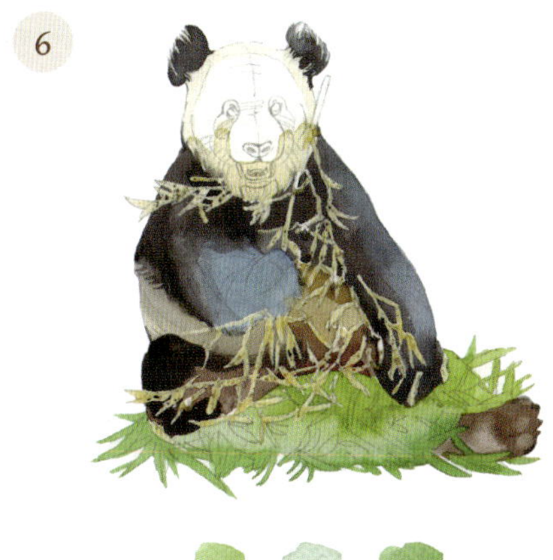

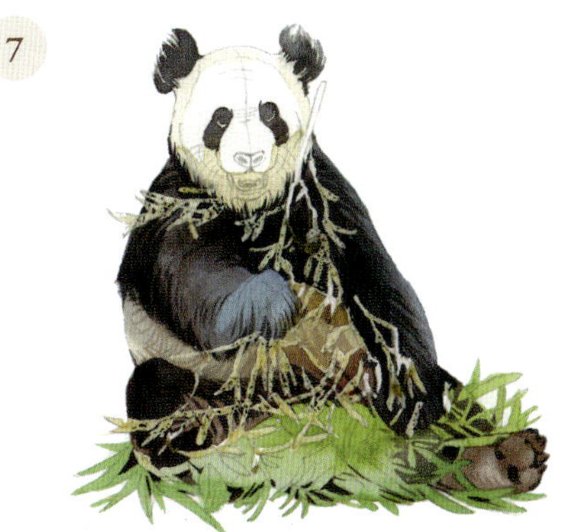

Mix A Mix B Mix C

Apply Mix B to the belly visible on the left and in the center. Apply Mix C to the foot, the leg on the left, and the lower part of the belly visible in the middle, between the bamboo leaves.

Apply Mix D to the right half of the arm on the right. Switch to Mix E and finish painting the left half. Do a similar thing with the other arm, starting by covering the hand, and once you reach halfway up the arm, switch to Mix E and continue to cover the rest of the arm. Then, bring this color near the head and cover the neck and chest. As a last step, take the same Mix E and apply it to the left part of the left leg and the toes of the foot on the right. Create a hairy texture on the edge of the ears using the tip of your small brush to make short, wavy strokes.

Step 6: Create three green color mixes for the bamboo:

- Mix A: cadmium yellow + green + water = medium vibrant grass green

- Mix B: green + cobalt blue or ultramarine + water (more water than pigment) = watery blue-green

- Mix C: green + cobalt blue or ultramarine + cadmium yellow + water = darker green

Apply Mix A to the individual bamboo leaves that extend beyond the outline of the panda on the right side, and then cover the top of the pile using the same color. Just cover everything uniformly; we will paint the dark details of the panda later. While Mix A is still wet, switch to the lighter Mix B and cover approximately two-thirds of the pile. Then, switch to the darker Mix C and finish painting the remaining pile. Also, outline the individual leaves on the lower side that go beyond the panda's surface with the same color. Wait for this layer to dry.

Step 7: Add some fur texture to the belly and the left hand with Mix 5C. Then, use Mix 5E to darken the eyes, leaving just the lower eyelids untouched. Use the same color to create the fur texture on the hands, applying curvy strokes that are thinner at the end and base but thicker in the middle. Use this color to outline the nails and individual toes on the right foot more clearly. Then, darken the chest and underline the white fur of the chin and lower side of the head with tiny, curvy strokes. Add some texture to the left leg and the left paw as well. As the last action of this step, use the same color to paint some of the panda's fur showing through the bamboo pile, especially on the left and lower sides. Follow the lines of the drawing to guide you. There's no need to add all the dark details now, as we will continue working on this area in the next steps. Let this dry.

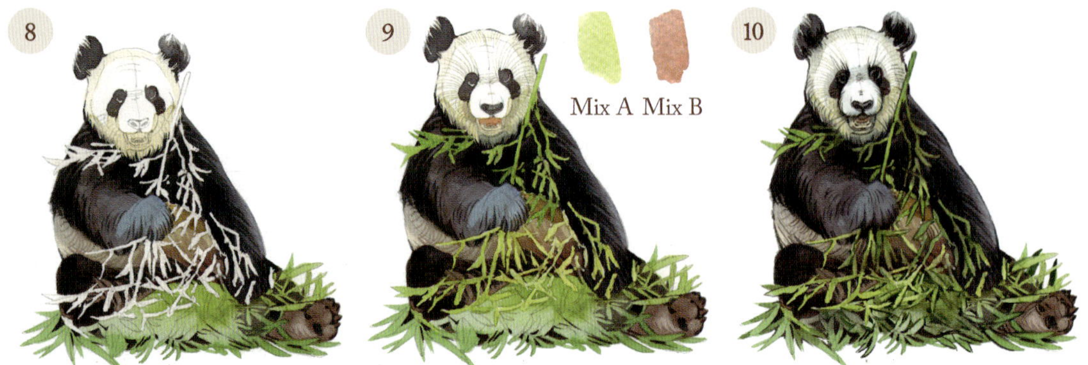

Step 8: It's time to peel off the masking fluid. Rub your finger against the surface covered by the masking fluid, preferably in the center of the painting and not near the edges, to avoid the possibility of smudging and staining the white background. Once you start rubbing your finger, you can take one of the tips of the masking fluid and begin pulling it so it peels away from the paper. Keep doing this until you have removed all the masking fluid. Make sure there's nothing left before proceeding.

Step 9: Create a new color mix:

- Mix A: cadmium yellow + a touch of green + water = vibrant yellow

Use this color and the tip of your brush to cover all the white leaves that were under the masking fluid. If you accidentally touch the dark surface, that color will be activated and affect the leaves. If that happens, don't worry too much, but just try to be careful and work with the tip of your brush. Then, paint the nose with Mix 5E.

Use Mix 5B to outline the shadows in the cheeks even more and create texture on the face using thin hairline strokes going from the center of the face toward its side around the circle. Avoid the nose, eyes, and mouth. Darken the outline of the head using one of the dark colors you already have on your palette.

As a final action, mix a color for the mouth:

- Mix B: a bit of cadmium yellow + cadmium red + some sepia + water = slightly muted light orange

Apply this mix to the inside part of the mouth with a small brush.

Step 10: Paint the nostrils with a very dark, almost black color like Mix 5E, and darken the eyes, ears, and nails on the right paw. Return to the face and add final touches to the mouth using the same mix, slightly diluted with water, and the very tip of your brush, following the pencil drawing. Add some tiny horizontal lines in the middle of the face between the eyes, and make the outline of the chin more visible with a thin, horizontal line. Soften the highlights on the eyelids a bit by blending that area with a small amount of clean water on your brush.

Once you're satisfied with the face, blend some of the areas of the bamboo pile with one of the medium-light green colors you have on your palette. Then, using the same color, create some leaves that appear behind darker ones. Finally, take Mix 5E and add some dark patches between the leaves to show the panda's body peeking through. After that, your painting is ready!

Amur Tiger

What a charismatic animal we're studying in this tutorial! The Amur tiger, also known as the Siberian tiger, is the largest tiger species and can be found in the cold, dense forests of the Russian Far East. These magnificent creatures have adapted to their harsh environment with a thick, insulating coat and powerful physique. In this lesson, we'll zoom in on the structure of its face and the textures of its fur in a realistic manner. You'll also gain a deeper understanding of the anatomy of felines, honing your skills in capturing the fine details of fur patterns, whiskers, and facial contours. Let's get started!

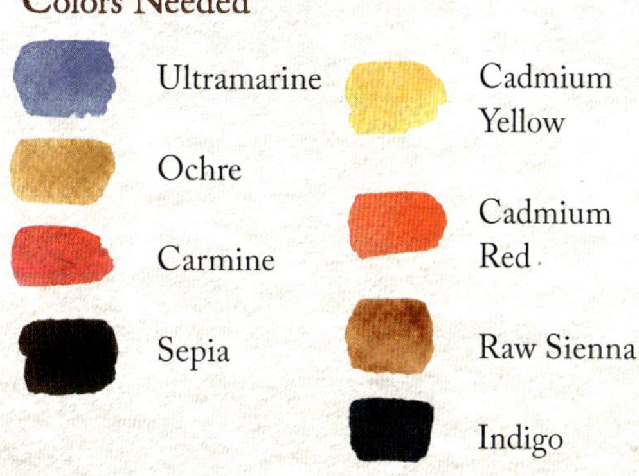

Colors Needed

- Ultramarine
- Ochre
- Carmine
- Sepia
- Cadmium Yellow
- Cadmium Red
- Raw Sienna
- Indigo

Suggested Paper Orientation: Vertical

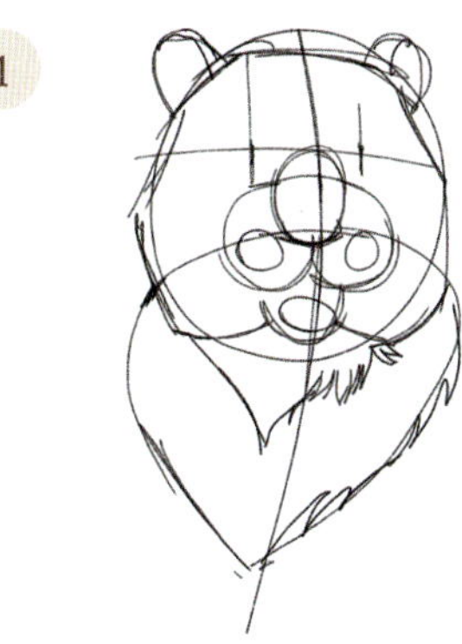

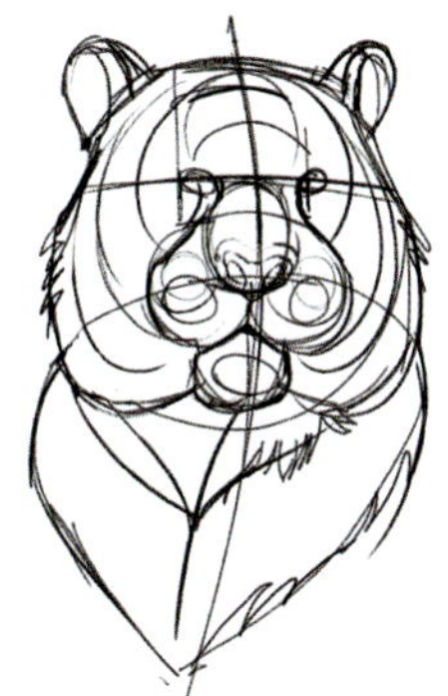

Step 1: Create two intersecting circles, and give a pointy tip to the lower circle, transforming it into a heart-like shape. The top circle will represent the head of the tiger and the lower heart shape will be the chest. Draw a long vertical arc that crosses both the head and the chest. Add a horizontal line to the head, slightly above its center—this will represent the eye level. Outline the eye placement with two vertical lines. Then, use small circles to outline the ears, cheeks, and jaw, and add an oval for the nose. Refine the shape of the head, making the top area narrower than the lower part. Draw a smaller triangle in the neck area to represent fur, then sketch some fur on the right side of this triangle and along the right outline of the chest.

Step 2: Use two vertical lines and the horizontal eye-level guide to place the eyes, using small horizontally positioned ovals. Refine the details on the nose by outlining the nostrils and other smaller features. Further define the cheeks and jaw, connecting the eyes to the cheeks with two curved lines. Improve the outline of the head and ears, and add a line to the chest to guide the direction of the fur in the next steps. Then, use curved lines to shape the forehead and left and right sides of the head.

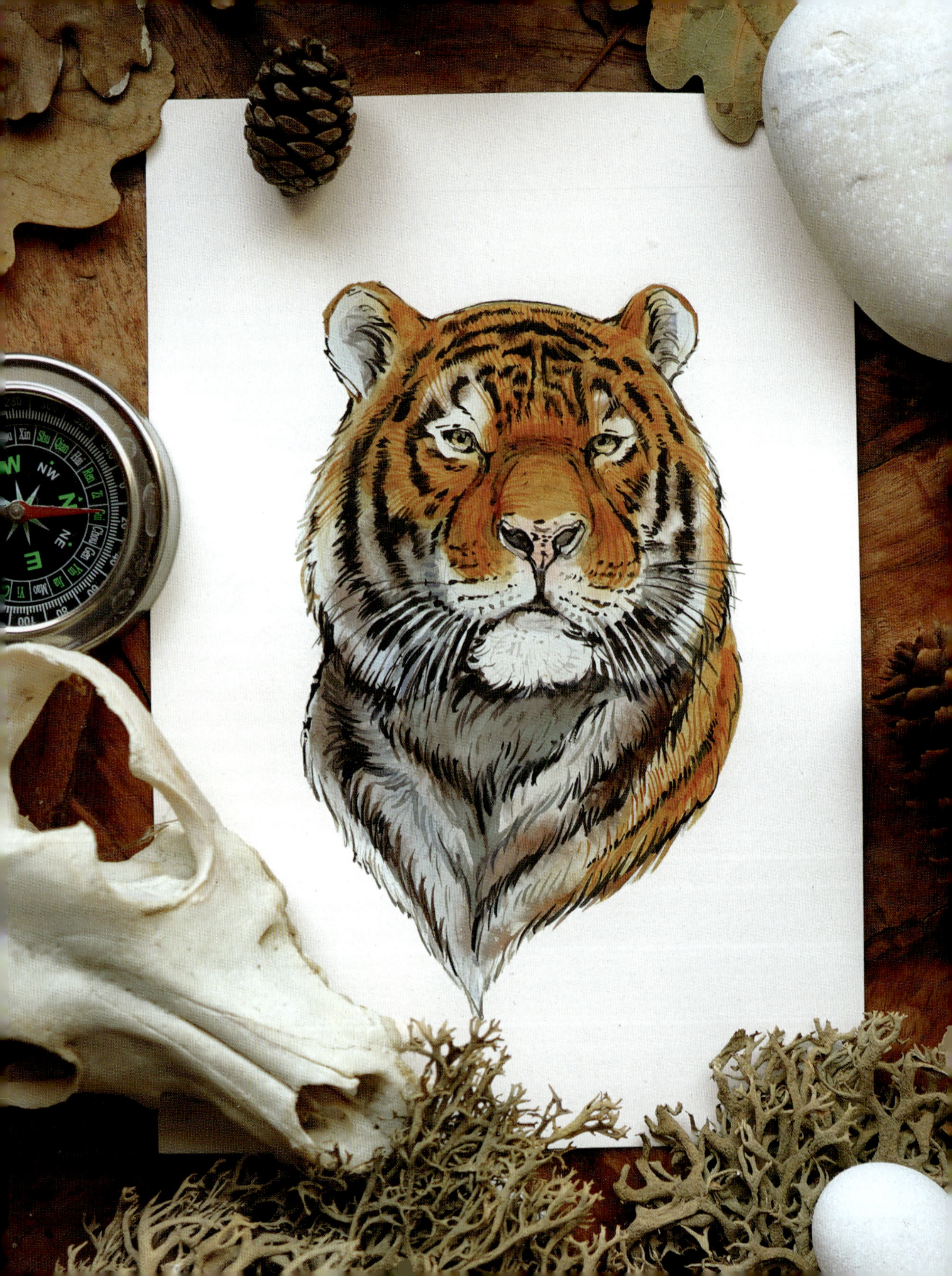

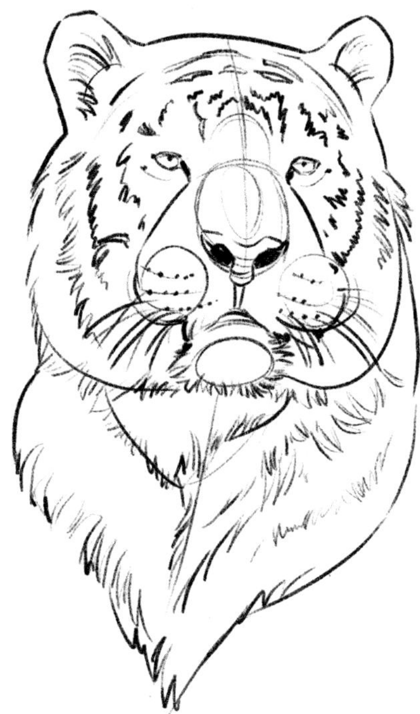

Step 3: Erase the guide lines and start defining the tiger's features in more detail. Refine the outline and add fur texture using zigzag lines, especially on the side of the head and the left side of the chest. Add fur texture to the face, starting with the ears, with vertical, parallel, curvy lines. Use short zigzag lines to add fur texture to the chin. Follow a similar method to outline the spots on the face. Then, continue with other areas of the tiger, like the chest, giving an organic look to the fur by varying the direction to follow its natural movement. Add the spots on the cheeks where the whiskers grow, and outline the whiskers with long, curvy lines. Add more details to the eyes, refining their shape and adding the pupils. Darken the nostrils.

Step 4: Make the general outline of the tiger bolder, emphasizing all the main features of the face, such as the folds near the eyes, nose, mouth, cheeks, and chin. Then, work on the placement of the stripes and spots on the face, the forehead, and near the eyes. Give the spots a defined, rounded shape. Add even more fur texture to the head and chest. Add additional whiskers, and refine details in the eyes and nose.

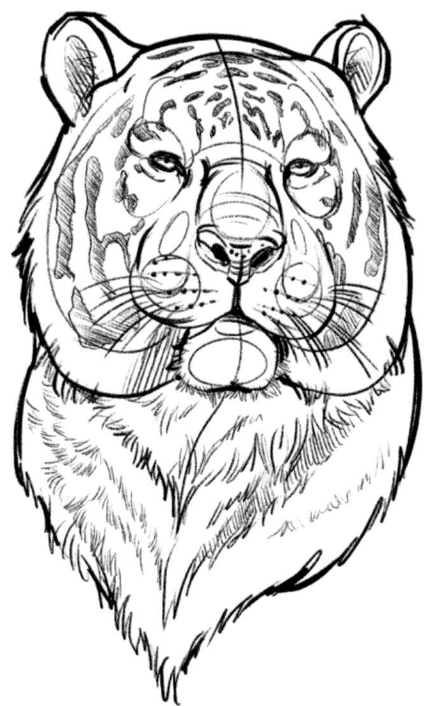

Step 5: Create two simple color mixes to separate different areas on the tiger's face. Mix ultramarine with water for a watery blue. Then, mix ochre with water to create a light yellowish mix. Then, create a new color mix for the tiger's nose:

- Mix A: carmine + ochre + water = warm, watery orangey-pink

Cover the entire tiger area with clean water. Work quickly without interruptions to apply all the colors using the wet-on-wet technique (page 17). Apply the ultramarine and water mix to the left side of the tiger, the inner ears, and the mouth. Then, use Mix A on the nose tip. If the color starts to spread too much, remove the excess with a clean, dry brush. Finally, apply the ochre and water mix to the nose, parts of the cheeks, some areas on the forehead, and the ears—these are spots for the yellow fur. Wait for this layer to dry.

Step 6: Mix two blue-gray colors that we'll use to create the shadow areas on the white parts of the tiger. We'll use the same colors from Step 5 but in different proportions.

- Mix A: ultramarine + a touch of sepia + water = medium blue-gray
- Mix B: Mix 6A (above) + more sepia = dark gray-blue

Apply Mix A to some areas of the face and neck. Use the tip of a medium brush to make wavy movements to imitate fur. Concentrate most of this color on the left side, under the face and cheeks. In this area, switch to a smaller brush and work between the whiskers, keeping them white for now by using thin strokes. Then, switch to Mix B and add it inside the ears with the same curvy strokes. Use this color to outline the top of the eye and nose, and cover the nostrils with it. Wait for this layer to dry.

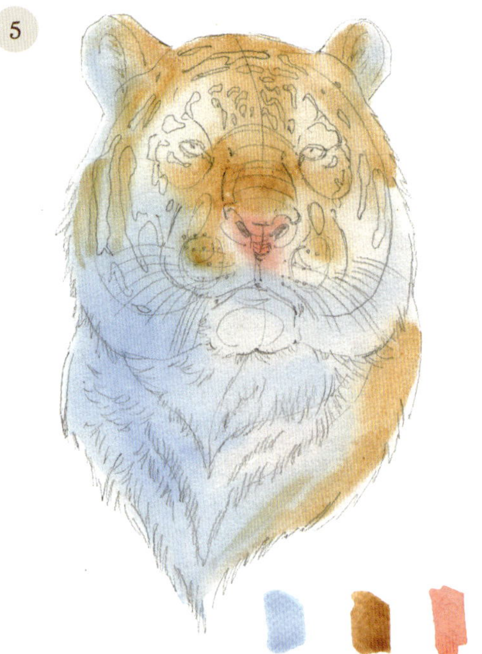

Ultramarine Ochre Mix A

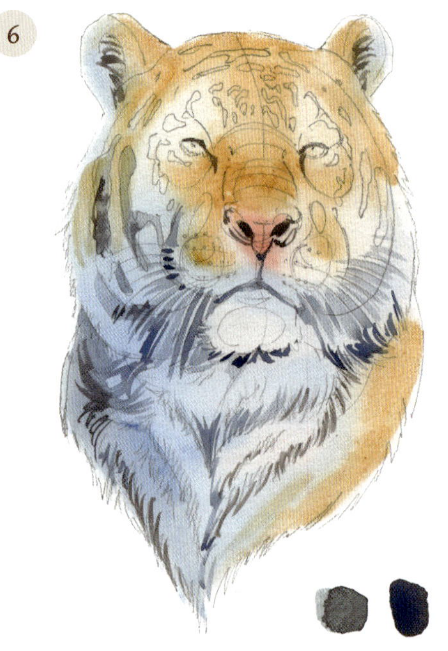

Mix A Mix B

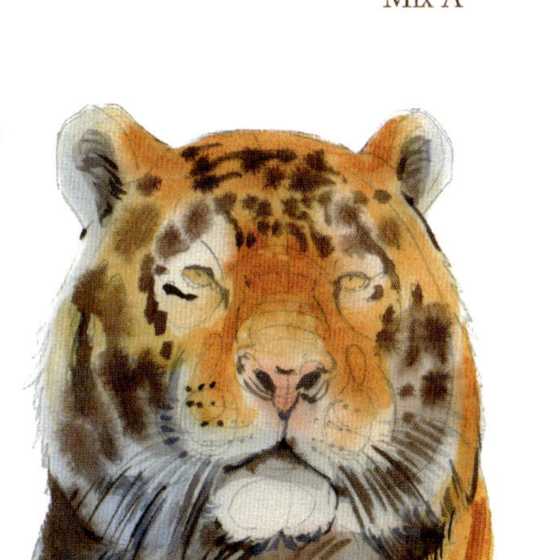

Mix A

Raw Sienna   Sepia

Step 7: Dilute Mix 6B with water, and apply it to the left half of the neck and under the neck, as well as around the cheeks and inside the ears. Then, mix a new color:

- Mix A: ochre + cadmium yellow + cadmium red + water = vibrant orange

Apply Mix A to the areas where the ochre and water mix from Step 5 was previously applied for more saturation. Use a more diluted version of the same color to cover the eyes.

Step 8: Combine raw sienna with water and then sepia with water. Cover the whole surface of the tiger with water. This will help unite what we've created so far and introduce new color seamlessly. Then, apply the raw sienna and water mix to the yellow areas. Apply the sepia and water mix to the dark spots. If the spots start to expand too much, clean the excess with a clean, dry brush. Use the same color to outline the texture of the fur on the neck. Wait for this layer to dry.

Step 9: Use the raw sienna and water mix from Step 8 to create saturation of the fur. Add this color to the nose, avoiding the tip. (Leave it untouched, and also avoid the under-eye area that should remain white.) Apply the raw sienna and water mix to the forehead, the ears, and the upper part of the cheeks, leaving the lower part white. Add the same color to the extreme right part of the neck. Then, mix a new color to darken the nose area between the eyes:

- Mix A: raw sienna + indigo + a touch of sepia + water = brown-green

Apply Mix A with a circular movement to the area where the nose connects to the forehead. Smooth the edges for a softer transition. Then, use the same color to outline the fur on the left and right sides of the head and neck. Then, mix a new color:

- Mix B: sepia + indigo + water = very dark, almost black color

Use Mix B to outline the eyes more clearly, using the very tip of your brush. Also use it to create the pupils in the eyes, define the nostrils and darken the insides, outline the mouth, and darken some of the fur that separates the lower part of the head from the neck.

Step 10: Mix a new color:

- Mix A: indigo + sepia + water = medium blue-gray

Use a big or medium brush to cover the whole triangular area in the middle of the neck with Mix A. Darken some of the left area of the neck as well, and then also darken the areas between the whiskers. Use Mix 9B to underline the area at the base of the whiskers, and draw small dots where the whiskers grow from. Finally, enhance the dark spots near the eyes.

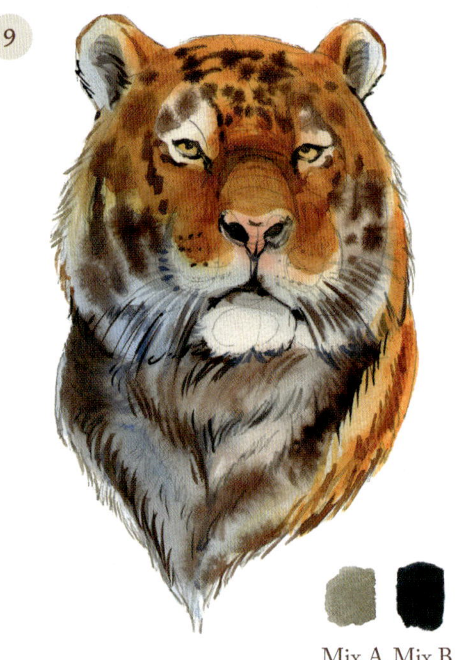

Mix A Mix B

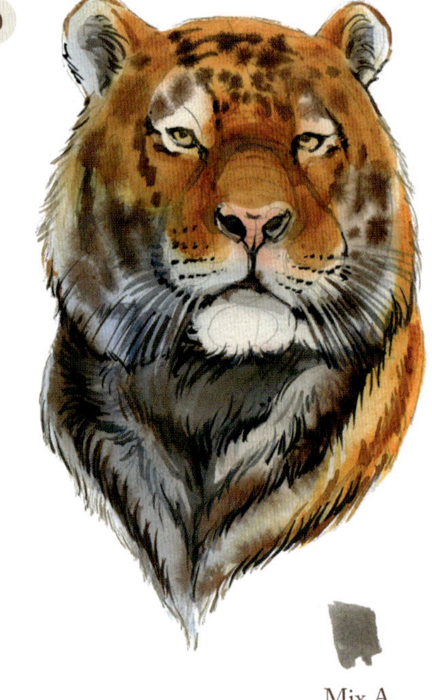

Mix A

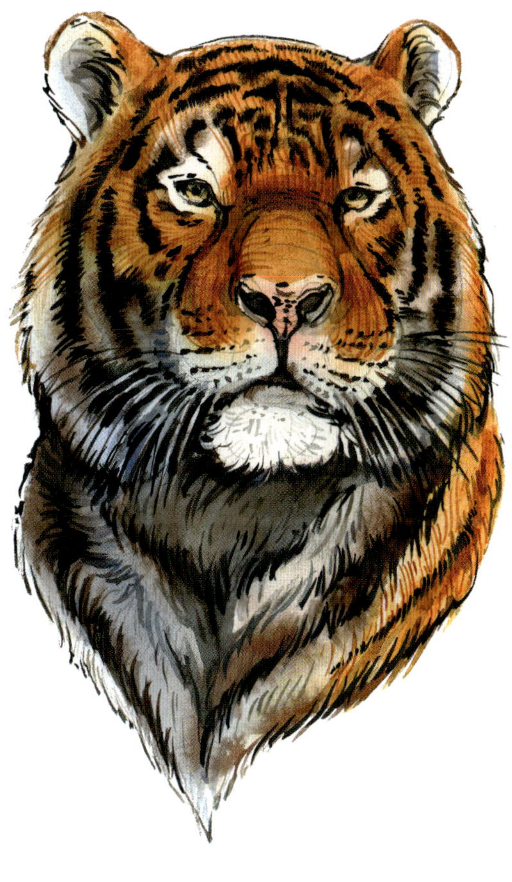

Mix A

Step 11: Take the raw sienna and water mix from Step 8, and with the tip of your small brush, create thin lines following the natural curves of the orange fur. Vary the length of the lines depending on where they are. For larger areas, like the right part of the neck, the lines can be longer. For smaller areas, such as the face, and especially near the eyes, the lines should be shorter.

Once you've finished the texture on the orange fur, move on to darkening the dark stripes on the face and neck. Use the very dark, almost black Mix 9B, and with the tip of your small brush, darken the lines and spots. As always, follow the natural direction of the fur when making your strokes. Use the same color and technique on the inside of the ears, add more dark details to the fur on the neck, and outline certain areas of the tiger, making sure the outline is not uniform. Add similar details to the tip of the nose using small dots. Also, add details near the eyes and underline the fur on the jaw and between the whiskers. Add even more small dots on the cheeks where the whiskers grow.

Then, mix a new color:

- Mix A: indigo + sepia + water = light gray (or use an existing gray color from your palette and dilute it with water if necessary)

Darken the top sides of the eye with Mix A. This will show the shadow cast from the eyebrows, giving the eyes more character and depth. After that, don't forget to restore the pupil and make it darker using Mix 9B. As a final step, use long, thin, wavy lines to draw additional whiskers, some of which can even extend beyond the outline of the tiger for a more spontaneous and realistic look. After that, your painting is ready!

Frangipani

The frangipani, with its delicate white petals, is a wonderful subject to explore in watercolor. This flower plays a significant role in Balinese culture and rituals. Often used in offerings, ceremonies, and as decoration, it embodies spiritual connection. In this tutorial, you'll learn a key watercolor technique: painting white subjects without using white paint. By leaving areas of paper untouched and painting around them, you'll create the illusion of white petals. This lesson will also show you how to add spontaneity and a sketchy charm to your illustrations with an expressive background. Let's begin!

Colors Needed

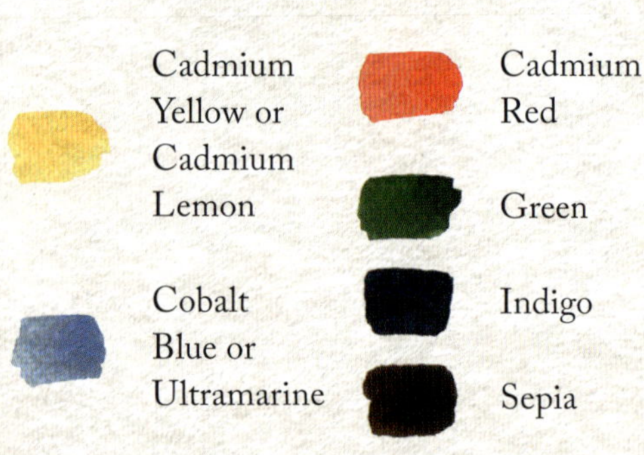

Cadmium Yellow or Cadmium Lemon

Cadmium Red

Green

Cobalt Blue or Ultramarine

Indigo

Sepia

Suggested Paper Orientation: Vertical

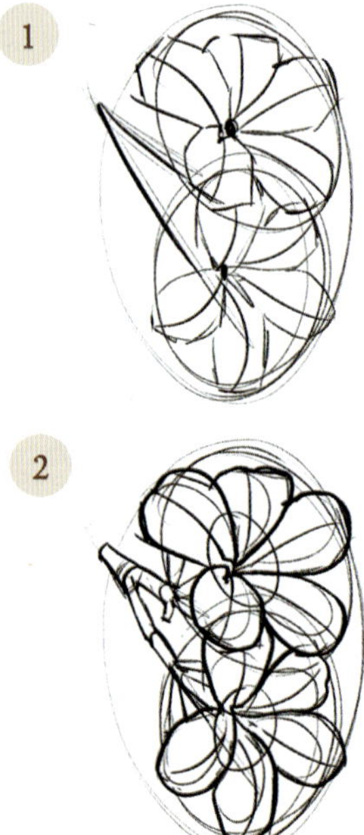

Step 1: Draw an oval in the middle of your paper. Draw two smaller intersecting ovals inside the main oval, one on top of the other. These smaller ovals will represent the two flowers. Place a point on the left side of the main oval, slightly above its center, and connect this point to the smaller ovals with two lines to indicate the stems. Next, add a point in the middle of each small oval; these will be the centers of the blooms. Sketch five individual petals of each flower. These are curved, so sketch them with curvy lines in different directions. Then, outline the shapes of the petals with ovals that are thicker toward the outside and thinner toward the center of the flower. Refine the shape of the petals further with short lines.

Step 2: Make the stems thicker, and add details by dividing them into smaller sections. Next, let's add more details to the flowers. Draw two smaller ovals in the center of each flower to represent the yellow area, which will guide us during the painting process. Then, refine the shape of each petal, making them more fluid and rounded.

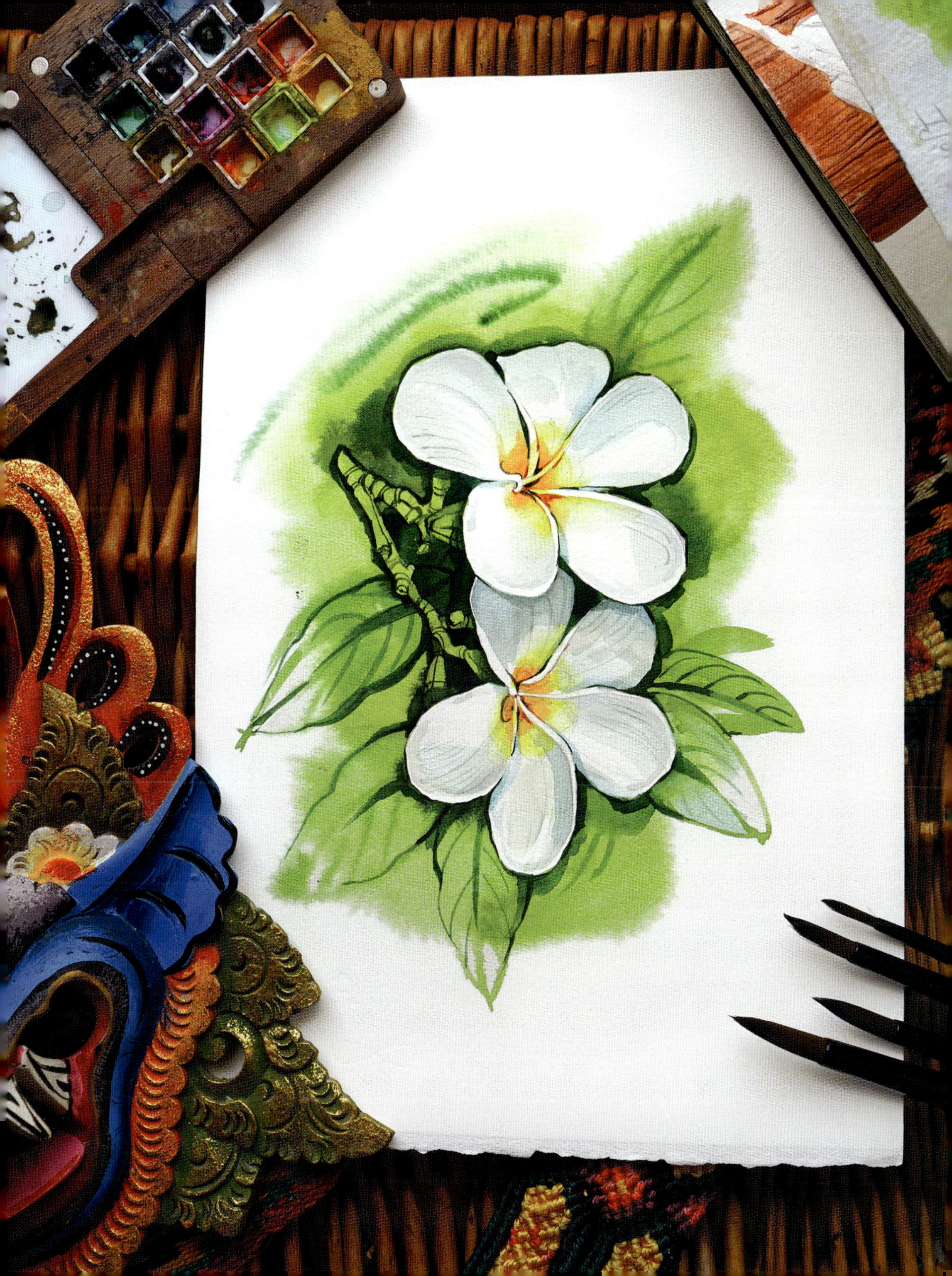

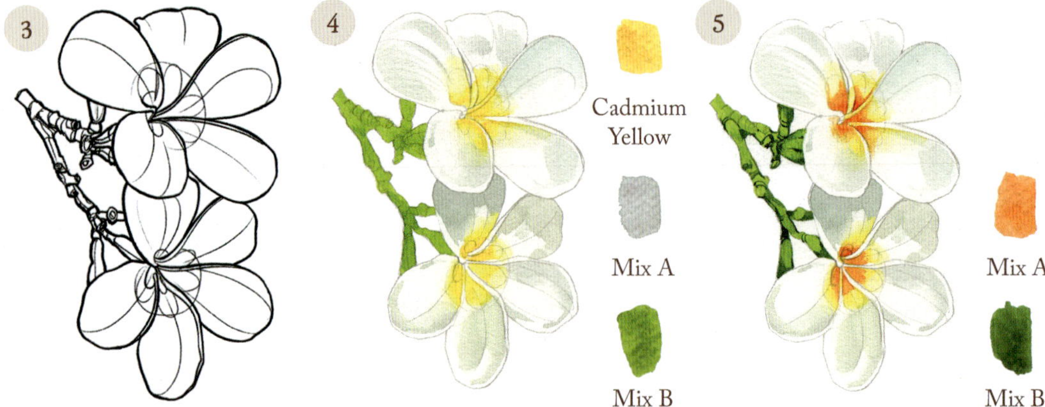

Step 3: Erase any guide lines that are no longer needed, including the initial oval. Add detail to the stem with short lines, as well as some bumps and imperfections. Add folds to the edges of the petals—this is characteristic of the frangipani flower and will help make it look more realistic. Also, add some curvy lines to the center of the flowers to outline the yellow areas more clearly. Once done, you can begin painting.

Step 4: Combine cadmium yellow or cadmium lemon with water for a light yellow mix. Next, create two color mixes:

- Mix A: cobalt blue or ultramarine + cadmium red + water = natural-cool gray
- Mix B: cadmium yellow or cadmium lemon + green + water = medium green

Apply the cadmium yellow and water mix to the center of one flower, avoiding the folds of the petals at the center. While the yellow is still wet, soften the edges with clean water to create a smooth color transition from the white petal to the yellow center. Repeat this for the second flower.

Use Mix A to outline the shadows on the petals, ensuring the gray is light; leave a good amount of pure white paper, especially on the top flower. Soften the edges of your strokes. The darkest petals should be those behind the top flower. Avoid painting the folds so they remain white. Finally, apply Mix B evenly to the stems. Let this layer dry before proceeding.

Step 5: Mix two additional colors:

- Mix A: cadmium yellow or cadmium lemon + cadmium red + water = yellow-orange
- Mix B: Mix 4B (cadmium yellow or cadmium lemon + green + water) + more green = saturated green

Apply Mix A to the very center of the flowers, between the petals, making sure to preserve the folds. The orange should cover approximately half of the current yellow area; when you reach halfway, soften the edges. Use Mix B to add shadows and details to the stems, especially near the petals, where shadows are cast by the flowers. Use larger strokes close to the petals and smaller strokes and lines along the rest of the stems.

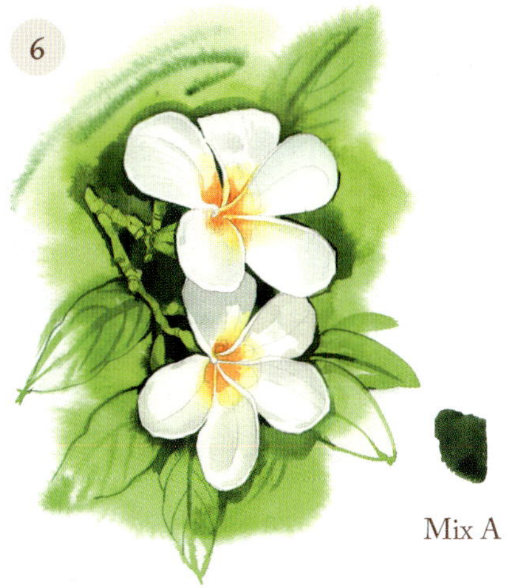

6

Mix A

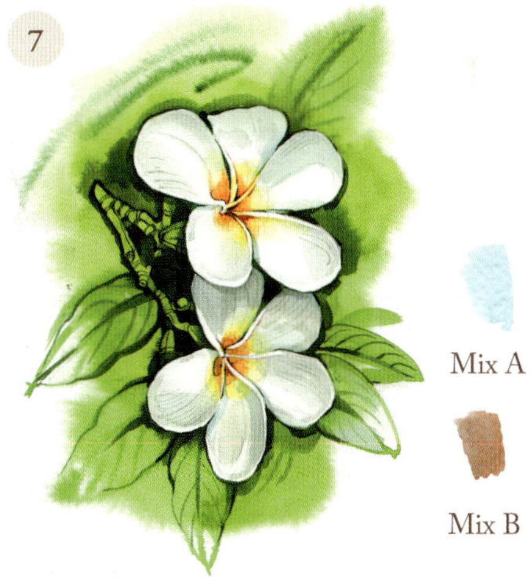

7

Mix A

Mix B

Step 6: One of the fundamental principles of watercolor is that we don't use white paint to represent white subjects; instead, we use the natural white of the paper. The best way to make a subject appear truly white is to place it against a darker background. That's exactly what we'll do here. Mix a generous amount of the following colors to avoid remixing during the process. You will need Mix 4B, Mix 5B, and a new color:

- Mix A: green + indigo + water = dark, saturated green

With a large brush or a mop brush, cover the background around the flowers with clean water, leaving some dry paper near the flowers—don't get too close to them. Ensure the paper is evenly wet, then quickly move on, as we'll use the wet-on-wet technique (page 17) to create an expressive, organic-looking background.

Apply Mix 4B around the flowers, allowing the color to expand and bloom—exactly the effect we're aiming for. This is your chance to get creative—since the effect is nearly impossible to replicate exactly, your outcome will be uniquely yours. Use Mix 4B to suggest leaves pointing in different directions. While the paper is still wet, switch to Mix 5B and add it close to the petals, especially in areas where you left the paper dry. Use the same

color to create expressive strokes and hints of leaf veins. Next, switch to Mix A and apply it between the petals and near the stems. By now, your paper may be drying; if so, use Mix 5B to define outlines and enhance leaf veins and details. Remember to add details only to some leaves, maintaining a spontaneous, sketchy appearance.

Step 7: Mix two new colors:

- Mix A: cobalt blue or ultramarine + a touch of sepia + water = light blue
- Mix B: cadmium red + sepia + water = medium, muted orange

Apply Mix A to the shadowed areas of the petals (on their right sides). Then, darken the two upper petals of the flower that's positioned behind. Use this same color in very thin, long strokes to create texture on some petals. Use Mix 5B and 6A to further define the outlines of the petals and add more detail to some of the background leaves. Make the outlines of the stems bolder, adding final details with the tip of your brush and thin lines along the stems. As a finishing touch, add a bit of Mix B to the very center of the flowers and use it to outline the folds within the petals for added contrast. This will make the flower appear more complete. Now, your painting is finished!

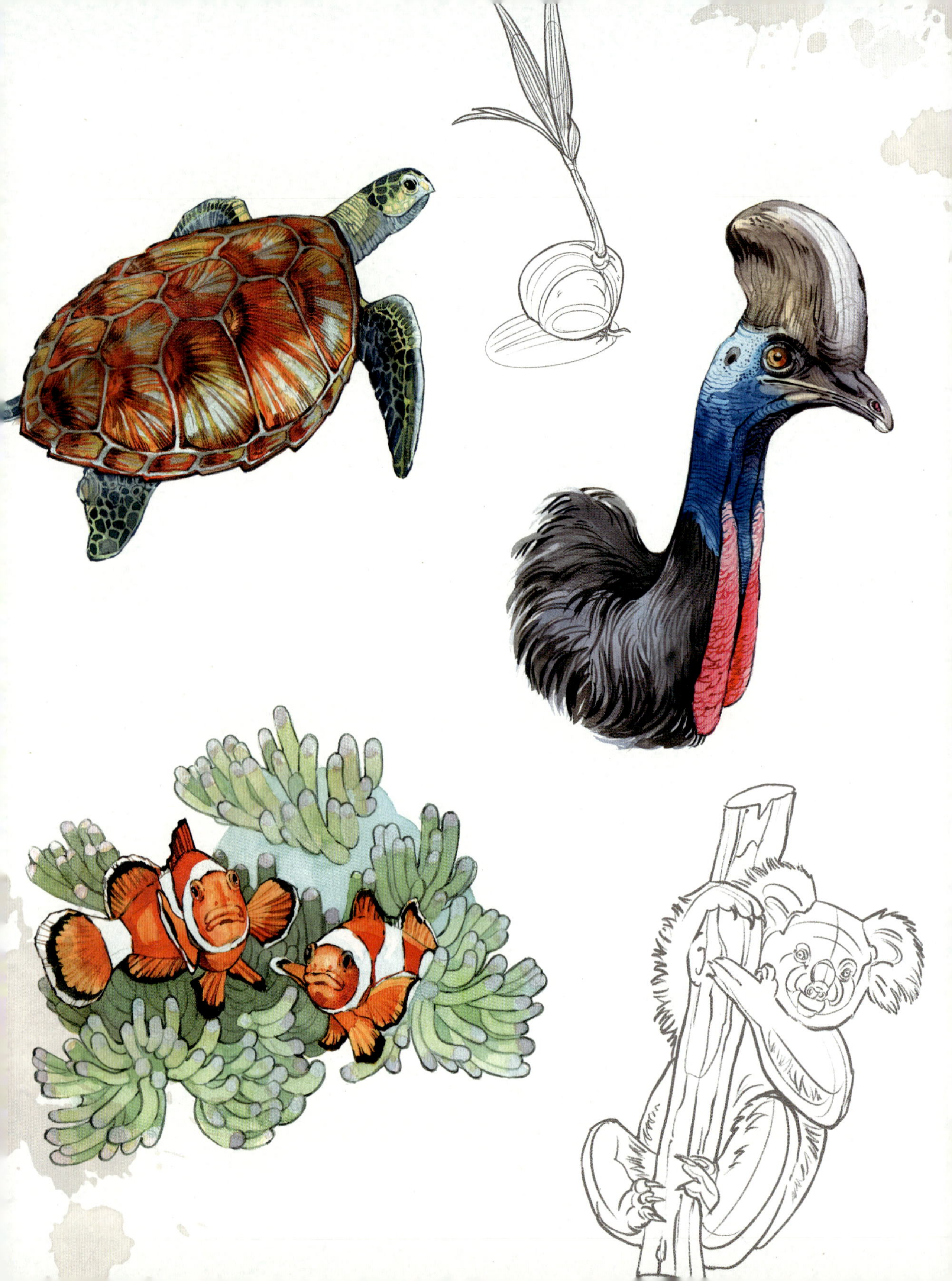

Oceania
The Wonders of Countless Islands

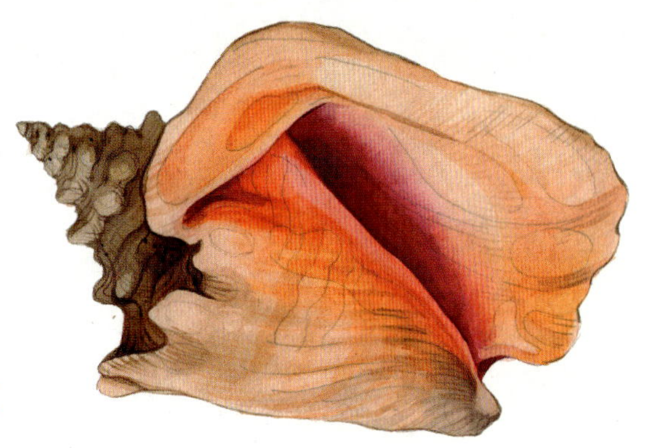

One lifetime isn't enough to explore the countless island of Oceania, a beautiful archipelago stretching from Southeast Asia to New Zealand. It's hard to pinpoint exactly how many islands make up this unique continent, but estimates suggest there are over 25,000. The name "Oceania" reflects the continent's deep connection to the sea, with its islands surrounded by numerous oceans and seas, including the Pacific Ocean and the Coral Sea—which is why the first project in this chapter is a Conch Shell (page 179)!

One of the most charming and recognizable inhabitants of Oceania's coral reefs is the Clownfish (page 199). Clownfish are incredibly territorial and will fiercely protect their homes. The anemones they live within provide them with protection, as their toxic tentacles are harmless to the clownfish, making it a perfect defense mechanism. I've had the chance to observe them in the wild, and it's amazing how they boldly defend their territory—even against predators many times their size!

No discussion of Oceania would be complete without mentioning the Hawksbill Sea Turtle (page 189), one of the longest-living creatures in the ocean. These graceful animals, which can live for over 100 years, are known for their long migrations. Interestingly, they return to the same beaches where they were born to lay their eggs. Their journey is a testament to the powerful instincts that guide these ancient mariners of the sea.

Oceania is also the land of marsupials—mammals that give birth to tiny, underdeveloped young, which finish growing in a pouch on their mother's belly. In this chapter, we'll focus on the Koala (page 194). These tree-dwelling creatures are primarily nocturnal and spend most of their lives munching on eucalyptus leaves—plants that are unique to Australia.

In the bird kingdom, one of the most striking and mysterious creatures of Oceania is the Cassowary (page 183). This large, flightless bird is often described as the world's most dangerous avian due to its powerful legs and sharp claws. Known for its strength and warrior-like nature, the cassowary is a symbol of the wild, untamed spirit of Oceania.

Oceania's ecosystems are home to some of the planet's most unique flora and fauna. From the tropical rainforests of New Guinea to the arid desert of Australia, the plant and animal life here is as diverse as it is fascinating. From Coconut Sprouts (page 204) to cassowaries, this chapter will take you on a colorful journey through incredible landscapes, brimming with life. So, let's get started!

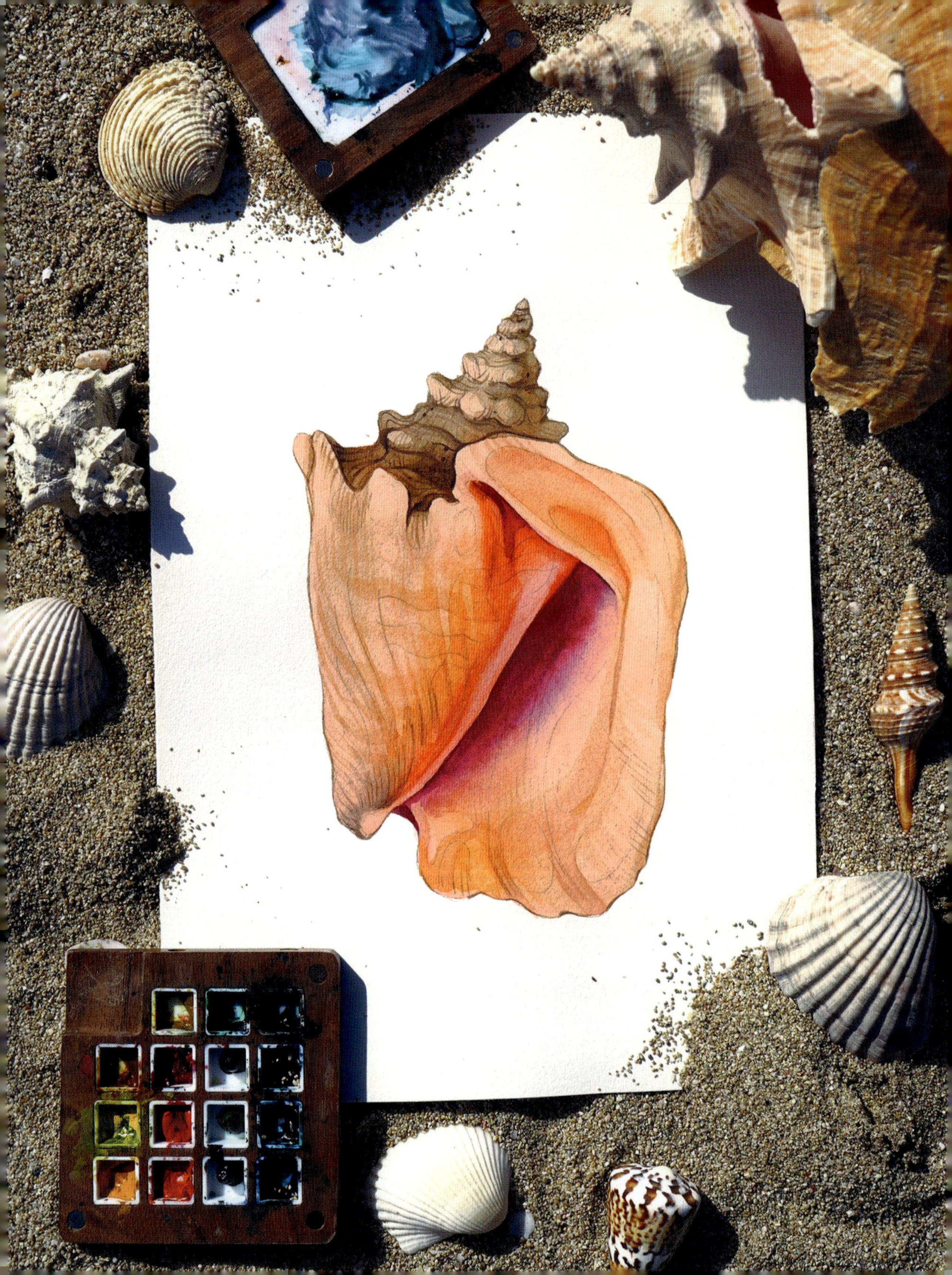

Conch Shell

Shells come in a stunning variety of shapes and sizes, but what unites them all is the perfect harmony behind their structure. The conch shell, known for its iconic spiral shape, is not only a treat for the eyes but also a remarkable example of nature's engineering. These shells follow the Fibonacci sequence, a pattern common in nature. In this tutorial, you'll explore how to paint the shell's intricate textures and smooth gradients. By practicing these techniques, you'll capture the depth and natural shine of the conch, while refining your shading skills and learning to represent complex structures.

Colors Needed

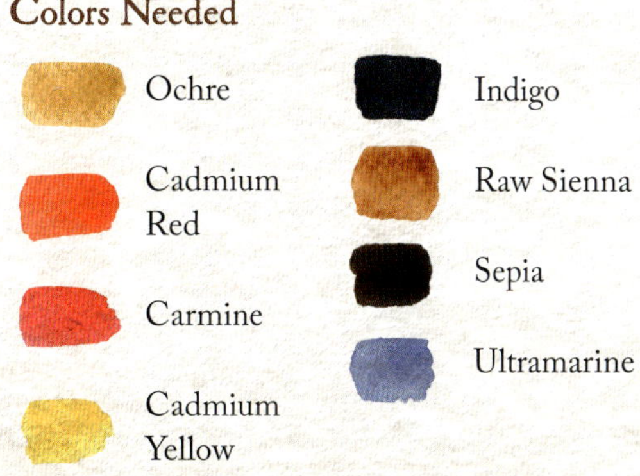

Suggested Paper Orientation: Vertical

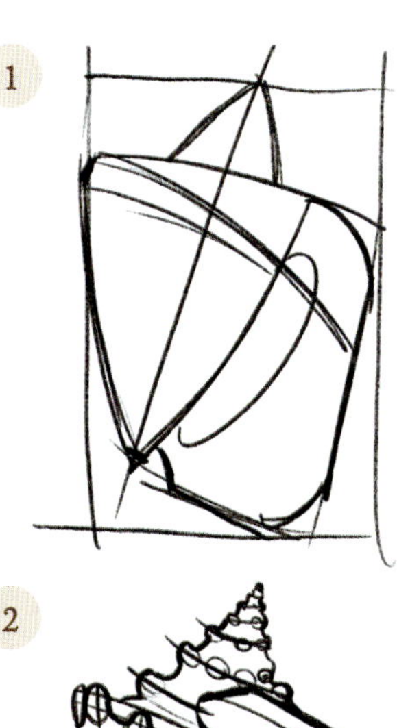

Step 1: Draw a rectangle that is taller than it is wide. Then, draw a diagonal line from the top center down to the lower left corner. This will represent the middle line of the shell. Next, outline the body of the shell with a triangle that has slightly curved sides. The triangle should be positioned around the middle of the diagonal line, slightly closer to the bottom than the top. Add another smaller triangle on the top of the base of the larger triangle, facing the opposite direction, with the tip at the beginning of the diagonal line. Next, outline the aperture of the shell with a straight line along the lower and right sides, and add more curved lines that connect these two lines to the body of the shell. Finally, create a diagonal line inside the shell, going from the top toward the aperture.

Step 2: Erase the exterior guide lines, and outline the spire using ovals. Place the lowest level of ovals along the guide line. Then, outline the upper levels and add your ovals. Remember, the higher the level, the smaller the ovals will be. Next, refine the outline, giving it a more organic, wavy appearance, and define the outline of the aperture. Add three ovals on the lower side of the aperture to help position the highlights during painting. Add a few lines that follow the natural shape of the shell to lead the viewer's eye inward.

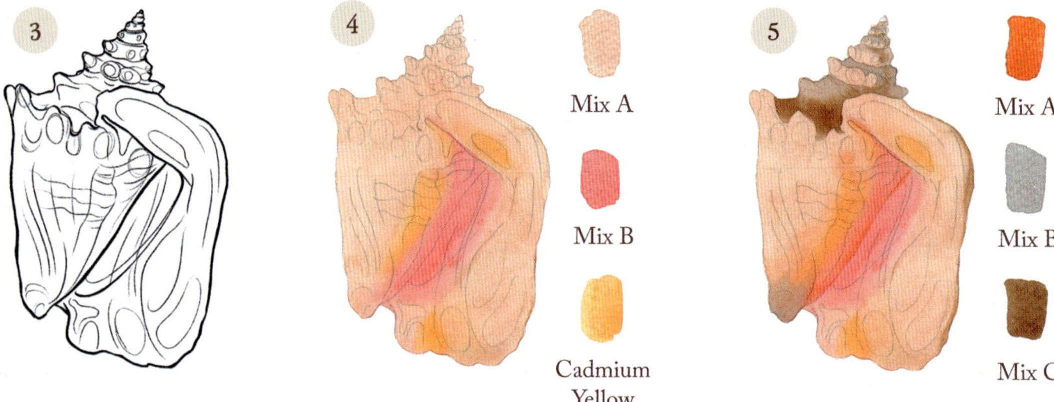

Step 3: Add similar lines to the body of the shell to emphasize its shape. Refine the shape of the horns, erase any distracting guide lines, and make the outline smoother. Add the final texture lines to the body and the opening. Once this is done, we can begin painting.

Step 4: We will mainly use the wet-on-wet technique (page 17) in the beginning steps of this tutorial, so make sure to paint quickly and mix enough paint to avoid needing to remix in the middle of the process. First, create the following color mixes:

- Mix A: ochre + cadmium red + water (more water than pigment) = light pinkish-beige
- Mix B: cadmium red + carmine + water (more pigment than water) = medium pink

Also, make another simple mix consisting of cadmium yellow with water.

Apply Mix A to the entire surface of the shell, except for the inside area and the right border of the cone body, near the concave area. Apply Mix B to the right side of the cone body and to the aperture of the shell. Then, apply the cadmium yellow and water mix to the lower part of the shell and some areas on the right side of the cone next to the medium pink Mix B. This should create brighter touches of color in the shell's surface. Wait for this layer to dry.

Step 5: Create these color mixes:

- Mix A: cadmium yellow + cadmium red + water = medium orange
- Mix B: indigo + a touch of cadmium red + water = medium grayish-blue
- Mix C: raw sienna + a touch of sepia + water = medium khaki

Start by painting the tip of the shell. Apply Mix B to the right part of the spiral area of the shell and the areas beneath the horns. You should create stripes of lighter and darker colors. Once you've painted about two-thirds of the section, without letting the color dry, switch to Mix C and apply it to the remaining area of the tip. You should achieve a seamless transition between the gray on top and the brown below. Use Mix C to accentuate the shadow area at the tip of the shell. If the layer is still wet, just add these spots and let them blend with the rest. If the area has dried, use the wet-on-dry technique (page 16) to introduce the color and smooth out the edges for a seamless transition. Since this color is already on your brush, outline the border of the right side of the shell with a thin line, especially on top. Then, smooth this out.

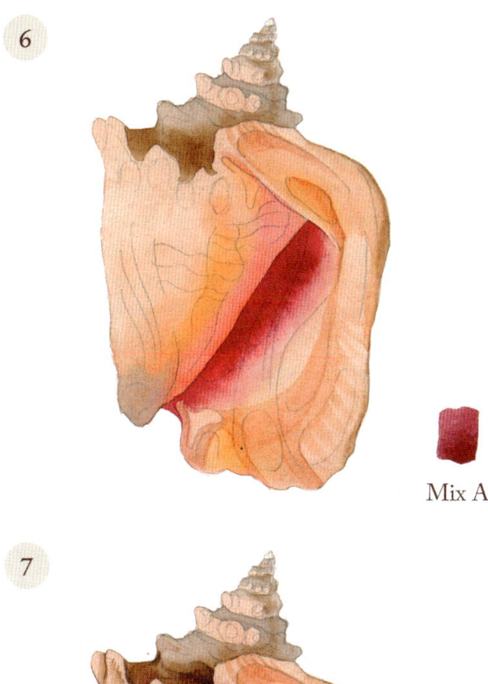

Next, let's focus on the cone section of the shell (body). Start by covering the upper portion of this area with water (this area starts beneath the Mix C we just applied). Once you've covered about one-third of the surface, continue applying water on the left side and switch to Mix A on the right side. This is where we will separate the cone part from the internal part (aperture), so be sure to respect the border of the cone. Once you just about reach the lower tip of the cone, switch to Mix B and paint the tip. Wait for this layer to dry.

Step 6: Let's start working on the aperture of the shell. We will need Mix 4A and a new color:

- Mix A: carmine + cadmium red + ultramarine + water = dark red

Apply Mix 4A to the shadow areas on the right side of the shell using the wet-on-dry technique. The goal here is to give more volume to that part of the shell by darkening only the areas in shadow, leaving the others lighter. Use lines to emphasize the natural concave movement in this part of the shell. Wait for this layer to dry.

To paint the darker inside part, start covering the inside area of the shell with clean water, starting from the right side. Before reaching the left side, switch to Mix A while the water is still wet, and continue painting this area until you reach the end of this area. As a result, the dark red Mix A will start to bleed into the water, creating a smooth color gradient from lighter pink to darker red in the deepest part of the shell. Wait for this layer to dry.

Step 7: Now, let's focus on the cone (body) part of the shell. You will need to make sure to have the following mixes prepared: 5A, 5B, 5C, and 6A. Cover the left side of the body with water. Then, add some texture on the shell using touches of Mix 5C under the largest horns. Switch to Mix 5B and create texture on the left part and the lower tip of the shell using curved lines that repeat the circular movement of the shell. Do the same on the right side, but use Mix 5A. Add some Mix 6A in the small top area (hole), and use Mix 5B to darken the area under the largest horns. Smooth the edges to make the dark brown color blend nicely into the rest of the surface.

Step 8: With a small brush, cover the entire right area of the shell's opening with water. This will unify the surface, smooth the strokes, and make it look more uniform. Let it dry. Meanwhile, start working on the spiral tip of the shell. We will use mixes 5B and 5C for this. First, cover the entire spiral cone of the shell with Mix 5B, then apply Mix 5C to the right side. This will make the spiral part look more cohesive and uniform, and give it a more three-dimensional look. While doing this, the aperture of the shell should have already dried. Cover the aperture with clean water, beginning at the right side. Then, before reaching the left side, switch to Mix 6A while the water is still wet, and continue painting until you reach the end of this area.

Step 9: Create texture on the spiral part of the shell using the very tip of your small brush, the dry brushing technique (page 18), and Mix 5C. Use the same technique with Mix 4A and Mix 5B to create very thin lines that will underline the shape of the shell and guide the viewer's eye inside the shell. Do the same for the tip of the shell using Mix 5B, but this time, emphasize the shape of the tip. Then, use Mix 5A to create wavy horizontal lines on the conic body of the shell. Start from right to left, making sure the left ends of the strokes are thinner than the right side. Create a mix of sepia and water to create a dark brown, and use it to create additional contrast on top of the main horns. Also add a few dots and lines to the spiral part of the shell for more interest. Apply Mix 6A in the area where the aperture transitions into the conic body. That's it! Your painting is complete.

8

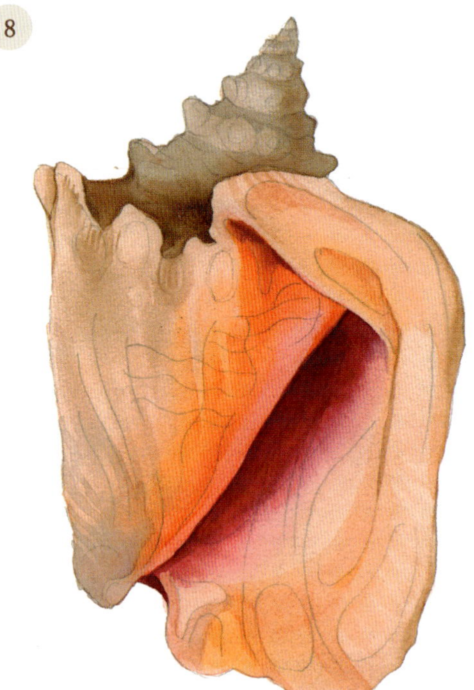

9

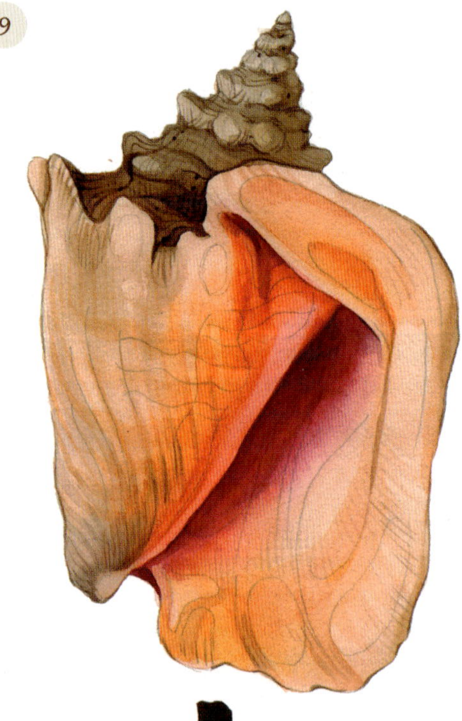

Sepia

Cassowary

The cassowary is a striking and fascinating bird, native to the tropical forests of Papua New Guinea, northern Australia, and nearby islands. Known for its vivid blue and black feathers and the helmet-like casque on its head, the cassowary is often considered one of the most dangerous birds in the world due to its powerful legs and sharp claws. In this tutorial, we will focus on painting the head of the cassowary, learning how to represent its unique facial features realistically. You will also discover techniques to paint the bird's hairlike feathers, capturing the texture and appearance of this extraordinary bird's crown and facial structure with precision.

Colors Needed

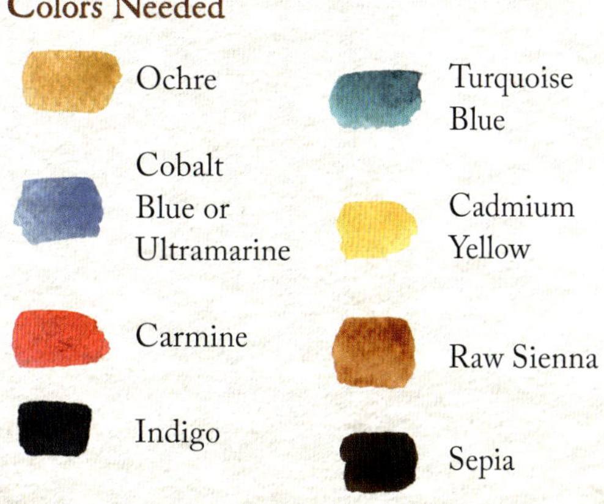

Suggested Paper Orientation: Vertical

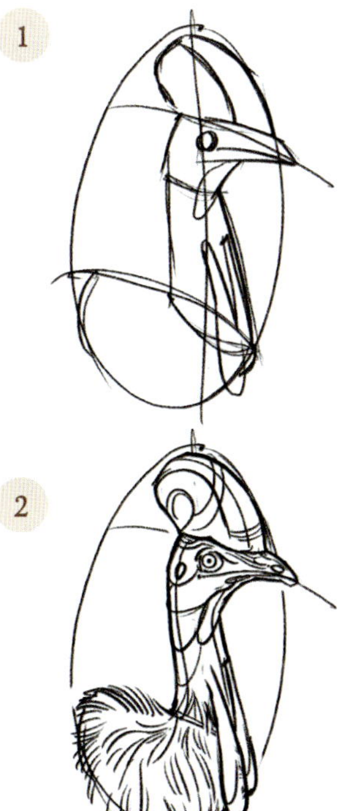

Step 1: Draw an oval in the middle of your paper. Draw a vertical line slightly to the right of the actual center of the oval. This is the line of the bird's neck. Next, divide the main oval horizontally into three parts, with the middle slightly bigger. The lower portion is the beginning of the body, and the top line represents the direction of the beak. Outline the neck with two parallel lines, the head with an oval, and the beak with a pointy triangle. Add a bony crest on top of the head using half an oval. Place the eye as a small circle, and sketch the wattles as long, thin ovals, narrower at the top and wider at the lower tips.

Step 2: Draw the eyelids and the pupil. Add texture to the beak and a nostril on the top side of the beak's tip. Add some texture to the neck by drawing a long line parallel to the outline, which will help define the light and shadow area later. Add texture to the bony crest using long lines, and begin outlining the feather texture on the body. The feathers of the cassowary are more similar to fur, so use long, wavy strokes in different directions.

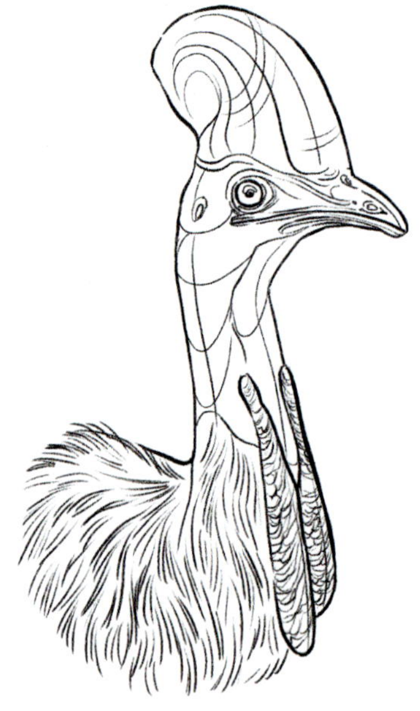

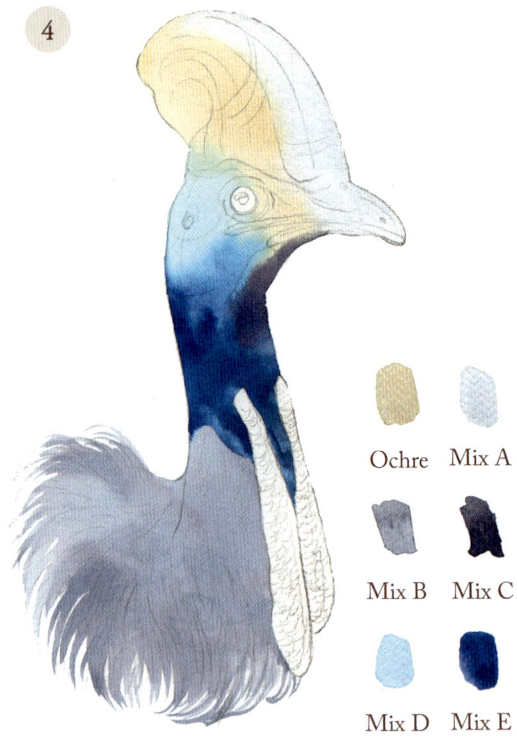

Step 3: Erase all unnecessary guide lines. Add more details and depth to the eye, outlining the highlight with a tiny circle. Use thin, long lines to outline the opening of the beak and the eyebrow. Add more fur-like feathers to the body and add texture to the wattles. Once you've added these details, you can start painting.

Step 4: Create a simple mix by combining ochre and water to make a watery, light yellow. Then, mix these colors:

- Mix A: cobalt blue or ultramarine + a touch of carmine + water = watery purple
- Mix B: same as Mix 4A (above) but with more pigment and less water = purple
- Mix C: same as Mix 4B (above) but with even more pigment and a touch of indigo = dark purple
- Mix D: ultramarine or cobalt + turquoise blue + water = light blue
- Mix E: same as Mix 4D (above) but with much more pigment and less water = saturated blue

Start painting from the top of the bird and gradually work your way down, trying to work through these steps without interruption to ensure seamless transitions. Apply Mix A to the right side of the bony head crest and to the beak. Without letting this color dry, switch to the yellow ochre and water mix and cover the left side of the crest and the area of the face to the right of the eye. Continue the blending without letting the colors dry by switching to Mix D and covering the part of the head to the left of the eye. Leave the eye white for now. Quickly switch to Mix E and apply it to the beginning of the neck, pulling the color downward until it reaches the feather area.

Don't forget to paint the space between the wattles. After that, apply Mix C under the beak and to the right of the area where the beak transitions into the neck. The most challenging part of this step is finished.

(Step 4 continued)

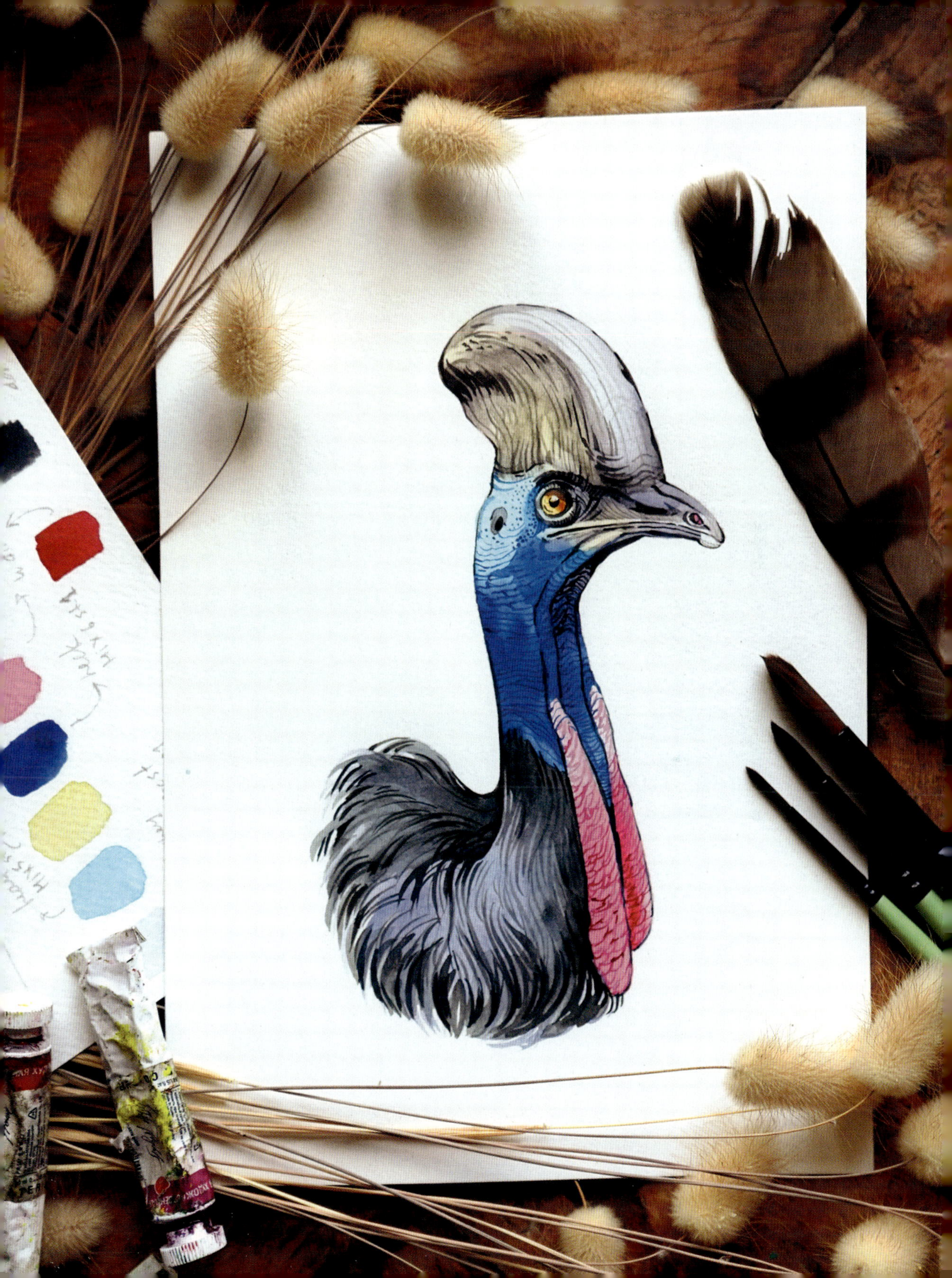

Apply Mix B to the remaining part of the neck and to outline the body. The trick here is to start outlining the "hairy" feathers. Begin filling this area with color from the center, then, instead of creating a neat outline on the edge of the body, use a feathery edge. Once the internal part of the body is covered, follow the lines of your drawing to create curvy brushstrokes. Start the strokes from the outer part and bring them inward to maintain more control and achieve a thinner tip. Vary the direction of the strokes to follow the pencil drawing, and avoid having the strokes look too uniform. Once the individual strokes are connected and the solid color fills the center of the body, you're done with this step. Wait for this layer to dry.

Step 5: Mix cadmium yellow with water and raw sienna with water. Apply the cadmium yellow and water mix to the left part of the eyeball. While it's still wet, cover the right part of the eye with the raw sienna and water mix, avoiding the highlight. Next, let's paint the wattles. Create two similar color mixes for these, different only in intensity. The first mix is carmine with water to obtain a light pink, and the second is the same but with more carmine and less water for a darker pink.

Start painting the left wattle with the light pink. Once you've reached about one-quarter of the way down, switch to the darker pink. Once the first wattle is dry, paint the second using the same method, only adding more of the darker pink near the left wattle to showcase the shadow in that area. Next, use the light pink to paint the nose hole.

Apply Mix 4B around the eyeball, leaving some white space for the eyelid. Bring the same mix closer to the nose and along the visual border between the purple and yellow colors of the crest. Paint the eyebrow, then use the lighter Mix 4A to create long vertical strokes on the crest. These strokes will highlight the texture and the direction of the crest.

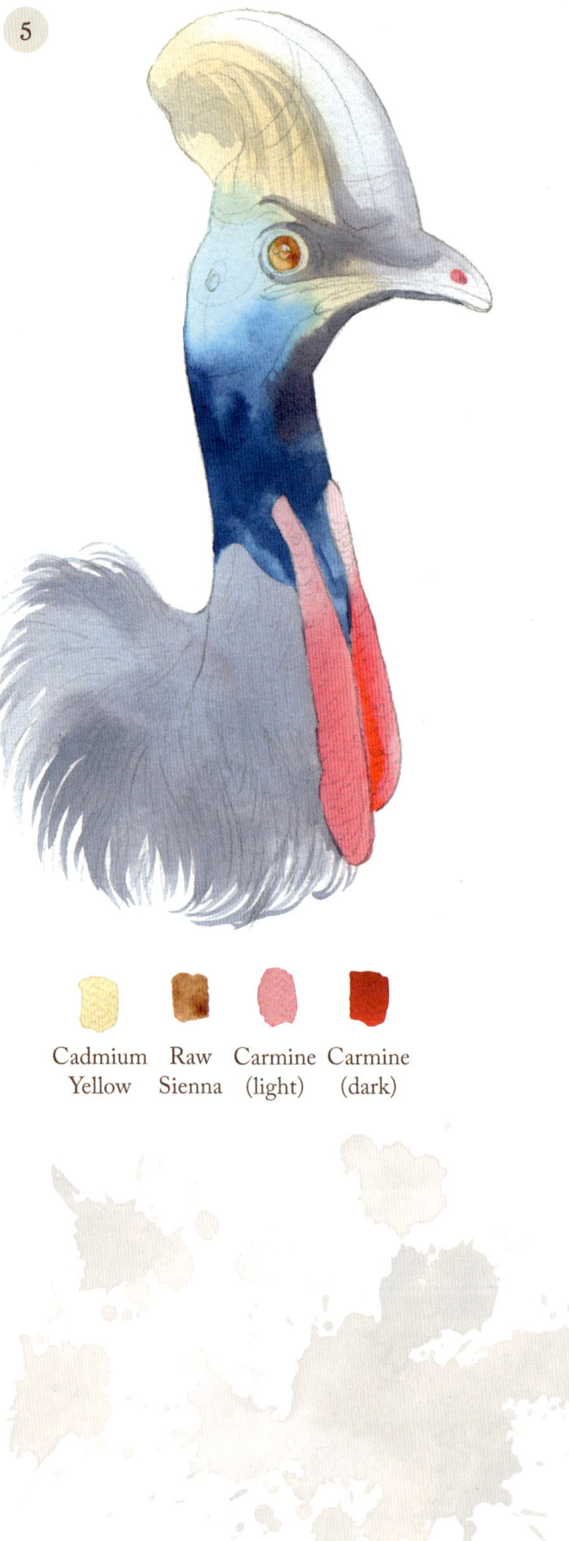

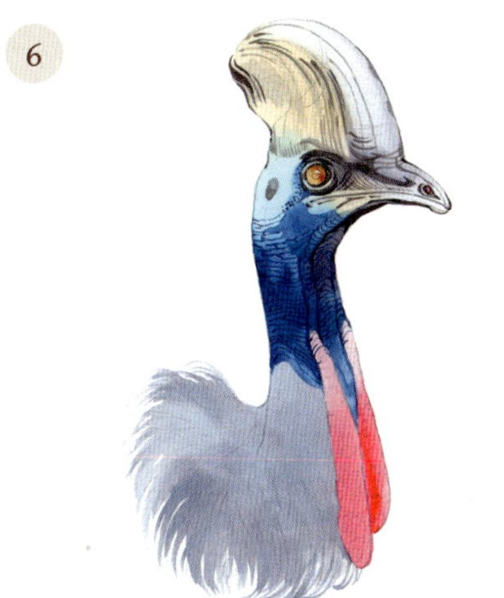

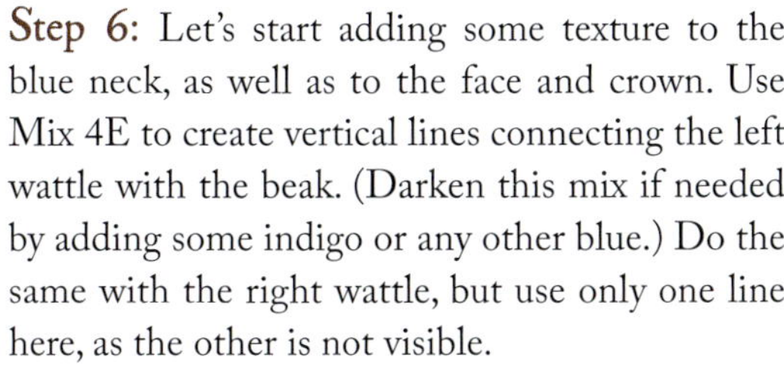

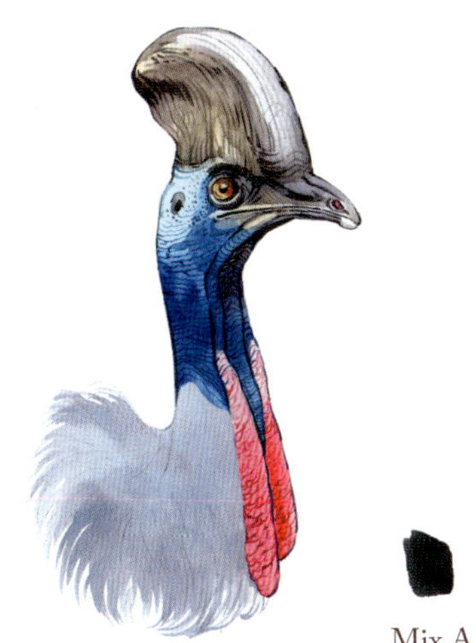

Mix A

Step 6: Let's start adding some texture to the blue neck, as well as to the face and crown. Use Mix 4E to create vertical lines connecting the left wattle with the beak. (Darken this mix if needed by adding some indigo or any other blue.) Do the same with the right wattle, but use only one line here, as the other is not visible.

Using the same color, add thin, wavy, almost hairlike, horizontal lines to the left part of the neck. Ensure they follow the natural movement of the neck, helping to showcase the folds and skin texture. Do the same for the area between the wattles. Add some short, curvy lines to the top of the wattles, continuing across the whole surface of the wattle attached to the neck until you reach the beak.

Apply the same Mix 4E to the left side of the eye, then smooth out the edge for a seamless transition. Add some dot texture near the eye in the same area. Switch to Mix 4B and create more texture on the crest by adding long, thin strokes—thinner than before. Use the same color to make the outline of the crest more visible but not uniform. Then, outline the opening of the beak and paint the eyebrow, bringing it to the point where it almost connects with the nose hole. This line will represent the fold in that area.

Then, use the very tip of your brush to create short, hairlike strokes to create texture, starting from the mouth and moving toward the eyebrow. Use Mix 4C to add more details around the eye, outline the eyelid, and add wrinkles on the right side of the eye. Also, outline the nose hole, darken the outline of the beak, and add shadow under the beak.

Step 7: Add texture to the wattles in a similar way as we did with the neck in the last step. Use the darker pink carmine and water mix from Step 5 to paint thin lines and create a scale texture on both wattles. The texture should be darker on the lower side and brighter on the upper, so adjust the color by switching to the lighter carmine and water mix from Step 5 or by diluting the darker mix with water as you go.

Create a new mix:

- Mix A: indigo + sepia + water = dark, almost black

Apply Mix A to the pupil using the tip of your small brush, and then add some final touches and texture to the face, outline the beak opening more clearly, and add more texture to the eyebrow using short, thin strokes.

(Step 7 continued)

Add some line texture under the beak. Then, switch to Mix 4B, and with the body of your medium or large brush, apply it to the transition between the front and side of the crest, as well as to the left side of the crest. Use the same color to create texture with long, thin, vertical strokes, starting from the transition between the blue area on the head and the crest. Then, with Mix 4C, add some final touches to the beak and the outline, and give additional texture to the crest.

Step 8: Create this mix:

- Mix A: sepia + indigo + a touch of carmine + water = medium neutral gray

With your medium or large brush, apply Mix A to the part of the back (to the left side of the neck), to the area where the blue of the neck transitions into the feathers of the body, to the left side of the left wattle, and also to the lower side of the body.

Then, switch to your smaller brush to create hair texture across the whole surface of the body by following your sketch lines and the hair texture you outlined. Make sure your lines are curvy and thin with pointy tips. If you need some practice before committing to adding these details to the final painting, you can do so on a spare sheet of paper.

Use Mix 7A to add the final touches of contrast to the hairlike feathers. Concentrate these last strokes on the shadow areas, such as the left side of the neck at the bottom and near the wattles in the middle, giving them a more visible but still irregular outline. After this, your painting is done!

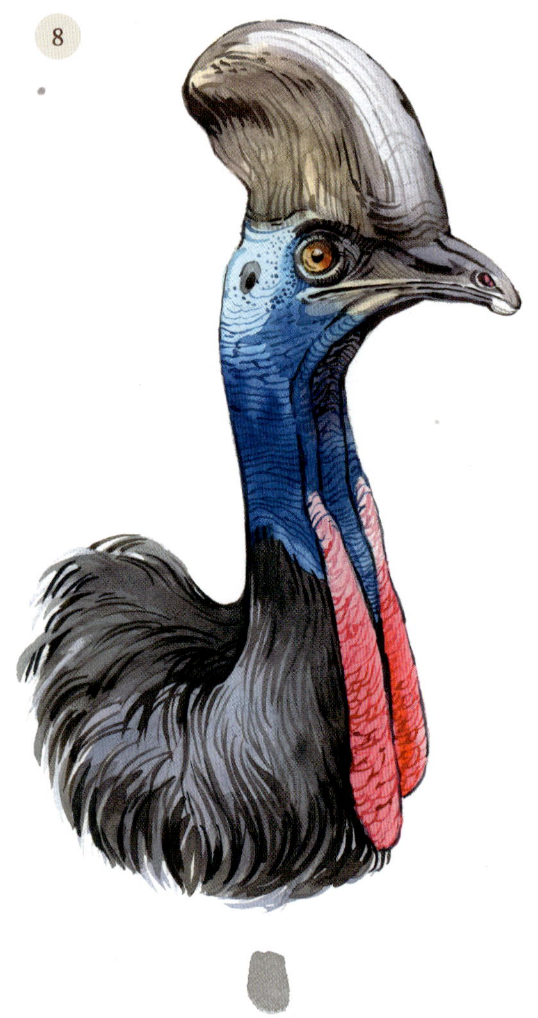

Mix A

Hawksbill Sea Turtle

The hawksbill sea turtle is known for its stunning, vibrant shell patterns and its vital role in maintaining healthy coral reefs. These turtles are skilled divers, spending most of their time in tropical and subtropical waters, where they help control the growth of sponges on coral reefs, allowing them to thrive. Here, you'll learn how to paint the turtle's intricate shell patterns and textures, using different watercolor techniques without masking fluid. This is a great opportunity to practice capturing complex textures and adding realistic details. Let's get started!

Colors Needed

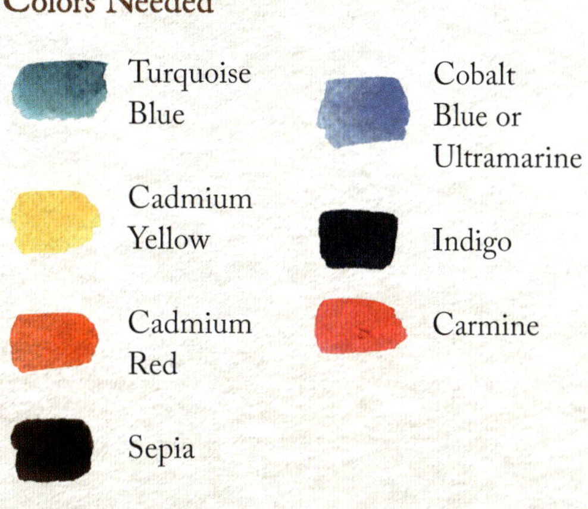

Turquoise Blue

Cobalt Blue or Ultramarine

Cadmium Yellow

Indigo

Cadmium Red

Carmine

Sepia

Suggested Paper Orientation: Horizontal

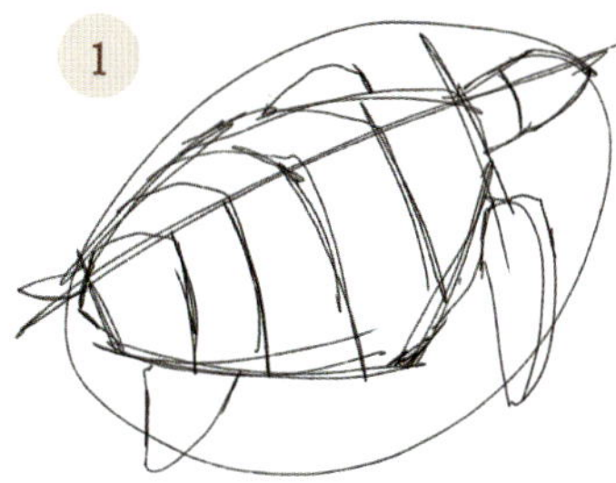

Step 1: Draw a diagonal oval, with the right slightly higher than the left. Draw a line not exactly in the middle, but make sure it divides the oval horizontally into two parts. The one closer to us should be larger. This line represents the top edge of the turtle's shell. The part closer to us appears larger due to perspective and foreshortening. Sketch the shell with a rhombus shape, and add four perpendicular lines in opposite directions, which will guide the texture of the turtle's shell. Then, use ovals to outline the head and fins—make the front fins larger than the back ones, as the back fins are partially hidden behind the shell due to perspective.

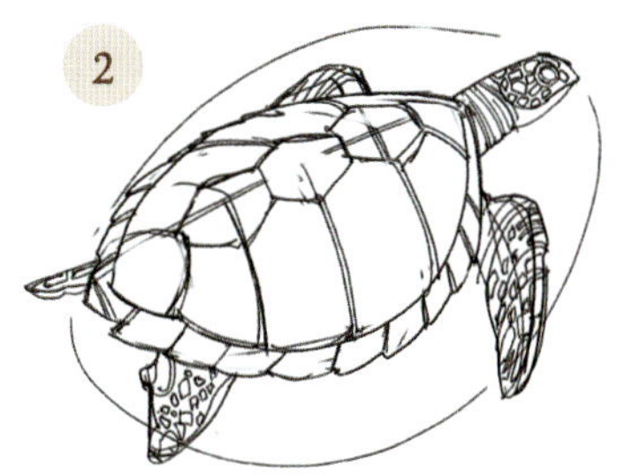

Step 2: Refine the structure of the shell, creating five rhombuses down the center of the shell, one below the other. Then, outline the shell's border with smaller rectangles. Give the shell edge a more pointed and spiky appearance by emphasizing the shape of these rectangles along the border. Next, refine the shape of the fins and head, making them slightly pointed. Begin outlining the texture on the fins and head with small, irregularly shaped rectangles. Add folds on the neck using long, perpendicular lines.

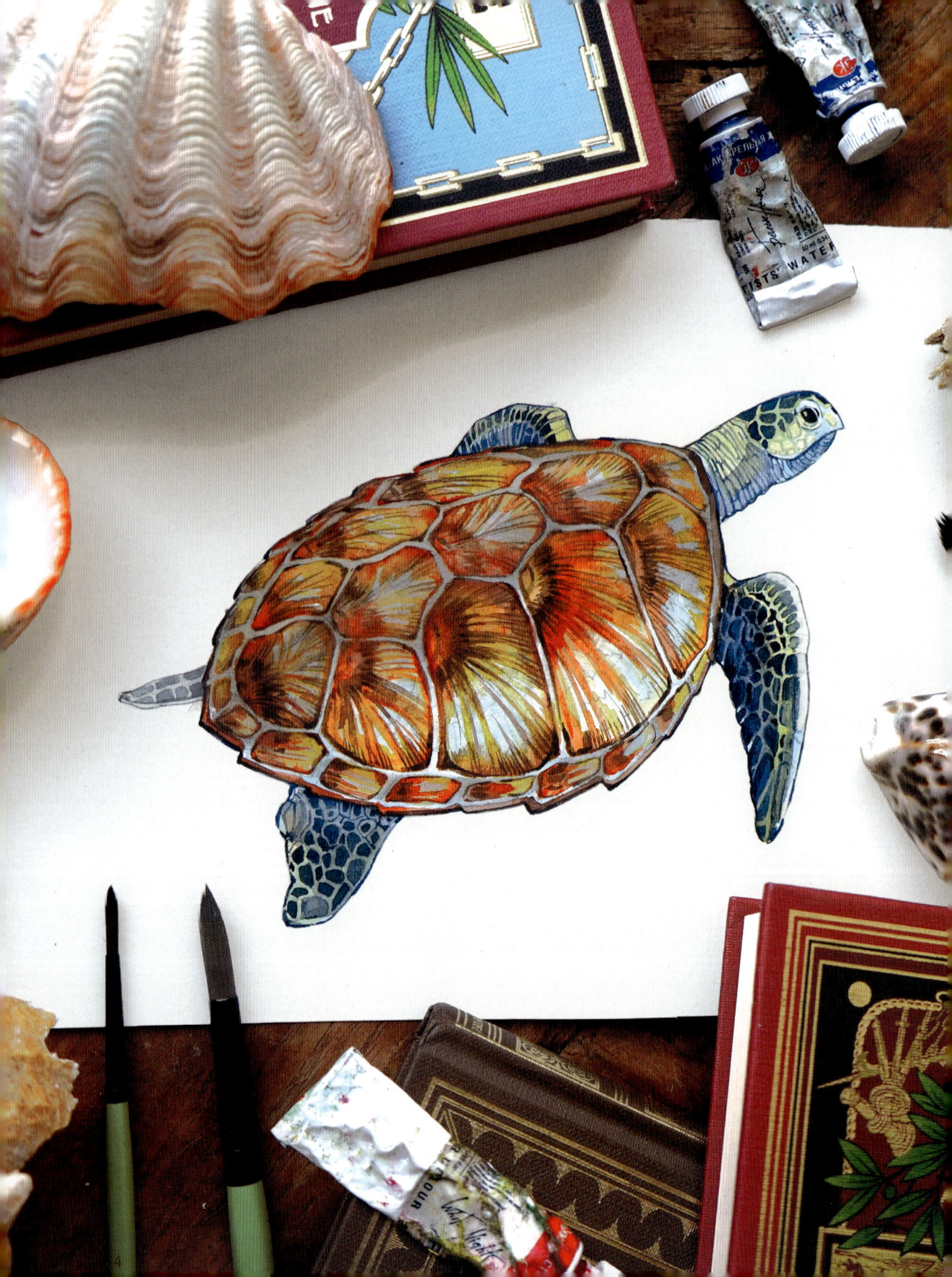

Step 3: Erase any unnecessary guide lines and start adding the final details to the turtle. Add thickness to the borders of the section of the shell, and create a pattern on the larger front sections using long, curved lines and irregular rectangles. Draw facial features by outlining the mouth and eye, and continue adding texture as you did in the previous step. Once you've filled the entire surface of the fins and head with texture, you're ready to move on to the next step.

Step 4: Mix a light blue by combining turquoise blue with water. Use the tip of a small brush to paint the thin gaps on the turtle's shell and body. This step may take some time, but try to work through it without rushing—it can be quite meditative! Wait for this layer to dry.

Step 5: Add some texture on each scale using the light blue from Step 4. You can follow the outlines you previously created or use long strokes starting from the lower right corner of each scale toward the turtle's line. Be sure to leave some space on each scale for now. While the blue is drying, mix cadmium yellow with water to create a medium yellow. Then, create a new mix:

- Mix A: cadmium yellow + cadmium red + water = saturated orange

Once the blue is dry, apply the cadmium yellow and water mix to the left side of each scale (working one at a time), avoiding the blue areas. As you reach the right/top part of the scale, switch to Mix A to cover the remaining area. While this layer is still wet, add Mix A to the scale edges to darken them, and add a few lines over the blue texture to enhance it. Be careful not to cover the blue completely. The result should be an interesting texture, lighter with yellow hues in the middle and darker along the edges. Make sure the gaps between the scales remain untouched.

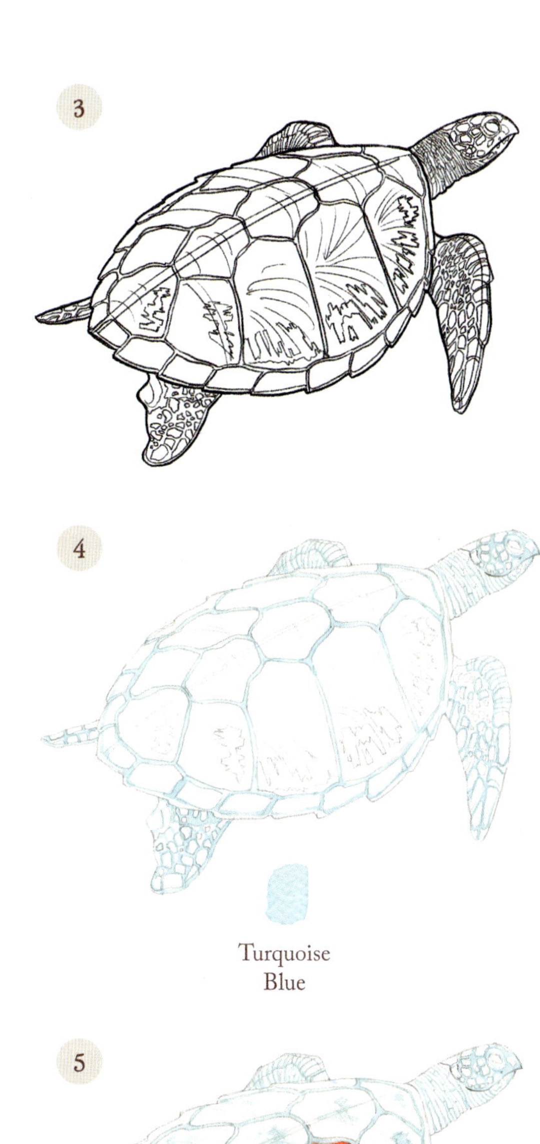

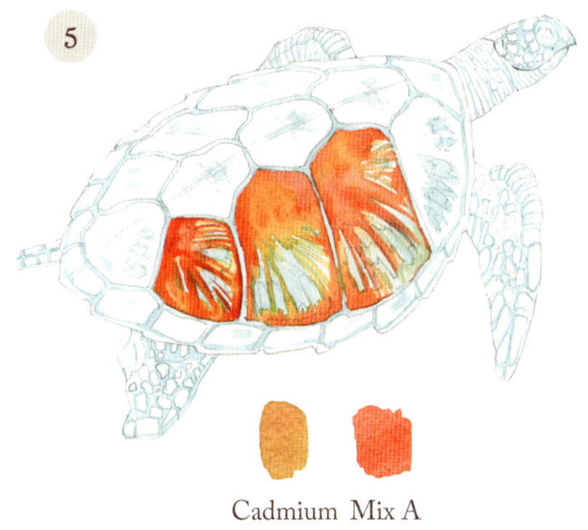

Turquoise
Blue

Cadmium Mix A
Yellow

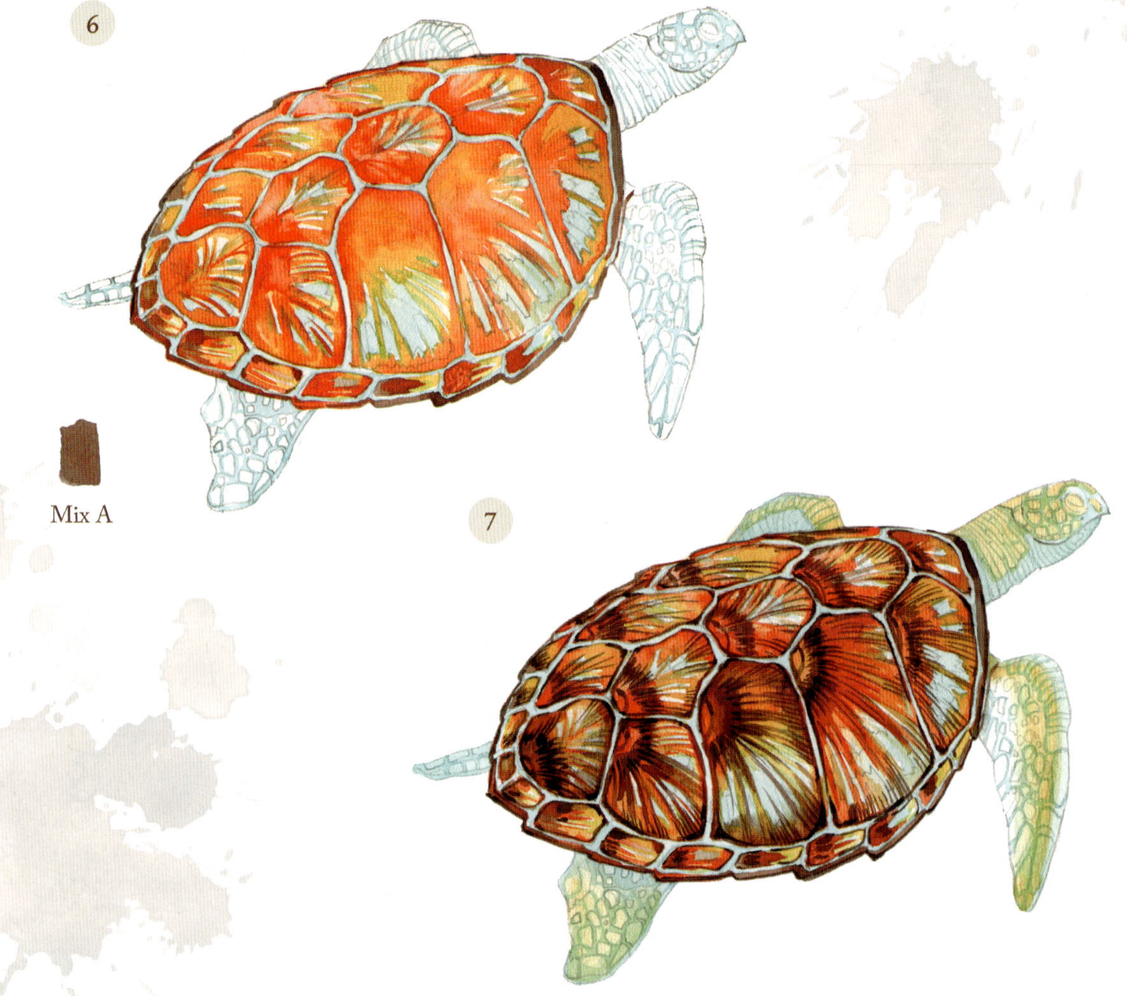

Step 6: Follow the same instructions from Step 5 for the remaining scales. After that, create a new color:

- Mix A: Mix 5A (cadmium yellow + cadmium red + water) + a bit of sepia = medium warm brown

Use Mix A to darken the border of the shell, especially along the front. You may also add this color to the row of smaller scales right before the border.

Step 7: Apply the turquoise blue and water mix from Step 4 to the lower portion of the turtle's head, the front right fin, the right side of the right back fin, the entire left back fin, and the lower side of the top left fin. Smooth the edges and let dry. Apply the cadmium yellow and water mix from Step 5 to the remaining white areas of the head and fins. Don't worry about the blue gaps; you can paint over them with yellow. Then, use Mix 6A to increase the saturation near the edges of the scales. Also, use thin, short and long lines to create a darker texture on the left side of each scale. Wait for this layer to dry.

Step 8: Mix two new colors:

- Mix A: cobalt blue or ultramarine + a touch of sepia + water = medium blue
- Mix B: Mix 8A (above) + more indigo = saturated dark blue

Start with the top right fin. Apply Mix A to the right side of the white scales of the fin, ensuring the extreme right sides remain untouched, smoothing out the edges for a seamless transition. This technique showcases the light hitting the extreme right part of the fin. Use Mix B for the remaining left part of the fin, leaving the blue gaps untouched to visually separate the dark scales from one another. Repeat the same process on the remaining fins. For the head, use thin lines and the tip of your small brush to outline the texture on the neck. This time, paint the lines rather than the spaces inside them. You can use Mix A, Mix B, or a combination of both. Then, switch to the head of the turtle, outlining the dark scales using the same methods. Outline the eyelids and color the eye with Mix B, making sure to leave a small highlight for added depth.

Step 9: Mix a new color:

- Mix A: indigo + carmine + a good amount of water = light, watery purple

Apply Mix A to the entire surface of the shell. While it's still wet, use a paper towel or napkin to blot the lightest blue-yellow area on the front side of the shell to make it lighter, as we want to preserve this light area. Next, apply the same color to the left side of each fin and to the lower side of the neck and chin. After that, let your paint dry, and it will be complete!

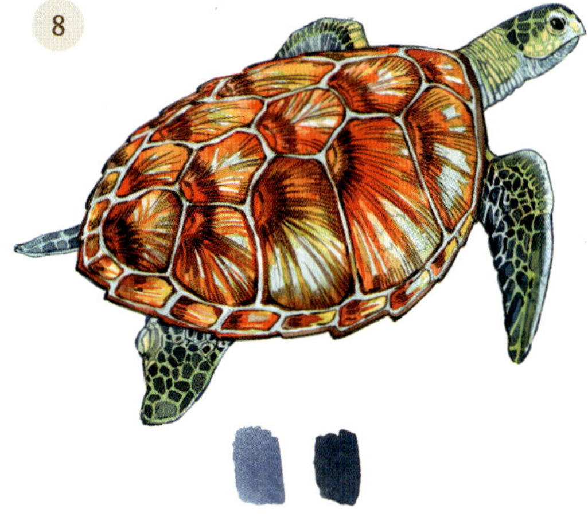

8

Mix A Mix B

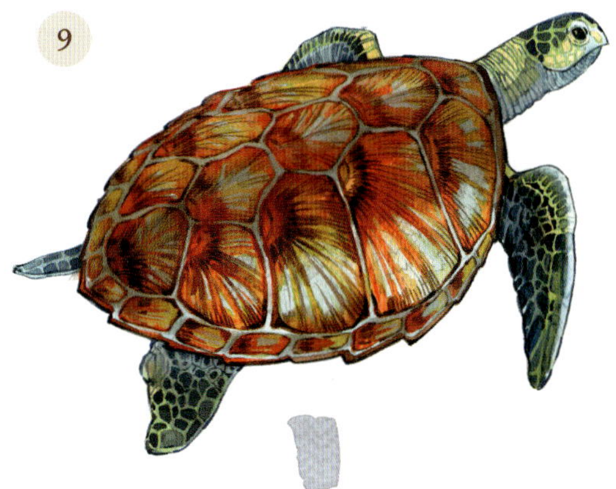

9

Mix A

Koala

Koalas, with their fluffy ears and endearing faces, are one of Australia's most iconic animals. These tree-dwelling marsupials spend most of their lives high in the eucalyptus trees, feeding on the leaves, which are their primary source of nutrition. Koalas sleep for up to 20 hours a day to conserve energy due to their low-nutrient diet. In this tutorial, you'll learn how to represent this curious creature realistically, giving you another chance to practice painting fur with fine details. You'll also discover how to add unexpected elements, like the eucalyptus leaves, even if they weren't part of your initial plan, adding depth and charm to your painting.

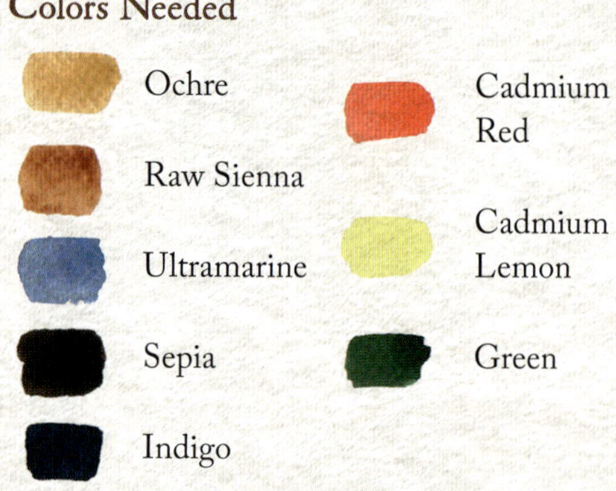

Colors Needed

Ochre

Raw Sienna

Ultramarine

Sepia

Indigo

Cadmium Red

Cadmium Lemon

Green

Suggested Paper Orientation: Vertical

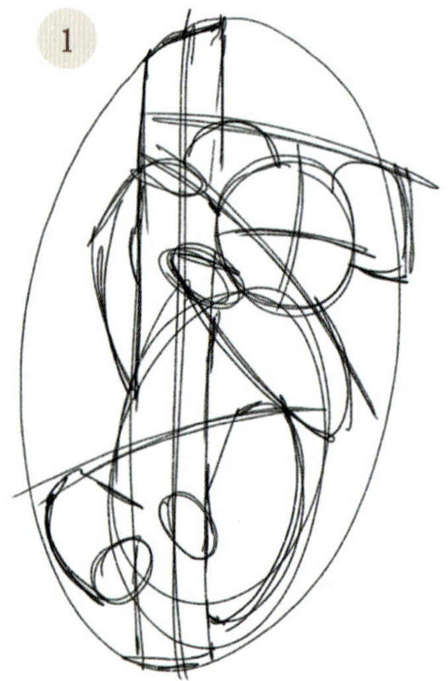

Step 1: Draw an oval in the middle of your paper. Draw a line connecting the top and bottom of the oval—this line should be straight with a slight lean to the left. This represents the branch the koala is holding onto. Add two parallel lines to the left and right sides of the branch for thickness. Next, outline the main shapes of the body. Start with the largest oval representing the body. Place it near the lower edge of the main oval, with its main portion on the right side of the branch. The oval's top edge should be a bit higher than the center of the main big oval. Place a circle on top of this oval for the head. Add a horizontal guide line on top of the head to help find the top edge and direction of the ears. Add the ears on the left and right sides of the head, making them appear slightly square.

Draw a cross on the head with two lines that intersect in the middle. These will help you identify the line of the head and guide you in placing the eyes correctly. Draw a line for the arms that leans to the left and another for the legs that's nearly horizontal, with the right tip higher than the left. Use larger ovals for the legs and arms, and smaller ovals for the hands and feet.

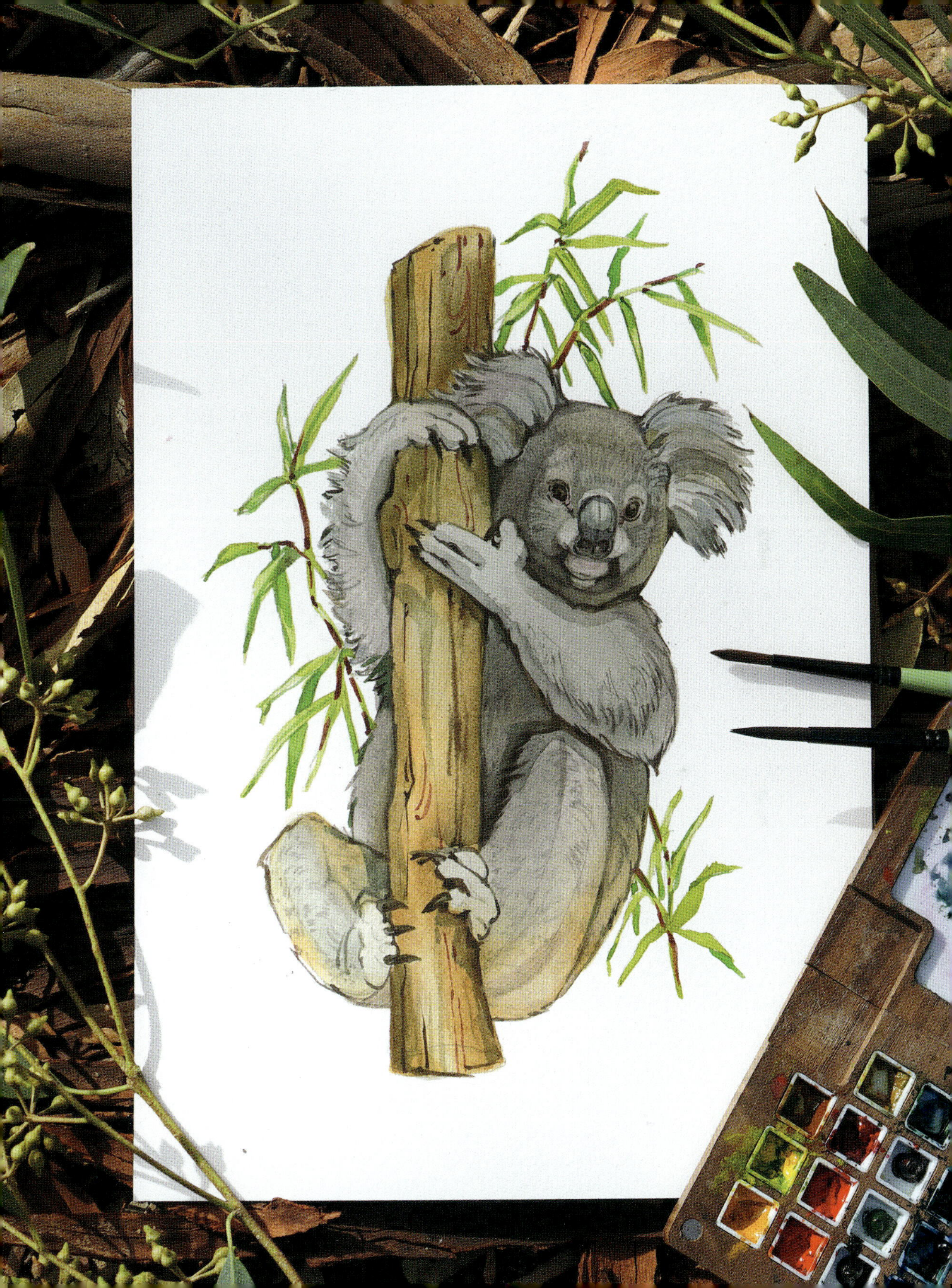

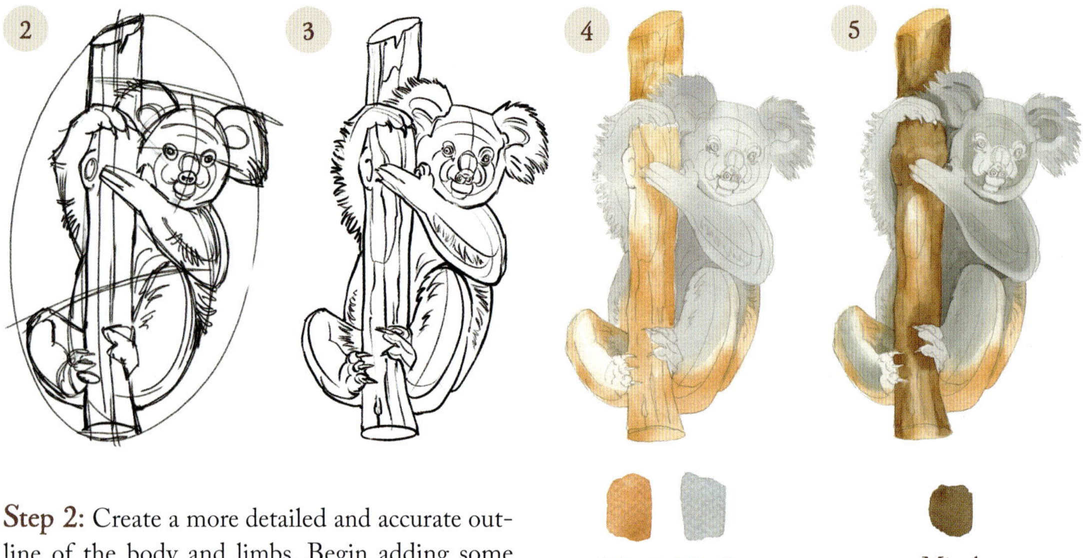

Step 2: Create a more detailed and accurate outline of the body and limbs. Begin adding some fur texture to the arms, back, and right leg using short zigzag lines. Define the facial features by placing the eyes in the middle of each half of the head. Position the nose in the center of the face, starting just below the midpoint. Use a bigger oval for the main portion of the nose and a smaller one for the tip. Add the nostrils using two tiny circles. Outline the jaw with a semicircle, define the cheeks, and add details to the ears using two small ovals. Include some details on the branch and improve the definition of the limbs, giving the koala toes and fingers with small, long ovals. You can also sketch some of the nails at this stage.

Step 3: Erase the initial oval and any other guide lines that you no longer need. Add more fur texture to the koala, especially the ears, using the same methods you used previously. Refine the facial features and add final details to the branch, hands, and toes. Outline the individual fingers more clearly and create the nails using long, pointy triangles. Once you're satisfied with the drawing, you can move on to the painting.

Step 4: Create two light mixes:

- Mix A: ochre + raw sienna + water = yellow

- Mix B: ultramarine + sepia + water = light gray

Paint the branch, the lower part of the koala, and the left side of the left leg with Mix A. Apply Mix B to the remaining surface of the koala. Once dry, add an additional layer of Mix B on the belly between the hand and the right leg. Wait for this layer to dry.

Step 5: Create a new mix:

- Mix A: raw sienna + sepia + water = brown

Use Mix A to paint the branch, blending the edges to achieve a smooth transition and create an instant light and shadow effect. Next, add cast shadows under the koala's arms and legs.

Apply Mix 4B to the legs, softening the edges for a gentle transition. Use the same mix to add shading to the center of the right arm, blending the edges. Then, apply it to the face, darkening the area around the cheeks and parts of the ears, following their natural curved shape. Outline the underside of the face and add shading to the belly, focusing on the areas darkened in the previous step.

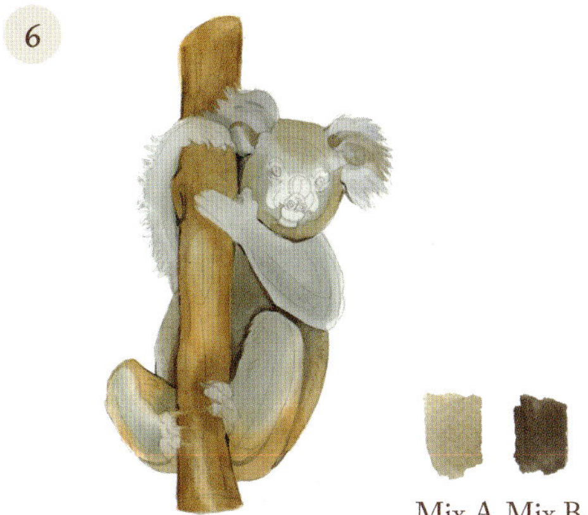

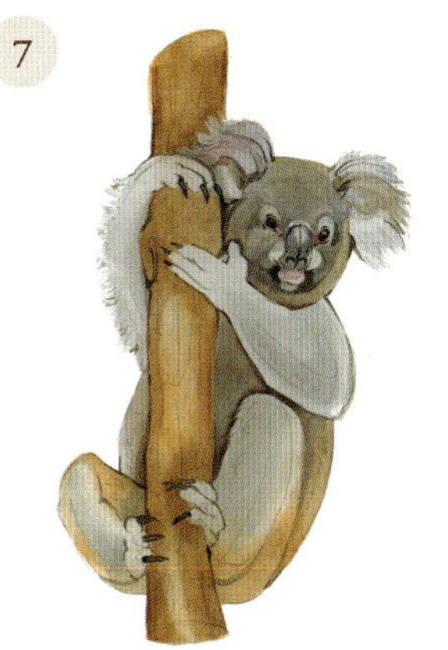

Mix A Cadmium Red

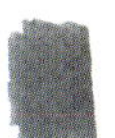
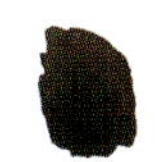

Mix A Mix B

Mix B   Mix C

Step 6: Here, you'll visually unify the tree and the koala. Apply Mix 4B as a uniform wash to the entire surface of the koala. Then, while the color is still wet, dab the face with a paper towel to lift some of the color, as we want the face to be lighter than the body. Allow this layer to dry completely before moving on. Create two new color mixes for the koala:

- Mix A: ochre + raw sienna + sepia + water = light beige
- Mix B: Mix 6A (above) + more sepia = medium brown

Apply Mix A to the right part of the body of the koala and smooth out that edge. Then, apply this mix to the lower part of the face to the ears. Paint the belly and under the right arm with Mix 5A. Use it to darken some parts of the ears as well. Use Mix B to define the branch in areas close to the koala. Use the same color and a thin line to outline the right arm, the right leg, and the small shadow on the left side of the head. Use the same thin outline to define a bump on the left side of the branch.

Step 7: Create a new mix:

- Mix A: indigo + sepia + water = medium gray-blue

Using a small brush, apply Mix A to the nose, leaving the highlight untouched. Then, mix a light pink color by combining a touch of cadmium red with water. Apply it to the mouth, the eyes, and to some areas of the ears, smoothing the edges on the ears. Darken the face of the koala with Mix 4B to unify the color of the koala.

Once the previous colors on the face have dried, create a new dark mix:

- Mix B: same as Mix 7A (left) but with more pigment = darker blue-gray

Use Mix B to add the darkest details to the nose with the tip of your small brush. Apply the same color to create dark shadows on the left and right sides of the mouth. Then, create a new mix:

- Mix C: indigo + sepia + almost no water = very dark, almost black color

With the tip of your small brush, paint the eyes and the folds around the eyes, remembering to leave the light highlight in each eye. Use the same color to outline the koala's nails. Next, with the tip of your brush, create the outline of the paws and other areas, such as the right side of the right hand. You can also use this color to add thin, curved lines to the ears to show the direction of the ear and imitate the texture of the fur.

Step 8: Now, let's add the fur to the body and head using the Mix 7B. Apply short strokes and zigzags to imitate fur on different parts of the body and face. Ensure your strokes are larger when working on bigger areas and smaller for the smaller areas. Then, apply Mix 7A to the shadow areas of the belly, arms, and legs, as well as to the shadow areas of the branch. Use Mix 6B to darken the outline of the koala in some areas, such as the nails, and to add details to the trunk with thin lines.

Step 9: Add more shadow to the lower side of the right arm using Mix 4B. When you're satisfied with the koala, add some eucalyptus leaves to the background behind the animal. These leaves were not outlined in your original sketch, but you can add them now. You can start painting right away if you feel confident, or begin with a pencil sketch if you're unsure about the shape of the leaves and their placement. Once you're done with the pencil drawing (if using one), create three mixes:

- Mix A: cadmium lemon + green + water = vibrant yellow-green

- Mix B: green + cadmium lemon + indigo + water = medium green

- Mix C: carmine + sepia + water = dark brown-red

Apply Mix A to all the leaves and branches. Paint some of the leaves with Mix B, especially the folds and those that are in the back. With the tip of your brush, apply Mix C to the branches using very thin lines. Use the same color and method to add the final touches to the branch. After that, your painting is ready!

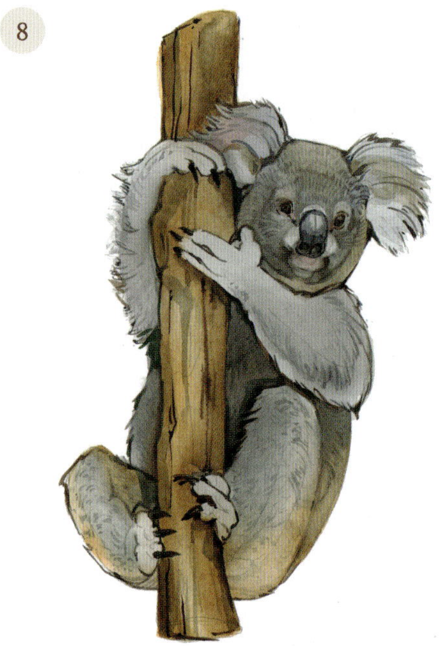

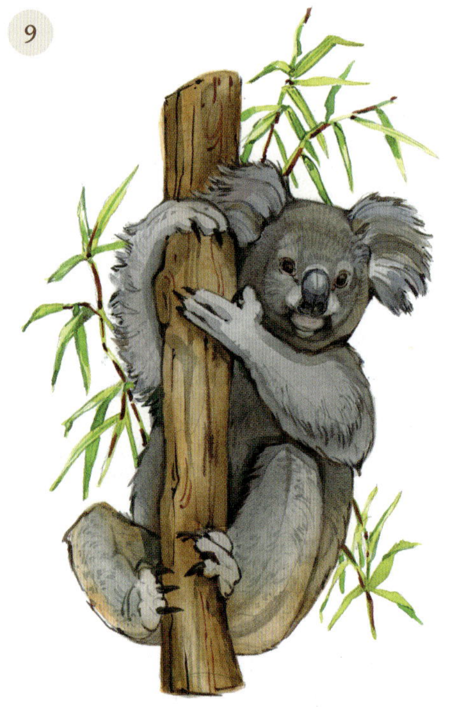

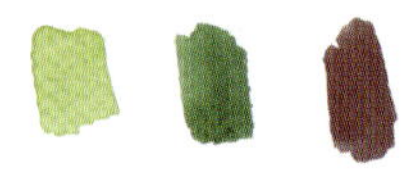

Mix A Mix B Mix C

Clownfish

Have you ever tried to approach a sea anemone, only to be met with an energetic and sometimes aggressive response from the clownfish that live there? These brave little fish are highly protective of their territory. Clownfish and sea anemones share a symbiotic relationship: The clownfish are immune to the anemone's stings, which makes this a perfect place to hide from predators, while the anemones get nutrient supply from the clownfish's waste. In this tutorial, you'll learn how to paint the clownfish in their vibrant habitat. You'll capture the delicate texture and color transitions of the anemones and bring the clownfish to life, showcasing their unique expressions.

Colors Needed

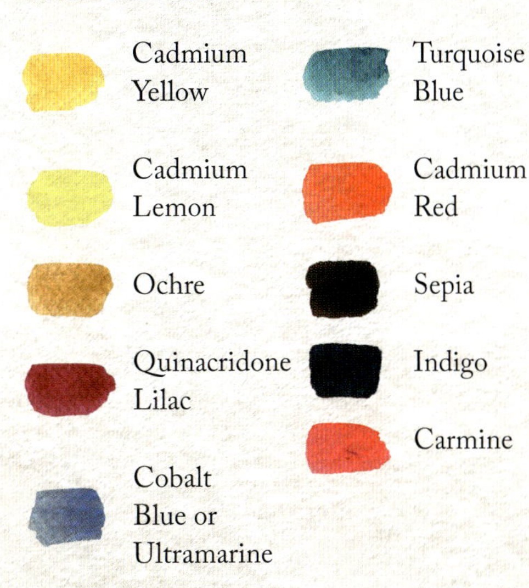

Cadmium Yellow

Cadmium Lemon

Ochre

Quinacridone Lilac

Cobalt Blue or Ultramarine

Turquoise Blue

Cadmium Red

Sepia

Indigo

Carmine

Suggested Paper Orientation: Horizontal

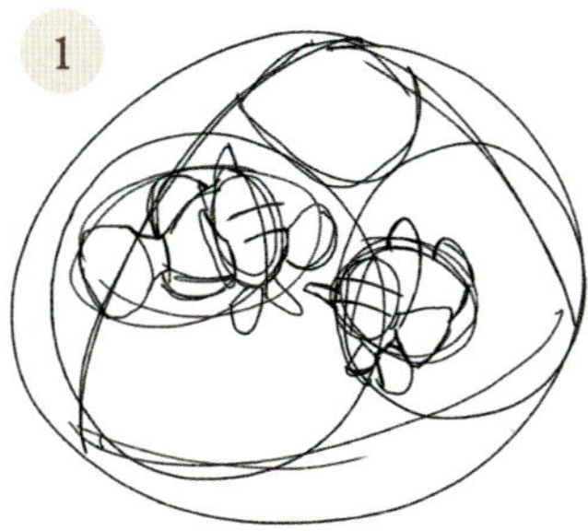

1

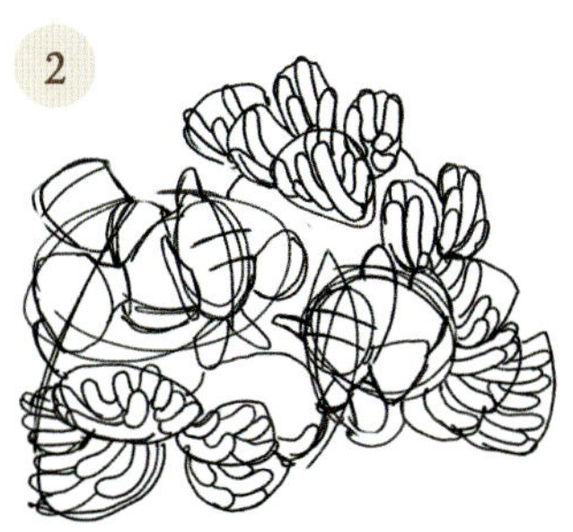

2

Step 1: Draw an oval in the middle of the paper. Then, draw three circles for the clusters of anemones. The two lower circles should be bigger than the top one. Then, connect these circles with lines to form a triangular-looking shape. This shape will represent the outline of the anemones. Now, let's start sketching the fish. Outline the left fish with a longer oval and the right one with a shorter one. (We see only half of the right fish, as it's somewhat covered by the anemones.) Sketch the heads of the fish with vertically placed ovals, and add vertical guide lines for the eyes and the mouth. Sketch the important body parts of the fish, such as the body, the tail, and the flippers, using simple lines and ovals.

Step 2: Erase general guide lines to avoid confusion. Start dividing the anemones into smaller clusters using ovals. Then, begin adding individual anemones inside each cluster. Make sure to draw longer and shorter anemones for more variety. To draw an anemone, create two parallel lines and add a round tip.

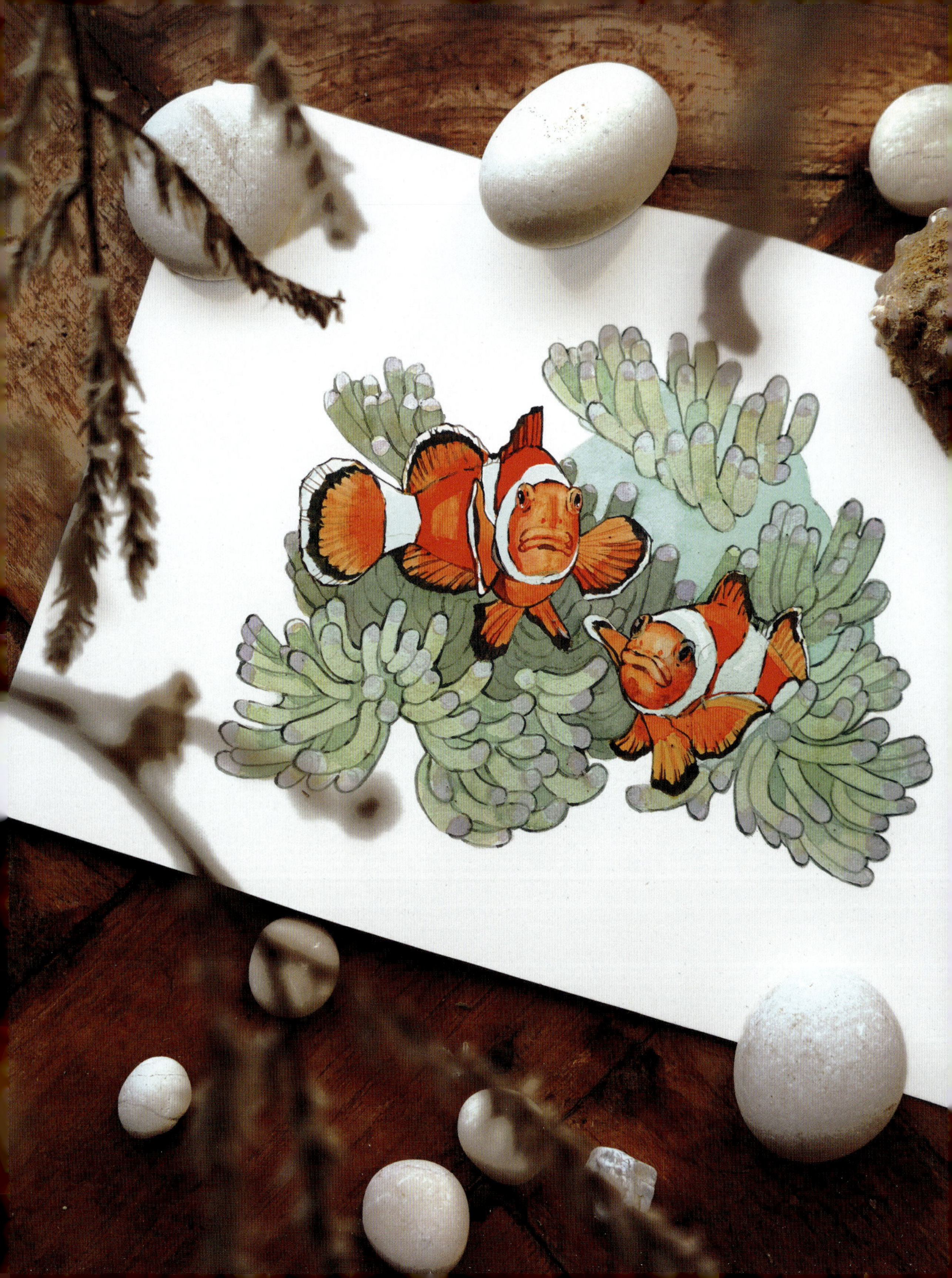

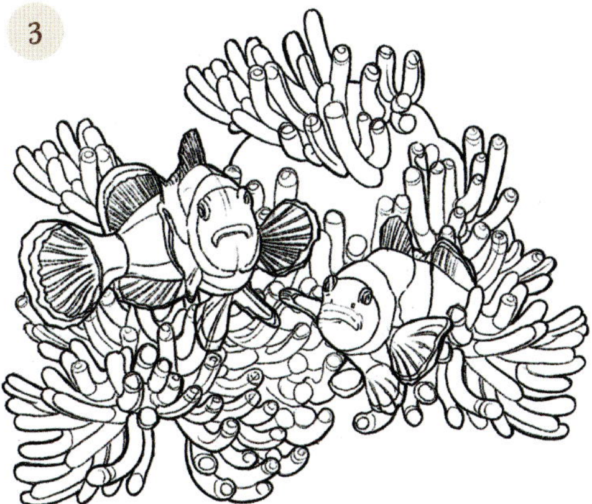

Step 3: Add facial features such as eyes, a mouth, and nose holes to the fish. Then, add more details to the flippers and tail of the left fish by drawing long, thin lines. Make sure to leave a border on some of the flippers. Finally, add the last details to the anemones. Add more anemones if you like. (I added an additional small cluster on top behind the left fish.) Then, refine the shape of the anemones even more and add tips to some of them by drawing circles. This will help during the painting process as you will give the tips a different color. Once you're happy with the look, you can proceed to the next step!

Step 4: Mix the colors for the anemones:

- Mix A: cadmium yellow + cadmium lemon + water = watery light yellow

- Mix B: cadmium yellow + ochre + water = light orange

- Mix C: quinacridone lilac + cobalt blue or ultramarine + water = light purple

Cover the anemones with Mix A and Mix B. You can cover some clusters of anemones with one or the other color for more variety, but make sure to leave the tips untouched. Once all the anemones are dry, apply Mix C to the tips.

Step 5: Mix a light blue by combining turquoise blue and water for the remaining white parts of the anemones and the white stripes of the clown-fish. Let this dry before proceeding.

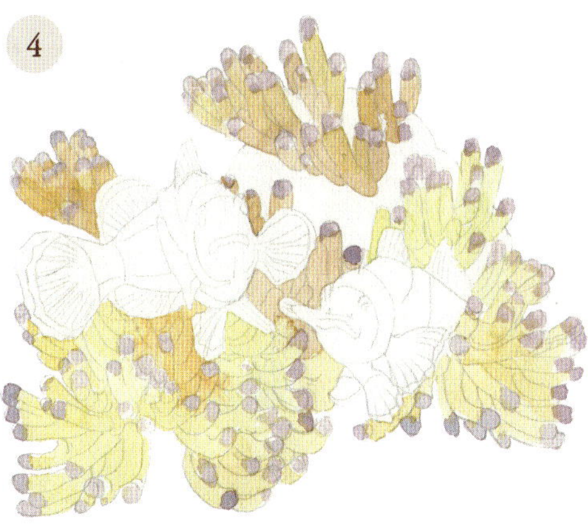

Mix A Mix B Mix C

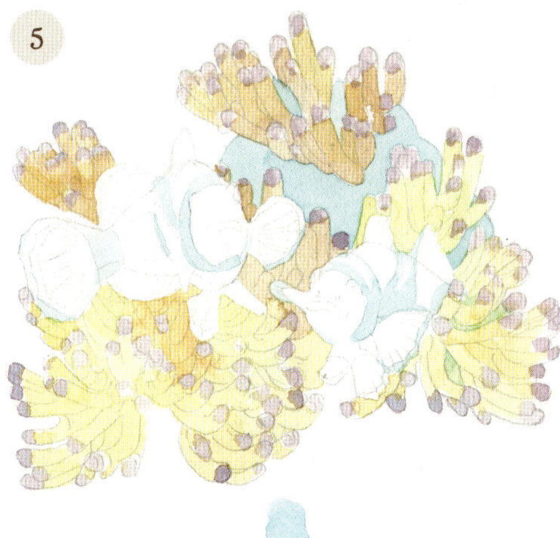

Turquoise Blue

Step 6: Mix these two oranges for the fish:

- Mix A: cadmium yellow + cadmium red + water = bright orange
- Mix B: Mix 6A (above) + more cadmium red = dark, saturated orange

Use Mix A to cover all the remaining white parts of the left fish, except for the top fin and the body; use the darker Mix B on them. Also, apply Mix B to the left and right parts of the face, but leave the center of the face lighter. For the right fish, use Mix A everywhere, but add Mix B to the right part of the head and to the body.

Step 7: Mix these colors to darken the anemones:

- Mix A: turquoise blue + a touch of sepia + water = light blue-green
- Mix B: same as Mix 7A (above) but with more pigment = medium blue-green
- Mix C: same as Mix 7B (above) but with even more pigment = dark blue-green

Paint the anemones under and behind the left fish with Mix B, but make sure to keep the purple tips untouched. Do the same with the anemones behind the right fish. Then, add depth to the lower front anemones by adding Mix A between them. Do the same on the top clusters of anemones, except for the darker ones. For those, use the darker Mix C to outline them. Let dry.

Step 8: In this step, we will give the anemones a more uniform look and a blue hue. With a large brush—ideally a mop brush—loaded with the turquoise blue and water mix from Step 5, paint a uniform wash over the entire surface of the anemones. Wait for this layer to dry.

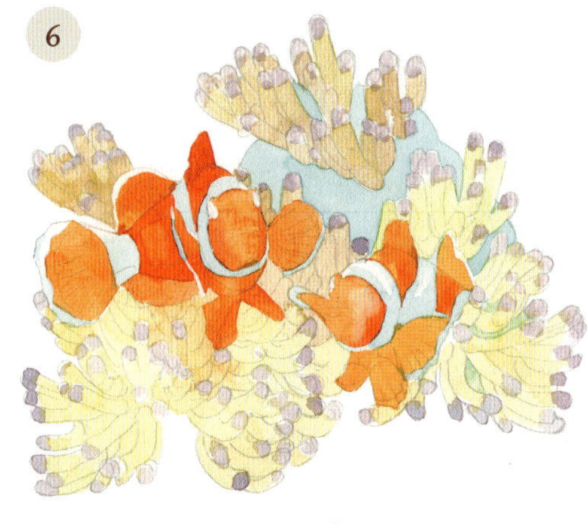

Mix A Mix B

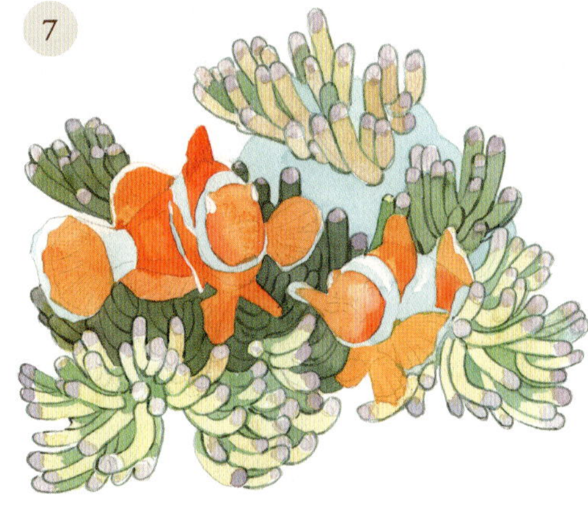

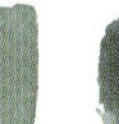

Mix A Mix B Mix C

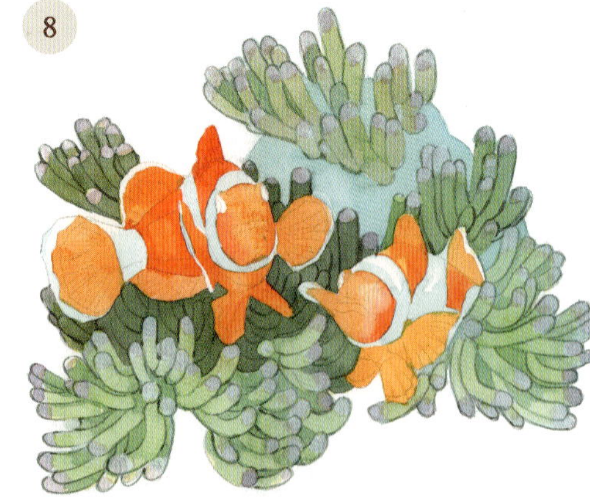

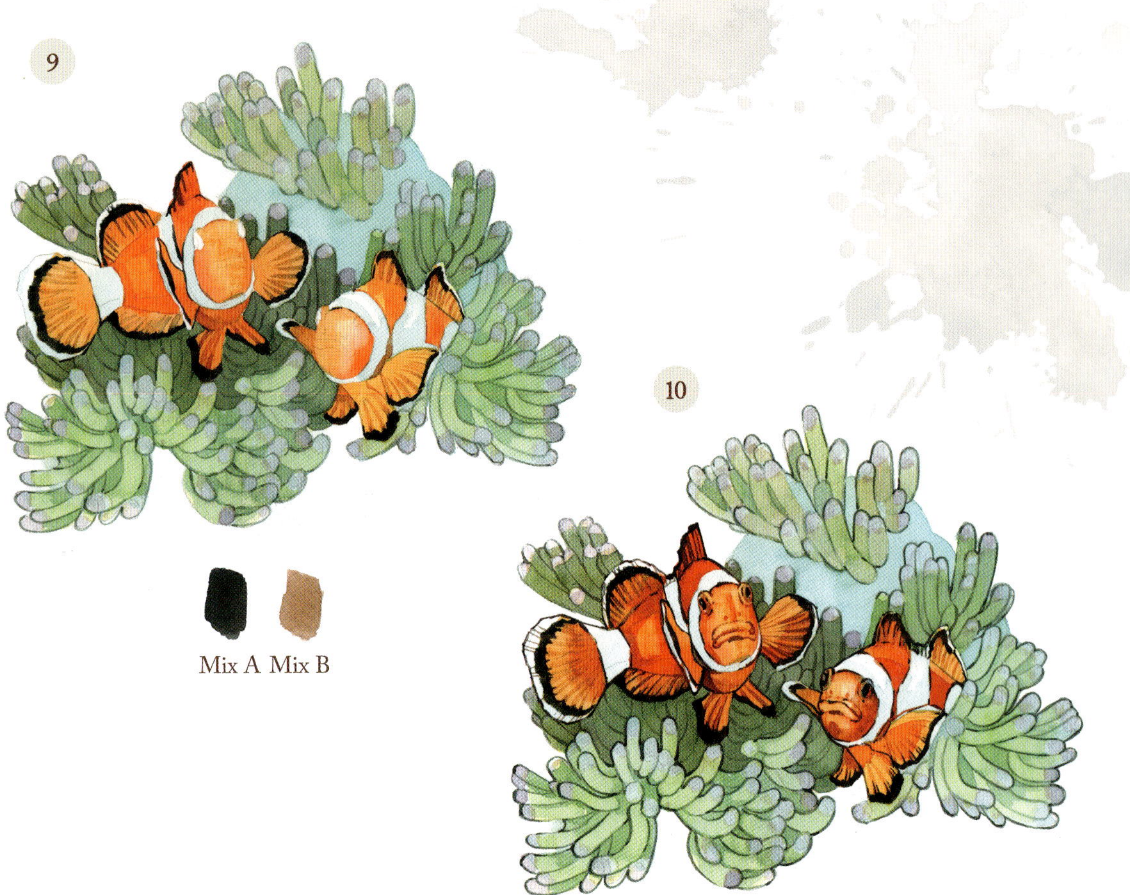

Step 9: Create this mix:

- Mix A: indigo + carmine + just a touch of water = dark gray

Use your small brush and work with the tip to apply Mix A to the borders and the flippers of both fish. Make sure to leave a light border on the tail and the top back flippers. Finally, mix a new color:

- Mix B: Mix 6A (cadmium yellow + cadmium red + water) + sepia = salmon

Use Mix B and the tip of your brush to create texture on the flippers and tail with thin lines.

Step 10: Use Mix 7C and the tip of a small brush to make the general external outline of the anemones more visible. With Mix 6B, darken the right side of the tail, the body, and the top flipper. Darken the body of the right fish, as well as the right part of its face.

Make the outline of the mouths of the fish darker with Mix 6B; you can even add some sepia to make it slightly darker. Add the nose holes and more line texture to the flippers and tail. Finally, use Mix 9A to paint the eyes. With the very tip of your small brush and the same color, add thin lines to visually separate the white parts from the orange parts of the body of the fish. After that, your painting will be ready!

Coconut Sprout

The coconut sprout, a symbol of resilience and growth, is a fascinating subject to bring to life with watercolor. In this beginner-friendly tutorial, you'll explore essential watercolor techniques on a simple-yet-intriguing subject. You'll have the opportunity to practice how light and shadow behave on rounded forms, adding depth and realism to your painting. Additionally, this lesson offers a chance to paint a new type of leaf, refining your skills in capturing its unique texture and structure. Let's dive into this vibrant study!

Colors Needed

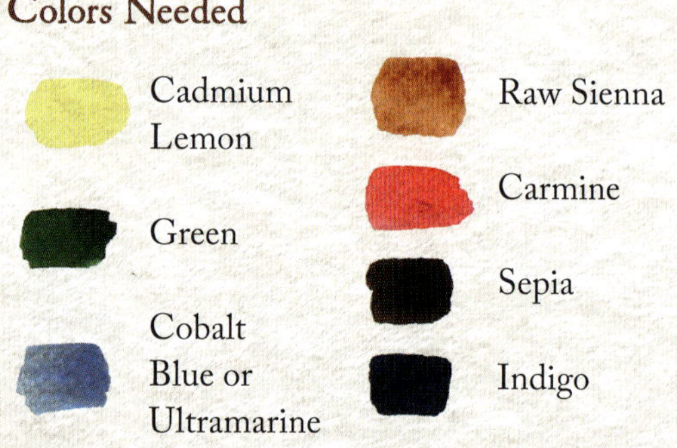

Suggested Paper Orientation: Vertical

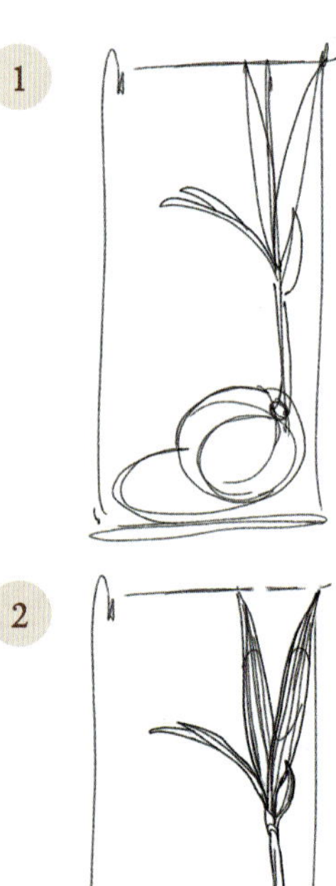

Step 1: Draw a tall rectangle that's twice as high as it is wide. Draw a vertical line on the right side of the rectangle, close to the edge, representing the direction of the sprout. Next, draw a circle on the lower part of this line to outline the coconut. Add a shadow on the ground cast by the coconut on its left side. Then, add some curved, arching lines to emphasize the natural shape of the coconut, which will help place light and shadow to accentuate folds. Now, outline the leaves from the sprout. First, give thickness to the sprout by adding a parallel line next to the existing one. Then, start sketching the leaves: The top leaves should be bigger, longer, and thicker, while the side leaves should be smaller and thinner, with the leaves to the left curving and facing left.

Step 2: Add vertical veins to the leaves, and sketch the tips and the base with curved, horizontal lines to help define light and shadow areas during the painting process. Make the shape of the coconut more realistic and slightly pointed, with the area where the sprout grows from a bit thinner. Outline the base of the sprout to clearly show where it begins to grow. Finally, start outlining the roots on the lower side of the coconut.

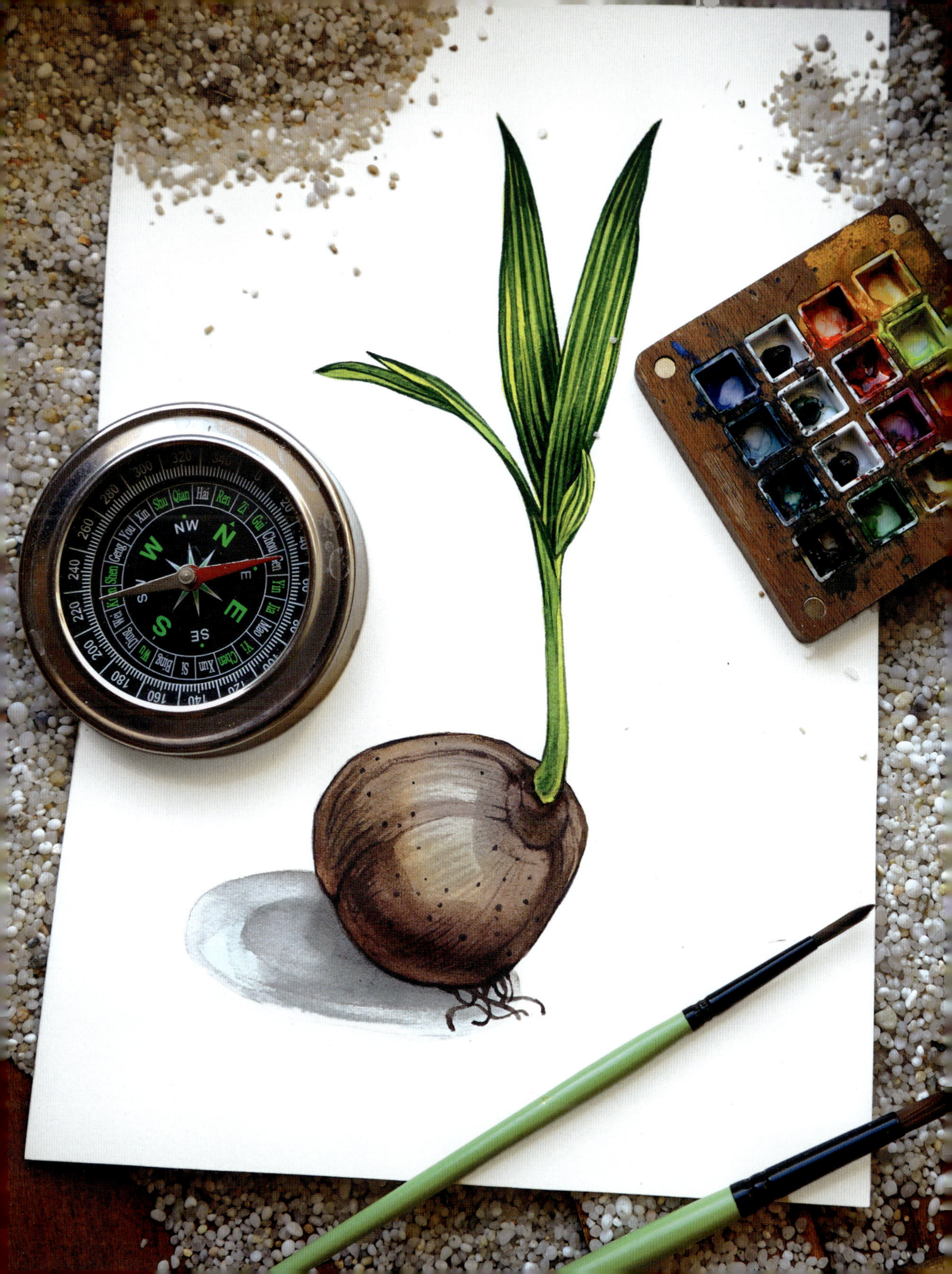

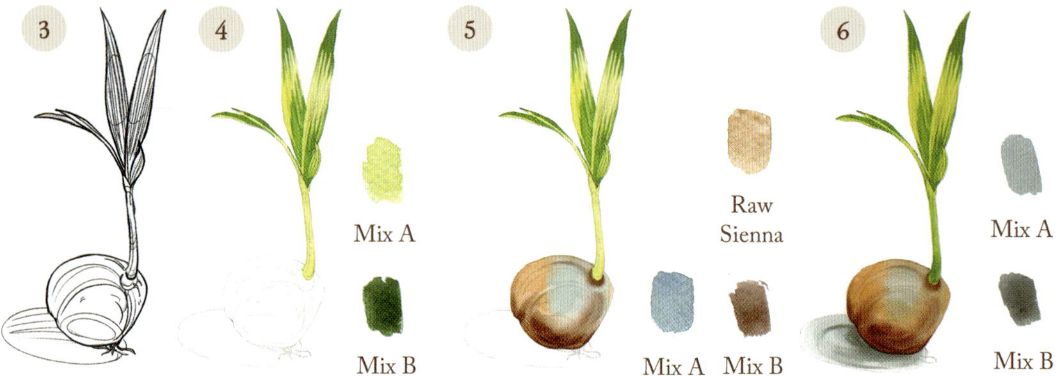

Step 3: At this stage, you can erase the guide lines and proceed with refining the shape of the coconut and the leaves. Make the outline a bit bolder and smooth out any transitions that are too pointy. Give the cast shadow a more realistic appearance and add final texture to the coconut and the roots. After that, you can proceed with painting.

Step 4: Create two color mixes for the leaves and stem:

- Mix A: cadmium lemon + a touch of green + water = bright yellow-green
- Mix B: green + a touch of cobalt blue or ultramarine + water = medium green

Apply Mix A to the whole surface of the leaves and the stem. Let it dry completely. Apply Mix B to the tips of the leaves. Once you reach approximately one-third of the way down the leaves, start outlining the individual veins with the tip of your small brush. Do this with the two larger leaves. Once dry, repeat the same step on the top sides of those leaves. Add Mix B to the smaller leaves as well, but use simple strokes since these leaves are too small for blending.

Step 5: Combine raw sienna and water for a light brown-orange. Then, create two color mixes:

- Mix A: cobalt blue or ultramarine + water = light blue

- Mix B: carmine + sepia + water = medium warm brown

Apply the raw sienna and water mix to the entire left part of the coconut, following its round shape. While the color is still wet, apply Mix A to the top right of the coconut, allowing it to blend with the previously applied color. Then, while the surface of the coconut is still wet, introduce the darker Mix B to the lower part of the coconut in the area from which the sprout grows out of the nut, and add some to the left outline. Next, use some circular strokes to emphasize the natural round shape of the nut in the middle and on the top. These lines will help visually enhance the shape, creating the illusion of folds and texture on the surface of the coconut.

Step 6: In this step, we will unite the leaves and the coconut and give them a more solid tone. Let's start with the leaves. Apply Mix 4A uniformly to the entire surface of the leaves and the stem. Then, use the raw sienna and water mix from Step 5 to cover the whole surface of the coconut uniformly. Once you reach the bottom, switch to Mix 5B. While the surface of the coconut is still wet, lift off some paint from the top right areas, just to the left of where the stem grows. This will create a highlight on the coconut and make it look more three-dimensional.

Create two gray mixes that are similar but different in intensity:

- Mix A: indigo + sepia + water = watery blue-gray
- Mix B: same as Mix 6A (above) but with more pigment and less water = dark blue-gray

Apply Mix A to the oval area of the shadow that you outlined with the pencil. While the color is still wet, smooth out the edge with a clean, dry brush. Next, while the color is still wet, introduce Mix B to the area of the shadow closer to the coconut. Use the same color to create circular lines that replicate the shape of the coconut in the shadow; this will give the shadow a more interesting and dynamic look.

Step 7: Create a new mix:

- Mix A: green + cobalt blue or ultramarine + a touch of water = dark green

Paint the leaves a bit with clean water, which will activate the green paint already present and help give them a darker tone. Let it dry, then use the very tip of your brush and Mix A to apply thin, long lines to darken the veins of the leaves. Then, darken the base of the leaves and create a clearer outline. Use a lighter green (you can dilute the existing green color with water) to darken the left side of the stem, as this is the shadow area. This will give the stem a finished look.

Step 8: Mix these:

- Mix A: sepia + carmine + a touch of indigo + water = medium-dark brown
- Mix B: same as Mix 8A (above) but with more pigment and almost no water = dark brown

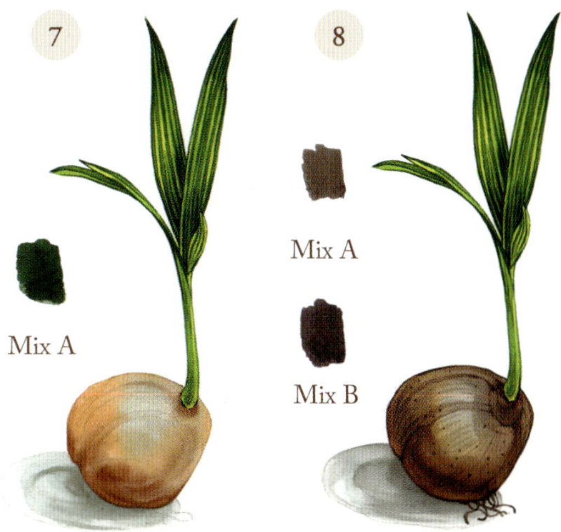

Apply Mix A to the left and lower sides of the coconut, as well as to the area under where the sprout grows. Then, smooth out the edges for a seamless transition. The surface of the coconut is probably not yet completely dry. This is perfect, as it will allow us to add texture using Mix B, which will blend nicely into the rest of the surface and create fuzzy lines. Use thin lines to underline the texture on the coconut in the shadow areas (left and lower sides). Make sure your lines are very thin.

Then, once the surface of the coconut is almost dry, add a few more thin lines to imitate the folds, especially near the area where the sprout is growing. Use the same color to create the outline of the coconut. If the surface of the coconut has already dried, you can now add final touches using Mix B. Add last lines and dots to enrich the texture.

Finally, darken the shadow near the coconut even more using Mix 6B. Let it dry, and then, using your small brush and Mix B, paint thin, wavy lines.

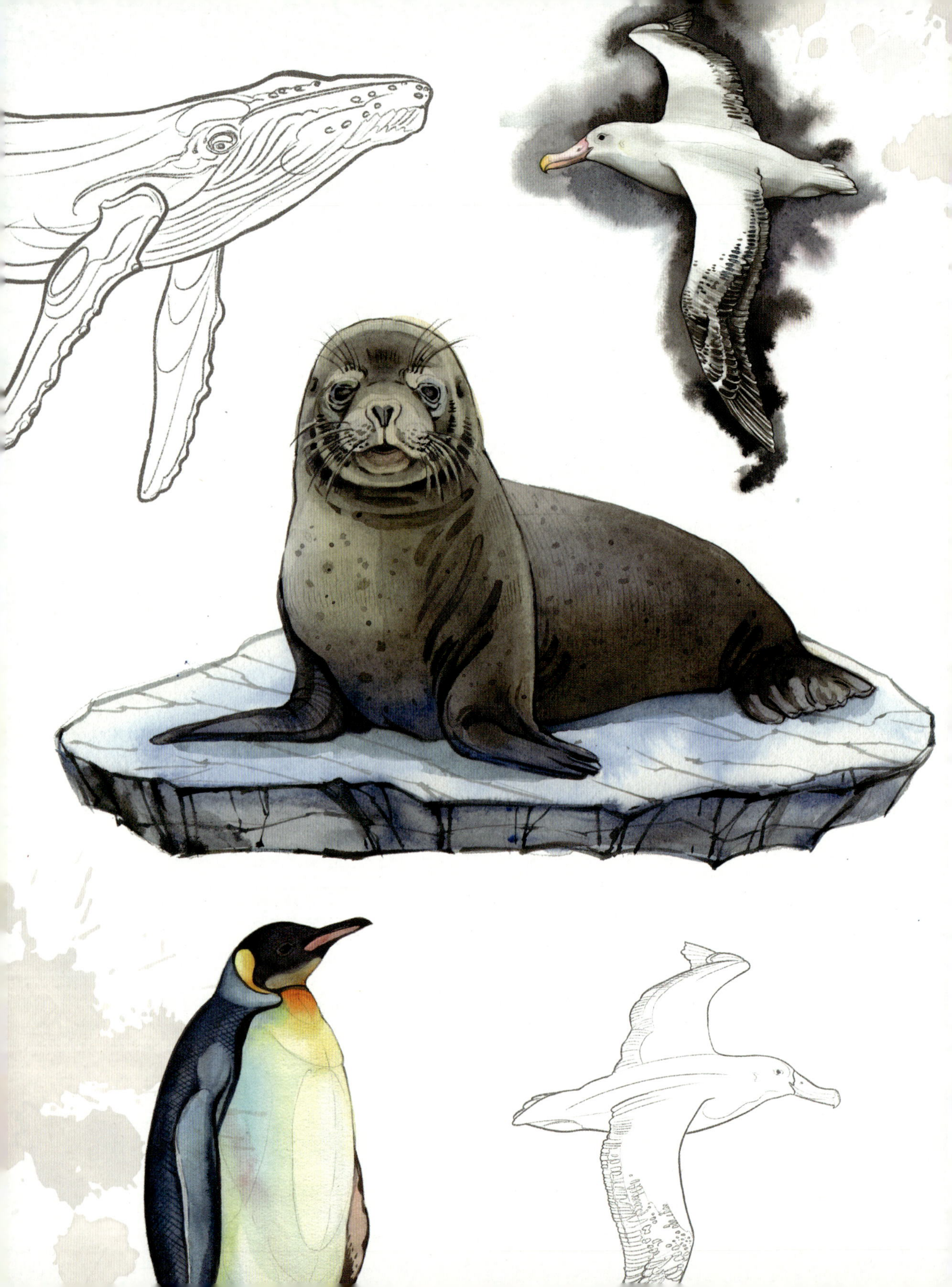

Antarctica
Life Amongst Ice

Antarctica may be the coldest, driest, and windiest place on Earth, but surprisingly, it teems with life in ways we often don't expect. This frozen land, known as the *white continent,* is not just a vast, icy desert—it's home to creatures with extraordinary adaptations that allow them to survive in one of the harshest environments on the planet. In this chapter, we'll explore the fascinating fauna that have adapted to conquer the cold.

Let's start with the Emperor Penguin (page 211), one of Antarctica's most iconic residents. These majestic birds, which can grow up to 4 feet (1 meter) tall, are the largest penguins in the world. They live in colonies that act as giant heat batteries, helping them survive the bitter cold. Emperor penguins also have a fascinating reproductive cycle. While the females head out to sea to forage for food, the males take over incubating the eggs. Their unique social behavior is key to thriving in the unforgiving Antarctic winter.

Next, we'll meet the Snowy Albatross (page 215), a true loner of the Southern Ocean. This magnificent bird is the northernmost species of albatross and is known for its remarkable ability to glide for days on end—without flapping its wings! Did you know that these birds can travel over 12,000 miles (19,000 kilometers) in a single year? The snowy albatross is also an expert fisherman, relying on the rich marine life of the Antarctic seas to sustain itself.

Among the mammals of Antarctica, one of the most fascinating is the Weddell Seal (page 221). Despite their playful, innocent appearance, these seals are tough survivors. They hunt birds, including emperor penguin chicks, and can dive to incredible depths to catch their prey. Their milk is one of the most calorie-rich in the animal kingdom, helping their pups grow strong and prepare for the dangers of the adult world, where predators like orcas are never far behind.

Then, we have the gentle giant of the Southern Ocean: the Humpback Whale (page 225). Despite their enormous size, humpbacks primarily feed on one of the smallest creatures in the ocean: krill. These tiny, shrimp-like organisms form the backbone of the Antarctic food chain. The ecosystem of Antarctica is delicately balanced, with the largest creatures relying on the smallest for survival.

Though it's nearly impossible to paint these animals in their natural habitat, you can still dive into the wonders of this frozen world from the comfort of your cozy studio. No need for a parka or gloves—just your favorite beverage and your art supplies! But be careful not to dip your brush in your drink instead of your water (we've all done it, right?). Get ready to explore the icy realms and meet the remarkable creatures that call this land of ice their home.

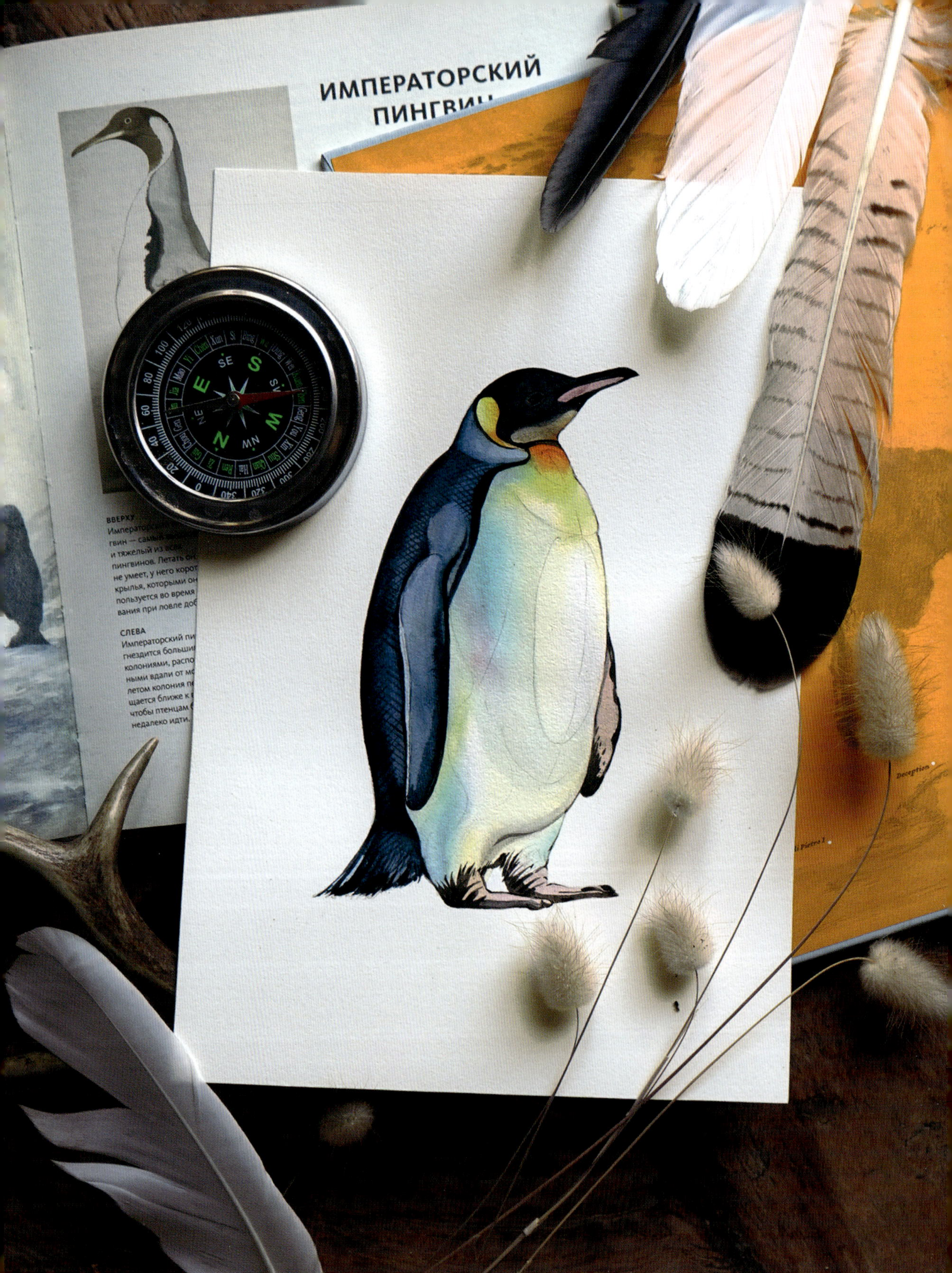

ИМПЕРАТОРСКИЙ
ПИНГВИН
ВВЕРХУ
Императо
гвин — самый
и тяжелый из
пингвинов. Летать
не умеет, у него корот
крылья, которыми он
пользуется во время
вания при ловле доб
СЛЕВА
Императорский пи
гнездится больши
колониями, распо
ными вдали от мо
летом колония пе
щается ближе к
чтобы птенцам
недалеко идти,

Emperor Penguin

The emperor penguin, an icon of the Antarctic, is the tallest and heaviest of all penguin species. In this tutorial, you'll master advanced techniques for painting white subjects without relying on contrasting backgrounds. You'll learn how to incorporate bolder colors on white areas while maintaining their bright appearance. Additionally, this lesson provides a perfect opportunity to practice the dry brushing technique (page 18) on the penguin's dark feathers, adding texture and realism to your artwork. Let's bring this majestic bird to life!

Colors Needed

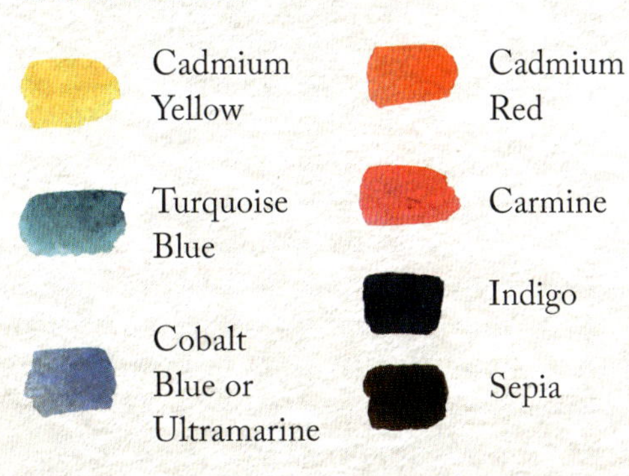

Suggested Paper Orientation: Vertical

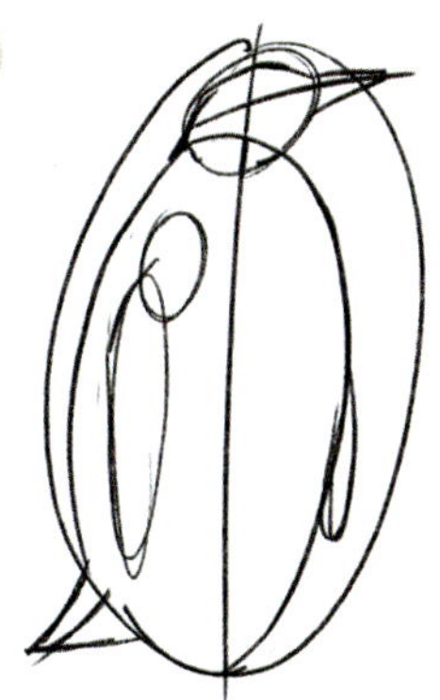

Step 1: Draw an oval in the middle of your paper. Draw a vertical guide line dividing it into two equal parts. Then, outline the head with a circle at the top of this line, inside the large oval. Create the outline of the body, which should be slightly to the left side of the main oval. Indicate the direction of the head with a line and outline the beak with a small pointy triangle extending slightly beyond the outline of the large oval. Next, outline the front wing with a small, round oval and a longer, thinner oval. Finally, outline the tail on the lower left side outside of the main oval.

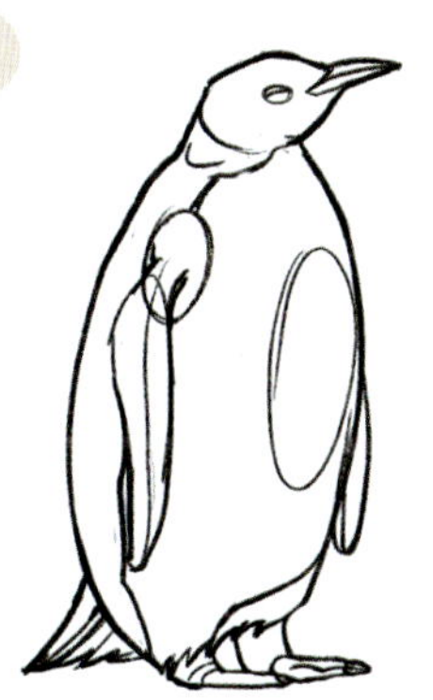

Step 2: Erase the guide lines and start defining the shape of the penguin more clearly. First, smooth the transition between the body and the head. Define the shape of the head better and give it a more pointed appearance by using shorter lines. Flatten the top of the head, as well as the left side of the neck. Add a line to visually separate the white belly from the black back. Then, create a long oval outlining the highlight on the belly. Refine the shape of the wings and add more lines to indicate the direction of the tail. Finally, draw the feet and give the lower outline of the penguin a more irregular zigzag edge to imitate feathers. Add an eye using a small oval and outline the opening of the beak.

Step 3: To add the final sketch details, draw some guide lines for the white belly to help us during the painting process. Add texture to the back and the left wing using long parallel lines, and better define the attachment of the wing to the back. Include some curvy lines to visually separate the head from the body. Add details to the eye and outline the spot on the left side of the head. Provide even more details to the feet with short parallel horizontal lines and refine the outline, especially on the right side, to better highlight the roundness of the chest. After that, let's start painting!

Step 4: We'll be using the wet-on-wet technique (page 17) for this step, so prepare all your colors before we start. We will need three simple mixes for this first layer: cadmium yellow and water, turquoise blue and water, and cobalt blue or ultramarine and water.

Begin by covering the entire surface of the penguin, except for the head and feet, with clean water. Once the penguin's surface is uniformly covered with water, act quickly and without interruption until the end of this step.

With a medium brush, apply the cadmium yellow and water mix to the top area of the chest (under the head), the lower part of the belly, the left leg, and the area to the right of the wing. It's important to preserve the white belly, as this is the lightest part of the penguin. Also add this color to the dry area on the left side of the head, where there will be no blooming since the paper is dry.

While the paper is still wet, apply the turquoise blue and water mix to the left part of the body, the left side of the left leg, and the right side of the right leg. While the paper is still wet, apply the cobalt blue and water mix to the entire left side of the penguin's body. This should blend seamlessly into the paper surface without affecting the white area. While this layer is still wet, take a clean, dry brush and lift some paint from the area on the left side of the wing and from the top area where the head transitions into the neck. Let this layer completely dry before proceeding.

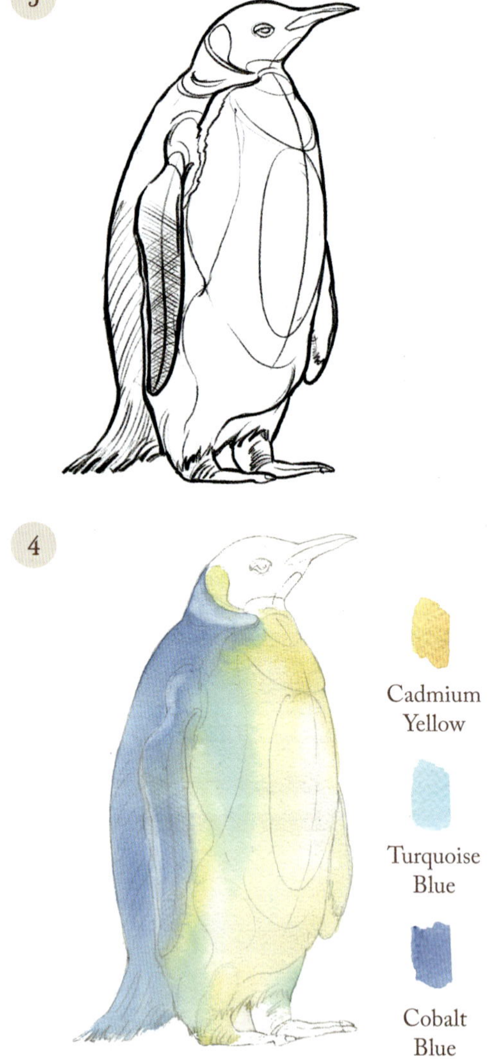

Step 5: Create three color mixes:

- Mix A: cadmium red + carmine + water = light pink
- Mix B: Mix 5A (above) + indigo = light purple-pink
- Mix C: carmine + cadmium yellow + water = saturated orange

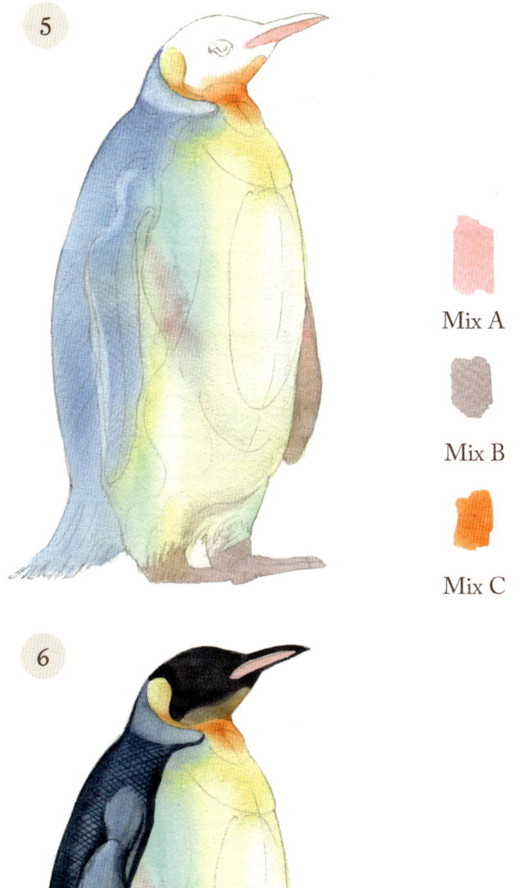

Mix A

Mix B

Mix C

Indigo

Mix A

Apply Mix A to the lower side of the beak and to the left part of the belly, then smooth out the edge using a large clean, dry brush. Next, add Mix B to the right wing and legs while avoiding the white feathers on the legs. Finally, apply Mix C to the areas where the head transitions into the chest, and then smooth out the edge so that the most intense orange color is in the middle of that area.

Step 6: Create a very dark mix by combining indigo and a touch of water. Then, create a new dark color mix:

- Mix A: indigo + carmine + sepia + a touch of water = dark purple

Apply water to the back of the penguin, including the tail, stopping before reaching the left wing. While wet, apply the indigo and water mix to the extreme left side of the back and allow this color to blend into the water. Do the same for the left wing, but make sure to leave a line between the left edge of the wing and the rest of the body untouched.

Then, start applying Mix A to the far right part of the wing, allowing this color to blend into the water. After that, outline the border between the end of the darker part of the belly. Use long, thin lines to create texture on the tail.

Wait until the body is completely dry before adding the last details, such as the outline of the wing. Next, add a grid texture to the dark part of the penguin using long, thin cross strokes and the indigo and water mix. Finally, use Mix A to cover the whole surface of the head, including the eye but excluding the pink part of the beak. Use clean water to unite the head with the orange area where the head transitions into the chest.

Step 7: Create these mixes:

- Mix A: carmine + sepia + indigo + water = neutral brown-gray
- Mix B: carmine + cadmium red + some water = bright pink
- Mix C: cobalt blue or ultramarine + turquoise blue + water = medium blue

Apply Mix A to the tip of the right wing and to its outline. Then, darken the left side of the feet. Use the tip of your brush with this color to visually separate the feet from the white body, and then use horizontal lines to create the folds of the feet. Outline the nails, again using the tip of your brush. Dilute this color slightly and use it to better outline the lower edge of the belly, the one that visually separates the legs from the belly. Smooth the edge for a more seamless transition. Finally, make the outline on the right side of the penguin more visible.

Apply Mix B to the left portion of the white part of the beak to make it more saturated. Then, use Mix C to darken the left wing and the left portion of the back of the penguin. Use the same color to darken the left portion of the neck.

Now, it's time to add the last details using the dark indigo and water mix from Step 6 to darken the edge that separates the white body from the blue back. Use the same color to paint the eye, darken the tip of the beak, and outline the yellow spot on the head of the penguin. Then, give the right part of the neck a more saturated and vibrant look by using the cadmium yellow and water mix from Step 4 on the lower side, smoothing out the lower edge. Add Mix 5C on the top side so that it blends into the yellow and creates a gradient from yellow to orange on the neck.

While this area dries, use Mix 6A to better define the outline on the left side of the penguin and to make the texture on the tail more visible. Finally, once the orange spot on the neck has dried, use the indigo and water mix from Step 6 to create a horizontal line that will visually separate the head from the neck. Add final touches to the feet and to the right wing using the same dark indigo and water mix from Step 6, and then your painting will be complete.

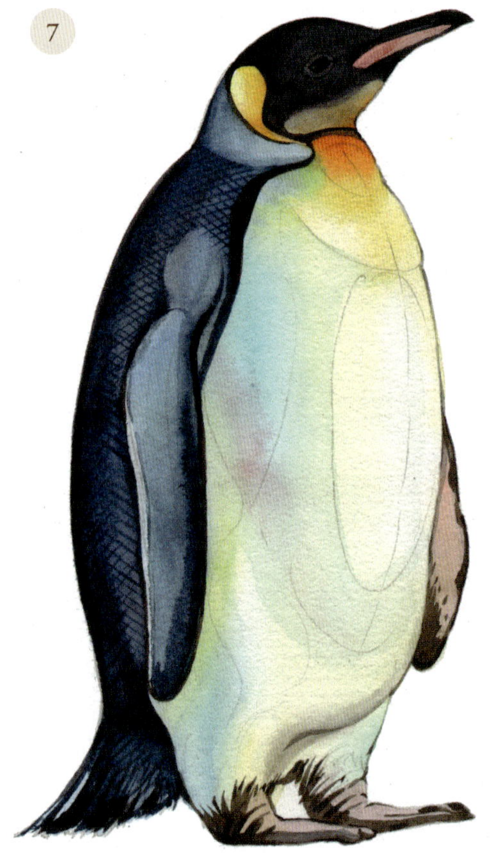

Mix A Mix B Mix C

Snowy Albatross

The snowy albatross, a splendid sea-bird known for its graceful wings and long-distance migrations, is a symbol of freedom over the vast oceans. These birds can fly for hours without flapping their wings, gliding effortlessly through the skies. In this tutorial, you'll learn how to paint the snowy albatross with a dynamic background, capturing the bird's beauty as well as a sense of the open, often gloomy, ocean. You'll also explore nontraditional techniques and materials to add a unique charm and atmosphere to your painting, making it feel as if the bird is soaring across a stormy sky.

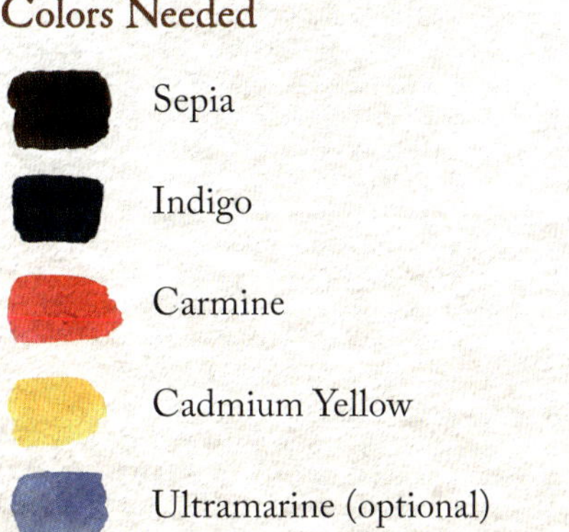

Colors Needed

Sepia

Indigo

Carmine

Cadmium Yellow

Ultramarine (optional)

Suggested Paper Orientation: Vertical

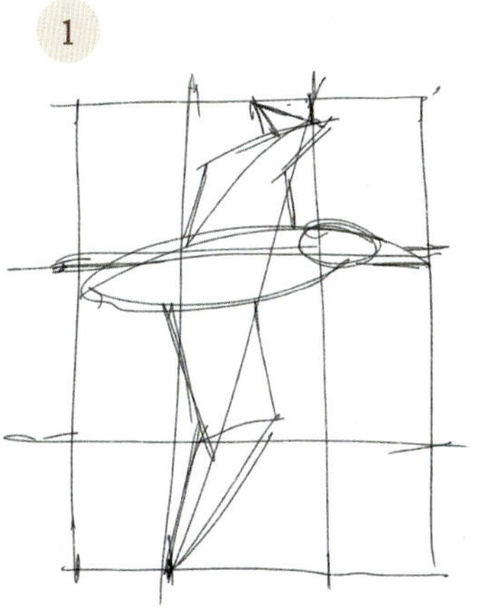

Step 1: Draw a rectangle that's higher than it is wide. Divide it into three equal parts horizontally and vertically, creating a grid. Add a diagonal line from the lower left corner of the bottom middle square to the upper right corner of the top middle square. This line will give direction to the wings.

Now, let's define the bird's proportions. Draw a long horizontal oval for the body. Use the grid in the image to the left to guide you. Attach a circle for the head at the right tip of the body oval. Connect the lower wing to the body using parallel diagonal lines that extend to the right. Once you reach two-thirds of the way down, change the direction of the lines. Draw a horizontal line to divide the two sections of the front wing. Do something similar for the upper wing, but add a third section to create a zigzag movement at the tip. The point of the top wing should be exactly in the middle at the top of the main rectangle. Finally, add a triangle for the beak.

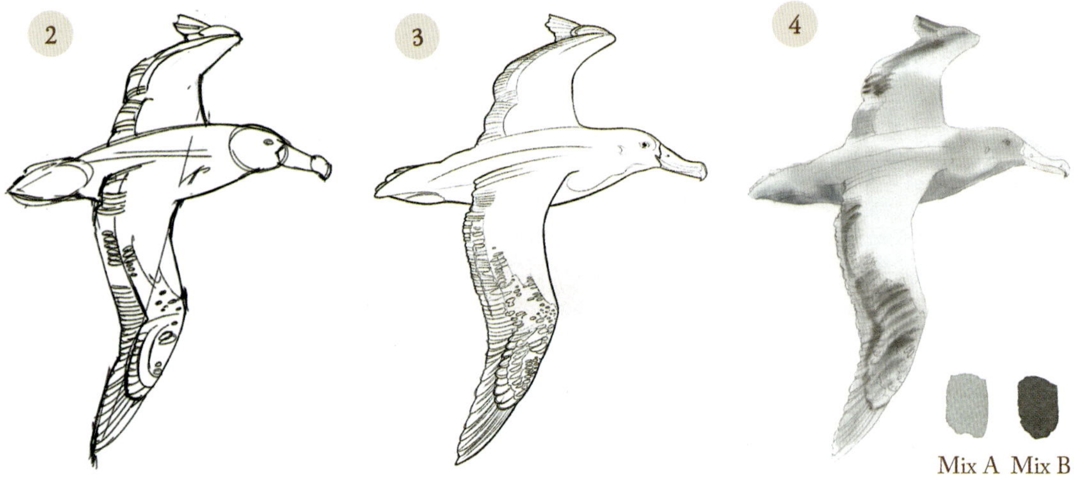

Step 2: Erase the guide lines. Connect the wings to the body, bringing the base of the front wing closer to the center of the body, and outline its base with a horizontal line. Outline the tail area with an oval and refine the shape of the beak. The tip of the beak should be thicker than its middle part, so outline it with a small oval. Define the base of the beak and place a small oval on the head to indicate the placement of the eye. Now, it's time to work on defining the feathers. There are two main layers of feathers on the front wing. Delineate this separation with two curvy lines that follow the shape of the wing outline. Then, begin outlining the individual feathers on the left side of the wing with long strokes. Ensure the feathers follow the natural shape of the wing, with the feathers of the right layer of the front wing using shorter strokes and ovals.

Step 3: Smooth any hard, pointy edges, and make sure the shape of the beak is well-defined, with a pointy tip facing down. Refine the feathers on the front wings. Add details to the tail and include more smaller feathers on both the back and front wings. Finally, create some long lines on the body of the bird to indicate the line of the back and use additional lines on the chest to visually separate the light and shadow areas. Enhance the details of the eye, add a nostril, and include more tiny ovals to symbolize feathers on the right portion of the front wing. The most texture should be on the front wing, as it is closer to us. Once you're finished adding texture, you can move on to the painting process.

Step 4: Create these mixes:

- Mix A: sepia + indigo + water = light neutral gray
- Mix B: same as Mix 4A (above) but with a bit more indigo and less water = darker bluish-gray

Cover the entire surface of the bird with clean water before applying Mix A to the belly, a bit of the body, and some of the wings, focusing on the tips. Apply Mix B to the extreme lower part of the belly. Also, add it to the wing feathers using short strokes. If the color blooms too much, remove the excess with a clean, dry brush. If you find you have no control over the color and it keeps blooming excessively, wait a bit until the water is damp but no longer completely wet. Lack of control over the blooming often means there is too much water or that the color you're trying to apply is too light.

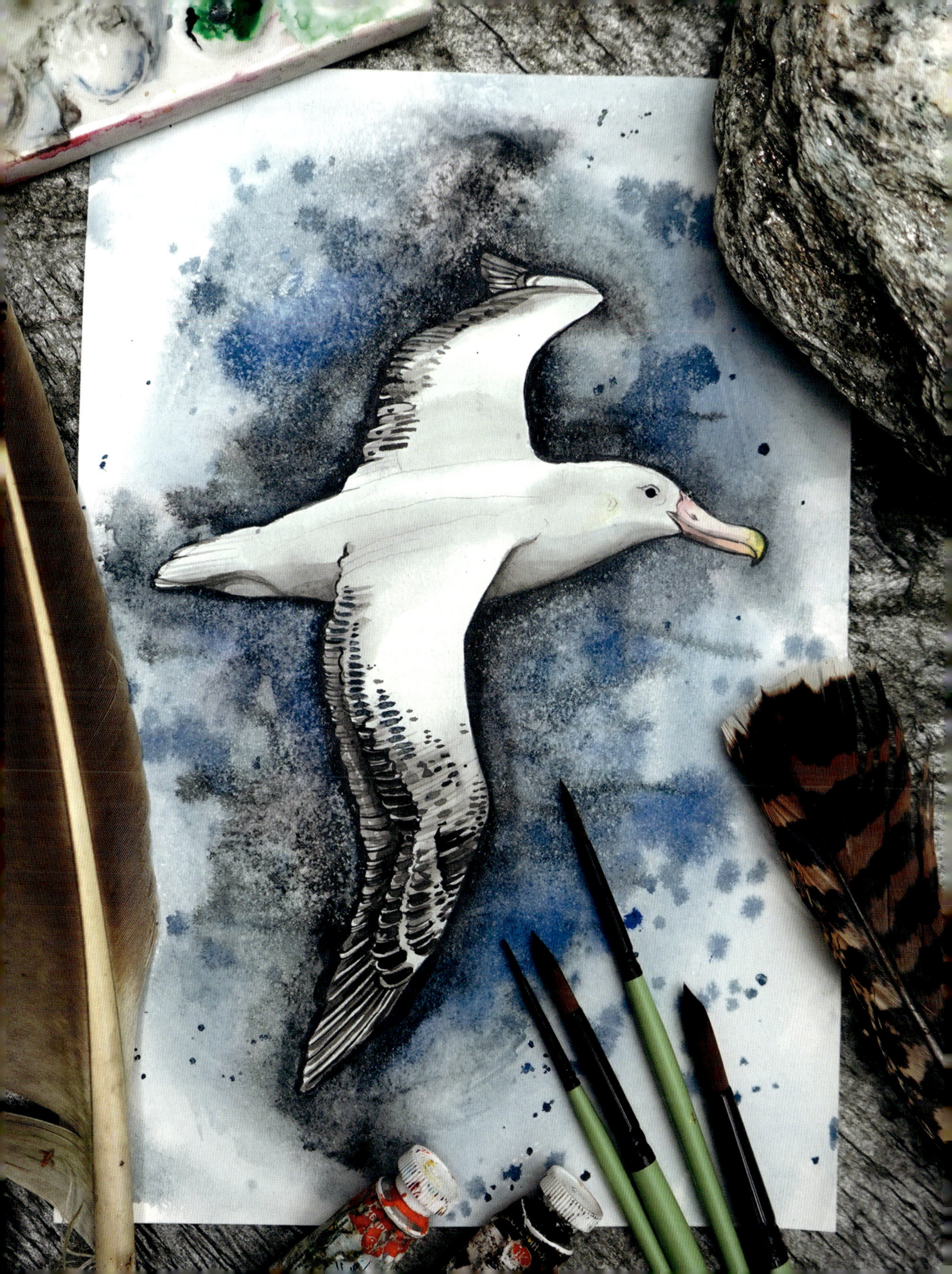

Step 5: Apply Mix 4B to the shadow areas of the belly and tail. Smooth out the edges for a seamless transition. Apply Mix 4A to the eye area and in the section where the back wing connects with the body. Smooth out the edges for seamless blending. Use Mix 4B and the wet-on-dry technique (page 16) to create texture on the wings. Begin by creating long, thin lines on the feathers at the tips of the wings. Don't forget to leave some white lines in that area to highlight the direction of the feathers.

Then, start working on the smaller feathers. Use short, round strokes to outline individual feathers on both the front and back wings. There's no need to smooth the edges this time, as we want this texture to remain visible.

Mix a touch of carmine with water and apply this watery pink to the base of the beak. Then, switch to a light mix of cadmium yellow with water. While the beak is still wet, apply a more concentrated version of the pink mix (add more carmine to the initial mix) to the very base of the beak and to the line of the opening of the beak. Let dry.

Step 6: Create this mix for the background:

- Mix A: sepia + ultramarine + carmine + water = dark blue-purple

Cover the whole area around the bird with water using a large brush, leaving just a thin line of dry paper between the water and the bird. Ensure that the entire surface of the paper is uniformly wet. If some areas are already dry, add more water. Apply Mix A around the bird, beginning from the dry part. You will see that the color will start to bloom, creating interesting and spontaneous effects. Let the watercolor play its game, as our goal is to create an artistic background that imitates a gloomy sky. If needed, add some additional color near the bird to help it pop. Once the background is dry, use the very tip of your small brush to make a thin outline around the bird.

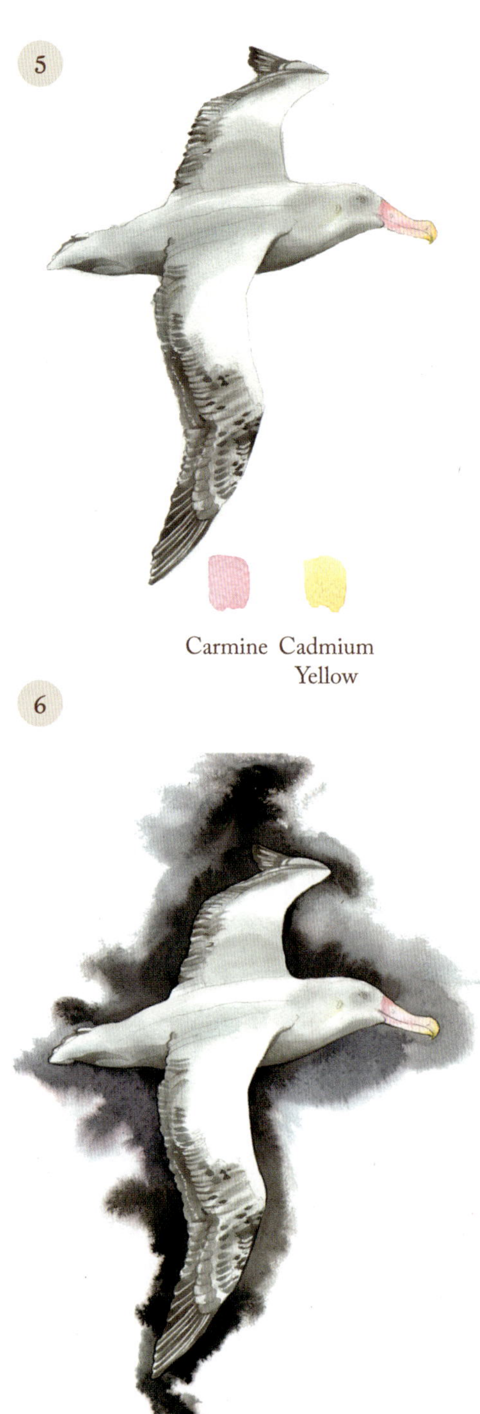

5

Carmine Cadmium
Yellow

6

Mix A

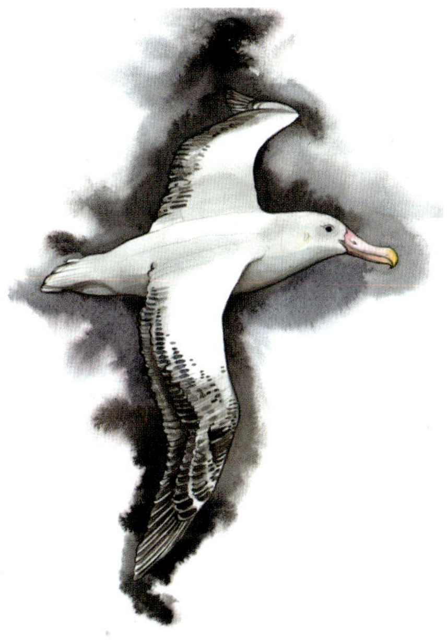

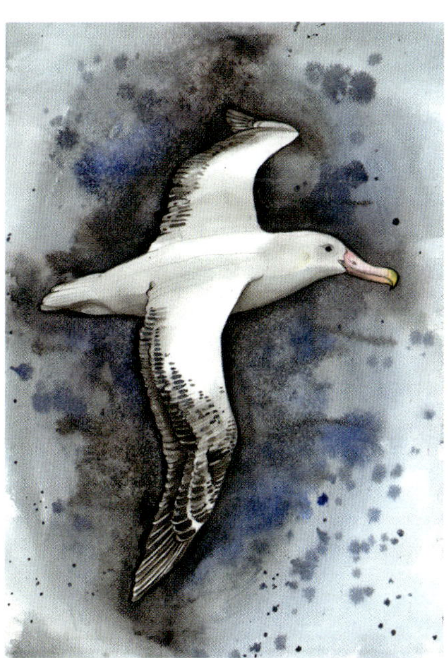

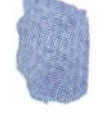

Ultramarine

Step 7: Use Mix 6A to paint thin lines and dots to add texture to the wings. Place the lines closer the left edge of the wing and the dots closer to the right edge. Meanwhile, paint the eye. Then, increase the saturation of the beak by applying more of the carmine and water and cadmium yellow and water mixes from Step 5.

Switch to Mix 4B to add a darker line to the opening of the beak. Then, use the tip of your brush to outline the nostril. If needed, darken the shadow on the lower side of the neck even further using the same gray mix and your large or medium brush, then smooth out the edge for a seamless transition. Finally, add any additional details to the wings and tail.

Step 8 (optional): Your painting can be considered finished at this stage, but if you want to add even more texture to the background, follow the next steps. Cover the whole surface near the albatross with Mix 6A and with a mix of ultramarine and water. Cover once again, leaving a thin line of dry paper between the water and the bird, just as you did in Step 6.

Apply Mix 6A near the bird and use splashes to create an even more spontaneous and moody effect. You can create the splashes of Mix 6A and ultramarine and water by tapping the brush handle with your fingers. Be careful not to cover the surface of the bird while doing so. If you want to create even more texture, sprinkle some coarse salt onto the wet surface of the paint and leave it to dry. This will result in an even more textured and snowy-looking background, as the salt will absorb some of the paint, leaving the surface beneath it whiter and creating a frosty effect. Make sure your painting is completely dry before removing the salt with your hands. After that, your painting is complete.

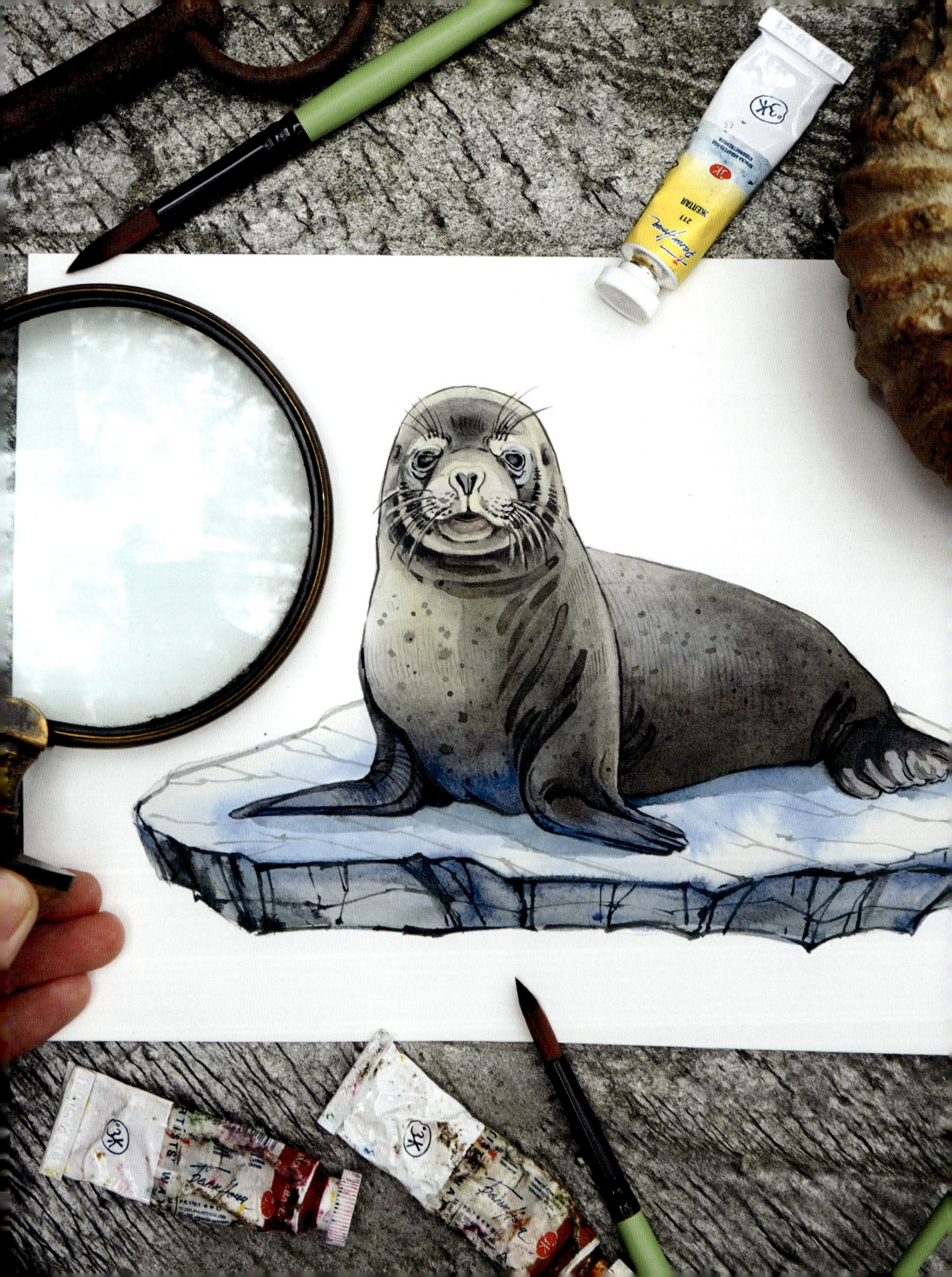

Weddell Seal

The Weddell seal, a charming creature with soulful eyes and a playful nature, is native to the icy waters of Antarctica. It spends much of its life lounging on ice platforms, where it rests. In this tutorial, you'll have the perfect opportunity to practice creating soft color blending, refining your skills in blending and shading. You'll also learn how to add extra charm and detail by including elements like the ice platform the seal is resting on, bringing the scene to life.

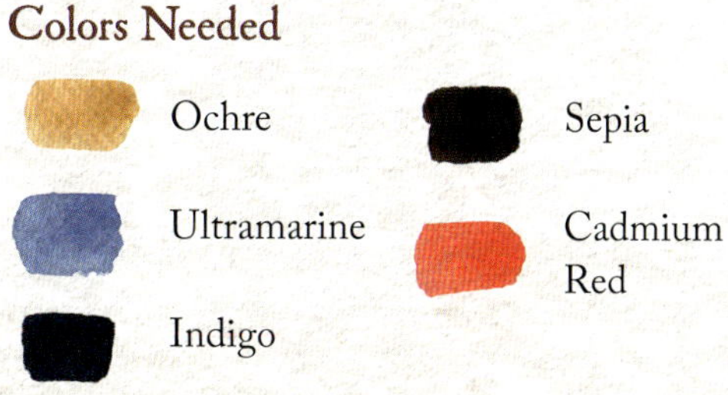

Colors Needed

Ochre

Sepia

Ultramarine

Cadmium Red

Indigo

Suggested Paper Orientation: Horizontal

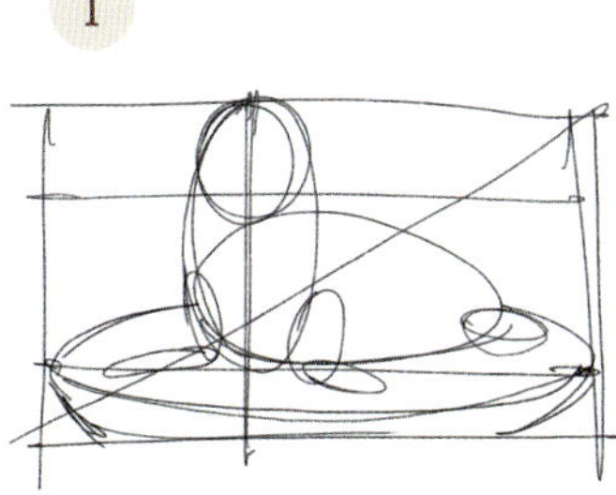

Step 1: Draw a wide rectangle. Draw a diagonal guide line from the lower left corner to the top right corner. Create one horizontal line one-quarter of the way from the top and a second line one-quarter of the way from the bottom. Draw a line slightly more than one-third of the way from the left top to the bottom. This is the guide line for the chest and head.

Draw an oval for the head and chest. Then, create another oval for the body. Make sure this oval is slightly thicker on the left, tapering as it transitions into the tail. The flippers are bent, so outline each with two thin ovals: one standing vertically and one horizontally. The left flipper starts at the middle of the chest oval. Then, draw another thin oval going to the left to outline the bent part that the seal rests on. The right flipper is the same but is placed lower (use the diagonal line as an indicator). The bent part of the flipper should face to the right and upward, with the top part of the flipper thicker. Additionally, the right flipper is a bit farther away from the line of the chest than the left one. Outline the tail with a horizontal oval that connects with the tip of the body oval. Finally, outline the ice platform. Draw an oval with the lower guide line at the center. Draw two curved lines to outline the sides of the platform.

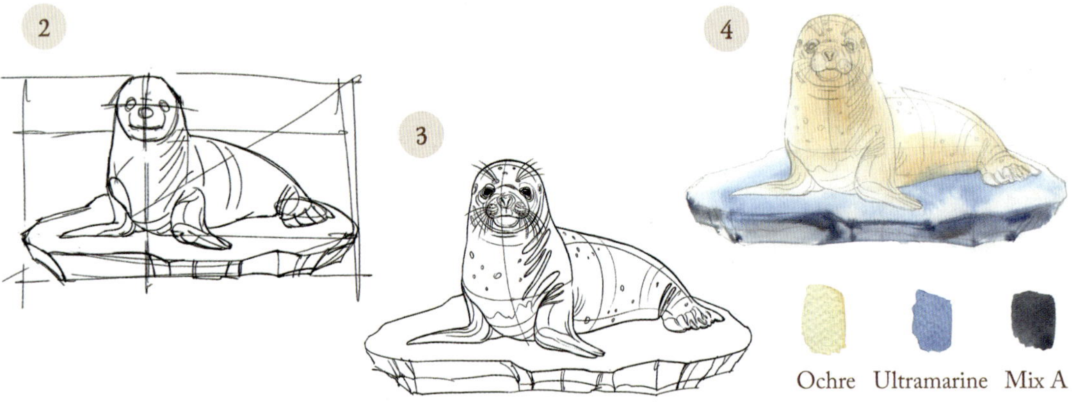

Step 2: Draw a horizontal guide line in the middle of the face circle. This line will help us position the eyes. Outline the eyes with two ovals, placing them in the middle of each side of the head. Then, position the nose between them, slightly lower, and also draw the mouth.

Sketch the folds of skin with long diagonal lines on the right side of the neck and on top of the right flipper. Then, sketch the folds on the body with even longer curved vertical lines. Unite the ovals of the flippers and give them a more realistic shape. Outline the folds on the flippers as well, using curved lines that follow their natural direction. Define the shape of the tail more clearly and add some folds by dividing it into smaller sections. Lastly, add more details to the platform. Define some sharp edges by adding short vertical lines on its front edge, and make the back side of the platform a bit more pointed.

Step 3: Erase the guide lines you no longer need. Refine the eyes and separate the eyelids from the eye itself. Outline the cheeks and jaw, adding folds around the face, especially on the lower side and forehead. Add the nostrils and some whiskers growing out of the cheeks, as well as eyebrows. Next, give the folds on the neck a more realistic appearance by transforming them from simple lines into very thin ovals.

Draw lines across the lower side of the chest, outlining the middle of the chest and separating the body from the tail. Add texture to the skin by creating tiny circles and dots, placing them randomly on the chest, body, and forehead. Define the folds on the flipper and tail more clearly. Lastly, clean up the shape of the ice platform, adding additional lines on the front to imitate cracks and hard edges. Congratulations, your drawing is ready, so let's start painting!

Step 4: Create a light yellow by mixing ochre with water and a light blue by mixing ultramarine with water. Then, create this mix:

• Mix A: indigo + sepia + water = darker blue

Apply the ochre and water mix to the lower part of the tail, the left and right fins, and the head and body. Smooth out the edges and lift some color from the cheeks and eyebrows. Cover the entire ice platform with clean water. Then, apply the ultramarine and water mix to the top near the seal. Apply Mix A to the lower part of the platform. If needed, add some extra color to the edges using an even more saturated version of Mix A (add more indigo to it). Let this layer dry completely before proceeding.

Step 5: Apply the ultramarine and water mix from Step 4 to parts of the body and chest. Smooth out the edges. Use Mix 4A to darken the forehead, under the eyes, neck, chest, the left side of the right fin, and some folds on the right side of the chest. Smooth out the edges. Wait for this layer to dry.

Step 6: Create these two mixes:

- Mix A: ultramarine + sepia + water = light gray
- Mix B: sepia + cadmium red + water = medium warm brown

Apply Mix A to the entire body of the seal except for the head. While this layer is still wet, add Mix 4A to the tail (except for the tips), the right fin, and the area where the head meets the body. Be careful not to cover the whiskers.

Next, apply the ultramarine and water mix from Step 4 to the eyes, under the eyes, and the area beneath the mouth. Apply Mix B to the mouth, then smooth the edges for a seamless transition. Once the body is dry, apply another layer of Mix A to the entire seal. Allow this layer to dry completely before proceeding.

Step 7: Create a new mix:

- Mix A: sepia + indigo + water = medium gray

This should be the darkest color we've mixed so far for this tutorial. Apply Mix A to the tail and the right and lower parts of the chest, smoothing out the edges. Apply the same color to the left and right sides of the left fin and to the fold on the right fin, but don't smooth out the edges this time. Add detail to the folds on the tail and on the belly near the right fin. Outline the details on the face, especially under the eyes, and add this

color to the nose, ears, and mouth using your small brush for more control. Also, add dots to the cheeks where the whiskers are growing from and outline the whiskers themselves. Finally, add some dots on the belly.

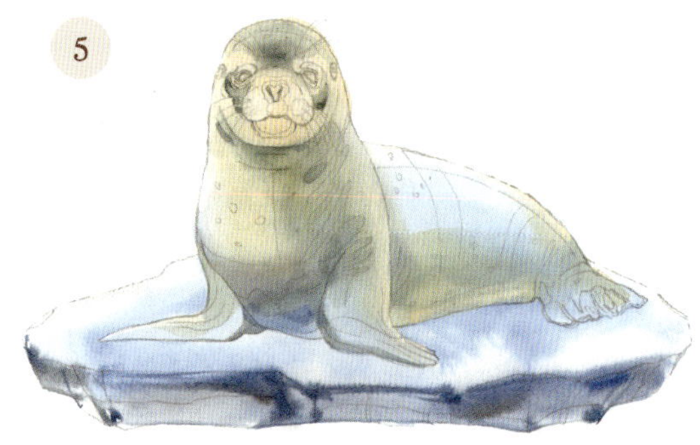

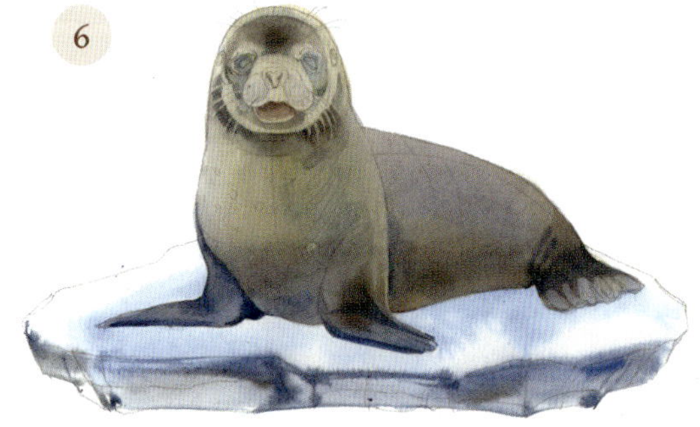

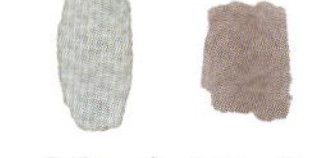

Mix A Mix B

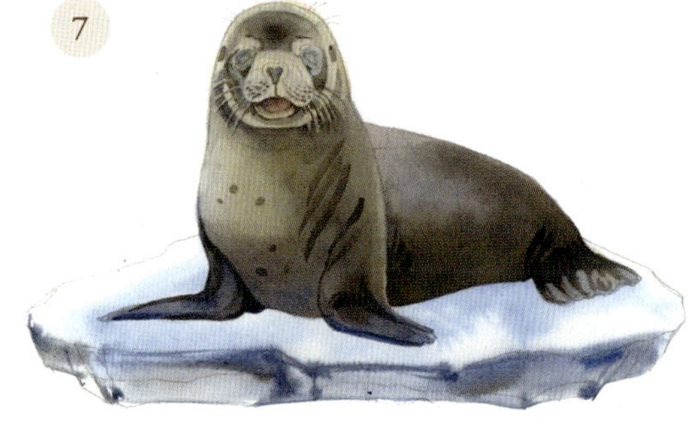

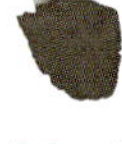

Mix A

Step 8: In this step, we will add more details to the face. Mix this color:

- Mix A: same as Mix 7A (sepia + indigo + water) but with more pigment and less water = dark brown-gray

Use the tip of your small brush loaded with Mix A to add details to the face. Darken the eyes while leaving a lighter highlight in the middle; then, smooth it out to reduce brightness. Outline the whiskers and the border from the head to the body. Use the tip of your brush to create the outline of the seal, ensuring that the lower outline is bolder while the outlines on the top of the seal are very thin.

Mix some indigo with water for a medium blue, and add it to the lower part of the chest, then smooth out the edge. Refine the outlines of the folds and add some additional small folds to the fins.

Create a new color:

- Mix B: same as Mix 7A (sepia + indigo + water) but with more water = lighter gray

Cover the area around the seal with your hand or some pieces of paper towels to ensure that only the body of the seal is exposed. Then, take a good quantity of Mix B on your brush and tap on it with your finger to make small drops of color fall onto the surface of the seal irregularly. To add even more variety to the texture, you can blot some of the drops with your paper towel so they appear lighter.

Step 9: Apply the ultramarine and water mix from Step 4 under the seal for shadow. Once dry, use Mix 8B and the very tip of your small brush to underline the cracks on the top surface of the ice. Use the same color to draw the back outline of the ice, ensuring it's not too dark or bold.

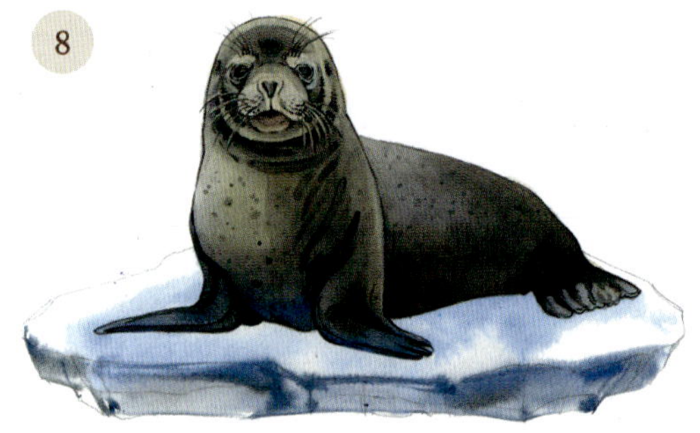

 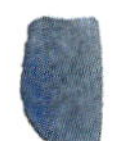 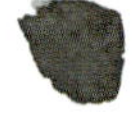

Mix A Indigo Mix B

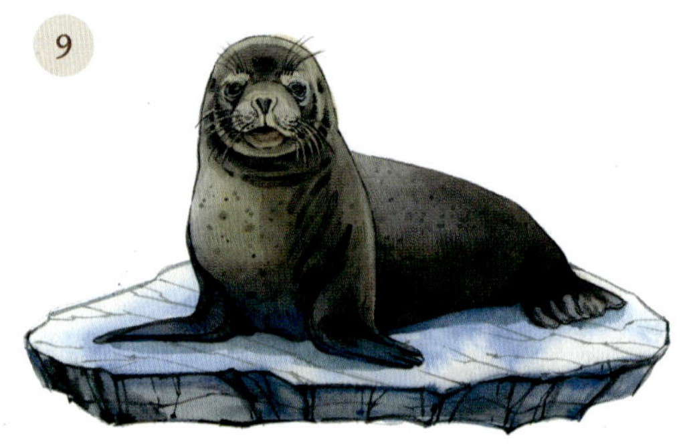

With the same color and a medium or large brush, cover the edge of the ice to make it look darker. Leave it to dry for a moment, and while the paper is damp, use a similar approach for the cracks but with Mix 7A and Mix 8A to create texture on the external side of the ice. This time, make the lines go from top to bottom, varying their direction and creating some points that form a "Y" shape for added variety. Once completely dry, add some additional touches using the same technique. Use the same colors and the tip of your brush to create the front outline, ensuring that your line is irregular. Once you're done working on the ice, your painting is complete.

Humpback Whale

The humpback whale is known for its incredible migrations. These majestic creatures feed in polar waters and travel to tropical seas to give birth, nurturing their calves in warm waters. In this tutorial, you'll focus on the smooth transitions of color on the whale's skin, mastering the art of painting a sleek surface with a subtle tonal shift. We'll also work on adding final details that enhance the realism, from reflections in the water to the texture of the whale's distinctive features. Let's dive in!

Colors Needed

 Cobalt Blue or Ultramarine

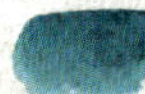 Turquoise Blue

 Indigo

Suggested Paper Orientation: Horizontal

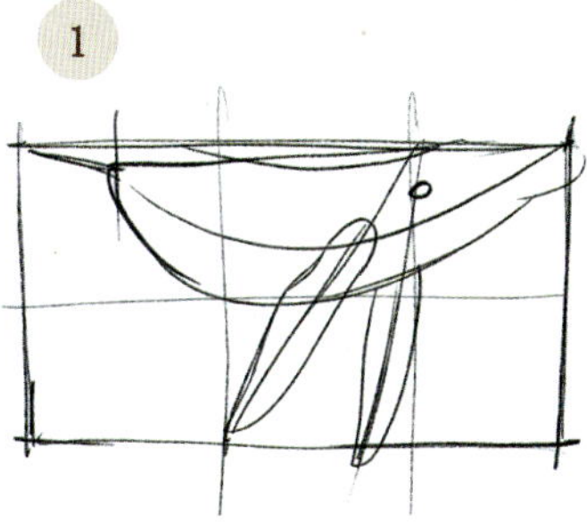

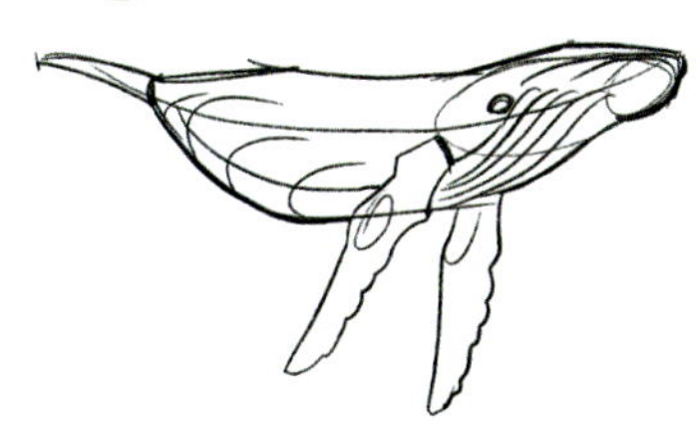

Step 1: Create a wide rectangle. Then, divide it in half horizontally and into three equal parts vertically. Suggest the movement of the whale's body with a wavy line, then define the shape of the body with a pointed oval that occupies the top half of the rectangle. The left side of the oval should end before reaching the left edge of the rectangle, as this area will be for the tail fin, which you can outline with a simple line for now.

Sketch the whale's mouth with a rounded shape on the right side of the body oval. Next, outline the direction of the two flippers by drawing two lines, both starting at the top left of the rightmost rectangle grid. For the left flipper, extend the line down to the bottom left corner of the bottom middle grid. For the right flipper, bring the line to the right edge of the same grid. Sketch the flippers with two thin ovals. Keep in mind that the right flipper is partially obscured by the body. Finally, draw the eye with a small oval on the right side of the body oval.

Step 2: Erase the guide lines and begin refining the outline. Add thickness to the tail and include some circular lines on the left part of the body to emphasize its volume. Use long, wavy lines to outline the folds (ventral pleats) on the right side of the whale's head. Finally, add more detail to the flippers by giving them a more irregular outline, particularly on the right side.

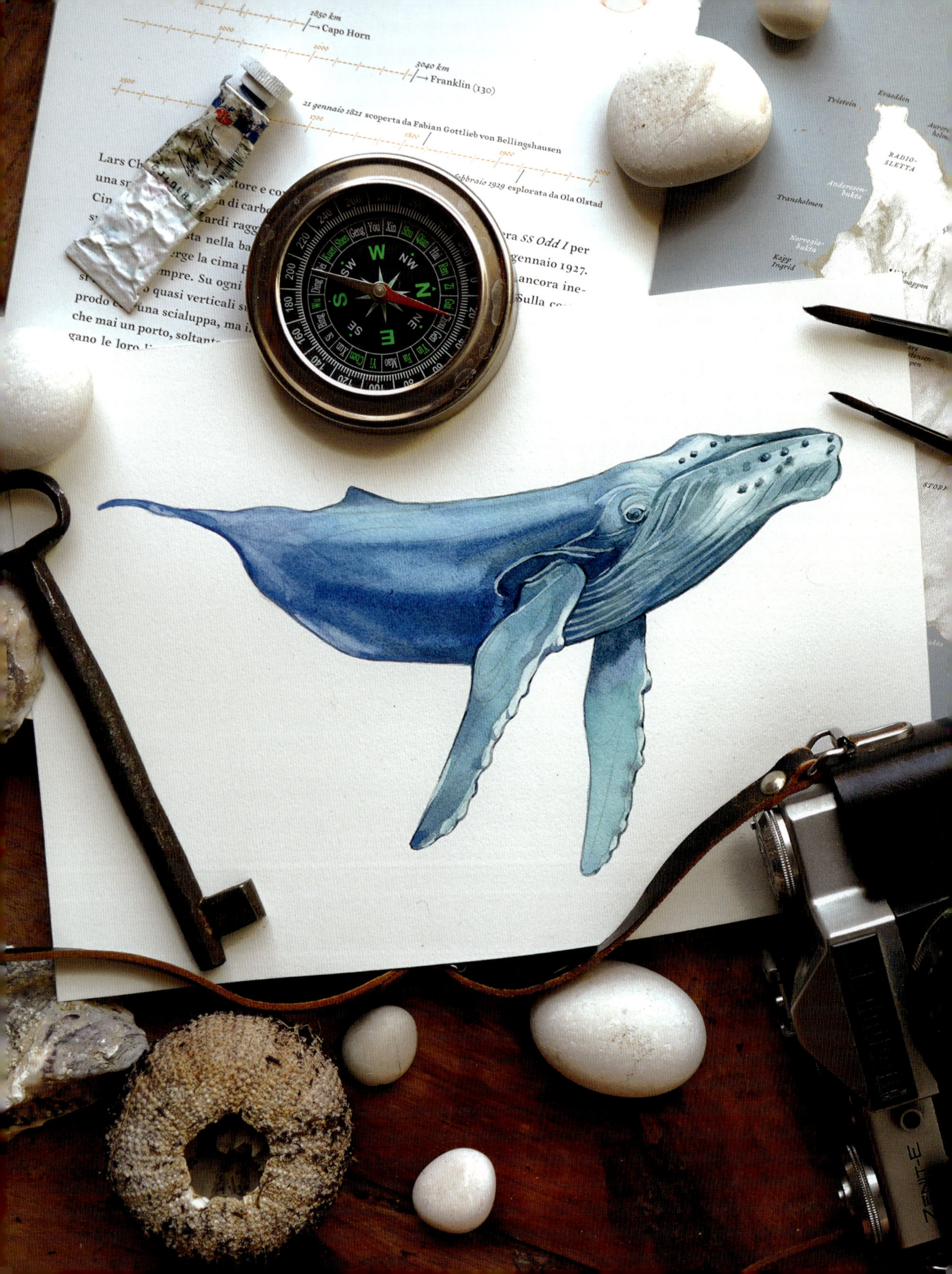

1850 km → Capo Horn
3040 km → Franklin (130)
21 gennaio 1821 scoperta da Fabian Gottlieb von Bellingshausen
febbraio 1929 esplorata da Ola Olstad
Lars Ch...
una s...
Cin...
...rdi ragg...
...sta nella ba...
...rge la cima...
...empre. Su ogni
prodo...una scialuppa, ma i...
che mai un porto, soltant...
gano le loro...
era SS Odd I per
gennaio 1927.
ancora ine-
Sulla co...
Tvistein
Evaodden
RADIO-SLETTA
Anderssen-bukta
Transholmen
Norvegia-bukta
Kapp Ingrid
STORY

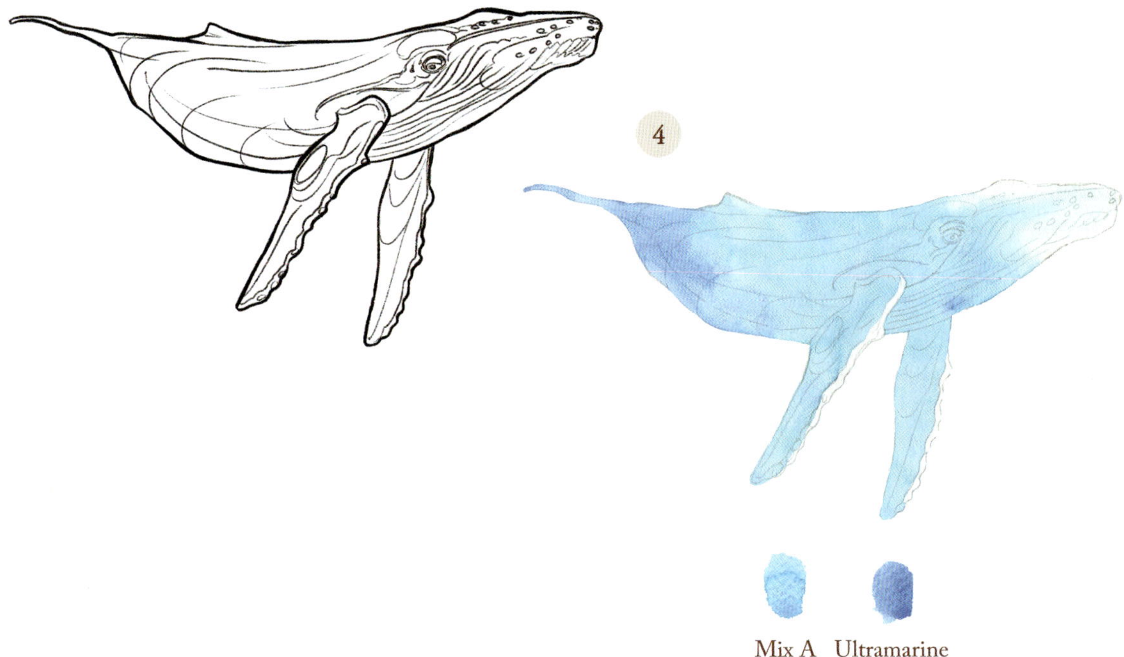

Step 3: Add a small top fin on the left part of the whale's body. Refine the shape of the tail to give it a more organic look. Add the final details to the flippers by defining their thickness with a parallel line at a small distance from the right edge of each flipper. Include additional details using curvy lines that will help define the shadow area. Enhance the eye by outlining the eyelid and the pupil, and add an eyebrow area with an oval. Draw a mouth line, add more lines to the lower part of the face, and include spots on the top and bottom near the mouth line to represent bumps. Once these details are complete, your drawing will be ready for painting.

Step 4: Create two color mixes:

- Mix A: cobalt blue or ultramarine + turquoise blue + water = blue

Then, mix another color by combining ultramarine with water for a pure medium blue color. Starting near the eye, begin applying Mix A with a medium or large brush. Add some to the opening of the mouth, leaving the tip of the face untouched. Continue bringing the paint toward the left side of the whale, maintaining a seamless wash without visible brushstrokes. Return to the face to smooth out the edge near the eye and around the mouth to create a seamless gradient from the lighter tip to the darker left side. Move back to the body and continue covering it with Mix A until you reach the small triangular fin on the whale's back. Once there, switch to the ultramarine and water mix and finish covering the rest of the whale's surface, including the tail. Allow this layer to dry completely before proceeding.

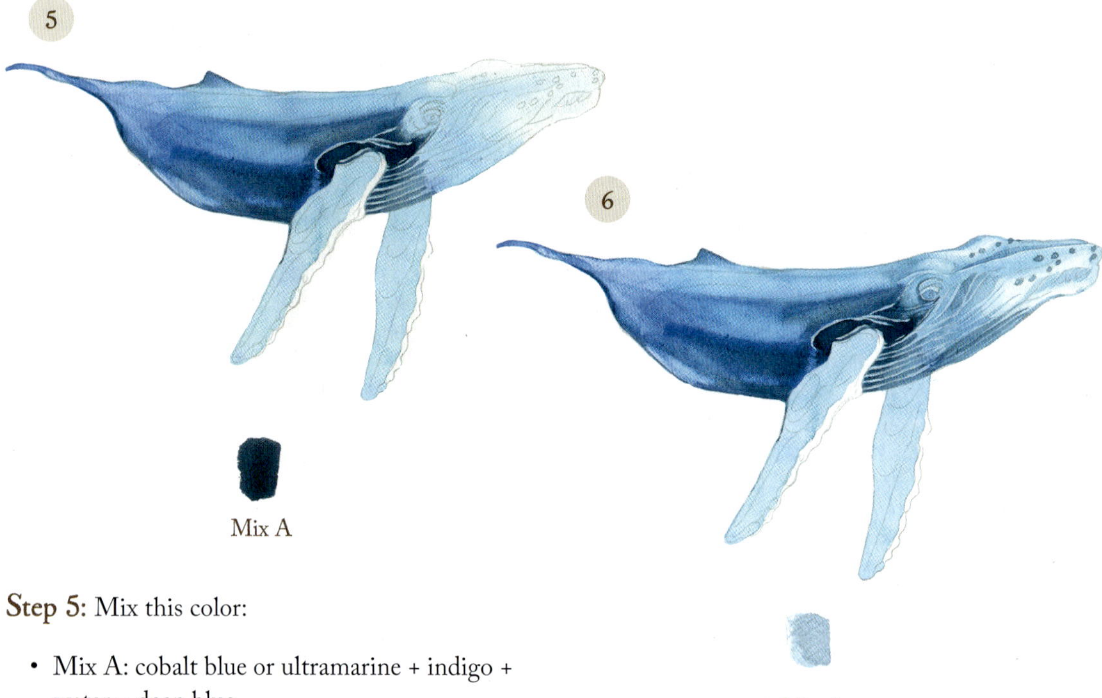

Mix A

Mix A

Step 5: Mix this color:

- Mix A: cobalt blue or ultramarine + indigo + water = deep blue

Use the ultramarine and water mix from Step 4 to darken the small triangular fin on the whale's back and the back fin of the tail. Then, use Mix 4A to cover the entire left side of the whale's body. While the color is still wet, switch back to the ultramarine and water mix and apply it to the middle part of the left side of the body. After that, switch to Mix A and apply it to the lower part of the whale's belly. Continue using Mix A on the area near the eye, above the left fin, and on the right side of it. Since that area is dry, there will be no blooming like on the left side where the wet-on-wet technique (page 17) was used. You will have more control over the color placement, so carefully apply it to this area with your small brush while avoiding the folds (ventral pleats) on top of the fin and to the right of it. Paint around these folds to keep them lighter.

Step 6: Create a new mix:

- Mix A: Mix 5A (cobalt blue or ultramarine + indigo) + more water = light blue

Use your medium or small brush loaded with Mix A to add shadows to the whale's face. Start with the shadow above the mouth opening, then smooth out the edge. Next, darken the area under the mouth and near the extreme right side, smoothing these edges as well. These actions will help make the whale's head look more detailed, three-dimensional, and realistic. Darken the bump on the top of the whale's head. Then, use the tip of your brush or a smaller brush to outline the ventral pleats more clearly by painting around them. Outline the folds around the eye and darken the eyeball, but avoid the eyelid for now. Finally, return to the tip and the top part of the face and add small round points to imitate the bumps on the whale's face.

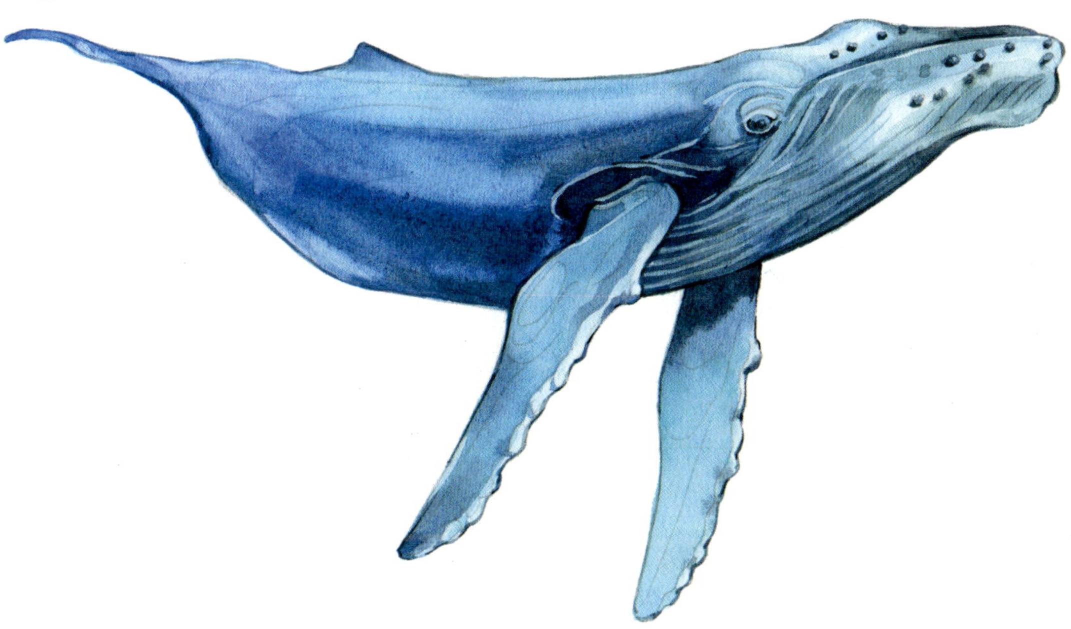

Step 7: Apply Mix 4A to the whole surface of the left fin, leaving the white right border and a couple of folds on top of the flipper untouched. Add more indigo to Mix 6A to make it slightly darker and add it to the upper part of the flipper and its tip while the previous color is still wet to create a smooth blend. After that, go over the right white side of the same flipper with a clean, dry brush to blend it better with the rest of the fin. Once that side is a bit drier, add Mix 5A to the bumps on the right side.

Then, move on to the right flipper. Start by covering the flipper (except for the right white side), beginning from the top with the ultramarine and water mix from Step 4. Once you reach about halfway down the flipper, switch to Mix 4A to finish covering the flipper. While the surface is still wet, apply Mix 5A to the top portion of the flipper, letting it blend with the initial color.

This will create a soft shadow in that area. Next, unite the white right strip of the fin with the rest of the fin using a clean, damp brush. After that, when the fin is a bit drier, outline the bumps on the right side even more with Mix 5A, just like we did for the left fin. That's it! Your painting is ready, and our odyssey around the globe has come to its end. I hope you enjoyed it!

Going Beyond the Projects
Finding Inspiration All Around You

I hope you enjoyed this creative odyssey around the globe and discovered new, fascinating details about the world we live in! Our planet is an extraordinary place, home to millions of unique creatures and breathtaking landscapes. When you start to view the world through a lens of observation and curiosity, you'll not only develop a deeper appreciation for nature but also realize that inspiration is often right in front of you—you don't have to travel far to find it!

Whether it's a peaceful walk in the park, a stroll through your local market, or simply noticing the flowers blooming in your window box, beauty is everywhere. The world is brimming with small, often overlooked details that can ignite the most profound artistic ideas. My hope is that this book serves as the beginning of your creative journey—a foundation for a lifetime of artistic exploration. In this final section, I'll share ideas for staying inspired throughout the year, even when you're not traveling, and offer tips for maintaining a consistent creative practice. Because in the end, consistency is the key to building confidence and mastering your craft!

How and What to Paint When You Don't Have a Lot of Time

Life gets busy, and it can feel like there's never enough time for a full painting session. But that doesn't mean you need to put your creative practice on hold! When time is limited, choosing a simple subject can help you make the most of the moments you have. I recommend starting with easy, accessible subjects like fruit, leaves, or flowers. These are not only readily available but also great for practicing your watercolor technique. Take a look around your kitchen, garden, or even the local grocery store for inspiration.

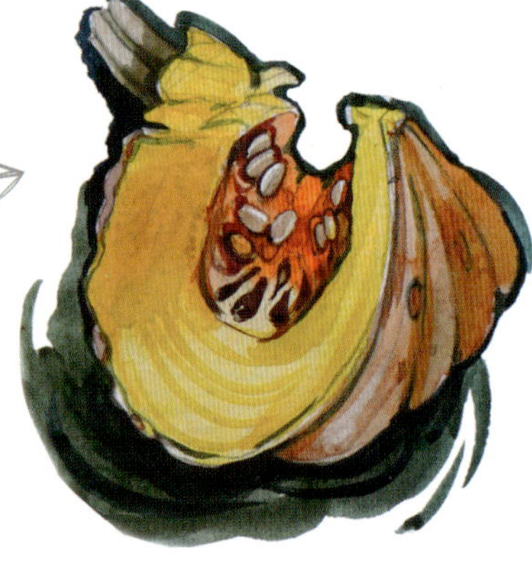

Choose a single subject that draws your attention—now you have an idea for your sketch!

In a busy market scene, it can be hard to focus and decide what to sketch, especially when short on time.

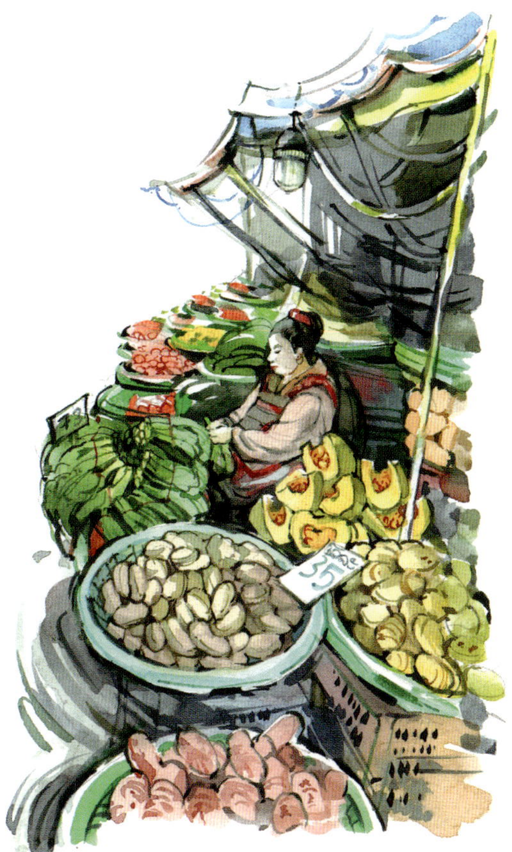

Look at a scene from a different angle
and notice what grabs your attention.

If your time is spread across multiple days, consider breaking the process up into smaller steps: Complete your drawing on the first day, then return to paint on the next. Another way to keep things manageable is to work on a smaller scale—still large enough to include the details you want but not so big that it feels overwhelming. Additionally, you can simplify your process by aiming to accomplish more in a single layer. While many tutorials in this book focus on layering, you could try a more direct, sketchy approach. This not only saves time but also creates a fresh, spontaneous look that doesn't rely heavily on fine details. With these strategies, you can stay creative and productive, even on your busiest days!

How to Establish a Creative Routine

Establishing a creative routine is a powerful way to grow as an artist and make art an integral part of your life. Start by setting aside dedicated time for your creativity, even if it's just 15 to 30 minutes a day. Pick a time that fits seamlessly into your schedule—early mornings, lunch breaks, or quiet evenings are all great options. Treat this time as a priority, like an appointment with yourself that you don't skip. Create a workspace that inspires you, and make sure your art supplies are easily accessible. Removing barriers to starting will help you jump right into your practice without hesitation. Begin each session with small, achievable goals, such as sketching a simple object or experimenting with a specific technique. These manageable steps make the process less intimidating and ensure steady progress. Over time, these regular, focused sessions will become a habit, allowing you to build momentum, nurture your creativity, and see meaningful growth in your skills.

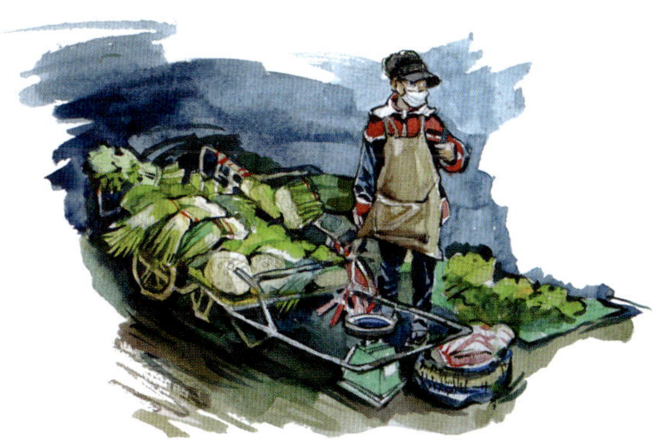

What Skills to Work on to Move Forward

Try to see the world through the new lens this book has revealed to you. Pay attention to the shapes and forms of the natural subjects around you, and think about how you would approach drawing and painting them. Practice quick sketches to train your observation skills and hand coordination. Sketching from life is particularly beneficial, as it allows you to observe the subject closely, turn it around, and examine its details in a way the photos can't offer. Real-life subjects provide this invaluable opportunity, and it's a great way to deepen your understanding.

It's also crucial to develop your drawing skills if you want to continue creating beyond the tutorials in this book. The more you practice drawing, the more confident and capable you'll become at representing any subject. You don't need to create highly detailed drawings every time, but regular sketching—even if it's just a quick one—will sharpen your skills. Try to capture the essence of what you see and gradually challenge yourself with more complex subjects as your confidence grows.

Above all, remember to have fun. Focus on the subjects that truly inspire you, and set small, achievable goals to build momentum before proceeding with more ambitious projects. This will boost your confidence and help you discover the direction you want to take your art in. Find someone to support your creative passion, or join a community, whether in-person or online. On my website, I offer various free and paid resources to help nature lovers and creatives develop their drawing and painting skills while expressing their love for travel and nature. You can find all of these at anastasiiamorozova.com.

Thank you for embarking on this creative journey with me. Let it be just the beginning of your amazing artistic path!

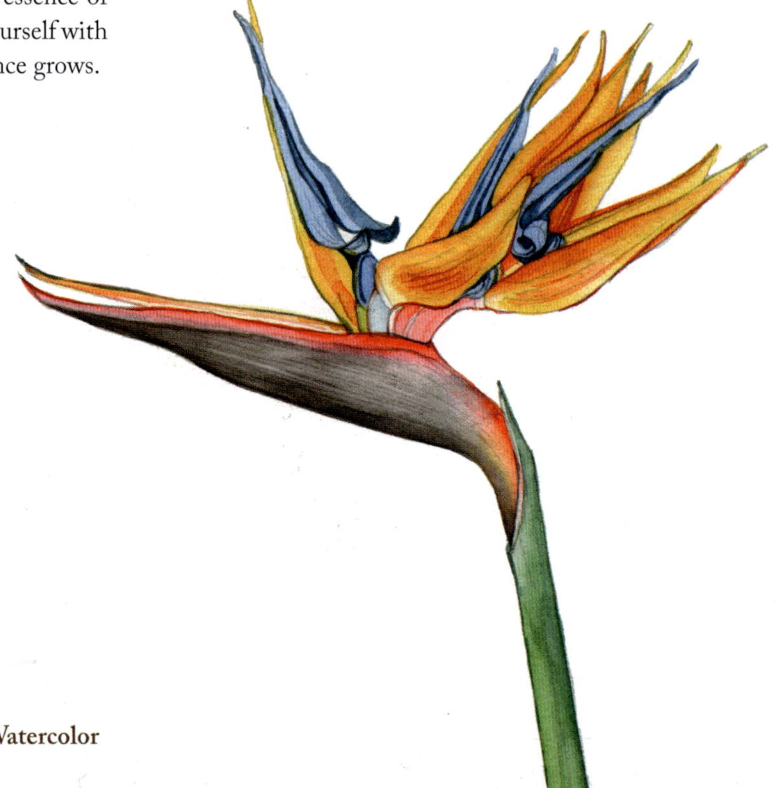

Acknowledgments

This book would not have been possible without the unwavering support and encouragement of so many remarkable people in my life.

First and foremost, to my husband, who has stood by me since the very beginning of my creative and teaching journey. Your belief in me and your constant support in realizing this book mean more than words can express. Thank you for being my rock and partner in this and other incredible adventures.

To my family, especially my parents, who supported my every passion and talent, and installed in me a deep curiosity and love for nature and the wonders of the world. Your example and guidance have fueled a lifelong passion for exploration and discovery.

To my grandmothers and godmother, thank you for showing me the magic and beauty of nature and for encouraging my creative spirit from an early age.

To my brother and my friends, thank you for your encouragement, love, and enthusiasm that have sustained me throughout the years.

To my incredible online community and students, a group of passionate individuals who share a love for nature, art, and joy of exploring the world—your enthusiasm and feedback have been invaluable.

A heartfelt thanks to the entire team at Page Street Publishing for bringing this dream of mine to life. Your dedication and expertise made this book a reality. To Sadie Hofmeester, your guidance, support, and invaluable feedback have been instrumental throughout this process. Thank you for believing in me and my vision.

This book is a labor of love, and I am endlessly grateful to everyone who has played a part in its creation, even without knowing it. Thank you for being part of this journey and for making it so meaningful.

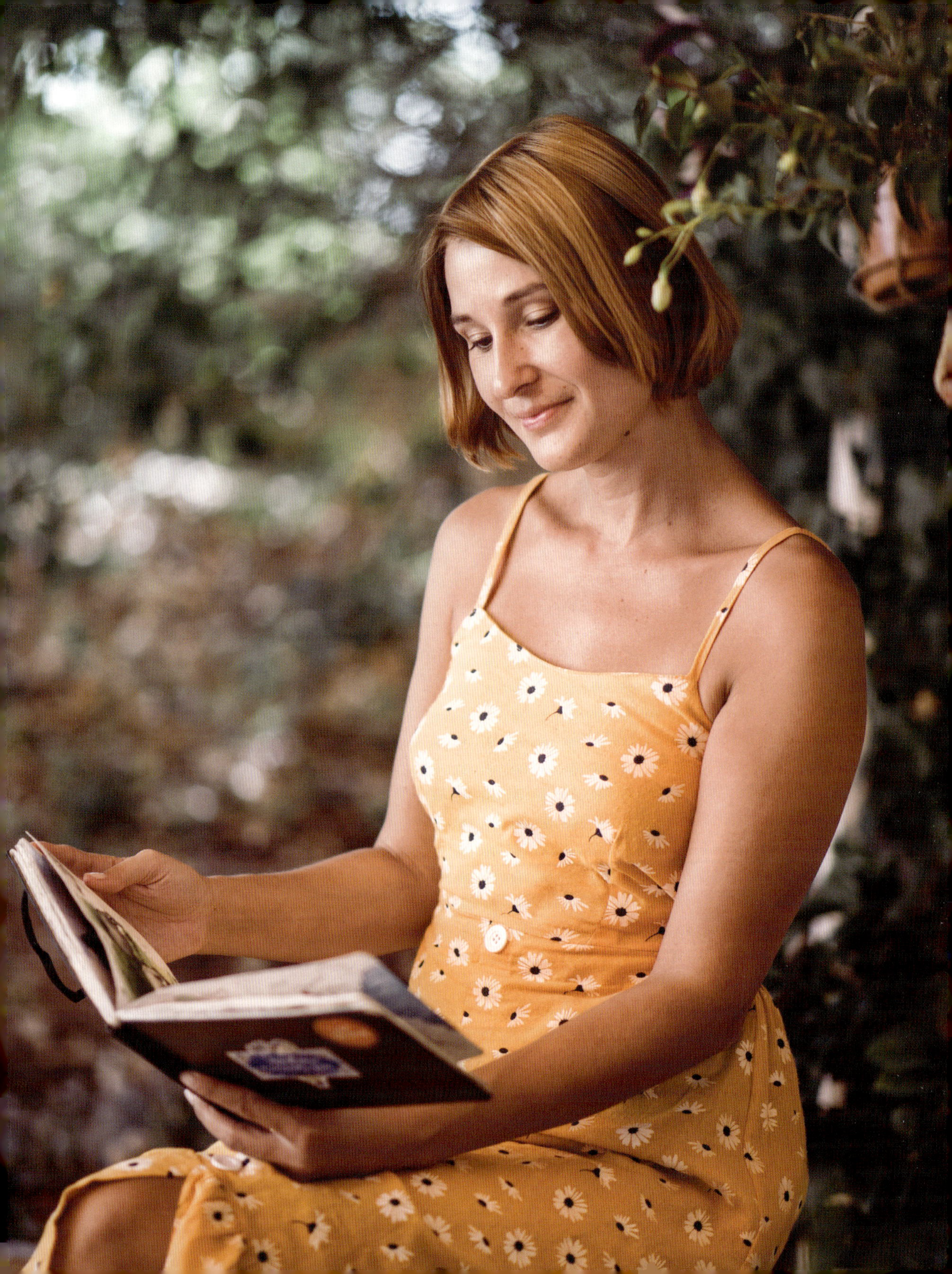

About the Author

Anastasiia Morozova was born and raised in the Ural Mountains region of Russia, where her connection to nature began during childhood holidays in her parents' forest house. This natural playground, along with her family's passion for the outdoors and traveling, fueled her curiosity and creativity from an early age. Her deep fascination with the natural world quickly found expression in art, and she was constantly creating something with her hands. As a teenager, she decided to pursue art as a career and began receiving professional art training.

After studying classical art at the Art Academy in her hometown, Anastasiia realized the challenges of pursuing a career as an artist, especially after witnessing her peers struggle to find art-related jobs. This led her to pursue a master's degree in Paris, France, where she shifted focus to art management and curation, working in Paris and New York. However, despite the excitement of the life in big cities, she deeply missed her connection to nature and felt a strong urge to return to creating.

After marrying her Italian husband, she moved with him to a small town in Southern Italy to start a new chapter. It was there that she rekindled her passion for watercolor, honing her skills and making nature a central theme of her work. After years of dedication and hard work, her art gained recognition online, leading to client commissions, book illustrations, and exhibitions.

During the COVID-19 pandemic, she focused on learning new skills online, which inspired her to launch her own online school. She now runs classes and programs that help students of all ages, locations, and skill levels improve their drawing and painting skills, develop their unique style, and discover ways to monetize their creativity.

After feeling confined by the restrictions during the pandemic, Anastasiia and her husband decided to embark on a long journey through Southeast Asia in 2024. This five-month trip inspired her to keep a daily sketchbook, capturing everything that caught her eye along the way. During this adventure, her focus on nature extended to include urban sketching, food, landscapes, portraits, and anything else that sparked inspiration.

This book combines her background as a botanical and animal-inspired artist with her ability to capture natural subjects on location, resulting in a unique blend of techniques that you will learn in these pages.

For art tips and inspiration, follow Anastasiia on social media or visit her website, anastasiiamorozova.com

instagram.com/natura.illustrata

facebook.com/naturaillustrata

youtube.com/@natura.illustrata

Index

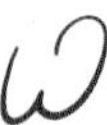